MW01125120

The Deleuze Dictionary
Revised Edition

To Ian Buchanan

The Deleuze Dictionary
Revised Edition

Edited by Adrian Parr

Edinburgh University Press

First published 2005

Edinburgh University Press Ltd
22 George Square, Edinburgh

Reprinted 2011, 2012, 2013

Typeset in Ehrhardt
by Servis Filmsetting Ltd, Stockport, Cheshire, and
printed and bound by CPI Group (UK) Ltd, Croydon, CR0 4YY

A CIP record for this book is available from the British Library

ISBN 978 0 7486 4147 5 (hardback)
ISBN 978 0 7486 4146 8 (paperback)

Contents

Acknowledgements

First I would like to thank all the authors who contributed to this project. Without you this dictionary would never have come into existence. Everyone who has entries included here and my editor, Carol Macdonald, have been tremendously cooperative and helpful in more ways than one. I would like to also thank Keith Ansell-Pearson, Ronald Bogue, Paul Patton, and James Williams for the comments and suggestions they provided for the first edition, all of which strengthened the theoretical rigour of this dictionary; any shortcomings are entirely my own. I am very grateful to the Department of Women's, Gender and Sexuality Studies; and the School of Architecture and Interior Design at the University of Cincinnati for their continuing support.

I thank all the authors for agreeing to donate all royalties from this new revised and expanded edition to the non-profit non-governmental organization Village Life Outreach Project.

Adrian Parr

Preface

Since the publication of the first edition of *The Deleuze Dictionary* in 2005 there has been a tremendous proliferation of scholarship that engages with the concepts and principles Deleuze developed throughout his life and in collaboration with Félix Guattari. As such when I was approached to revise and update the dictionary I was excited at the opportunity to respond to this growing scholarship. The challenge was how to continue with the spirit of the first edition as well as address some of the new scholarship in the field. I decided to focus on putting Deleuze's terms and concepts to work in some of the areas that had not been covered in the first edition, and primarily this was in the disciplines of architecture and science.

In this new revised and expanded edition of *The Deleuze Dictionary*, the connectives continue to be the most important feature. This is because they encourage us to think about how the Deleuzian conceptual apparatus functions. To a certain degree I always conceived of the dictionary as an intervention of sorts. Put differently, the 'definitions' were not conceived of as a way to order reality; rather, I approached them as a destabilising condition. The question was, and still is, one of how to use Deleuzian concepts in such a way that they push the concrete conditions of what currently is in new and unforeseeable directions? That is, when I originally decided upon producing connectives with the definitions I was hoping to prompt the reader to literally get a sense of how the Deleuzian conceptual apparatus might intensify, activate, and tease out the affective potential of Deleuze's thinking. The hope was, and still is, that the connectives might disorganise the rigidity of a 'definition' by opening it up to its own internal difference. For these reasons, with this new expanded and revised edition I have been much more interested in producing more connectives than adding to the list of definitions. I should add at this point, this is not to say that there are no new definitions in the second edition. Two very important concepts that were not previously included – Assemblage and Fabulation – now appear in this new edition.

I have had to remove some of the less used terms and concepts of the first edition to make way for a fresh influx of material. These edits are in no way a reflection upon the quality of work, they are purely the result of having to make room for new material. I have also used this as an opportunity to update the bibliography. The expanded bibliography includes recent scholarship in the area of Deleuze studies. I should add however, the bibliography is not intended to be exhaustive. It is quite simply a guide.

Adrian Parr

Introduction

Claire Colebrook

Why a Deleuze dictionary? It might seem a particularly craven, disrespectful, literal-minded and reactive project to form a Deleuze dictionary. Not only did Deleuze strategically change his lexicon to avoid the notion that his texts consisted of terms that might simply name extra-textual truths, he also rejected the idea that art, science or philosophy could be understood without a sense of their quite specific creative problem. A philosopher's concepts produce connections and styles of thinking. Concepts are intensive: they do not gather together an already existing set of things (extension); they allow for movements and connection. (The concept of 'structure' in the twentieth century, for example, could not be isolated from the problem of explaining the categories of thinking and the image of an impersonal social subject who is the effect of a conceptual system; similarly, the concept of the 'cogito' relates the mind to a movement of doubt, to a world of mathematically measurable matter, and to a distinction between thought and the body.) To translate a term or to define any point in a philosopher's corpus involves an understanding of a more general orientation, problem or milieu. This does not mean that one reduces a philosophy to its context – say, explaining Deleuze's 'nomadism' as a reaction against a rigid structuralism or linguistics. On the contrary, to understand a philosophy as the creation of a plane, or as a way of creating some orientation by establishing points and relations, means that any philosophy is more than its manifest terms, more than its context. In addition to the produced texts and terms, and in addition to the explicit historical presuppositions, there is an unthought or outside – the problem, desire or life of a philosophy. For Deleuze, then, reading a philosopher requires going beyond his or her produced lexicon to the deeper logic of production from which the relations or sense of the text emerge. This sense itself can never be said; in repeating or recreating the milieu of a philosopher all we can do is produce another sense, another said. Even so, it is this striving for sense that is the creative drive of reading a philosopher. So, when Deleuze reads Bergson he allows each term and move of Bergson's philosophy to revolve around a problem: the problem of intuition, of how the human observer can think from beyond its own constituted, habituated and all too human world.

It would seem, then, that offering definitions of terms in the form of a dictionary – as though a word could be detached from its philosophical life and problem – would not only be at odds with the creative role of philosophy; it would also sustain an illusion that the philosophical text is nothing more than its 'said' and that becoming-Deleuzian would be nothing more than the adoption of a certain vocabulary. Do we, in systematising Deleuze's thought, reduce an event and untimely provocation to one more doxa?

If Deleuze's writings are difficult and resistant this cannot be dismissed as stylistically unfortunate, as though he really *ought* to have just sat down and told us in so many words what 'difference in itself ' or 'immanence' really meant. Why the difficulty of style and vocabulary if there is more to Deleuze than a way of speaking? A preliminary answer lies in the nexus of concepts of 'life', 'immanence' and 'desire'. The one distinction that Deleuze insists upon, both when he speaks in his own voice in *Difference and Repetition* and when he creates his sense of the history of philosophy, is the 'image of thought'. Philosophy begins from an image of what it is to think, whether that be the grasp of ideal forms, the orderly reception of sense impressions, or the social construction of the world through language. The concepts of a philosophy both build, and build upon, that image. But if the history of philosophy is a gallery of such images of thought – from the conversing Socrates and mathematical Plato, to the doubting Descartes and logical Russell – some philosophers have done more than stroll through this gallery to add their own image. Some have, in 'schizo' fashion, refused to add one more proper relation between thinker and truth, and have pulled thinking apart. One no longer makes one more step within thought – tidying up a definition, or correcting a seeming contradiction. Only when this happens does philosophy realise its power or potential.

Philosophy is neither correct nor incorrect in relation to what currently counts as thinking; it creates new modes or styles of thinking. But if all philosophy is creation, rather than endorsement, of an image of thought, some philosophers have tried to give a sense or concept to this creation of thinking: not one more image of thought but 'thought without an image'. Deleuze's celebrated philosophers of univocity confront the genesis, rupture or violence of thinking: not man who thinks, but a life or unthought within which thinking might happen. When Spinoza imagines one expressive substance, when Nietzsche imagines one will or desire, and when Bergson creates the concept of life, they go some way to towards really asking about the emergence of thinking. This is no longer the emergence of the *thinker*, or one who thinks, but the emergence of something like a minimal relation, event or perception of thinking, from which 'thinkers' are then effected. This means that the real history of philosophy requires understanding the way philosophers produce singular points, or the orientations within which subjects, objects, perceivers and images are ordered.

Any assemblage such as a philosophical vocabulary (or an artistic style, or a set of scientific functions) faces in two directions. It both gives some sort of order or consistency to a life which bears a much greater complexity and dynamism, but it also enables – from that order – the creation of further and more elaborate orderings. A philosophical vocabulary such as Deleuze's gives sense or orientation to our world, but it also allows us to produce further differences and further worlds. On the one hand, then, a Deleuzian concept such as the 'plane of immanence' or 'life' or 'desire' establishes a possible relation between thinker and what is to be thought, giving us some sort of logic or order. On the other hand, by coupling this concept with other concepts, such as 'affect' 'concept' and 'function', or 'plane of transcendence' and 'image of thought', we can think not just *about* life or the plane of immanence but also of how the brain imagines, relates to, styles, pictures, represents and orders that plane. This is the problem of how life differs from itself, in itself. The role of a dictionary is only one side of a philosophy. It looks at the way a philosophy stratifies or distinguishes its world, but once we have seen how 'a' philosophy thinks and moves this should then allow us to look to other philosophies and other worlds.

There is then a necessary fidelity and infidelity, not only in any dictionary or any reading, but also in any experience or any life. Life is both effected through relations, such that there is no individual or text in itself; at the same time, life is not reducible to effected or actual relations. There are singularities or 'powers to relate' that exceed what is already given. This is the sense or the singularity of a text. Sense is not what is manifestly said or denoted; it is what is opened *through* denotation. So, we might say that we need to understand the meaning of Deleuze's terminology – how 'territorialisation' is defined alongside 'deterritorialisation', 'assemblage', 'Body without Organs' and so on – and then how these denoted terms express what Deleuze wants to say, the intention of the Deleuzian corpus. But this should ultimately then lead us to the *sense* of Deleuze, which can only be given through the production of another text. *I* can say, here, that the sense of Deleuze's works is the problem of how thinking emerges from life, and how life is not a being that is given but a power to give various senses of itself (what Deleuze refers to as '?being'). But in saying this I have produced another sense. Each definition of each term is a different path from a text, a different production of sense that itself opens further paths for definition. So, far from definitions or dictionaries *reducing* the force of an author or a philosophy, they create further distinctions.

This does not mean, as certain popular versions of French poststructuralism might indicate, that texts have no meanings and that one can make anything mean what one wants it to mean. On the contrary, the life or problem of Deleuze's philosophy lay in the event: both the event of philosophical texts and the event of works of art. The event is a disruption, violence or dislocation of thinking. To read is not to recreate oneself, using the text as a mirror or medium through which one repeats already habitual orientations. Just as life can only be lived by risking connections with other powers or potentials, so thinking can only occur if there is an encounter with relations, potentials and powers not our own. If we take Deleuze's definition of life seriously – that it is not a given whole with potentials that necessarily unfold through time, but is a *virtual* power to create potentials through contingent and productive encounters – then this will relate directly to an ethics of reading. We cannot read a thinker in order to find what he is saying 'to us', as though texts were vehicles for exchanging information from one being to another. A text is immanent to life; it creates new connections, new styles for thinking and new images and ways of seeing. To read a text is to understand the problem that motivated its assemblage. The more faithful we are to a text – not the text's ultimate message but its construction, or the way in which it produces relations among concepts, images, affects, neologisms and already existing vocabularies – the more we will have an experience of a style of thought not our own, an experience of the power to think in creative styles as such.

One of the most consistent and productive contributions of Deleuze's thought is his theory and practice of reading, both of which are grounded in a specific conception of life. If there is one understanding of philosophy and good reading as grounded in consistency and doxa, which would return a text to an assimilable logic and allow thought to remain the same, Deleuze places himself in a counter-tradition of distinction and paradox. Neither philosophy nor thinking flows inevitably and continuously from life; reason is not the actualisation of what life in its potential was always striving to be. More than any other thinker of his time Deleuze works against vitalism or the idea that reason, thinking and concepts somehow serve a function or purpose of life, a life that is nothing more than change or alteration for the sake of efficiency or self-furthering. If there is a concept of life in Deleuze it is a life at odds with itself, a potential or power to create divergent potentials. Admittedly, it is possible to imagine thinking, with its concepts, dictionaries and organon, as shoring 'man' against the forces of chaos and dissolution, but we can also – when we extend this potential – see thinking as a confrontation with chaos, as allowing more of what is *not* ourselves to transform what we take ourselves to be. In this sense thought has 'majoritarian' and 'minoritarian' tendencies, both a movement towards reducing chaotic difference to uniformity and sameness and a tendency towards opening those same unities to a 'stuttering' or incomprehension. Deleuze, far from believing that one might return thought to life and overcome the submission to system, recognises that the creation of a system is the only way one can really live non-systemically. One creates a minimal or dynamic order, both to avoid absolute deterritorialisation on the one hand and reactive repetition of the already-ordered on the other. In this sense, Deleuze is a child of the Enlightenment. Not only does he inhabit the performative self-contradiction, 'Live in such a way that one's life diverges from any given principle,' he also deduces this 'principle that is not one' from life. If one is to *live*, there must both be a minimal connection or exposure to the outside alongside a creation or perception of that outside, with perception being a difference.

Deleuze's ontology – that relations are external to terms – is a commitment to perceiving life; life is connection and relation, but the outcome or event of those relations is not determined in advance by intrinsic properties. Life is not, therefore, the ground or foundation differentiated by a set of terms, such that a dictionary might provide us with one schema of order among others. The production or creation of a system is both an exposure to those powers of difference not already constituted as proper categories of recognising 'man' and a radical enlightenment. Enlightenment is, defined dutifully, freedom from imposed tutelage – the destruction of masters. Deleuze's destruction of mastery is an eternal, rather than perpetual, paradox. Rather than defining thought and liberation against another system, with a continual creation and subsequent destruction, the challenge of Deleuze's thought is to create a system that contains its own aleatory or paradoxical elements, elements that are both inside and outside, ordering and disordering. This is just what Deleuze's great concepts serve to do; life is both that which requires some form of order and system (giving itself through differences that are perceived and synthesised) *and* that which also opens the system, for life is just that power *to differ* from which concepts emerge but that can never be included in the extension of any concept.

We can only begin to think and live when we lose faith in the world, when we no longer expect a world to answer to and mirror ourselves and our already constituted desires. Thinking is paradox, not because it is simple disobedience or negation of orthodoxy, but because if thinking has any force or distinction it has to work against inertia. If a body were only to connect with what allowed it to remain relatively stable and self contained – in image of the autopoietic system that takes only what it can master and assimilate – then the very power of life for change and creation would be stalled or exhausted by self involved life forms that lived in order to remain the same. Despite first appearances a dictionary can be the opening of a self-enclosed system. If we are faithful to the life of Deleuze's thought – recognising it as a creation rather than destined effect of life – then we can relive the production of this system and this response as an image of production in general.

'I must create a system or be enslaved by another man's' – so declares Blake's ideal poet in the highly contested and chaotic agonistics of his great poem *Jerusalem*. Blake's aphorisms were indebted to an enlightenment liberationism that found itself in a seemingly paradoxical structure. If we are condemned to live in some form of system then we can either inhabit it passively and reactively, or we can embrace our seeming submission to a system of relations not our own and respond creatively. Blake's early response provided an alternative to the inescapability of the categorical imperative which still haunts us today: if I am to speak and act as a moral being then I can neither say nor do what is particular or contingent for me; living with others demands that I decide what to do from the point of view of 'humanity in general'. To speak or to live is already to be other than oneself, and so morality demands a necessary recognition of an initial submission. Such a final consensus or intersubjectivity may never arrive, but it haunts all life nevertheless. By contrast, Deleuze's paradoxical and eternal affirmation of creation begins from the inescapability of a minimal system – to perceive or live is already to be connected, to be other – but far from this requiring a striving for a system of consensus or ideal closure, this produces an infinite opening. It might seem that the Enlightenment imperative – abandon all external authority – comes to function as yet one more authority, and it might also seem that a fidelity to Deleuze is a crime against the thinker of difference. But the problem of Deleuze's thought is just this passage from contradiction to paradox. To *not* be oneself is contradictory if one must be *either* this or that, if life must decide or stabilise itself (form a narrative or image of itself). 'Becoming-imperceptible', by contrast, is an enabling and productive paradox. One connects or perceives in order to live, in order to *be*, but this very tendency is also at the same time a becoming-other: not a nonbeing but a? being. A Deleuzian dictionary comes into being only in its use, only when the thoughts that it enables open the system of thought to the very outside and life that made it possible.

A

ACTIVE/REACTIVE

Lee Spinks

The distinction between active and reactive forces was developed by Friedrich Nietzsche in his *On the Genealogy of Morality* and the notes posthumously collected as *The Will to Power*. In his seminal reading of Nietzsche, Deleuze seized upon this distinction (and what it made possible) and placed it at the very heart of the Nietzschean revaluation of values. For Nietzsche, the distinction between active and reactive force enabled him to present 'being' as a process rather than 'substance'. The world of substantial being, he argued, is produced by the recombination of multiple effects of force into discrete ideas, images and identities. There is no essential 'truth' of being; nor is there an independent 'reality' before and beyond the flux of appearances; every aspect of the real is already constituted by quantities and combinations of force. Within this economy of becoming, every force is related to other forces and is defined in its character by whether it obeys or commands. What we call a body (whether understood as political, social, chemical or biological) is determined by this relation between dominating and dominated forces. Meanwhile Deleuze maintains that any two forces constitute a body as soon as they enter into relationship. Within this body the superior or dominant forces are described as 'active'; the inferior or dominated forces are described as 'reactive'. These qualities of active and reactive force are the *original* qualities that define the relationship of force with force.

If forces are defined by the relative difference in their quality or power, the notion of quality is itself determined by the difference in quantity between the two forces that come into relationship. The character of any relation, that is, is produced through forces. There are no intrinsic properties that determine how forces will relate: a master becomes a master through the act of over-powering. In the encounter between forces, each force receives the quality that corresponds to its quantity. Forces are dominant, or dominated, depending upon their relative difference in quantity; but they manifest themselves as active or reactive according to their difference in quality. Once the relation has been established the quality of forces – dominant or dominated – produces an active power (that commands the relation) and a reactive power (defined by the relation). The difference between forces defined according to their quantity as active or reactive is described in terms of a *hierarchy*. An active force is the stronger term and goes to the limit of what it can do. Its characteristics are dominating, possessing, subjugating and commanding. The expression of activity is the expression of what is necessarily unconscious; all consciousness does is express the relation of certain reactive forces to the active forces that dominate them. Active force affirms its difference from everything that is weaker than and inferior to itself; meanwhile reactive force seeks to limit active force, impose restrictions upon it, and to recast it in the spirit of the negative. Crucially, reactive force cannot transform itself into a fully active force; nor can a collection of reactive forces amalgamate themselves into something greater than active force. A slave who gains power, or who bonds with other slaves, will remain a slave and can only be freed from slavery by abandoning *consciousness*. Consciousness remains what it is, and is unlike the active force of difference. Consciousness *represents* and recognises active forces, thereby separating activity from what it can do. Such separation constitutes a subtraction or division of active force by making it work against the power of its own affirmation. The remarkable feature of the becoming-reactive of active force is that historically it has managed to form the basis of an entire vision of life. This vision embodies the principle of 'ressentiment': a movement in which a reactive and resentful denial of higher life begins to create its own moral system and account of human experience. The reactive triumph expressed in movements of consciousness like ressentiment, bad consciousness and the ascetic ideal depends upon a mystification and reversal of active force: at the core of these new interpretations of life reactive force *simulates* active force and turns it against itself. It is at precisely the historical moment when the slave begins to triumph over the master who has stopped being the spectre of law, virtue, morality and religion.

An active force becomes reactive when a reactive force manages to separate it from what it can do. The historical development of reactive forces is itself predicated upon the affinity between reaction and negation, an affinity which is itself a weak form of the Will to Power in so far as it is an expression of nihilism or the will to nothingness. The will to asceticism or world-renunciation is, after all, still an expression of *will*. Thus, while reactive forces are weaker than active forces, they also possess a potentially sublime element in as much as they are able to advance a new interpretation of life (the world of moral ideas, for example) and they supply us with an original, although nihilistic, version of the Will to Power. By inventing a transcendent idea of life in order to judge life, reactive forces separate us from our power to create values; but they also teach us new feelings and new ways of being affected. What needs to be understood is that there is a variation or internal difference in the disposition of reactive forces; these forces change their character and their meaning according to the extent to which they develop their affinity for the will to nothingness. Consequently one of the great problems posed to interpretation is to determine the degree of development reactive forces have reached in relation to negation and the will to nothingness; similarly we need always to attend to the nuance or relative disposition of active force in terms of its development of the relation between action and affirmation.

Connectives

Bergson
Genealogy
Nietzsche
Will to Power

ACTUALITY

Claire Colebrook

It might seem that Deleuze's philosophy is dominated by an affirmation of the virtual and is highly critical of a western tradition that has privileged actuality. To a certain extent this is true, and this privilege can be seen in the way philosophy has traditionally dealt with difference. First, there are deemed to be actual terms, terms that are extended in time – having continuity – and possibly also extended in space. These terms are then related to each other, so difference is something *possible* for an already actualised entity. Difference is between actual terms, such as the difference between consciousness and its world, or is a difference grounded upon actuality, such as something actual bearing the capacity for possible changes. This understanding of actuality is therefore tied to the concept of possibility. Possibility is something that can be predicated of, or attributed to, a being, which remains the same. Now against this understanding of actuality, Deleuze sets a different couple: actuality/potentiality. If there is something actual it is not because it takes up time, nor because time is that which links or contains the changes of actual beings; rather, actuality is *unfolded* from potentiality. We should see the actual not as that from which change and difference take place, but as that which has been effected from potentiality. Time is not the synthesis or continuity of actual terms, as in phenomenology where consciousness constitutes time by linking the past with the present and future. Rather, time is the potential for various lines of actuality. From any actual or unfolded term it should be possible (and, for Deleuze, desirable) to intuit the richer potentiality from which it has emerged.

As an avowed empiricist Deleuze seems to be committed to the primacy of the actual: one should remain attentive to what appears, to what is, without invoking or imagining some condition outside experience. However, while it is true that Deleuze's empiricism affirms life and experience, he refuses to restrict life to the actual. In this respect he overturns a history of western metaphysics that defines the potential and virtual according to already present actualities. We should not, Deleuze insists, define what something is according to already actualised forms. So we should not, for example, establish what it is to think on the basis of what is usually, generally or actually thought. Nor should we think that the virtual is merely the possible: those things that, from the point of view of the actual world, may or may not happen. On the contrary, Deleuze's empiricism is that of the Idea, and it is the essence of the Idea to actualise itself. There is, therefore, an Idea of thinking, the potential or power to think, which is then actualised in any single thought. We can only fully understand and appreciate the actual if we intuit its virtual condition, which is also a real condition. That is, real conditions are not those which must be presupposed by the actual – such as assuming that for any thought there must be a subject who thinks – rather, real conditions are, for Deleuze, the potentials of life from which conditions such as the brain, subjectivity or mind emerge.

For example, if we want to understand a text historically we need to go beyond its actual elements – not just what it says but also beyond its manifest context – to the virtual problem from which any text is actualised. For instance, we should not read John Milton's *Paradise Lost* (1667) as a historical document responding to the English revolution, a revolution that we might understand by reading more texts from the seventeenth century. Rather, we need to think of the potential or Idea of revolution as such: how Milton's text is a specific actualisation, fully different, of the problem of how we might be free, of how power might realise itself, of how individuals might release themselves from imposed servitude. Any actual text or event is possible only because reality has a virtual dimension, a power to express itself in always different actualities: the English revolution, the French revolution, the Russian revolution, are specific and different only because actuality is the expression of an Idea of revolution which can repeat itself infinitely.

Connective

Virtual/Virtuality

AFFECT

Felicity J. Colman

Watch me: affection is the intensity of colour in a sunset on a dry and cold autumn evening. Kiss me: affect is that indescribable moment before the registration of the audible, visual, and tactile transformations produced in reaction to a certain situation, event, or thing. Run away from me: affected are the bodies of spectres when their space is disturbed. In all these situations, affect is an independent thing; sometimes described in terms of the expression of an emotion or physiological effect, but according to Deleuze, the affect is a transitory thought or thing that occurs prior to an idea or perception.

Affect is the change, or variation, that occurs when bodies collide, or come into contact. As a body, affect is the transitional product of an encounter, specific in its ethical and lived dimensions and yet it is also as indefinite as the experience of a sunset, transformation, or ghost. In its largest sense, affect is part of the Deleuzian project of trying-to-understand, and comprehend, and express all of the incredible, wondrous, tragic, painful, and destructive configurations of things and bodies as temporally mediated, continuous events. Deleuze uses the term 'affection' to refer to the additive processes, forces, powers, and expressions of change – the mix of affects that produce a modification or transformation in the affected body.

There are distinctions to be noted in the use of the idea of 'affect'. In philosophy, the word affect is used to signal physical, spiritual, cognitive, and intellectual processes and states. This form of affect is addressed in the context of issues such as life and death; emotions such as pleasure, pain, boredom; attitudes such as fatalism and scepticism, legal states such as justice and obligations (Immanuel Kant, Martin Heidegger). In psychology, the term affect is used to attribute emotional corporeal and psychological reactions and denote states of being, such as delusion, euphoria, sadness, grief, trauma (Silvan Tompkins). There is also the strand of affective neuroscience of theoretical and medical work that examines the affective nature of culture, brain and body relations (Antonio Damasio, Francisco Varela, Joseph LaDoux). While these terms of 'affect' are used to chart corporeal, neurological, subjective responses, and perceptual practices, Deleuze takes a different approach (although overlaps in methodologies occur, for example the Spinozist core in Damasio's approach). The Deleuzian sense of affect is to be distinguished as a philosophical concept that indicates the result of the interaction of bodies; an affective product. In his study of contemporary society, *Parables for the Virtual: Movement, Affect, Sensation*, Brian Massumi makes the crucial distinction between affect and its purported synonym emotion, arguing that this is an inappropriate association, since 'emotion and affect – if affect is intensity – follow different logics and pertain to different orders' (M 2002: 27).

Deleuze engages and extends Baruch Spinoza and Friedrich Nietzsche's philosophical conceptions of affect in order to describe the processes of becoming, transformation through movement and over duration. Through his work on David Hume, Henri Bergson, and work with Félix Guattari, and his books on the Cinema, Deleuze rejects the philosophical tradition of passive reflection, and the value-laden associations of ascribing emotions to subjective experience or perceptions. For Deleuze, affect can produce a sensory or abstract result and is physically and temporally produced. It is determined by chance and organisation and it consists of a variety of factors that include geography, biology, meteorology, astronomy, ecology and culture. Reaction is a vital part of the Deleuzian concept of affective change. For instance, describing Spinoza's study of the transformation of a body, a thing, or a group of things over a period of space and time, Deleuze (with Guattari) writes in *A Thousand Plateaus*: 'Affects are becomings' (DG 1987: 256). Affect expresses the modification of experiences as independent things of existence, when one produces or recognises the consequences of movement and time for (corporeal, spiritual, animal, mineral, vegetable, and, or conceptual) bodies. Affect is an experiential force or a power source, which, through encounters and mixes with other bodies (organic or inorganic), the affect becomes enveloped by affection, becoming an idea, and as such, as Deleuze describes, it can compel systems of knowledge, history, memory, and circuits of power.

Deleuze's conception of affect develops through his entire oeuvre. In his study of Hume in *Empiricism and Subjectivity*, Deleuze discusses the linkages between ideas, habits of thought, ethics, patterns, and repetitions of systems; all the while describing the relationship between affect and difference in terms of temporally specific subjective situations. *Empiricism and Subjectivity* also signals Deleuze's interest in Bergson, a key thinker in the Deleuzian development of a theory of affect. Bergson's book *Matter and Memory* addresses the corporeal condition of what he terms 'affection' in relation to perception (B 1994). Deleuze also engages the work of Spinoza and draws extensively on Spinoza's address of affections and affect in terms of a modality of 'taking on' something in the *Ethics* (1677). In his essay 'On the Superiority of Anglo-American Literature', Deleuze describes affect as verbs becoming events – naming affects as perceivable forces, actions, and activities. In relation to art in *What is Philosophy?* he (with Guattari) describes affects as more than sensate experience or cognition. Through art, we can recognise that affects can be detached from their temporal and geographic origins and become independent entities.

In accounting for experience in a non-interpretive manner, Deleuze's conception of affect exposed the limits of semiotics that tends to structure emotional responses to aesthetic and physical experiences. Undeniably a romantic concept within his discussion of the regulation and production of desire and energy within a social field, Deleuze's writings of affect and affection nevertheless enable a material, and therefore political critique of capital and its operations. Within a Deleuzian framework, affect operates as a dynamic of desire within any assemblage to manipulate meaning and relations, inform and fabricate desire, and generate intensity – yielding different affects in any given situation or event. Perception is a non-passive continual moulding, driven and given by affect.

Closely linked to Deleuze (and Guattari's) concepts of 'multiplicity', 'experience' and 'rhizomatics', the concept of 'affect' should also be considered in relation to the concepts of 'arborescence' and 'lines of flight.' Situated as part of the Deleuzian 'and' of becoming, the molecular thresholds of bodies and things as events are described by Deleuze in terms of affective happenings; occasions where things and bodies are altered. To this end, affect describes the forces behind all forms of social production in the contemporary world, and these affective forces' ethical, ontological, cognitive, and physiological powers. In Deleuze's singular and collaborative work with Guattari, affective forces are depicted as reactive or active (following Nietzsche), tacit or performed. As Deleuze portrays it, affective power can be utilised to enable ability, authority, control and creativity. Embrace me.

Connectives

Active/Reactive
Arborescent schema
Becoming
Experience

Hume
Lines of flight
Multiplicty
Rhizome

ARBORESCENT SCHEMA

Cliff Stagoll

The arboreal schema is one of Deleuze's many potent and prominent biological and organic images. His criticism, and his use of the schema, is scattered across his corpus, at various times targeting approaches to philosophy, psychiatry, literature, science, theoretical criticism and even everyday living. The notion of an arborescent or tree-like schema is Deleuze's counterpoint to his model of the rhizome, which he uses to challenge tendencies in thinking and to suggest ways of rehabilitating 'thought' as a creative and dynamic enterprise.

Deleuze's model of the tree-like structure appears to be quite simple. Typically, at its top, is some immutable concept given prominence either by transcendental theorising works on epistemology and ontology, he identifies Plato's Forms, the models of the subject espoused by René Descartes and Immanuel Kant, as well as the 'Absolute Spirit' of Georg Wilhelm Friedrich Hegel as examples. All other concepts or particulars are organised vertically under this concept in a tree/trunk/root arrangement. The ordering is strictly hierarchical, from superior to subordinate, or transcendent to particular, such that the individual or particular element is conceived as less important, powerful, productive, creative or interesting than the transcendent. The subordinate elements, once so arranged, are unable to 'move' horizontally in such a way as to establish creative and productive interrelationships with other concepts, particulars or models. Rather, their position is final, according to an organising principle implied or determined by the superior concept.

Furthermore, the tree is a self-contained totality or closed system that is equal just to the sum of its parts. Relations between elements of the system are interior to and inherent within the model. They are stable or even essential in so far as, first, the superior concept is the all-powerful defining force that dictates the position or meaning of all else in the system and, second, the tendency is to think of the system either as complete in itself or else unconnected to other systems in any meaningful way. The tree is 'fixed to the spot' and static. Any remaining movement is minimal and internal to the system rather than exploratory or connective. Because the creative potential of disorder and inter-connectivity is precluded, the potential inherent in conceptualising and thinking in this manner is very limited.

Deleuze's model calls to mind the porphyrian tree, a device used by the philosopher Porphyry to show how reality and our concepts are ordered and how logical categorisation proceeds. The concept of 'Substance' can be placed at the top of the tree, and dichotomous branching at each level obtained by adding a specific difference such that, at the lowest level, some individual can be identified as a sub-set of 'Substance'. This version of the arboreal model also highlights something of its complexity and ontological importance for Deleuze. The difference evident between particulars is subsumed by the similarity that defines them in terms of superior concepts in general and the transcendent concept (Substance) in particular. Rather than deriving concepts from individual particulars (or interactions between them), an abstract concept is used to organise individuals and determine their meaning relative just to the organisational hierarchy. Difference has to be added back to each element in order to define it as a particular, rather than having individual elements serve as the starting point for conceptualisation. In contrast, Deleuze holds that lived experience comprises particularity and uniqueness in each moment, experience and individual, the inherent differences of which ought always to be acknowledged. By positing the concept over the particular, thinking of the arboreal kind abstracts from lived experience in its very structure. For Deleuze, thinking in such a way stifles creativity, leaves superior concepts relatively immune to criticism and tends to close one's mind to the dynamism, particularity and change that is evident in lived experience. Not only is such thinking necessarily abstract, it also serves to protect the status quo and relieve dominant concepts and positions from productive critique.

Connectives

Rhizome
Substance

ART

Felicity J. Colman

Deleuze's descriptions of art remind us that it is one of the primary mediums with which humans learn to communicate and respond to the world. Art excited Deleuze for its ability to create the domains that he saw, felt, tasted, touched, heard, thought, imagined and desired. Besides publishing books on singular writers and artists, including making specific manifesto style statements concerning art as a category of critical analysis, Deleuze's specific activities in respect to art extended to writing short exhibition catalogue essays for artists (for example on the French painter Gérard Fromanger), and making experimental music (with Richard Pinhas).

Deleuze's preferred art works for his discussions encompassed a range of mediums, including music and sounds (birdsong), cinema, photography, the plastic arts (sculpture, painting and drawing), literature and architecture. Deleuze's philosophical interests also led him to discuss a number of performative and theatrical works, using examples from anthropology to make cultural and philosophical distinctions. Deleuze addresses the visual, aesthetic and perceptual terms of art through distinctive polemical methodologies drawn from the sciences, such as biological evolution, geological formations and concepts, and mathematics.

Deleuze leans upon a critical assortment of art history critics, film critics, literary critics, architectural critics and musical critics throughout his philosophical practice: Wilhelm Worringer, Aloïs Riegl, Paul Claudel, Clement Greenberg, Lawrence Gowing, Georges Duthuit, Gregory Bateson, André Bazin, Chistian Metz, and Umberto Eco. As a writer, Deleuze's literary predecessors figure prominently (see work in *Essays Critical and Clinical*). His cognitive approach toward art comes from his adopted philosophical fathers including Immanuel Kant, Baruch Spinoza and Friedrich Nietzsche. In *Nietzsche and Philosophy*, Deleuze employs 'art' as a category of 'Critique', taking on Nietzsche's observation that the world is emotive and sensory, but any analysis of this world is bound by epistemological structures. For Deleuze, the descriptive nature of art lies with art's ability not merely to redescribe; rather art has a material capacity to evoke and to question through non-mimetic means, by producing different affects.

Deleuze treats plastic art movements including Byzantine, the Gothic, the Baroque, Romanticism, Classicism, Primitive, Japanese, and Art Brut, as trans-historical concepts that contribute to the field of art through their various propositions and development of forms, aesthetics and associated affects. Singular artists, writers and composers including William Blake, Vincent Van Gogh, Paul Cézanne, Paul Klee, Thomas Hardy, Marie Henri-Beyle Stendhal, Samuel Beckett, Antonin Artaud, William S. Burroughs, Lewis Carroll, Leopold von Sacher-Masoch, Franz Kafka, and Alain Robbe-Grillet are critically absorbed by Deleuze in terms of their respective enquiries into the creation of art forms that translate, illustrate and perform the forces of the world (such as desire), by making them visible. Deleuze mentions in passing an enormous range of artists of various mediums to make a point or an observation – from Igor Stravinsky to Patti Smith, from Diego Velásquez to Carl Andre. The means and methods by which art is able to transform material into sensory experience is of course part of the modernist contribution to art in the twentieth century. In his discussions concerning art, Deleuze is thus a contributor to the twentieth-century modernist canon.

The methodology of art forms the core of Deleuze's study of Marcel Proust's work *À la recherche du temps perdu* (1913–27), a book that examines aspects of temporality, desire and memory. As in his book co-authored with Guattari on *Kafka*, in *Proust,* Deleuze understands art as being much more than a medium of expression.

Deleuze's book *Francis Bacon: The Logic of Sensation* works through the complicated connections of Deleuze and Guattari's Body without Organs (BwO) and English painter Francis Bacon's treatment of the power and rhythms of the human body, to a discussion of the differences from and similarities to the work of French painter Cézanne of Bacon's own work. In this book, Deleuze privileges painting as an art form that affords a concrete apprehension of the forces that render a body. In Deleuze's final work co-authored with Guattari, *What is Philosophy?* 'art' is accorded a privileged position in their triad of philosophy, art and science. Art is an integral component of their three level operations of the cerebral quality of things (the brain-becoming-subject). In this book, 'art' as a category has developed into the means by which Deleuze and Guattari can operate affect, temporality, emotion, mortality, perception and becoming. The active, compounding creativity of artists' work are described as 'percepts' – independent aggregates of sensation that live beyond their creators. Deleuze and Guattari significantly comment that the inspiration for art is given by sensations; the affect of methods, materials, memories and objects: 'We paint, sculpt, compose, and write with sensations' (D&G 1994:166).

Connectives

Affect
Bacon
Experience
Kafka

ARTAUD, ANTONIN (1895–1948) – refer to the entries on 'art', 'becoming + performance art', 'Bergson', 'Body without Organs', 'ethics', 'feminism', 'Foucault + fold', 'hysteria', 'Lacan' and 'lines of flight + art + politics'.

ASSEMBLAGE

Graham Livesey

The concept of assemblage, developed by Deleuze and Guattari, derives from the English translation of their concept in French of *agencement* (arrangement), or the processes of arranging, organising, and fitting together. According to Deleuze and Guattari there is both a horizontal and a vertical axis associated with assemblages. The horizontal axis deals with '*machinic assemblages* of bodies, actions and passions' and a '*collective assemblage of enunciation*, of acts and statements, of incorporeal transformations of bodies' (D&G 1987: 88). The vertical axis has both '*territorial sides*, or reterritorialized sides, which stabilize it, and *cutting edges of deterritorialization*, which carry it away' (D&G 1987: 88). Through its multiplicity an assemblage is shaped by and acts on a wide range of flows.

Assemblages, as conceived of by Deleuze and Guattari, are complex constellations of objects, bodies, expressions, qualities, and territories that come together for varying periods of time to ideally create new ways of functioning. Assemblages operate through desire as abstract machines, or arrangements, that are productive and have function; desire is the circulating energy that produces connections. An assemblage transpires as a set of forces coalesces together, the concept of assemblages applies to all structures, from the behaviour patterns of an individual, the organisation of institutions, an arrangement of spaces, to the functioning of ecologies.

Assemblages emerge from the arranging of heterogeneous elements into a productive (or machinic) entity that can be diagrammed, at least temporarily. The diagram defines the relationships between a particular set of forces; a diagram is, according to Deleuze, the 'map of destiny' (D 1988b: 36). Effectively, the diagram is the code or arrangement by which an assemblage operates, it is a map of the function of an assemblage; assemblages produce affects and effects. The machinic dimension underscores the objectivity, lack of specific location, and the primary role of being productive fundamental to assemblages.

The territorial aspects of assemblages deals with those forces that unmake and make territories, what Deleuze and Guattari define as deterritorialisation and reterritorialisation. The interrelationship between a territory, however defined, and the forces of deterritorialisation and reterritorialisation are necessary for the spatial definition of the earth. Forces, both internal and external, that create deterritorialisation and reterritorialisation, do so as a special function of the territory, or as a refunctioning of a territory. Specific actions can find, define, and assemble territories, and the forces of deterritorialisation and reterritorialisation themselves develop new territories. Deleuze and Guattari, in defining a territory, state that functionality is a product of a territory, rather than the more conventional inverse (D&G 1987: 315-27).

An assemblage emerges when a function emerges; ideally it is innovative and productive. The result of a productive assemblage is a new means of expression, a new territorial/spatial organisation, a new institution, a new behaviour, or a new realisation. The assemblage is destined to produce a new reality, by making numerous, often unexpected, connections.

Connectives

Desire
Deterritorialisation/Reterritorialisation
Space

ASSEMBLAGE + ARCHITECTURE

Jeffrey A. Bell

In his influential analysis of *Ten Canonical Buildings: 1950-2000*, architect and theoretician Peter Eisenman draws upon Deleuze, Derrida, and others in demonstrating how the history of architecture has been a continual attack upon traditional dualisms within architectural practice – namely, the dualistic relations between subject/object, figure/ground, solid/void, and part/whole (E 2008). Eisenman draws particular attention to Deleuze's concept of the figural and Derrida's understanding of the undecidable as effective starting points for rethinking architecture as a practice that is irreducible to an either/or relationship. Eisenman could equally well have stressed Deleuze's concept of an assemblage. An assemblage, for Deleuze, entails a consistency of elements that is irreducible to a traditional dualism – e.g. form–substance relation – and yet assemblages 'swing between territorial closure that tends to restratify them and a deterritorializing movement that on the contrary connects them with the Cosmos' (D&G 1987: 337). Assemblages therefore risk, yet avoid collapsing into actualised stratification or actualised deterritorialisation. An assemblage is thus a dynamic assemblage, a multiplicity that is drawn into a plane of consistency that maintains itself without being reduced to either side of a dualistic relation.

Crucial to connecting Deleuze's understanding of assemblages with architecture is the important role multiplicity plays for Deleuze in developing a philosophy that avoids dualism. In response to the claim that

Deleuze (and Deleuze and Guattari) put forth a philosophy that relies on numerous dualisms – such as virtual/actual, deterritorialisation/reterritorialisation, intensive/extensive, etc. – Deleuze denies the claim and argues that what he and Guattari have sought to do is to 'find between the terms. . .whether they are two or more, a narrow gorge like a border or a frontier which will turn the set into a multiplicity, independently of the number of parts' (D 1987: 132). Similarly, the architect avoids dualism by finding an assemblage that is a multiplicity irreducible to the dualistic terms that are used to identify what it is the architect is doing.

To clarify by way of example, an important dualism among architectural theorists in thinking about modernism is that between autonomy and heteronomy. Modern architecture, as exemplified by Le Corbusier among others, stresses the autonomy of function in opposition to an architecture that relies upon historically and culturally dependent designs and motifs. It is for this reason that Le Corbusier, in his *Towards a New Architecture*, will look to American grain elevators for inspiration and criticise the ornately designed buildings found in the Baroque revival architecture of his day (C 1986). The ideal for an autonomous architecture is to produce a building whose design is independent of the cultural context, including references to earlier styles and periods. This is evidenced in Le Corbusier's Chandigarh project in India as well as his proposals for Algiers. The design of these buildings bears no relationship to the architectural styles one would find in India or Algiers, and hence the autonomy of the architecture. Peter Eisenman will also stress the autonomy of architecture, which for him means that an architect ought to concern himself with addressing purely architectural problems and solutions and they should avoid drawing non-architectural elements into their work. Eisenman's Houses I-XI, for example, are thus for Eisenman purely architectural assemblages that do not refer to anything other than architectural elements. Architect Michael Graves, by contrast, has defended the use of the figurative in architecture and has designed buildings that clearly represent other historical and cultural elements – take his Swan and Dolphin resort at Walt Disney World, where a large swan statue is prominently used in the design. Despite Eisenman's concern for avoiding dualistic relations within architecture, it appears he exemplifies an autonomous as opposed to a heteronomous architecture.

With Deleuze's concept of an assemblage we can rethink this dualism between autonomous and heteronomous architecture. As a dynamic and consistent multiplicity of elements, an architectural assemblage 'swing[s] between', to recall Deleuze and Guattari's formulation cited above, 'territorial closure' on the one hand and a deterritorialising movement on the other. An autonomous architecture thus swings in the direction of territorial closure for it excludes and disenfranchises elements that are not part of the architectural territory; and a heteronomous architecture swings towards a deterritorialising movement in that it includes non-architectural elements (e.g. swans, dolphins, etc.). As an assemblage, however, the point precisely is the swing between these two tendencies, the dynamic tension that neither resolves the tension dialectically, nor becomes actualised as one tendency in opposition to the other. From this perspective, architecture is an assemblage that involves both territorial and architectural elements and deterritorialising non-architectural elements.

The concept of an assemblage also elucidates Aldo Rossi's understanding of the city in *Architecture of the City* (R 1984). With his notion of locus, or place, Rossi is able to set forth an understanding of the city that neither reduces it to being a single place, an organic totality, nor reduces the city to being the result of a totalising plan or function (as was Le Corbusier's ideal). Rather, a city consists of a series of significant places – or loci – that together constitute an assemblage that is irreducible to the places themselves but which is not a totality separable and distinct from these places. A city is thus an assemblage or emergent property of these significant places.

More recently Reiser + Umemoto have incorporated Deleuze's concepts of multiplicity and assemblage into their architectural design procedures (RU 2006). In contrast to an Aristotelian model that would seek to find a mean between two extremes, Reiser + Umemoto call for an architecture that entails both extremes. They seek, in short, to pursue assemblages that simultaneously swing towards territorial closure and deterritorialising movement, and in doing so develop an architecture that avoids the traditional dualisms of form/matter and order/disorder. The concept of an assemblage is therefore not only a productive way of using Deleuze's thought to rethink architectural practice, it has increasingly become incorporated by architects themselves as an integral part of how they both conceptualise and carry out their work.

AXIOMATIC

Alberto Toscano

A term used to define the operation of contemporary capitalism within the universal history and general semiology proposed by Deleuze and Guattari in *A Thousand Plateaus*. Originating in the discourse of science and mathematical set theory in particular, axiomatic denotes a method that need not provide definitions of the terms it works with, but rather orders a given domain with the adjunction or subtraction of particular norms or commands (axioms). Axioms thus operate on elements and relations whose nature need not be specified. They are indifferent to the properties or qualities of their domain of application and treat their objects as purely functional, rather than as qualitatively differentiated by any intrinsic features. Axioms are in turn accompanied by theorems, or models of realisation, which apply them to certain empirical or material situations.

If we take flows (and their cuts or breaks) as the basic constituents of Deleuze and Guattari's transcendental materialism, an axiomatic system differs from systems of coding and overcoding by its capacity to operate directly on decoded flows. In this respect, whilst it too implies a form of capture, its degree of immanence and ubiquity is far greater than that of coding systems, all of which require an instance of externality or transcendence (e.g. the Emperor). That is why Deleuze and Guattari defend the thesis of a difference in kind between capitalist and pre-capitalist formations: the latter code flows, while the former operates without coding. Within universal history the immanent axiomatic of capitalism is activated with the passing of a threshold of decoding and deterritorialisation, at the moment when, following Marx, we are confronted with 'free' labour and independent capital. The axiomatic method, as instantiated by contemporary capitalism and royal science, can be juxtaposed to schizoid practice, which is capable of combining decoded flows without the insertion of axioms, as well as to the problematic method in the sciences, which is concerned with events and singular points rather than systemic consistency.

One of the bolder claims made by Deleuze and Guattari is that we should not think of the axiomatic as a notion analogically exported from science to illustrate politics. On the contrary, within science itself the axiomatic collaborates with the State in the fixation of unruly flows, diagrams and variations. It is an essentially stratifying or semioticising agency, which subordinates the transversal communications and conjunctions of flows to a system of fixed points and constant relations. As Deleuze and Guattari indicate, the unity of an axiomatic system, and of capitalism in particular, is itself very difficult to pin down: the opportunistic character of the adjunction and subtraction of axioms opens up the question of the saturation of the system and of the independence of the axioms from one another. Moreover, though their dependence on axioms makes models of realisation isomorphic (e.g. all states in one way or another satisfy the axiom of production for the market) these models can demonstrate considerable amounts of heterogeneity and variation (e.g. socialist, imperialist, authoritarian, social-democratic, or 'failed' states). The axiomatic system is therefore not a dialectical totality, since it also generates 'undecidable propositions' that demand either new axioms or the overhaul of the system, and it is interrupted by entities (e.g. non-denumerable infinite sets) whose power is greater than that of the system, and which thus open up breaches onto an outside. It is the capacity to conjugate and control flows without the introduction of a transcendent or totalising agency which makes the capitalist axiomatic the most formidable apparatus of domination.

The capitalist axiomatic's ability to establish relations and connections between decoded flows that are otherwise incommensurable and unrelated, and to subordinate these flows to a general isomorphy (i.e. all subjects must produce for the market), leads Deleuze and Guattari to posit a resurgence – beyond citizenship, sovereignty and legitimation – of a machinic enslavement which, no longer referred to an emperor or a transcendent figure, is made all the more cruel by its impersonality. Inasmuch as its mode of operation can entirely bypass subjective belief or the coding of human behaviour, such an axiomatic moves us from a society of discipline to a society of control, where power acts directly on a decoded 'dividual' matter. Not only do flows continue to evade and even overpower the axiomatic, but the global and non-qualified subjectivity of capital never attains absolute deterritorialisation, and is always accompanied by forms of social subjection, in the guise of nation-states, and a panoply of territorialisations at the level of its modes of realisation.

Connectives

Capitalism
Marx
Schizoanalysis

B

BACON, FRANCIS (1909–92)

John Marks

Deleuze's aim in *Francis Bacon: The Logic of Sensation*, as with all his other works on art, is to produce philosophical concepts that correspond to the 'sensible aggregates' that the artist has produced. The 'logic of sensation' that Deleuze constructs shows how Francis Bacon uses 'Figures' to paint sensations that aim to act directly on the nervous system. 'Sensation', here, refers to a pre-individual, impersonal plane of intensities. It is also,

Deleuze claims, the opposite of the facile or the clichés of representation. It is at one and the same time the human subject and also the impersonal event. It is directed towards the sensible rather than the intelligible.

In developing the use of the 'Figure', Bacon pursues a middle path between the abstract and the figural, between the purely optical spaces of abstract art and the purely 'manual' spaces of abstract expressionism. The 'Figure' retains elements that are recognisably human; it is not a representational form, but rather an attempt to paint forces. For Deleuze, the vocation of all non-representational art is to make visible forces that would otherwise remain invisible. It is for this reason that Bacon's figures appear to be deformed or contorted, sometimes passing through objects such as washbasins or umbrellas: the body seeks to escape from itself. There are even some paintings in which the 'Figure' is little more than a shadow within a 'scrambled whole', as if it has been replaced entirely by forces. In short, Bacon's paintings can be considered as an artistic expression of Deleuze and Guattari's concept of the Body without Organs.

Generally in his work, Deleuze seeks to contradict the received wisdom that artists such as Bacon or Franz Kafka are in some way expressing a deep terror of life in their art. For this reason, he is at pains to point out that Bacon has a great love of life, and that his painting evinces an extraordinary vitality. Bacon is optimistic to the extent that he 'believes' in the world, but it is a very particular sort of optimism. Bacon himself says that he is cerebrally pessimistic – in that he paints the horrors of the world – but at the same time nervously optimistic. Bacon's work may be imbued with all sorts of violence, but he manages to paint the 'scream' and not the 'horror' – the violence of the sensation rather than the violence of the spectacle – and he reproaches himself when he feels that he has painted too much horror. The forces that cause the scream should not be confused with the visible spectacle before which one screams. The scream captures invisible forces, which cannot be represented, because they lie beyond pain and feeling. So, cerebrally, this may lead to pessimism, since these invisible forces are even more overwhelming than the worst spectacle that can be represented. However, Deleuze claims that, in making the decision to paint the scream, Bacon is like a wrestler confronting the 'powers of the invisible', establishing a combat that was not previously possible. He makes the active decision to affirm the possibility of triumphing over these forces. He allows life to scream *at* death, by confronting terror, and entering into combat with it, rather than representing it. The 'spectacle' of violence, on the other hand, allows these forces to remain invisible, and diverts us, rendering us passive before this horror.

Deleuze talks at some length about the importance of 'meat' in Bacon's paintings. For Deleuze, Bacon is a great painter of 'heads' rather than 'faces'. Bacon seeks to dismantle the structured spatial organisation of the face in order to make the head emerge. Similarly, Bacon sometimes makes a shadow emerge from the body as if it were an animal that the body was sheltering. In this way, Bacon produces a zone of indiscernibility. The bones are the spatial organisation of the body, but the flesh in Bacon's paintings ceases to be supported by the bones. Deleuze remarks upon Bacon's preference for 'Figures' with raised limbs, from which the drowsy flesh seems to descend. This flesh, or meat, constitutes the zone of indiscernibility between man and animal. The head, then, constitutes what Deleuze calls the 'animal spirit' of man. Bacon does not ask us to pity the fate of animals (although this could well be one effect of his paintings), but rather to recognise that every human being who suffers is a piece of meat. In short, the man that suffers is an animal, and the animal that suffers is a man. Deleuze talks of this in terms of a 'religious' aspect in Bacon's paintings, but a religious dimension that relates to the brutal reality of the butcher's shop. The understanding that we are all meat is not a moment of recognition or of revelation, but rather, for Deleuze, a moment of true becoming. The separation between the spectator and the spectacle is broken down in favour of the 'deep identity' of becoming.

Connectives

Art
Becoming
Intensity
Sensation

BECKETT, SAMUEL (1906–89) – refer to the entries on 'art', 'minoritarian + cinema' and 'space'.

BECOMING

Cliff Stagoll

Together with 'difference', 'becoming' is an important component of Deleuze's corpus. In so far as Deleuze champions a particular ontology, these two concepts are its cornerstones, serving as antidotes to what he considers to be the western tradition's predominant and unjustifiable focus upon being and identity. This focus is replicated, Deleuze argues, in our everyday thinking, such that the extent of the variety and change of the experienced world has been diluted by a limited conception of difference: difference-from-the-same. Deleuze works at two levels to rectify such habitual thinking. Philosophically, he develops theories of difference, repetition and becoming. For the world of practice, he provides challenging writings designed to upset our thinking, together with a range of 'tools' for conceiving the world anew. At both levels, becoming is critical, for if the primacy of identity is what defines a world of re-presentation (presenting the same world once again), then becoming (by which Deleuze means 'becoming different') defines a world of presentation anew.

Taking his lead from Friedrich Nietzsche's early notes, Deleuze uses the term 'becoming' (*devenir*) to describe the continual production (or 'return') of difference immanent within the constitution of events, whether physical or otherwise. Becoming is the pure movement evident in changes *between* particular events. This is not to say that becoming represents a phase between two states, or a range of terms or states through which something might pass on its journey to another state. Rather than a product, final or interim, becoming is the very dynamism of change, situated between heterogeneous terms and tending towards no particular goal or end-state.

Becoming is most often conceived by deducing the differences between a start-point and end-point. On Deleuze's account, this approach means first subtracting movement from the field of action or thinking in which the states are conceived, and then somehow reintroducing it as the means by which another static state has 'become'. For Deleuze, this approach is an abstract exercise that detracts from the richness of our experiences. For him, becoming is neither merely an attribute of, nor an intermediary between events, but a characteristic of the very production of events. It is not that the time of change exists between one event and another, but that every event is but a unique instant of production in a continual flow of changes evident in the cosmos. The only thing 'shared' by events is their having become different in the course of their production.

The continual production of unique events entails a special kind of continuity: they are unified in their very becoming. It is not that becoming 'envelops' them (since their production is wholly immanent) but that becoming 'moves through' every event, such that each is simultaneously start-point, end-point and mid-point of an ongoing cycle of production. Deleuze theorises this productive cycle using Nietzsche's concept of 'eternal return'. If each moment represents a unique confluence of forces, and if the nature of the cosmos is to move continually through states without heading towards any particular outcome, then becoming might be conceived as the eternal, productive return of difference.

Deleuze believes that each change or becoming has its own duration, a measure of the relative stability of the construct, and the relationship between forces at work in defining it. Becoming must be conceived neither in terms of a 'deeper' or transcendental time, nor as a kind of 'temporal backdrop' against which change occurs. Becoming-different *is its own time*, the real time in which changes occur, and in which all changes unfold. This is not the Kantian *a priori* form of time that depends upon attributes of a particular kind of consciousness. Rather it is the time of production, founded in difference and becoming and consequent to relations between internal and external differences. For Deleuze, the present is merely the productive moment of becoming, the moment correlating to the productive threshold of forces. As such, it represents the disjunction between a past in which forces have had some effect and a future in which new arrangements of forces will constitute new events. In other words, becoming per se is Deleuze's version of pure and empty time.

Such a view of the world has important implications for concepts traditionally considered central to philosophy. It undercuts any Platonic theory that privileges being, originality and essence. For Deleuze, there is no world 'behind appearances', as it were. Instead of being about transitions that something initiates or goes through, things and states are now viewed as *products* of becoming. The human subject, for example, ought not to be conceived as a stable, rational individual, experiencing changes but remaining, principally, the same person. Rather, for Deleuze, one's self must be conceived as a constantly changing assemblage of forces, an epiphenomenon arising from chance confluences of languages, organisms, societies, expectations, laws and so on.

Connectives

Duration
Nietzsche

BECOMING + MUSIC

Marcel Swiboda

'Becoming' and 'music' are two terms that can be brought together such that a becoming is capable of proceeding through music, for example through the musical operation known as 'counterpoint', or the interweaving of several different melodic lines horizontally where the harmony is produced through linear combinations rather than using a vertical chordal structure or setting. Counterpoint might most usually constitute a specifically 'musical' case in that when one speaks of musical counterpoint the assertions made regarding the term usually refer back to a given musical example: in short, counterpoint is something that we normally *hear*. However, when counterpoint describes the interweaving of different lines as something other than what we can hear, then it opens up to a different function, a function that frees the term from a direct relation to properly musical content. Consider the work of the ethologist Jakob von Uexküll on the relationship between animal behaviour among certain species and the environments inhabited by these species that led him to propound a theory of this relationship based on a conception of counterpoint. To this extent, nature – in the very ways in which it can be figured through the interaction of different *lines* of movement, between animals and their environments, or between and across different species of animals – can be understood as constituting a counterpoint in a sense that extends beyond a strictly metaphorical deployment of the term. From the perspective outlined here, music enters into a relation of proximity to nature where *music becomes nature*.

If in cultural theory the term 'nature' is somewhat problematic it is to the extent that it cannot be unquestioningly presupposed as having any objective existence beyond the terms that define it, terms that are often loaded. In the present case, the term aims at neither an objective conception nor a discursive one. Rather, this description attempts to restore to 'nature' a material dimension that extends beyond the confines of discourse, to the extent that discourse *implies* material processes that cannot be reduced to interpretation or the status of fixed objects. To im-ply, in this instance, is to en-fold, whereby language can in some instances be deployed in ways that foreground its enfolding of material processes. Implication in this sense is illustrated by the use of the term 'counterpoint', a term which has largely been retained by Deleuze and Guattari in *A Thousand Plateaus* because it is highly amenable to a thinking oriented towards *process*. As was mentioned earlier, the term is most often used in a musical context to figure the (harmonic) interactions of melodic lines. As such it does not describe a fixed object and the term's linguistic or semantic sense is insufficient to account for *what actually happens* when counterpoint takes place as it draws its contingent connections between different melodic lines.

This characteristic of the term makes it amenable to the task of constructing a different conception of nature, in that it is detachable from its strictly musical context in such a way that it still retains its capacity both to describe and *at the same time* to imply, or enfold process. This capacity is what allows us to use the term to describe non-musical as well as musical interactions, where the idea of the melodic line, strictly speaking, gives way to an expanded conception of linear interactions, such as those taking place between the bodies of different animals, animal species, their environments, and one another. This expanded sense of the term permits the construction of a renewed conception of nature that puts it in proximity to music, where *nature becomes music*. An example of this proximity is embodied in the work of the French composer Olivier Messiaen who famously transcribed the songs of different bird species before incorporating them into his musical compositions. The territorial codings between and across certain bird species and their environments (transcodings) are carried over into the music in the use of birdsong, such that there can no longer be a binary or hierarchical distinction drawn between the productions of 'culture' and those of 'nature'.

Music becomes nature and nature becomes music and their resulting indiscernibility is the product of a philosophical labour: to *select terms best suited to the task of thinking and describing process*. Counterpoint is such a term because it is capable of putting music and nature into proximity and describing the material implications that orient thought towards process.

BECOMING + PERFORMANCE ART

Adrian Parr

The early era of performance art from the mid-1960s and through the1970s included such figures as Allan Kaprow, Vito Acconci, Bruce Nauman, Chris Burden, Adrian Piper, Laurie Anderson, Lacy and Labowitz, Hannah Wilke, Carolee Schneemann, and Ana Mendieta in the United States; Joseph Beuys, Marina and Ulay, Valie Export, Hermann Nitsch and the Vienna Actionismus in West Europe; Jan Mlcoch, Petr Stembera, Milan Knizak, Gabor Attalai, Tamas Szentjoby in East Europe; Stuart Brisley, and Gilbert and George in England; and Jill Orr, Stelarc and Mike Parr in Australia. More recently performance has become a significant, if not primary, ingredient of many artistic practices. Examples include but are not restricted to: Coco Fusco, Guillermo Gómez-Peña, Ricardo Dominguez, Santiago Sierra, Franco B., Vanessa Beecroft, Matthew Barney, Tehching Hsieh, and Andrea Fraser.

Strongly influenced by Antonin Artaud, Dada, the Situationists, Fluxus and Conceptual Art, performance art in its early days tended to define itself as the antithesis of theatre, in so far as the event was never repeated the same way twice and did not have a linear structure with a clear beginning, middle and end. More importantly though, all performance art interrogates the clarity of subjectivity, disarranging the clear and distinct positions that the artist, artwork, viewer, art institution and art market occupy.

Trying to articulate the changed relationship between artist, artwork and viewer that performance art inaugurated can at times be difficult but the Deleuzian concept of 'becoming' is especially useful here in that it allows us to consider art in terms of a transformative experience as well as conceptualise the process of subjectification performance art sustains. 'Becoming' points to a non-linear dynamic process of change and when used to assist us with problems of an aesthetic nature we are encouraged not just to reconfigure the apparent stability of the art object as 'object' defined in contradistinction to a fully coherent 'subject' or an extension of that 'subject' but rather the concept of art's becoming is a fourfold becoming-minor of the artist, viewer, artwork and milieu. It is in this regard that performance prompts us to consider the production and appreciation of art away from the classical subject/object distinction that prevailed by and large up until the 1960s.

A good example of this would have to be Acconci's *Following Piece* (1969) that began with a proposition randomly to follow people in New York. The idea was that the performance would independently arrive at a logical endpoint, regardless of the artist's intention and despite the 'goal' of the work being achieved. Instead, it was the person being followed who brought the work to its final conclusion, such as when she entered her apartment or got into her car and drove off. In this instance the work was provisionally structured by a proposition, 'to follow another person', but the eventual form the work took was structured by the movements of the person being followed. In fact, here the art can be considered as a process sensitive to its own transformation; as the artist was led around the city at the whim of someone else. There is a proposition to do 'X' then the activity of doing 'X' activates new previously unforeseen organisations to take place; the art is in the 'becoming of art' that is in itself social. Art of this kind may be best articulated as 'art without guarantees'; this is because it exists entirely in duration and amidst the play of divergent forces that typifies Deleuze's understanding of 'becoming'.

What is more, with performance art artistic value is produced socially; it is not an abstract value that is imposed outside the creative process itself. Hence, what we find is that this kind of artistic practice concomitantly provides a radical challenge against the whole concept of labour in a capitalist context. Value is not decided according to profit margins and the market, rather it is a particular kind of social organisation. For example, when Beuys arrived at the René Block Gallery in New York (May 1974) where he lived with a wild coyote for seven days in the gallery, the art was in how the two slowly developed a sense of trust in the other to the point where they eventually slept curled up together. The meaning that emerged out of the piece was not universal, nor was it absolutely relative; as an a-signifying process this was an art practice occurring at the limits of signification.

In the examples given, the art was both socially produced and conceived in terms of 'social formation', one that converged differences in their mutual becoming. Hence, what this demonstrates is that performance art turns its back on the optical emphasis that once governed art. Instead, such practices aim at producing an encounter or event, not in the simplistic sense that it 'happened' at a particular moment in time, but in so far as it aspires to bring a variety of elements and forces into relation with one another. Ultimately, performance art involves a multiplicity of durations, each of which is implied in the artwork as a whole. The crucial point is that performance art cannot be described within traditional aesthetic parameters that reinforce the validity of subject/object distinctions, consequently the conceptual apparatus 'becoming' offers us is descriptive. It helps us describe the process of change indicative of performance art; an event that in its singularity concomitantly expresses a multiplicity of relations, forces, affects and percepts.

BERGSON, HENRI (1859–1941)

Felicity J. Colman

Deleuze has been credited with restoring French philosopher Henri Bergson to the canon of key thinkers of his generation, and Bergson's work continues to impact disciplines concerned with time, movement, memory and perception. Along with the thoughts of Gottfried Wilhelm von Leibniz, Baruch Spinoza, Friedrich Nietzsche, David Hume, Antonin Artaud, Guattari and Lucretius, Deleuze engages Bergson's empiricism as a challenge to the rigidity of philosophy, especially in its use of transcendental elements, phenomenological assumptions, and the quest for 'knowledge' and 'truth'. Deleuze's philosophical interest in Bergson is manifold and central to his entire oeuvre. Although neglected in philosophical canons of the second half of the twentieth century, in the early decades of that century, Bergson's work was well known and widely discussed in many artistic and literary arenas, from the French Cubists to the English writer T. E. Hulme.

In Bergson Deleuze finds an intellectual partner for some of his core philosophical pursuits: concepts and ideas of temporality, the affective nature of movement and duration, the political implications of multiplicity and difference, the morphological movement of genetics, and the temporal causality of events as habitual and associated series. Deleuze signals his interest in Bergson in his essay on Hume, *Empiricism and Subjectivity*. Then, in 1966, Deleuze published his book *Bergsonism*, in which he called for 'a return to Bergson', through an extended consideration of what he saw as Bergson's three key concepts: intuition as method, the demand for an invention and utilisation of a metaphysical orientation of science, and a logical method and theory of multiplicities. Bergson not only questions the logistics of existence in terms of movement, but his writing indicates his genuine fascination with the subjects and objects of life – appealing to Deleuze's own propositions concerning vitalism.

Bergson's concepts are influential for Deleuze's work in *Difference and Repetition*, where Deleuze develops ideas of difference and repetition, memory and repetition, the intensive and extensive forms of time, and the physical movements of time; all of which are indebted to Bergson's discussion of the paradoxical modalities of time in his book, *Matter and Memory* [*Matière et Mémoire*] (1896). Bergson proposes a moving model of duration – a concept of duration that is not spatially predetermined but continually alters its past through cognitive movement. Then, later in *Creative Evolution* Bergson incorporates the cinematic model into his philosophical expression, noting the cinematographical character of ancient philosophy in its apprehension of the thought of ordinary knowledge (B 1911: 331–33). From this model (and the Kantian notion of time, and Hegelian conception of thought and movement) Deleuze develops his explication of how the perceptual recognition of moving images of the cinematic screen operates not through the apprehension of that movement, but through specific moments of sound and optical registration. This Deleuze discusses at length in his two books on the cinema, *Cinema 1: The movement-image* and *Cinema 2: The Time-Image.*

Bergson conceives memory as a temporal blending of perceptual imagery, and this idea becomes central to Deleuze's hypothesis in his discussion of the philosophical importance of cinema. In his second book on cinema, *The Time-Image*, Deleuze draws from Bergson's interest in the different types of possible memory states – dreams, amnesia, déjà-vu, and death. To these Deleuze adds a breadth of memory functions: fantasy, hallucinations, Nietzsche's concept of 'promise-behaviour' where we make a memory of the present for the future use of the present (now as past), theatre, Alain Robbe-Grillet's concept of the 'recognition' process where the portrayal of memory is through invention and elimination, and numerous others.

Following Bergson, Deleuze describes how the perceptual and cognitive abilities of the dream or wakeful receptor of memory events or imagery are dependent upon a complex network of factors. As Bergson discusses in *Matter and Memory*, systems of perceptual attention are contingent upon the 'automatic' or 'habitual' recognition of things. These different modes of remembering are further tempered through the degree of attention given in the perception of things, affecting not only the description of the object, but the features of the object itself. From Bergson, Deleuze's mature conception of duration and the movements and multiplicities of time are developed.

Connectives

Cinema
Difference
Duration
Hume
Memory
Multiplicity

BLACK HOLE

Kylie Message

Deleuze and Guattari believe that the role of philosophy is to invent new concepts that challenge the way that philosophy itself is written and formulated. Because of this, they draw both from new ideas and from those of a multiplicity of already existing disciplines, including biological and earth sciences, and physics. This interdisciplinary coverage is designed to make their philosophical project have concurrent significance or effect (no matter how small) within the field of conceptual matrices that they both appropriate from and contribute to; philosophical or otherwise. These engagements are at times fleeting and at times more sustained, and contribute to their strategy of preventing their position from stabilising into an ideology, method, or single metaphor. In other words, they encourage philosophy to occupy the space of slippage that exists between disciplinary boundaries, and to question how things are made, rather than simply analysing or interpreting the taken-for-granted final result or image. This provides the foundation for the work presented in *Anti-Oedipus* and *A Thousand Plateaus*, and the series of renewed terms proposed by these texts (including schizoanalysis, rhizomatics, pragmatics, diagrammatism, cartography, and micropolitics).

Appearing predominantly in *A Thousand Plateaus*, the term 'black hole' has been sourced from contemporary physics. Referring to spaces that cannot be escaped from once drawn into, Deleuze and Guattari describe the black hole as a star that has collapsed into itself. While although this term exists literally rather than as a metaphor (because it maintains an effect that is fully actualised, affective and real), it has been relocated away from its original source in scientific discourse. As with many of the terms appropriated by *A Thousand Plateaus*, it is presented as being engaged in its own process of deterritorialisation that is independent from the text that it has been woven into; these concepts do not exist for the newly bricolaged together text, but happen to come into contact with it or move through it as a condition or process of their own moving trajectory or line of flight.

In the context of *A Thousand Plateaus*, the black hole is presented as being one – unwanted but necessary – outcome for a failed line of flight. Deterritorialising movement strays away from the concept and state of molar identity and aims to force splinters to crack open into giant ruptures and cause the subsequent obliteration of the subject as he becomes ensconced within a process of becoming-multiple. Engaged in this process, the subject is deconstituted, and becomes a new kind of assemblage that occupies what Deleuze and Guattari call the 'plane of consistency', which is a space of creativity and desire. However, because this plane is also that of death and destruction, traps are scattered throughout this process. Existing as micro-fascisms across this plane, black holes threaten self conscious acts of transcendence and self-destruction alike, which is why Deleuze and Guattari advise nomads to exercise caution as they disorganise themselves away from the molar organisations of the State. So, in simple terms, the black hole is one possible outcome of an ill-conceived (which often equates to overly self-conscious) attempt at deterritorialisation that is caused by a threshold crossed too quickly or an intensity become dangerous because it is no longer bearable.

Another way of thinking about the black hole is in terms of how Deleuze and Guattari rewrite the relationship philosophy and psychoanalysis has with desire and subjectivity. If the black hole is one possible outcome faced by the overly convulsive, self-consumed desiring subject, then it works to illustrate their contention that every strong emotion – such as consciousness or love – pursues its own end. As a potential outcome for both paths of transcendence and destruction, the lure of the black hole indicates the subject's attraction toward an absolute (lack) of signification. This expresses the absolute impossibility of representation at the same time as it actively works to show how grand narrative statements continually intertwine subjectivity and signification. In appealing to a deterritorialising activity, Deleuze and Guattari problematise the process of subjectification, which, they claim, results either in self-annihilation (a black hole), or re-engagement with different planes of becoming.

In addition to presenting the black hole as a possible end-point to certain acts of deterritorialisation, Deleuze and Guattari use it as a way of further conceptualising their notion of faciality. In this context, black holes exist as the binary co-requisite of the flat white surface, wall or landscape that nominally symbolises the generic white face of Christ. In order to break through the dominating white face, or wall of the signifier, and avoid being swallowed by the black hole, one must renounce the face by becoming imperceptible. However, Deleuze and Guattari advise caution when embarking on such a line of flight. Indeed, they claim madness to be a definite danger associated with attempts to break out of the signifying system represented by the face. We must not, they warn, entirely reject our organising boundaries because to do so can result in the complete rejection of subjectivity. Recalling the slogan of schizoanalysis, they tell us not to turn our backs on our boundaries, but to keep them in sight so that we can dismantle them with systematic caution.

Connectives

Molar
Schizoanalysis
Space

BODY

Bruce Baugh

'Body' for Deleuze is defined as any whole composed of parts, where these parts stand in some definite relation to one another, and has a capacity for being affected by other bodies. The human body is just one example of such a body; the animal body is another, but a body can also be a body of work, a social body or collectivity, a linguistic corpus, a political party, or even an idea. A body is not defined by either simple materiality, by its occupying space ('extension'), or by organic structure. It is defined by the relations of its parts (relations of relative motion and rest, speed and slowness), and by its actions and reactions with respect both to its environment or milieu and to its internal milieu. The parts of a body vary depending on the kind of body: for a simple material object, such as a rock, its parts are minute particles of matter; for a social body, its parts are human individuals who stand in a certain relation to each other. The relations and interactions of the parts compound to form a dominant relation, expressing the 'essence' or a power of existing of that body, a degree of physical intensity that is identical to its power of being affected. A body exists when, for whatever reason, a number of parts enter into the characteristic relation that defines it, and which corresponds to its essence or power of existing. Since nature as a whole contains all elements and relations, nature as a whole is a body, a system of relations among its parts, expressing the whole order of causal relations in all its combinations.

Deleuze is fond of quoting Baruch Spinoza's dictum that 'no one knows what a body can do'. The more power a thing has, or the greater its power of existence, the greater number of ways in which it can be affected. Bodies are affected by different things, and in different ways, each type of body being characterised by minimum and maximum thresholds for being affected by other bodies: what can and what cannot affect it, and to what degree. Certain external bodies may prove insufficient to produce a reaction in a body, or fail to pass the minimum threshold, whereas in other cases, the body being affected may reach a maximum threshold, such that it is incapable of being affected any further, as in a tick that dies of engorgement. A body being affected by another, such that the relations of its parts are the effect of other bodies acting on it, is a passive determination of the body, or passion. If an external body is combined or 'composed' with a body in a way that increases the affected body's power of being affected, this transition to a higher state of activity is experienced as joy; if the combination decreases the affected body's power of being affected, this is the affect of sadness. It is impossible to know in advance which bodies will compose with others in a way that is consonant with a body's characteristic relation or ratio of its parts, or which bodies will decompose a body by causing its parts to enter into experimental relations.

Whether the effect is to increase or decrease a body's power of acting and being affected, one body affecting another, or producing effects in it, is in reality a combining and a mixing of the two bodies, and most often 'bit by bit', or part by part. Sometimes this mixing alters one of the bodies (as when food is altered in being assimilated, or when a poison destroys a body's vital parts); sometimes it alters both and produces a composite relation of parts that dominates the relations of both components (as when chyle and lymph mix to form blood, which is of a different nature from its components); and sometimes it preserves the relation of parts among them both, in which case the two bodies form parts of a whole. The characteristic relation that results from harmoniously combining the relations of the two component bodies into a 'higher individual' or 'collective person', such as a community or an association, corresponds to a collective power of being affected, and results in collective or communal affects.

Since a body is a relation of parts corresponding to an essence, or a degree of physical intensity, a body need not have the hierarchical and dominating organisation of organs we call an 'organism'. It is rather an intensive reality, differentiated by the maximum and minimum thresholds of its power of being affected.

Connectives

Body without Organs
Power
Space
Spinoza

BODY WITHOUT ORGANS

Kylie Message

A phrase initially taken from Antonin Artaud, the Body without Organs (BwO) refers to a substrate that is also identified as the plane of consistency (as a non-formed, non-organised, non-stratified or destratified body or term). The term first emerged in Deleuze's *The Logic of Sense*, and was further refined with Guattari in *Anti-Oedipus* and *A Thousand Plateaus*. The BwO is proposed as a means of escaping what Deleuze and Guattari perceive as the shortcomings of traditional (Freudian, Lacanian) psychoanalysis. Rather than arguing that desire is based on Oedipal lack, they claim desire is a productive-machine that is multiple and in a state of constant flux. And whereas psychoanalysis proclaims closure and interpretation, their critique of the three terms (organism, significance and subjectification) that organise and bind us most effectively suggests the possibility of openings and spaces for the creation of new modes of experience. Rather than proceeding directly to invert or deconstruct terms dominant in the production of identity and consciousness, they suggest that implicit within, between, and all around these are other – possibly more affective – fields of immanence and states of being.

Attention is refocused away from the subjectivity (a term they feel is too often mistaken for the term 'consciousness') traditionally privileged by psychoanalysis as Deleuze and Guattari challenge the world of the articulating, self-defining and enclosed subject. The BwO is the proposed antidote (as well as precedent, antecedent and even correlate) to this articulate and organised organism; indeed, they claim that the BwO has no need for interpretation. The BwO does not exist in opposition to the organism or notions of subjectivity, and it is never completely free of the stratified exigencies of proper language, the State, family, or other institutions. However, it is, despite this, both everywhere and nowhere, disparate and homogeneous. In terms of this, there are two main points to note: firstly, that the BwO exists within stratified fields of organisation at the same time as it offers an alternative mode of being or experience (becoming); secondly, the BwO does not equate literally to an organ-less body.

In reference to the first point, Deleuze and Guattari explain that although the BwO is a process that is directed toward a course of continual becoming, it cannot break away entirely from the system that it desires escape from. While it seeks a mode of articulation that is free from the binding tropes of subjectification and signification, it must play a delicate game of maintaining some reference to these systems of stratification, or else risk obliteration or reterritorialisation back into these systems. In other words, such subversion is an incomplete process. Instead, it is continuous and oriented only towards its process or movement rather than toward any teleological point of completion. Consistent with this, and in order to be affective (or to have affect) it must exist – more or less – within the system that it aims to subvert.

Deleuze and Guattari take Miss X as their role model. A hypochondriac, she claims to be without stomach, brain, or internal organs, and is left with only skin and bones to give structure to her otherwise disorganised body. Through this example, they explain that the BwO does not refer literally to an organ-less body. It is not produced as the enemy of the organs, but is opposed to the organisation of the organs. In other words, the BwO is opposed to the organising principles that structure, define and speak on behalf of the collective assemblage of organs, experiences or states of being. Whereas psychoanalysis privileges 'lack' as the singular and productive force that maintains desire, Deleuze and Guattari claim that by binding and judging desire in this way, our understanding and relationship with the real or Imaginary becomes further removed and compromised.

Elaborating further on the nature of the BwO, Deleuze also invokes the German biologist, August Weismann, and his 'theory of the germplasm' (1885, published 1893) to contend that – like the germplasm – the BwO is always contemporary with and yet independent of its host organism. Weismann believed that at each generation, the embryo that develops from the zygote not only sets aside some germplasm for the next generation (the inheritance of acquired features) but it also produces the cells that will develop into the soma – or body – of the organism. In Weismann's view, the somaplasm simply provides the housing for the germplasm, to ensure that it is protected, nourished and conveyed to the germplasm of the opposite sex in order to create the next generation. What comes first, the chicken or the egg? Weismann would insist the chicken is simply one egg's device for laying another egg. Similarly, Deleuze presents the BwO as equivalent to the egg; like the egg, the BwO does not exist before or prior to the organism, but is adjacent to it and continuously in the process of constructing itself.

Instead of slotting everything into polarised fields of the norm and its antithesis, Deleuze and Guattari encourage us to remove the poles of organisation but maintain a mode of articulation. They advise that in seeking to make ourselves a BwO, we need to maintain a mode of expression, but rid language of the central role it has in arbitrating truth and reality against madness and the pre-symbolic real. Relocating desire away from a dichotomous linguistic trajectory, Deleuze and Guattari present it as being contextualised by the field of immanence offered by the BwO rather than by the conclusive field of language. As such, desire is always already engaged in a continuous process of becoming. However, despite occupying (and in some cases embodying) a field of immanence or a plane of consistency, which are often described as being destratified, decoded and deterritorialised, the BwO has its own mode of organisation (whose principles are primarily derived from Baruch Spinoza). Rather than being a specific form, the body is more correctly described as uncontained matter or a collection of heterogeneous parts.

Connectives

Becoming
Body
Desire
Lacan
Psychoanalysis
Spinoza

BREUER, JOSEPH (1842–1925) – refer to the entries on 'hysteria' and 'feminism'.

BURROUGHS, WILLIAM (1914–97) – refer to the entries on 'art' and 'post-structuralism + politics'.

C

CANGUILHEM, GEORGES (1904–95) – refer to the entry on 'schizophrenia'.

CAPITALISM

Jonathan Roffe

In the period before his death, Deleuze announced in an interview that he would like to compose a work, which would be called *The Grandeur of Marx*. This fact clearly indicates Deleuze's positive attitude towards the philosophy of Karl Marx, which he never abandoned despite altering many of its fundamental elements. Certainly the most important of these elements is capitalism. The Marxism of Deleuze comes from his insistence that all political thought must take its bearings from the capitalist context we live in. While mentioning capitalism in passing in a number of places, it is the two volumes of *Capitalism and Schizophrenia*, which contain the most sustained and radical treatment of this theme.

Deleuze and Guattari insist any given social formation restricts or structures movements or flows. They claim that these flows are not just the flows of money and commodities familiar to economists, but can be seen at a variety of levels: the movement of people and traffic in a city, the flows of words that are bound up in a language, the flows of genetic code between generations of plants, and even the flow of matter itself (the movement of the ocean, electrons moving in metals, and so forth). Thus, Deleuze and Guattari's political thought begins with the premise that nature itself, the Whole of existence, is at once a matter of flows, and that any society must structure these flows in order to subsist. All State and pre-State societies – all those which according to Marx are pre-capitalist – on Deleuze and Guattari's account, have such a restriction of flows as their basic principle.

Deleuze and Guattari call this process of restriction, or structuring, 'coding'. They conceive coding as at once restrictive and necessary. Societies, as regimes of coding, aim to bring about certain fixed ways of existing (living, talking, working, relating) while denying other more malleable ways. However, without some structure – our own coherent individuality and agency for example, which Deleuze and Guattari consider specific to each social formation and always oppressive – there would be no basis upon which to challenge and attempt to alter the given coding regime. Both *Anti-Oedipus* and *A Thousand Plateaus* include lengthy analyses of different kinds of societies and the ways in which they code flows.

Capitalism is the radical exception to this basic central understanding of the nature of society. There are four features to this exceptional status of capitalism for Deleuze and Guattari. First, instead of working by coding flows, capitalism is a regime of decoding. Second, and in tandem with this, the recoding that would take place in non-capitalist societies to recapture decoded flows is replaced by the process of axiomatisation. For example, the coding of sexual relations through marriage, the church, morals and popular culture – which in different societies locate the practice of sex in certain contexts, whether that is marriage, prostitution or youth culture – has been decoded in capitalist societies. This is first of all, for Deleuze and Guattari, a good thing, making possible new kinds of relations that were excluded by the coding regimes in question. In capitalism, however, a correlative axiomatisation has taken place making possible the sale of sex as a product (what Karl Marx called a 'commodity'). Axioms operate, in short, by emptying flows of their specific meaning in their coded context (sex as the act of marriage, the meal as the centre of family life, and so on) and imposing a law of general equivalence in the form of monetary value. These flows remain decoded in so far as they are fluid parts of the economy. They cannot, as commodities, be bound to a certain state of affairs to have value – for food to be a product it must be possible to eat it in a context other than the family home, or tribe.

The third important aspect of capitalism for Deleuze and Guattari – drawing on Marx – is that this process of decoding/axiomatisation has no real limit. Given that all such limits would be codes, this movement effectively and voraciously erodes all such limits. This accounts for the sense in capitalist societies of perpetual novelty and innovation, since coded flows are continually being turned into commodities through this process, further extending the realm of monetary equivalence.

However, such a process could never be total. Thus, fourthly, the fact that capitalist society proceeds in this way does not mean for Deleuze and Guattari that coded elements of social formation are entirely absent. Rather, certain fragments of State society (in particular) are put to work in the service of capitalism. Obviously, structures like the government and the family still exist in capitalism. As they note, there could be no total decoded society – an oxymoronic phrase. Governments and monarchies remain, while having their real juridical power substantially reduced, as regulative mechanisms stabilising the growth of decoding/axiomatisation. The nuclear family in particular, the kind of coded entity that one might imagine would be dissolved by the decoding/axiomatising movement of capitalism, is for Deleuze and Guattari the site of a surprising miniaturisation of State society, where the father takes the position (structurally speaking) of the despotic and all-seeing ruler.

None of these points, however, makes for a celebration of the liberatory effects of capitalism. Deleuze and Guattari remain Marxists in so far as they consider real freedom to be unavailable in the world of monetary equivalence enacted by capitalism. While imitating the decoding that makes possible the freeing up of flows and new ways of existing, capitalist society only produces a different, more insidious, kind of unfreedom.

Connectives

Freedom
Marx
Oedipalisation

CAPITALISM + UNIVERSAL HISTORY

Eugene Holland

Deleuze and Guattari are alone among post-structuralists in their resuscitation of the notion of universal history. But by drawing on Karl Marx rather than Georg Wilhelm Friedrich Hegel, they insist that this is an 'ironic' universal history, for three reasons: it is retrospective, singular and critical. It is retrospective in that the perspective of schizophrenia only becomes available toward the end of history, under capitalism; yet at the same time, capitalism does not represent the *telos* of history, but rather a contingent product of fortuitous circumstance. This confirms the singularity of capitalist society: it is not some hidden similarity between capitalism and previous social forms that makes capitalism universal, but rather what Marx (in the *Grundrisse*) calls the 'essential difference' between it and the others: it exposes the source of value that previous societies kept hidden. And hence capitalism offers the key to universal history because with capitalism, society can finally become self-critical.

Capitalist modernity represents the key turning point in this view of universal history, for a crucial discovery is made in a number of different fields: by Martin Luther; by Adam Smith and David Ricardo; somewhat later by Sigmund Freud, who will therefore be considered 'the Luther and the Adam Smith of psychiatry'. The key discovery is that value does not inhere in objects but rather gets invested in them by human activity, whether that activity is religious devotion, physical labour or libidinal desire. In this fundamental reversal of perspective, objects turn out to be merely the support for subjective value-giving activity. Yet in each of the three fields, the discovery of the internal, subjective nature of value-giving activity is accompanied by a resubordination of that activity to another external determination: in the case of Luther, subjective faith freed from subordination to the Catholic Church is nevertheless resubordinated to the authority of Scripture; in Smith and Ricardo, wage-labour freed from feudal obligations is resubordinated to private capital accumulation; in Freud, the free-form desire of polymorphous libido is resubordinated to heterosexual reproduction in the privatised nuclear family and the Oedipus complex. To free human activity from these last external determinations is the task of world-historical critique: Marx provides the critique of political economy to free wage-labour from private capital; Friedrich Nietzsche provides the critique of religion and moralism to free Will to Power from nihilism; Deleuze and Guattari provide the critique of psychoanalysis to free libido from the private nuclear family and the Oedipus complex.

If capitalism makes history universal, this is ultimately because it promotes multiple differences, because the capitalist market operates as a 'difference-engine'. For Marx, the key human universal was production: the species-being of humanity was defined in terms of its ever-growing ability to produce its own means of life rather than simply consume what nature offered. For Deleuze and Guattari, the key universal is not just production (not even in the very broad sense they grant that term in *Anti-Oedipus*), but specifically the production of difference free from codification and representation. The market fosters an increasingly differentiated network of social relations by expanding the socialisation of production along with the division of labour, even though capital extracts its surplus from the differential flows enabled by this network, by means of exploitation and the never-ending repayment of an infinite debt. Even though the difference-engine of capital fails fully to realise universal history, it nonetheless makes universality possible; puts it on the historical agenda. So while the capitalist market inaugurates the *potential* for universal history in its production of difference, it is the elimination of capital from the market that will multiply difference and realise the freedom inherent in universal history.

CAPTURE

Alberto Toscano

The concept of capture is used by Deleuze and Guattari to deal with two problems of relationality: (1) how to conceive of the connection between the state, the war machine and capitalism within a universal history of political life; (2) how to formulate a non-representational account of the interaction between different beings and their territories adequate to a thinking of becoming. In the first instance, capture defines the operation whereby the state (or Urstaat) binds or 'encasts' the war machine, thereby turning it into an object that can be made to work for the state, bolstering it and expanding its sovereignty.

Apparatuses of capture constitute the machinic processes specific to state societies. They can be conceived as primarily a matter of signs. Whence the figure of the One-Eyed emperor who binds and fixes signs, complemented by a One-Armed priest or jurist who codifies these signs in treaties, contracts and laws. Capture constitutes a control of signs, accompanying the other paradigmatic dimension of the state, the control of tools. The principal ontological and methodological issue related to this conception of capture has to do with the type of relation between capture and the captured (namely in the case of the war machine as the privileged correlate of the apparatus). Deleuze and Guattari's notion of universal history evades any explanation in terms of strict causality or chronological sequence. It turns instead to notions drawn from catastrophe theory and the sciences of complexity to revive the Hegelian intuition that the state has always been there – not as an idea or a concept, but as a threshold endowed with a kind of virtual efficacy, even when the state as a complex of institutions and as a system of control is not yet actual.

The logic of capture is such that what is captured is both presupposed and generated by the act of capture, at once appropriated and produced. Deleuze and Guattari return to many of the key notions in the Marxian critique of political economy to affirm the thesis of a constructive character of capture, arguing, for instance, that surplus labour can be understood to engender labour proper (though it can also be understood as the attempt to block or manipulate a constitutive flight from labour). Capture is thus an introjection and determination of an outside as well as the engendering of the outside qua outside of the apparatus. It is in this regard that capture is made to correspond to the Marxian concept of primitive accumulation, interpreted as a kind of originary violence imposed by the state to prepare for the functioning of capital. Deleuze and Guattari are very sensitive here to the juridical aspects of the question, such that state capture defines a domain of 'legitimate' violence, inasmuch as it always involves the affirmation of a right to capture. In its intimate link with the notion of machinic enslavement, the apparatus of capture belongs both to the initial imperial figure of the state and to full-blown global or axiomatic capitalism, rather than to the intermediary stage represented by the bourgeois nation-state and its forms of disciplinary subjectivation.

The notion of capture can also be accorded a different inflection, associated with the privileging of ethological models of intelligibility within a philosophy of immanence. Here the emphasis is no longer on the expropriation and appropriation of an outside by an instance of control, but on the process of convergence and assemblage between heterogeneous series, on the emergence of blocs of becoming, as in the case of the wasp and the orchid. What we have here is properly speaking a double capture or intercapture, an encounter that transforms the disparate entities that enter into a joint becoming. In Deleuze and Guattari's Kafka, such a process is related to a renewal of the theory of relation, and specifically to a reconsideration of the status of mimesis, now reframed as a type of symbiosis.

Under the heading of capture we thus encounter two opposite but entangled actions, both of which can be regarded as schemata alternative to a dominant hylemorphic mode of explaining relation: the first, understood as the political control of signs, translates a coexistence of becomings (as manifested by the war machine) into a historical succession, making the state pass from an attractor which virtually impinges upon non-state actors to an institutional and temporal reality; the second defines a coexistence and articulation of becomings in terms of the assemblage of heterogeneous entities and the formation of territories. What is paramount in both instances is the affirmation of the event-bound and transformative character of relationality (or interaction), such that capture, whether understood as control or assemblage, is always an ontologically constructive operation and can never be reduced to models of unilateral causation.

Connective

Capitalism

CAPTURE + POLITICS

Paul Patton

Deleuze and Guattari deny that the State is an apparatus that emerged as the result of prior conditions such as the accumulation of surplus or the emergence of private property. Instead, they argue that States have always existed and that they are in essence always mechanisms of capture. The earliest forms of State involved the capture of agricultural communities, the constitution of a milieu of interiority and the exercise of sovereign power. The ruler became 'the sole and transcendent public-property owner, the master of the surplus or stock, the organiser of large-scale works (surplus labour), the source of public functions and bureaucracy' (D&G 1987: 428). Historically the most important mechanisms of capture have been those exercised upon land and its products, upon labour and money. These correspond to Karl Marx's 'holy trinity' of the modern sources of capital accumulation, namely ground rent, profit and taxes, but they have long existed in other forms. In all cases, we find the same two key elements: the constitution of a general space of comparison and the establishment of a centre of appropriation. Together, these define the abstract machine which is expressed in the different forms of State, but also in non-state mechanisms of capture such as the capture of corporeal representation by faciality, or the capture of political reason by public opinion.

Consider first the capture of human activity in the form of labour. Deleuze and Guattari argue that 'labour (in the strict sense) begins only with what is called surplus labour' (D&G 1987: 490). Contrary to the widespread colonial presumption that indigenous peoples were unsuited for labour, they point out that 'so-called primitive societies are not societies of shortage or subsistence due to an absence of work, but on the contrary are societies of free action and smooth space that have no use for a work-factor, anymore than they constitute a stock' (D&G 1987: 491). In these societies, productive activity proceeds under a regime of 'free action' or activity in continuous variation. Such activity only becomes labour once a standard of comparison is imposed, in the form of a definite quantity to be produced or a time to be worked. The obligation to provide taxes, tribute or surplus labour imposes such standards of comparison, thereby effecting the transformation of free action into labour.

The same two elements are present in the conditions that enable the extraction of ground rent, which Deleuze and Guattari describe as 'the very model of an apparatus of capture' (D&G 1987: 441). From an economic point of view, the extraction of ground rent presupposes a means of comparing the productivity of different portions of land simultaneously exploited, or of comparing the productivity of the same portion successively exploited. The measurement of productivity provides a general space of comparison; a measure of qualitative differences between portions of the earth's surface which is absent from the territorial assemblage of hunter-gatherer society. Thus, 'labour and surplus labour are the apparatus of capture of activity just as the comparison of lands and the appropriation of land are the apparatus of capture of territory' (D&G 1987: 442).

One further condition is necessary in order for ground rent to be extracted: the difference in productivity must be linked to a landowner (D&G 1987: 441). In other words, from a legal point of view, the extraction of ground rent is 'inseparable from a process of relative deterritorialization' because 'instead of people being distributed in an itinerant territory, pieces of land are distributed among people according to a common quantitative criterion' (D&G 1987: 441). The conversion of portions of the earth inhabited by so-called primitive peoples into an appropriable and exploitable resource therefore requires the establishment of a juridical centre of appropriation. The centre establishes a monopoly over what has now become land and assigns to itself the right to allocate ownership of portions of unclaimed land.

This centre is the legal sovereign and the monopoly is the assertion of sovereignty over the territories in question. That is why the fundamental jurisprudential problem of colonisation is the manner in which the territories of the original inhabitants become transformed into a uniform space of landed property. In the colonies acquired and governed in accordance with British common law, the sovereign right of the Crown meant it had the power both to create and extinguish private rights and interests in land. In this sense, Crown land amounts to a uniform expanse of potential real property that covers the earth to the extent of the sovereign territory. It follows that, within these common-law jurisdictions, the legal imposition of sovereignty constitutes an apparatus of capture in the precise sense that Deleuze and Guattari give to this term. The imposition of sovereignty effects an instantaneous deterritorialisation of indigenous territories and their reterritorialisation as a uniform space of Crown land centred upon the figure of the sovereign.

CARROLL, LEWIS (1832–98) – refer to the entries on 'art' and 'incorporeal'.

CÉZANNE, PAUL (1839–1906) – refer to the entries on 'art', 'sensation', and 'sensation + cinema'.

CHAOS

Alberto Toscano

This term receives two main treatments in the work of Deleuze (and Guattari), one intra-philosophical, the other non-philosophical. In the first acceptation, chaos designates the type of virtual totality that the philosophy of difference opposes to the foundational and self-referential totalities proposed by the philosophies of representation, and by the dialectic in particular. In polemical juxtaposition to those systems of thought for which what lies beyond the powers of representation is undetermined or null, this Deleuzian chaos, in which all intensive differences are contained – 'complicated' but not 'explicated' – is equivalent to the ontologically productive affirmation of the divergence of series; it is what envelops and distributes, without identifying them, the heterogeneities that make up the world. In other words, this chaos is formless, but it is not undifferentiated. Deleuze thus opposes this Joycean and Nietzschean chaosmos, in which the eternal return selects simulacra for their divergence, to the chaos that Plato attributes to the sophist, which is a privative chaos of non-participation. Moreover, he considers such a chaosmos as the principal antidote to the trinity that sustains all philosophies of representation and transcendence: world, God and subject (man). In *A Thousand Plateaus* however, having moved away from the structuralist-inspired terminology of series (which chaos was seen to affirm), Deleuze and Guattari provide a critique of both chaosmos and eternal return as an insufficient bulwark against a (negative) return of the One and of representation, juxtaposing them with the concepts of rhizome and plane of immanence.

When chaos makes its reappearance in *What is Philosophy?*, it is as the shared correlate of the three dimensions of thought (or of the brain), also designated as 'chaoids': science, art and philosophy. In this context, chaos is not defined simply by how it contains (or complicates) differences, but by its infinite speed, such that the particles, forms and entities that populate it emerge only to disappear immediately, leaving behind no consistency, reference or any determinate consequences. Chaos is thus defined not by its disorder but by its fugacity. It is then the task of philosophy, through the drawing of planes of immanence, the invention of conceptual personae and the composition of concepts, to give consistency to chaos whilst retaining its speed and productivity. Chaos is thus both the intimate threat and the source of philosophical creation, which is understood as the imposition onto the virtual of its own type of consistency, a consistency other than those provided by functions or percepts, for example.

Philosophy can thus be recast in terms of an ethics of chaos, a particular way of living with chaos – and against the sterile clichés of opinion (doxa) – by creating conceptual forms capable of sustaining the infinite speed of chaos whilst not succumbing to the stupidity, thoughtlessness or folly of the indeterminate. Philosophical creation is thus poised between, on the one hand, the subjection of the plane of immanence to some variety of transcendence that would guarantee its uniqueness and, on the other, the surging up of a chaos that would dissolve any consistency, any durable difference or structure.

Chaos and opinion thus provide the two sources of inconsistency for thought, the one determined by an excess of speed, the other by a surfeit of redundancy. Though chaos is a vital resource for thought, it is also clear that philosophy's struggle is always on two fronts, inasmuch as it is the inconsistency or idiocy of a chaotic thought that often grounds the recourse to the safety and identity of opinions. In Deleuze's later work with Guattari it is essential to the definition of philosophical practice and its demarcation from and interference with the other chaoids that chaos not be considered simply synonymous with ontological univocity, but that it instead be accorded a sui generis status as the non-philosophical dimension demanded by philosophical thought.

Connectives

Plato
Representation
Thought

CINEMA

Constantine Verevis

Following his work on *A Thousand Plateaus*, Deleuze's *Cinema* books – *Cinema 1: The movement-image* and *Cinema 2: The time-image* – understand film as a multiplicity, a phenomenon simultaneously oriented toward a network of reproductive forces, which make it a-signifying totality (a 'being-One'), and equally toward a network of *productive* forces, that facilitate the connection and creation of an encounter (a 'becoming-Other'). The first interpretation of film finds its clearest expression in two great mechanisms of cinematic overcoding – historical poetics and textual analysis – that have dominated anglophone, academicised film interpretation since the mid-1970s. Each of these approaches understands repetition as a kind of redundancy, one that contributes to the *habitual* recognition of the same: an industrial representational model, a symbolic blockage. Within these totalising and homogenising approaches to film, repetition (redundancy) functions as a principle of unification, limiting – but never totally arresting – cinema's potentially active and creative lines of flight. In place of these nomalising – informational and/or symbolic – accounts of cinema, another approach develops an experimental-creative understanding of film in which an attentive misrecognition abandons representation (and subjectification) to sketch circuits – and . . . and . . . and – between a series of images. The latter describes Deleuze's 'crystalline regime', an intensive system which resists a hierarchical principle of identity in the former present, and a rule of resemblance in the present present, to establish a communication *between* two presents (the former and the present) which co-exist in relation to a virtual object – the absolutely different. This direct presentation of time – a becoming-in-the-world – brings cinema into a relation not with an ideal of Truth, but with powers of the false: opening, in the place of representation, a sensation of the present presence of the moment, a creative stammering (and . . . and . . . and).

These two critical interpretations of film correspond to, yet cut across, the separate aspects of cinema dealt with in each of the *Cinema* books. In *Cinema 1*, Deleuze identifies the classical or 'movement-image' as that which gives rise to a 'sensory-motor whole' (a unity of movement and its interval) and grounds narration (representation) in the image. This movement-image, which relates principally to pre-World War II cinema, contributes to the realism of the 'action-image', and produces the global domination of the American cinema. In *Cinema 2*, Deleuze describes a post-war crisis in the movement image, a break-up of the sensory-motor link that gives rise to a new situation – a neo-realism – that is not drawn out directly into action, but is 'primarily optical and of sound, invested by the senses' (D 1989: 4). As Deleuze describes it, even though this opticalsound image implies a beyond of movement, movement does not strictly stop but is now grasped by way of connections which are no longer sensory-motor and which bring the senses into direct relation with time and thought. That is, where the movement-image and its sensory-motor signs are in a relationship only with an indirect image of time, the pure optical and sound image – its 'opsigns' and 'sonsigns' – are directly connected to a time-image – a 'chronosign' – that has subordinated movement.

Appealing to Henri Bergson's schemata on time, Deleuze describes a situation in which the optical-sound perception enters into a relation with genuinely *virtual* elements. This is the large circuit of the dream-image ('onirosign'), a type of intensive system in which a virtual image (the 'differenciator') becomes actual not directly, but by actualising a different image, which itself plays the role of the virtual image being actualised in another, and so on. Although the optical-sound image appears to find its proper equivalent in this infinitely dilated circuit of the dream-image, for Deleuze the opsign (and sonsign) finds its true genetic element only when the actual image crystallises with *its own* virtual image on a *small circuit*. The time-image is a direct representation of time, a *crystal-image* that consists in the indivisible unity of an actual image and its own virtual image so that the two are indiscernible, actual *and* virtual at the same time. Deleuze says: 'what we see in the crystal is time itself, a bit of time in the pure state' (D 1989: 82).

In a brief example, *Chinatown* (1973) is a perfectly realised (neoclassical) Hollywood genre film but one that exhibits an ability to *exceed* itself. *Chinatown* can be understood as a representational and symbolic text – a detective film and an Oedipal drama. But its subtle patterning of repetitions – the motifs of water and eye – while contributing to the film's narrative economy sketch the complementary panoramic vision of a *large circuit* indifferent to the conditions of meaning and truth. Additionally, the film's final repetition – a woman's death in Chinatown – brings the detective Gittes' past and present together with hallucinatory exactitude to form a small circuit in which the virtual corresponds to the actual. The final act gestures toward neither a diegetic nor oneiric temporality, but a crystalline temporality.

Connectives

Crystal
Lines of flight
Time image

COGITO

James Williams

Deleuze's critical approach to the cogito of René Descartes, the 'I think, therefore I am' from the *Discourse on Method* or the 'I think, I am' from the *Meditations*, can be divided into a critique of the Cartesian analytic method, a critique of the self-evidence of the cogito and an extension of the Cartesian view of the subject.

Descartes' foundational method is the rationalist construction of a system of analytic truths. That is, he believes that certain propositions are true independently of any others and that therefore they can stand as a ground for the deduction of further truths according to reason. Deleuze's synthetic and dialectical method, developed in *Difference and Repetition*, depends on the view that all knowledge is partial and open to revision.

Thus, any relative truth is open to extension through syntheses with further discoveries and through further experiments. The relation between these truths is dialectical rather than analytical and foundational. There is a reciprocal process of revision and change between them, as opposed to Cartesian moves from secure and inviolable bases out into the unknown. Where Descartes situates reason at the heart of his method, as shown by the role of thinking in the cogito, Deleuze emphasises sensation.

Sensation is resistant to identity in representation. Thought must be responsive to sensations that go beyond its capacity to represent them. These point to a realm of virtual conditions defined as intensities and Ideas (the capital indicates that these are not ideas to be thought of as empirical things in the mind, rather they are like Kantian Ideas of reason).

Deleuze holds that no thought is free of sensation. The cogito cannot be self-evident, because sensation always extends to a multiplicity of further conditions and causes. The Cartesian hope of defeating systematic doubt through the certainty of the cogito must therefore fail. Deleuze often turns to dramatisations from art, literature and cinema to convince us of the insufficiency of the cogito. Wherever we presume to have found pure thought, or pure representations, the expressivity of the arts points to sensations and deeper Ideas.

A thought, such as the cogito, is therefore inseparable from sensations that themselves bring a series of intensities and Ideas to bear on the subject. The 'I' is therefore not independent but carries all intensities and all Ideas with it. These are related to any singular thought in the way it implies different arrangements of intensities and different relations of clarity and obscurity between Ideas.

You do not think without feeling. Feeling defines you as an individual. That singular definition brings some intensities to the fore while hiding others (more hating, less anger, greater caring, less jealousy). In turn, these intensities light up Ideas in different ways making some relations more obscure and others more distinct (The Idea of love for humanity took centre stage, after their sacrifice).

The subject is therefore extended through the sensations of singular individuals into virtual intensities and Ideas. Unlike the Cartesian cogito, which is posited on the activity of the thinking subject, Deleuze's individual has an all-important passive side. We cannot directly choose our sensations, we are therefore passive with respect to our virtual 'dark precursors'.

Deleuze's philosophy depends on Descartes' rationalist critics, notably Baruch Spinoza, for the synthetic method and for the opposition to the free activity of the subject, and Gottfried Wilhelm von Leibniz, for the extension of the subject or monad to the whole of reality. Deleuze is not simply anti-Cartesian; rather, he extends the active subject through passivity and through the conditions for sensation. The cogito is an important moment in philosophy, but it requires completing through syntheses that belie its independence.

Connectives

Kant
Sensation

CONCEPTS

Cliff Stagoll

Deleuze understands philosophy as being the art of inventing or creating concepts, or putting concepts to work in new ways. He does not consider it to be very useful or productive, however, when it creates and uses concepts in the manner that he thinks has typified much of western philosophy to date. Too often, Deleuze argues, philosophy has used real experience merely as a source for extracting or deducing abstract conceptual means for categorising phenomena. It has tended then to employ these same concepts either to determine or express the essence of phenomena, or else to order and rank them in terms of the concept. An example is Plato's concept of Forms, the absolute and changeless objects and standards of knowledge against which all human knowledge is but an inferior copy. Such a concept does not help us appreciate or contribute to the richness of lived experience, Deleuze argues, but only to order, label and measure individuals relative to an abstract norm. It is true, he argues, that concepts help us in our everyday lives to organise and represent our thoughts to others, making communication and opinion-formation simpler; but Deleuze insists such simplicity detracts from the variety and uniqueness evident in our experiences of the world.

For Deleuze and Guattari, concepts ought to be means by which we move beyond what we experience so that we can think of new possibilities. Rather than bringing things together under a concept, he is interested in relating variables according to new concepts so as to create productive connections. Concepts ought to express states of affairs in terms of the contingent circumstances and dynamics that lead to and follow from them, so that each concept is related to particular variables that change or 'mutate' it. A concept is created or thought anew in relation to every particular event, insight, experience or problem, thereby incorporating a notion of the contingency of the circumstances of each event. On such a view, concepts cannot be thought apart from the circumstances of their production, and so cannot be hypothetical or conceived *a priori*.

Deleuze's theory of concepts is part of a potent criticism of much philosophy to date. He is arguing that any philosophy failing to respect the particularity of consciousness in favour of broad conceptual sketches is subject to metaphysical illusion. The application of abstract concepts merely gathers together discrete particulars *despite* their differences, and privileges concepts over what is supposed to be explained. For example, one might understand things as instances of Being or usefulness, thereby presupposing an ontological or epistemological privilege for the concept of 'Being' or 'utility' that is not evident in immediate experience. By bearing in mind that the concept at work relates just to *this* being or *this* useful thing, here and now, such illusions are avoided.

In Deleuze's work, concepts become the means by which we move beyond experience so as to be able to think anew. Rather than 'standing apart' from experience, a concept is defined just by the unity that it expresses amongst heterogeneous elements. In other words, concepts *must* be creative or active rather than merely representative, descriptive or simplifying. For this reason, in his work on David Hume, Deleuze goes to some lengths to show how causation is a truly creative concept by explaining how it brings us to expect and anticipate outcomes before they occur, and even outcomes that we don't observe at all. In such cases, anticipatory creation is so powerful that it becomes a normal part of life, and causation is a concept that represents the creation of other concepts without the requirement for sense perceptions to ground them.

Moving from a reiterative history of philosophy to the practice of philosophy means engaging with inherited concepts in new ways. This means for Deleuze that philosophers ought to engage in new lines of thinking and new connections between particular ideas, arguments and fields of specialisation. Only then does philosophy take on a positive power to transform our ways of thinking. In his own work, Deleuze reappropriates numerous concepts inherited from the great philosophers of the past in terms of new problems, uses, terms and theories. Henri Bergson's concepts of duration and intuition, Gottfried Wilhelm von Leibniz's monad, Hume's associationism, and numerous concepts from literature, film, criticism, science and even mathematics are reworked and put to work in new and creative ways. The apparent inconsistency of their meanings and uses is a sign of Deleuze's refusal to give any concept a single purpose or referent. By cutting routinely across disciplinary boundaries, Deleuze abides by his proposal that concept-creation be an 'open ended' exercise, such that philosophy creates concepts that are as accessible and useful to artists and scientists as to philosophers.

Connectives

Bergson
Duration

Hume
Plato

CONTROL SOCIETY

John Marks

Deleuze develops his notion of the 'control society' at the beginning of the 1990s. In the 1970s Michel Foucault showed how, during the eighteenth and nineteenth centuries, a *disciplinary* society had developed that was based on strategies of confinement. As Deleuze points out, Foucault carried out this historical work in order to show what we had inherited of the disciplinary model, and not simply in order to claim that contemporary society is disciplinary. This is the sense of the *actual* in Foucault's work, in the sense of what we are in the process of differing from. Deleuze uses Foucault's insights as a starting point to claim that we are moving towards *control* societies in which confinement is no longer the main strategy.

Deleuze reminds us that disciplinary societies succeeded 'sovereign' societies, and that they concentrated on the organisation of life and production rather than the exercise of arbitrary entitlements in relation to these two domains. Disciplinary societies developed a network of sites and institutions – prisons, hospitals, factories, schools, the family – within which individuals were located, trained and/or punished at various times in their life. In this way, the figure of the 'population' emerges as an observable, measurable object, which is susceptible to various forms of manipulation. Essentially, the disciplinary system is one of contiguity: the individual moves from site to site, beginning again each time. In contrast to this, societies of control – which emerge particularly after World War II – are continuous in form. The various forms of control constitute a network of inseparable variations. The individual, in a disciplinary society, is placed in various 'moulds' at different times, whereas the individual in a contemporary control society is in a constant state of *modulation*. Deleuze uses as an example the world of work and production. The factory functioned according to some sort of equilibrium between the highest possible production and the lowest possible wages. Just as the worker was a component in a regulated system of mass production, so unions could mobilise mass resistance. In control societies, on the other hand, the dominant model is that of the business, in which it is more frequently the task of the individual to engage in forms of competition and continuing education in order to attain a certain level of salary. There is a deeper level of modulation, a constant variation, in the wages paid to workers. In general terms, the duality of mass and individual is being broken down. The individual is becoming a 'dividual', whilst the mass is reconfigured in terms of data, samples and markets. Whereas disciplinary individuals produced quantifiable and discrete amounts of energy, 'dividuals' are caught up in a process of constant modulation. In the case of medicine, which claims to be moving towards a system 'without doctors or patients', this means that the figure in the individual is replaced by a dividual segment of coded matter to be controlled.

Although he is in no way suggesting that we should return to disciplinary institutions, Deleuze clearly finds the prospect of the new control society alarming. In the domains of prison, education, hospitals and business, the old institutions are breaking down and, although these changes may be presented as being more closely tailored to the needs of individuals, Deleuze sees little more than a new system of domination. It may even be the case, he suggests, that we may come to view the harsh confinements of disciplinary societies with some nostalgia. One reason for this is obviously that techniques of control threaten to be isolating and individualising. We may regret the loss of previous solidarities. Another reason would be that we are constantly coerced into forms of 'communication'. This means that we are denied the privilege of having nothing to say, of cultivating the particular kind of creative solitude that Deleuze values. It appears that we will increasingly lack a space for creative 'resistance'. He suggests that the move towards continuous assessment in schools is being extended to society in general, with the effect that much of life takes on the texture of the gameshow or the marketing seminar.

The critique of contemporary societies that the notion of control society entails might in some ways be unexpected in Deleuze's work, given that it sometimes looks like a conventional defence of the individual threatened by the alienating forces of global capitalism. One might expect Deleuze to be in favour of a move towards societies which do away with the constraints of individuality. However, it is the precise way in which control societies dismantle the individual that alarms Deleuze. Rather than encouraging a real social engagement with the pre-personal, they turn the individual into an object that has no resistance, no capacity to 'fold' the line of modulation. Although the Body without Organs lacks the discreteness of what we conventionally know as an individual that is not to say it does not have resistance. On the contrary, it is a zone of intensity. It may be traversed by forces, but it is not simply a relay for those forces.

Connectives

Body without Organs
Fold

Foucault
Intensity

CONTROL SOCIETY + STATE THEORY

Kenneth Surin

In his short but prescient essay 'Postscript on Control Societies' Deleuze says that in the age of the societies of control (as opposed to the disciplinary societies of the previous epoch famously analysed by Michel Foucault), capital has become a vast 'international ecumenical organization' that is able to harmonise into a single overarching assemblage even the most disparate forms (commercial, religious, artistic, and so forth) and entities. In this new dispensation, productive labour, dominated now by the myriad forms of intellectual labour and service provision, has expanded to cover every segment of society: the exponentially extended scope of capital is coterminous with the constant availability of everything that creates surplus-value. Human consciousness, leisure, play, and so on, are no longer left to 'private' domains but are instead directly encompassed by the latest regimes of accumulation. The boundary between home and workplace becomes increasingly blurred, as does the demarcation between 'regular' work and 'casual' labour. Capitalism becomes informalised, even as it becomes ubiquitous. Capitalism's *telos* has always involved the creation of an economic order that will be able to dispense with the State, and in its current phase this *telos* has become more palpably visible. Where Deleuze is concerned, this development does not require the State and its appurtenances to be abolished. Rather, the traditional separation between State and society is now no longer sustainable. Society and State now form one all-embracing matrix, in which all capital has become translatable into social capital, and so the production of social cooperation, undertaken primarily by the service and informational industries in the advanced economies, has become a crucial one for capitalism.

This need to maintain constant control over the forms of social cooperation in turn requires that education, training, business, never end: the business time-scale is now '24/7' so that the Tokyo stock exchange opens when the one in New York closes, in an unending cycle; training is 'on the job' as opposed to being based on the traditional apprenticeship model (itself a holdover from feudalism); and education becomes 'continuing education', that is, something that continues throughout life, and is not confined to those aged six to twenty-two. This essentially dispersive propensity is reflected in the present regime of capitalist accumulation, where production is now meta-production, that is, no longer focused in the advanced economies on the use of raw materials to produce finished goods, but rather the sale of services (especially in the domain of finance and credit) and already finished products. Social control is no longer left to schools and police forces, but is now a branch of marketing, as even politics has become 'retail politics', in which politicians seek desperately for an image of themselves to market to the electorate, and when public relations consultants are more important to prime ministers and presidents than good and wise civil servants. Recording, whether in administration or business, is no longer based on the written document kept in the appropriate box of files, but on bar-coding and other forms of electronic tagging.

The implications of the above-mentioned developments for state theory are momentous. The state itself has become fragmented and compartmentalised, and has accrued more power to itself in some spheres while totally relinquishing power in others. However, if the State has mutated in the era of control societies, it retains the function of regulating, in conjunction with capital, the 'accords' that channel social and political power. In his book on Gottfried Wilhelm von Leibniz, Deleuze maintains that state and non-state formations are constituted on the basis of such 'concerts' or 'accords'. These 'accords' are organising principles which make possible the grouping into particular configurations of whole ranges of events, personages, processes, institutions, movements, and so forth, such that the resulting configurations become integrated formations. As a set of accords or axioms governing the accords that regulate the operations of the various components of an immensely powerful and comprehensive system of accumulation, capital is situated at the crossing-point of all kinds of formations, and thus has the capacity to integrate and recompose capitalist and non-capitalist sectors or modes of production. Capital, the 'accord of accords' par excellence, can bring together heterogeneous phenomena, and make them express the same world, that of capitalist accumulation.

Accords are constituted by selection criteria, which specify what is to be included or excluded by the terms of the accord in question. These criteria also determine with which other possible or actual accords a particular accord will be consonant (or dissonant). The criteria that constitute accords are usually defined and described by narratives governed by a certain normative vision of truth, goodness and beauty (reminiscent of the so-called mediaeval transcendentals, albeit translated where necessary into the appropriate contemporary vernacular). A less portentous way of making this point would be to say that accords are inherently axiological, value-laden. What seems to be happening today, and this is a generalisation that is tendentious, is that these superimposed narratives and the selection criteria they sanction, criteria which may or may not be explicitly formulated or entertained, are being weakened or qualified in ways that deprive them of their force. Such selection criteria, policed by the State, tend to function by assigning privileges of rank and order to the objects they subsume ('Le Pen is more French than Zidane', 'Turks are not Europeans', and so on), as the loss or attenuation of the customary force of such accords makes dissonances and contradictions difficult or even impossible to resolve, and, correlatively, makes divergences easier to affirm. Events, objects and personages can now be assigned to several divergent and even incompossible series. The functioning of capital in the control societies requires that the State become internally pluralised.

CREATIVE TRANSFORMATION

Adrian Parr

In developing the idea of 'creative transformation' Deleuze draws on a variety of philosophical sources. Initially in his work on Henri Bergson he picks up on the philosopher's concept of 'creative evolution' and 'duration', revamping these in *Difference and Repetition* into a discussion of the productive understanding of repetition, all the while embracing a concept of difference that belies the negative structure of a 'difference to or from' in favour of 'difference in itself'. Keen to expand upon the generative and dynamic implications of Bergsonian creative evolution he turns to Baruch Spinoza's *Ethics*, in particular the conception of bodies that Bergson and Spinoza share: a body is constituted on an immanent plane. The next philosophical influence in Deleuze's use of creative transformation would have to be Friedrich Nietzsche's concept of the 'eternal return'. Then, in his collaboration with Guattari, creative transformation takes a turn through biophilosophy, bypassing both the human condition and teleological theories of evolution characteristic of Jean-Baptiste Lamarck in favour of a transhuman theory of heredity.

The question of 'life', namely the force that persists over time and the changes that ensue, is addressed by Deleuze as an experimental, spontaneous, and open process of transformation. As it was articulated in *Difference and Repetition*, evolution is construed as a process of repetition that is inherently creative: it is productive of difference. In the hands of Deleuze (remember, like Michel Foucault, concepts are tools for Deleuze), creative transformation becomes a system of involution where transversal movements engage material forces and affects.

In both his 1956 essay on Bergson and his 1966 book *Bergsonism* (D 1988a) Deleuze utilises the idea of 'evolution' proposed by Bergson in terms of transmission. Expanding on this a little more, Deleuze shifts the focus of inheritance away from determination and the continuance of a fixed essence that is passed on over time. Like Bergson, Deleuze chooses to bring to our attention the creative dimension inherent in evolution. It is the force of life that persists, thus, through change, the vitality of life and difference are affirmed. According to this schema creative transformation is immanent, taking place on a plane of consistency that precedes univocal Being. In Bergson Deleuze finds the possibility for a philosophy that grasps life in terms of duration and the inhuman. The temporality of duration is not conceived of chronologically, whereby the end of one moment marks the beginning of the next; nor is it a measurable time, that is broken down into seconds, minutes, hours, days, months, or years. Put differently, Deleuzian duration needs to be construed as the flow of time; it is intensive as much as it is creative in so far as it is the movement of time that marks the force of life. Hence, duration maintains life in an open state of indeterminacy.

The theory of creative inheritance and the emphasis placed on non-organic life is then given a makeover and turned into the concept of the 'rhizome' in his collaboration with Guattari. Early on in *A Thousand Plateaus* Deleuze and Guattari characterise a rhizome as indeterminate and experimental. Steering the emphasis away from representational interpretative frameworks, they clearly state that a rhizome is a map not a trace. Explaining this distinction they write that what 'distinguishes the map from the tracing is that it is entirely oriented toward an experimentation in contact with the real' (D&G 1987: 12). The rhizome is conceived of as an open multiplicity, and all life is a rhizomatic mode of change without firm and fixed boundaries that proceeds 'from the middle, through the middle, coming and going rather than starting and finishing' (D&G 1987: 25). It is, however, important to note that their use of 'open' here is not conceived of negatively, which is to say it is not the antithesis of being 'closed'; rather, the machinic character of a rhizome arises out of the virtual and the dynamic boundaries that constitute it.

In *A Thousand Plateaus* the force of life is described by Deleuze and Guattari as inherently innovative and social. Inheritance is not articulated within an essentialist framework that places the emphasis on species, genes and organisms, because Deleuze and Guattari recognise that it is the power of affect that is creative – to produce affects and being open to being affected. Here creativity is taken to be a machinic mode of evolution that is productive in and of itself. The whole question of transformation is clearly situated by both Deleuze and Guattari in an experimental milieu and the creativity of this milieu is necessarily social.

Connectives

Bergson
Difference
Representation
Spinoza

CREATIVE TRANSFORMATION + BIOLOGY

John Protevi

Biology seeks to explain resemblance and novelty in living things across multiple spatial (molecular, organic, systemic, organismic, specific, and ecological) and temporal (developmental, physiological, reproductive, and evolutionary) scales.

Deleuze has a strong and a weak sense of the creative transformation involved in the production of biological novelty. The strong sense is novelty that does not produce substantial filiation (i.e. does not produce an organism with descendants); this can be connected to the notions of 'niche-construction' and 'life cycle' in Developmental Systems Theory (DST). The weak sense is novelty that does produce substantial filiation (an organism with desendants); this can be connected to the notions of serial endosymbiosis in the macroevolutionary work of Lynn Margulis and developmental plasticity in the microevolutionary work of Mary Jane West-Eberhard (M 1998; WE 2003).

The strong sense, which excludes substantial filiation, is expressed in *A Thousand Plateaus*:

> Finally, becoming is not an evolution, at least not an evolution by descent and filiation. . . It concerns alliance. If evolution includes any veritable becomings, it is in the domain of *symbioses* that bring into play beings of totally different scales and kingdoms, with no but from which no wasp-orchid can ever descend. (D&G 1987: 238)

We can connect this to the thoughts of 'niche construction' and 'life cycle' in DST (O 2000). Here, 'niche construction' looks to the way organisms actively shape the environment and, thus, the evolutionary selection pressures for themselves and their offspring. Thus evolution should be seen as the change in organism-environment systems, that is, the organism in its constructed niche. It's the 'becoming' of the organism-in-its-niche that needs to be thought as the unit of evolution (e.g. the wasp-orchid).

In generalising and radicalising the thought of niche construction, DST thinkers propose the 'life cycle' as the widest possible extension of developmental resources that are reliably present (or better, re-created) across generations. DST thinkers thus extend the notion of inheritance beyond the genetic to the cytoplasmic environment of the egg (an extension many mainstream biologists have come to accept) and onto intra-organismic and even (most controversially) extra-somatic factors. In other words, to the relevant, constructed, features of the physical and social environments (for example, normal brain development in humans needs positive corporeal affect and language exposure in critical sensitive windows). This notion of 'life cycle' as the unit of evolution encompassing intranuclear, cytoplasmic, organic, and extra-somatic elements comes close to what Deleuze and Guattari refer to above as 'symbioses that bring into play beings of totally different scales and kingdoms.'

The weak sense of biological novelty is that which does result in a substantial filiation, that is, organisms with descendants. There is still the emphasis on heterogenous elements entering a symbiosis, but the result has organismic form. The foremost connection here is with the work of Lynn Margulis (M 1998) who posits that symbiosis, rather than mutation, is the most important source of variation upon which natural selection works. Her most famous example is mitochondrial capture at the origin of eukaryotic cells. Magulis holds that mitochondria were previously independent aerobic bacteria engulfed by anaerobic (proto-nucleated) bacteria; eukaryotic cells thus formed produce the lineage for all multicellular organisms. Serial endosymbiosis thus short-circuits the strict neo-Darwinist doctrine of mutation as origin of variation upon which we find selection of slight adaptations. Although there is organismic filiation, Margulis's notion of evolution via the symbiosis of different organisms seems at least in line with the spirit of what Deleuze and Guattari call 'involution' (D&G 1987: 238-9).

We see a second connection with the weak sense of creative transformation in biology in the mircoevolutionary work of Mary Jane West-Eberhard (WE 2003). West-Eberhard proposes that genetic control mechanisms can be exposed to selection by the phenotypic adaptation of organisms to new kinds of environment. This is not Lamarckian, West-Eberhard emphasises, because there is no direct influence of environment on genotype. Lamarck thought that adaptive phenotypic changes were the source of variants that could be inherited. But West-Eberhard says that some adaptive phenotypic change is the result of developmental plasticity calling upon previously hidden, i.e. unexpressed, genetic variation. In other words, neither the phenotype nor the environment produces genetic variation, but their interaction enables the tapping into of previously unexpressed genetic variation or what Deleuze and Guattari refer to as the 'surplus value of code' (D&G 1987: 53).

In *Difference and Repetition*, Deleuze insists that individuation precedes differenciation. Individuation is real material development; differenciation is the relation of differences to each other, that is, how one individuation relates to another. To make the connection with West-Eberhard, recall how developmental plasticity is the creativity of the phenotype and environment (not the genotype and environment). When an adaptive phenotypic change has a genetic component, the distributed networks regulating gene expression (arguably extending to the entire 'life cycle') for this adaptive phenotypic variant will now be selected (if the environmental change reliably recurs). Now these accommodated or now newly/creatively expressed networks regulating gene expression were only virtual, that is, only potentials of the pre-existing but unexpressed genetic variation.

Here we see the meaning of West-Eberhard's phrase that gene networks are followers as opposed to leaders in evolution. That is, it's the developmental plasticity (in Deleuze's terms, 'intensive processes of individuation') that takes the lead and brings out previously unexpressed potentials of hereditary DNA (strings of nucleotides on chromosomes), that is, they bring out their potential to take part in new regulatory gene networks. But the potential of hereditary DNA to take part in new gene expression networks is 1) dependent on the distributed system (up to the 'life cycle') and 2) not preformed, in the sense that there is no program in the DNA that determines the actualisation of the potential for these new networks. In Deleuzian terms, the virtual realm of potential networks regulating gene expression is not self-determining, it is determined on the spot, each time, by the individuation process. It's the individuation process that takes the lead in creatively producing biological novelty.

D

DEATH

Bruce Baugh

Death is many things: a state of affairs, when a body's parts, through external causes, enter into a relation that is incompatible with that body's continued existence; an impersonal event of dying, expressed through an infinitive verb (*mourir*, to die); the experience of zero 'intensity' that is implicit in a body's feeling or experience of an increase or decrease in its force of existence; a 'model' of immobility and of energy that is not organised and put to work; and finally, the 'death instinct', capitalism's destruction of surplus value through war, unemployment, famine and disease.

A body exists when its parts compose a relation that expresses the singular force of existence or 'essence' of that body, and ceases to be when its parts are determined by outside causes to enter into a relation that is incompatible with its own. Death in this sense always comes from outside and as such is both fortuitous and inevitable: it is the necessary and determined result of a body's chance encounters with other bodies, governed by purely mechanical laws of cause and effect. Since every body interacts with other bodies, it is inevitable that at some point it will encounter bodies that 'decompose' the vital relation of its parts, and cause those parts to enter into new relations, characteristic of other bodies.

Death, as the decomposition of a body's characteristic relation, forms the basis of the personal and present death of the Self or ego.To this death, as founded in the personal self and the body, Deleuze contrasts the 'event' of dying, which is impersonal and incorporeal, expressed in the infinitive verb 'to die' and in the predicate mortal. Dying is not a process that takes place in things, nor is 'mortal' a quality that inheres in things or subjects. Rather, the verb and the predicate express meanings that extend over the past and future, but which are never physically present in bodies and things, even though the death of a body effectuates or actualises this dying. In impersonal dying, 'one' dies, but one never ceases or finishes dying. The death of the Self or 'I' is when it ceases to die and is actually dead: when its vital relations are decomposed, and its essence or power of existence is reduced to zero intensity. Yet, at this very instant, impersonal dying makes death lose itself in itself, as the decomposition of one living body is simultaneously the composition of a new singular life, the subsumption of the dead body's parts under a new relation.

During its existence, bodies experience increases or diminutions of their power or force of existing. Other bodies can combine with a body either in a way that agrees with the body's constitutive relation, that results in an increase in the body's power felt as joy, or in a way that is incompatible with that relation, resulting in a diminution of power felt as sadness. Power is physical energy, a degree of intensity, so that every increase or decrease in power is an increase or decrease in intensity. When the body dies, and the Self or the ego with it, they are returned to the zero intensity from which existence emerges. Every transition from a greater to a lesser intensity, or from a lesser to a greater, involves and envelops the zero intensity with respect to which it experiences its power as increasing or decreasing. Death is thus felt in every feeling, experienced 'in life and for life'.

It is in that sense that the life instincts and appetites arise from the emptiness or zero intensity of death. The 'model' of zero intensity is thus the Body without Organs (BwO), the body that is not organised into organs with specific functions performing specific tasks, the energy of which is not put to work, but is available for investment, what Deleuze calls death in its speculative form (taking 'speculative' in the sense of financial speculation). Since the BwO does not perform any labour, it is immobile and catatonic. In *The Logic of* Sense, the catatonic BwO arises from within the depths of the instincts, as a death instinct, an emptiness disguised by every appetite. In *Anti-Oedipus*, Deleuze retains his definition of the death instinct as desexualised energy available for investment, and as the source of the destructiveness of drives and instincts, but argues that rather than a principle, the death instinct is a product of the socially determined relations of production in the capitalist system. Death becomes an instinct, a diffused and immanent function of the capitalist system – specifically, capitalism's absorption of the surplus value it produces through anti-production or the production of lack, such as war, unemployment, and the selection of certain populations for starvation and disease. The death instinct is thus historical and political, not natural.

Connectives

Body
Body without Organs

DERRIDA, JACQUES (1930–2004) – refer to the entries on 'becoming + cinema', 'nonbeing' and 'virtual/virtuality'.

DESCARTES, RENÉ (1596–1650) – refer to the entries on 'arborescent schema', 'cogito', 'Hume', 'immanence', 'plane', 'Spinoza' and 'thought'.

DESIRE

Alison Ross

'Desire' is one of the central terms in Deleuze's philosophical lexicon. In his work with Guattari, Deleuze develops a definition of desire as positive and productive that supports the conception of life as material flows. In each of the features used to define this conception of desire, an alternative conception of desire as premised on 'lack' or regulated by 'law' is contested. The psychoanalytic conception of desire as an insatiable lack regulated by Oedipal law is one of the main inaccuracies of desire that Deleuze tries to correct. Instead of desire being externally organised in relation to prohibitions that give it a constitutive relation to 'lack', for Deleuze desire is defined as a process of experimentation on a plane of immanence. Added to this conception of desire as productive, is the conception of desire as positive. Whereas in psychoanalytic theory desire is located within the individual as an impotent force, the positive and productive dimension Deleuze ascribes to desire makes it a social force. Thus reinterpreted, desire is viewed not just as an experimental, productive force, but also as a force able to form connections and enhance the power of bodies in their connection. These two features are used to distinguish the experimentation of desire from any variant of naturalism; and Deleuze defines desire accordingly in his work with Guattari as assembled or machined. This conception of desire works across a number of themes in Deleuze's writing with Guattari. Productive and positive desire works in their writing as an operative vocabulary through which they explain fascism in politics as the desire for the repression of desire, and they advance a new ethics of 'schizoanalysis' whose task is the differentiation between active and reactive desires, all the while explaining simple activities such as sleeping, walking or writing as desires.

Desire is also a crucial element in Deleuze's critique of philosophical dualism. Such dualism, whether in Immanuel Kant or psychoanalysis, is able to submit desire to a juridical system of regulation precisely because it first distinguishes the domain of existence from those transcendent values that arrange it in relation to ordering principles. In the case of psychoanalysis this exercise of transcendent regulation erroneously contains desire to the field of the subject's sexuality and turns it into a problem of interpretation. Against psychoanalysis, Deleuze tries to de-sexualise and de-individualise desire. Sexuality is one flow that enters into conjunction with others in an assemblage. It is not a privileged infrastructure within desiring assemblages, nor an energy able to be transformed, or sublimated into other flows (D 1993b: 140).

Deleuze is particularly critical of the alliance between desire-pleasure-lack in which desire is misunderstood as either an insatiable internal lack, or as a process whose goal is dissolution in pleasure. Whether desire is related to the law of lack or the norm of pleasure it is misunderstood as regulated by lack or discharge. Against this alliance Deleuze describes desire as the construction of a plane of immanence in which desire is continuous. Instead of a regulation of desire by pleasure or lack in which desire is extracted from its plane of immanence, desire is a process in which anything is permissible. Desire is accordingly distinguished from that which 'would come and break up the integral process of desire' (D 1993b: 140). This integral process is described in *A Thousand Plateaus* as the construction of assemblages. The term, which is developed in response to the subjectivist misinterpretation of the desiring machines of *Anti-Oedipus*, underlines the view that desire is experimental and related to an outside. It is this relation to an outside that underpins the social dimension given to desire in Deleuze's thought. Understood as an assemblage, desire in Deleuze's vocabulary is irreducible to a distinction between naturalism/artifice, or spontaneity/law. For this reason when Deleuze argues against the dualism that prohibits or interrupts desire from the external points of lack or pleasure, he also makes ascesis an important condition for the processes that construct assemblages of desire.

Connectives

Immanence
Kant
Lacan
Oedipalisation
Psychoanalysis
Schizoanalysis

DESIRE + SOCIAL-PRODUCTION

Eugene Holland

Schizoanalysis uses the pivotal term 'desiring-production', in tandem with 'social-production', to link Sigmund Freud and Karl Marx: the term conjoins libido and labour-power as distinct instances of production-in-general. Just as bourgeois political economy discovered that the essence of economic value does not inhere in objects but is invested in them by subjective activity in the form of labour-power, bourgeois psychiatry discovered that the essence of erotic value does not inhere in objects but is invested in them by subjective activity in the form of libidinal cathexis. Schizoanalysis adds the discovery that labour-power and libido are in essence two sides of the same coin, even though they are separated by capitalism in its historically unique segregation of reproduction from production at large via the privatisation of reproduction in the nuclear family.

The concept of desiring-production prevents desire from being understood in terms of 'lack' (as it has been in western metaphysics from Plato to Freud): desiring-production actually produces what we take to be reality (in the sense that a lawyer produces evidence) through the investment of psychical energy (libido), just as social-production produces what we take to be reality through the investment of corporeal energy (labour-power). Desire is thus not a fantasy of what we lack: it is first and foremost the psychical and corporeal production of what we want – even though under certain conditions what we want subsequently gets taken away from us by the repressive figure of a castrating father or the oppressive figure of an exploitative boss (among others). By restoring the link between desiring- production and social-production, schizoanalysis deprives psychoanalysis of its excuse for and justification of repression; that psychic repression is somehow autonomous from social oppression, and exists independent of social conditions. Schizoanalysis insists on the contrary that 'social-production is purely and simply desiring-production itself under determinate conditions' (D&G 1983: 29), and that psychic repression therefore derives from social oppression: transform those social conditions, and you transform the degree and form of psychic repression as well.

There are two basic forms of desiring-production: schizophrenia, the free form of desire promoted half-heartedly by capitalism and wholeheartedly by schizoanalysis; and paranoia, the fixed form of desire subjected to socially-authorised belief (in God, the father, the boss, the teacher, the leader, and so on). There are three modes of social-production, each of which oppresses/represses desiring-production in a specific way. Of the three, capitalism is the most promising, because it at least is ambivalent: it actively fosters both forms of desiring-production, whereas its predecessors always did their utmost to crush the one in favour of the other. Capitalism frees desiring-production from capture and repression by codes and representations, while at the same time it recaptures and represses desiring-production in mostly temporary codes and representations, but also in the more enduring forms of State-sponsored nationalism, the Oedipus complex and the nuclear family.

It is because schizoanalysis insists that social-production always provides the determinate conditions under which desiring-production takes shape that it can hold the mode of social-production responsible for that shape; that is, schizoanalysis evaluates a mode of social-production according to the form of desiring-production it makes possible. The value of capitalism as a mode of social-production is not only the extraordinary material productivity so admired by Marx, but even more its propensity for generating schizophrenia as the radically free form of desiringproduction. And the corresponding challenge to schizoanalysis as a revolutionary psychiatry is to eliminate the countervailing forces that recapture free desire and subject it to paranoia and belief, forces operating in institutions ranging from the nuclear family and Oedipal psychoanalysis, to the bureaucracy of private enterprise, all the way up to and including the State.

DETERRITORIALISATION / RETERRITORIALISATION

Adrian Parr

There are a variety of ways in which Deleuze and Guattari describe the process of deterritorialisation. In *Anti-Oedipus* they speak of deterritorialisation as 'a coming undone' (D&G 1983: 322). In *A Thousand Plateaus* deterritorialisation constitutes the cutting edge of an assemblage (D&G 1987: 88). In their book on the novelist Franz Kafka, they describe a Kafkaesque literary deterritorialisation that mutates content, forcing enunciations and expressions to 'disarticulate' (D&G 1986: 86). In their final collaboration – *What is Philosophy?* – Deleuze and Guattari posit that deterritorialisation can be physical, mental or spiritual (D&G 1994: 68). Given this seemingly broad spectrum of descriptions two questions emerge. First, how does the process of deterritorialisation work? Second, how is deterritorialisation connected to reterritorialisation? Perhaps deterritorialisation can best be understood as a movement producing change. In so far as it operates as a line of flight, deterritorialisation indicates the creative potential of an assemblage. So, to deterritorialise is to free up the fixed relations that contain a body all the while exposing it to new organisations.

It is important to remember that Deleuze, as well as Guattari, is concerned with overcoming the dualistic framework underpinning western philosophy (Being/nonbeing, original/copy and so on). In this regard, the relationship deterritorialisation has to reterritorialisation must not be construed negatively; it is not the polar opposite of territorialisation or reterritorialisation (when a territory is established once more). In fact, in the way that Deleuze and Guattari describe and use the concept, deterritorialisation inheres in a territory as its transformative vector; hence, it is tied to the very possibility of change immanent to a given territory.

Qualitatively speaking there are two different deterritorialising movements: absolute and relative. Philosophy is an example of absolute deterritorialisation and capital is an example of relative deterritorialisation. Absolute deterritorialisation is a way of moving and as such it has nothing to do with how fast or slow deterritorialising movements are; such movements are immanent, differentiated and ontologically prior to the movements of relative deterritorialisation. Relative deterritorialisation moves towards fixity and as such it occurs not on a molecular but molar plane as an actual movement. Put succinctly, absolute deterritorialising movements are virtual, moving through relative deterritorialising movements that are actual.

There are several different theoretical contexts Deleuze and Guattari discuss and use deterritorialisation in. These include: art, music, literature, philosophy and politics. For instance, in the western visual arts, faces and landscapes are deterritorialised. Meanwhile in philosophy, thought is deterritorialised by all that is outside of thought. In this regard, it is not the question that is deterritorialising but the problem, because the question seeks an answer, whereas the problem posits all that is unrecognisable or unknowable. They suggest that what is deterritorialised in music are human voices and the refrain (*ritournelle*). A helpful example here would be the composer Olivier Messiaen who, from around 1955 on, used birdsong in his compositions. In these works he did not just imitate the songs of birds; rather he brought birdsong into relation with the piano in a manner that transformed the territory of the musical instrument (piano) and the birdsong itself. Here the distinctive tone, timbre and tempo of birdsongs were fundamentally changed the moment these elements connected with musical organisation. Similarly Messiaen's compositional style also changed when it entered into a relation with birdsong, whereby these compositions could be described in terms of a becoming-bird.

Yet as the bird sings its song is it simply being territorial? Here we may consider the way in which the bird refrain is a territorial sign. Deleuze and Guattari use the biological understanding of 'territoriality' as discussed in the studies of birds conducted during the early to mid-twentieth century; however, they push this work in a different direction. Bernard Altum, Henry Eliot Howard and Konrad Lorenz all suggested male birds aggressively defend a particular territory as a way of socially organising themselves. These studies of bird activity understood territoriality as a biological drive pitched towards the preservation of species. Instead, Deleuze and Guattari address territoriality from the position of what is produced by the biological function of mating, hunting, eating and so forth, arguing that territoriality actually organises the functions. The problem they have with Lorenz, for example, is that he makes 'aggressiveness the basis of the territory' (D&G 1987: 315). They claim functions, such as mating, are organised 'because they are territorialised' (D&G 1987: 316). In this way, they use the understanding of territory advanced by the ethologist Jakob von Uexküll, to help shift the focus away from a mechanistic understanding of life onto an expressive one.

Von Uexküll proposed that there is no meaning outside of a milieu

(*Umwelt*). For him a 'territory' refers to a specific milieu that cannot be separated from the living thing occupying and creating the milieu, so that the meaning of a milieu for Von Uexküll is affective. This is important when we come to consider the supposed slippage between deterritorialisation and decoding that happens in *Anti-Oedipus* but not in *A Thousand Plateaus*. To decode, in the way that Deleuze and Guattari intend it, means to strike out at the selfsame codes that produce rigid meanings as opposed to translating meaning. Rather than understanding deterritorialisation as destabilising that which produces meaning, in *A Thousand Plateaus* Deleuze and Guattari regard it as a transversal process that defines the creativity of an assemblage: a nonlinear and nonfiliative system of relations.

Apart from biology the term 'territorialisation' can also be found in psychoanalysis. As early as 1966 Guattari used the psychoanalytic term – 'territorialisation' – in his book *Psychoanalyse et Transversalité*. Here, it was the French psychoanalyst Jacques Lacan who influenced Guattari. For Lacan, 'territorialisation' refers to the way in which the body of an infant is organised around and determined by erogenous zones and the connections it forms with part-objects. This organizational process is one of libidinal investment. As the infant undergoes a process of territorialisation its orifices and organs are conjugated. In the psychoanalytic sense, to deterritorialise is to free desire from libidinal investment. This freeing up of desire includes setting desire free from Oedipal investment (desire-as-lack). Accordingly, the upshot of Deleuze and Guattari's reconfiguration of Lacanian 'territorialisation' is that the subject is exposed to new organisations; the principal insight being: deterritorialisation shatters the subject.

In addition to the bioethological and psychoanalytic antecedents for the concepts of deterritorialisation and reterritorialisation, Deleuze and Guattari extend a political use to them. Leaning upon Karl Marx, they posit that labour-power is deterritorialised the moment it is freed from the means of production. That selfsame labour-power can be described as being reterritorialised when it is then connected to another means of production. Eugene Holland explains, when the English Enclosure Acts (1709–1869) enclosed common land for purposes of sheep-grazing, the peasants were concomitantly banished (or 'freed') from one means of production only to have their labour-power reterritorialised onto other means of production, such as when they became factory workers in the textile industry (H 1999: 19–20). During the early phases of industrialisation when capitalism was really gaining momentum, a system of deterritorialising flows prevailed: markets were expanding, social activities were undergoing radical changes, and populations moved from rural to urban environments. In one sense rural labour-power was deterritorialised (peasant and landowner) but in another sense it was reterritorialised (factory worker and industrial capitalist). Commenting on capitalism, Deleuze and Guattari insist that deterritorialised flows of code are reterritorialised into the axiomatic of capitalism and it is this connection between the two processes that constitutes the capitalist social machine.

Connectives

Assemblage
Becoming
Lacan
Lines of flight
Nomadicism
Partial Object
Rhizome

DETERRITORIALISATION + POLITICS

Paul Patton

The concept of deterritorialisation lies at the heart of Deleuze and Guattari's mature political philosophy. Processes of deterritorialisation are the movements which define a given assemblage since they determine the presence and the quality of 'lines of flight' (D&G 1987: 508). Lines of flight in turn define the form of creativity specific to that assemblage, the particular ways in which it can effect transformation in other assemblages or in itself (D&G 1987: 531). From the point of view of social or political change, everything hinges on the kinds of deterritorialisation present. Deleuze and Guattari define deterritorialisation as the movement by which something escapes or departs from a given territory (D&G 1987: 508). The processes of territory formation, deterritorialisation and reterritorialisation are inextricably entangled in any given social field: 'The merchant buys in a territory, deterritorialises products into commodities, and is reterritorialised on commercial circuits' (D&G 1994: 68).

Deterritorialisation is always a complex process involving at least a deterritorialising element and a territory, which is being left behind or reconstituted. Karl Marx's account of primitive accumulation in *Capital* illustrates the operation of 'vectors of deterritorialisation' in a social and economic territory: the development of commodity markets deterritorialises the socio-economic territory of feudal agriculture and leads to the emergence of large-scale commercial production. Deterritorialisation is always bound up with correlative processes of reterritorialisation, which does not mean returning to the original territory but rather the ways in which deterritorialised elements recombine and enter into new relations. Reterritorialisation is itself a complex process that takes different forms depending upon the character of the processes of deterritorialisation within which it occurs. Deleuze and Guattari distinguish between the 'connection' of deterritorialised flows, which refers to the ways in which distinct deterritorialisations can interact to accelerate one another, and the 'conjugation' of distinct flows which refers to the ways in which one may incorporate or 'overcode' another thereby effecting a relative blockage of its movement (D&G 1987: 220). Marx's account of primitive accumulation shows how the conjugation of the stream of displaced labour with the flow of deterritorialised money capital provided the conditions under which capitalist industry could develop. In this case, the reterritorialisation of the flows of capital and labour leads to the emergence of a new kind of assemblage, namely the axiomatic of capitalism.

When Deleuze and Guattari suggest that societies are defined by their lines of flight or by their deterritorialisation, they mean that fundamental social change happens all the time, even as the society reproduces itself on other levels. Sometimes change occurs by degrees, as with the steady erosion of myths about sexual difference and its role in social and political institutions. Sometimes, change occurs through the eruption of events which break with the past and inaugurate a new field of social, political or legal possibilities. The rioting of May 1968 was an event of this kind, 'a becoming breaking through into history' (D 1995: 153). Other examples include the sudden collapse of Eastern European communism or the dismantling of apartheid in South Africa. These are all turning points in history after which some things will never be the same as before. The key question is not whether change is slow or sudden; but, whether it is animated by a force of absolute deterritorialisation.

Deleuze and Guattari distinguish four types of deterritorialisation along the twin axes of absolute and relative, positive and negative (D&G 1987: 508–10). Deterritorialisation is relative in so far as it concerns only movements within the actual order of things. Relative deterritorialisation is negative when the deterritorialised element is immediately subjected to forms of reterritorialisation which enclose or obstruct its line of flight. It is positive when the line of flight prevails over secondary reterritorialisations, even though it may still fail to connect with other deterritorialised elements or enter into a new assemblage. Deterritorialisation is absolute in so far as it concerns the virtual order of things, the state of 'unformed matter on the plane of consistency' (D&G 1987: 55–6). Absolute deterritorialisation is not a further stage that comes after relative deterritorialisation but rather its internal dynamic, since there is 'a perpetual immanence of absolute deterritorialisation within relative deterritorialisation' (D&G 1987: 56). The difference between positive and negative forms of absolute deterritorialisation corresponds to the difference between the connection and the conjugation of deterritorialised flows. Absolute deterritorialisation is positive when it leads to the creation of a new earth and new people: 'when it connects lines of flight, raises them to the power of an abstract vital line or draws a plane of consistency' (D&G 1987: 510). Since real transformation requires the recombination of deterritorialised elements in mutually supportive ways, social or political processes are truly revolutionary only when they involve assemblages of connection rather than conjugation.

DIAGRAM – refer to the entries on 'axiomatic', 'black hole', 'fold', 'Foucault + fold', 'plateau', 'semiotics' and 'virtual/virtuality'.

DIFFERENCE

Cliff Stagoll

Deleuze is often labelled as a 'philosopher of difference', an assessment that highlights the critical place of 'difference' in his work. He is concerned to overturn the primacy accorded identity and representation in western rationality by theorising difference as it is experienced. In doing so, Deleuze challenges two critical presuppositions: the privilege accorded Being and the representational model of thought. He considers both to have important and undesirable political, aesthetic and ethical implications that a disruption of traditional philosophy can help to surmount. Deleuze uses his notion of empirical and non-conceptual 'difference in itself' in the service of such a disruption.

Difference is usually understood either as 'difference from the same' or difference of the same over time. In either case, it refers to a net variation between two states. Such a conception assumes that states are comparable, and that there is at base a sameness against which variation can be observed or deduced. As such, difference becomes merely a relative measure of sameness and, being the product of a comparison, it concerns external relations between things. To think about such relations typically means grouping like with like, and then drawing distinctions between the groups. Furthermore, over and above such groupings might be posited a *universal* grouping, such as Being, a conception of presence that alone makes the groups wholly consistent and meaningful. It is because Georg Wilhelm Friedrich Hegel drew a comprehensive and cohesive world of Being that made him such a significant target for Deleuze's critique.

On such an account, difference is subordinated to sameness, and becomes an object of representation in relation to some identity. As such, it is never conceived in terms of 'difference-in-itself ', the uniqueness implicit in the particularity of things and the moments of their conception and perception. Rather, difference is understood in terms of resemblance, identity, opposition and analogy, the kinds of relations used to determine groupings of things. Yet this tendency to think in terms of sameness detracts from the specificity of concrete experience, instead simplifying phenomena so that they might 'fit' within the dominant model of unity. Deleuze's 'liberation' of difference from such a model has two parts. First, he develops a concept of difference that does not rely on a relationship with sameness and, second, he challenges the philosophy of representation.

Deleuze argues that we ought not to presume a pre-existing unity, but instead take seriously the nature of the world as it is perceived. For him, every aspect of reality evidences difference, and there is nothing 'behind' such difference; difference is not grounded in anything else. Deleuze does not mean to refer, however, to differences of degree, by which he means distinctions amongst items that are considered identical or in any sense the same. Instead, he means the particularity or 'singularity' of each individual thing, moment, perception or conception. Such difference is *internal* to a thing or event, implicit in its being that particular. Even if things might be conceived as having shared attributes allowing them to be labelled as being of the same kind, Deleuze's conception of difference seeks to privilege the individual differences between them.

Such individuality is, for Deleuze, the primary philosophical fact, so that, rather than theorising how individuals might be grouped, it is more important to explore the specific and unique development or 'becoming' of each individual. The genealogy of an individual lies not in generality or commonality, but in a process of individuation determined by actual and specific differences, multitudinous influences and chance interactions.

Deleuze's difference-in-itself releases difference from domination by identity and sameness. Indeed, on this account, identity must always be referred to the difference inherent in the particulars being 'swept up' in the process of constructing a relationship between them. To realise this is to meet Deleuze's challenge of developing a new perspective in order to resist transcendence. However, to do so routinely is not easy. Only by destabilising our thinking, disrupting our faculties and freeing our senses from established tendencies might we uncover the difference evident in the lived world, and realise the uniqueness of each moment and thing.

Deleuze's theory of difference also challenges the traditional theory of representation, by which we tend to consider each individual as re-presenting ('presenting again') something as just another instance of a category or original. On such a view, difference is something that might be predicated of a concept, and so logically subordinated to it, whilst the concept can be applied to an infinite number of particular instances. To think in terms of difference-in-itself means to set the concept aside and focus instead on the singular, and the unique circumstances of its production. Awareness of such specific circumstances means that the notion of some 'thing in general' can be set aside in favour of one's experience of *this* thing, here and now.

Connectives

Creative transformation
Eternal return
Repetition

DIFFERENCE + POLITICS

Paul Patton

Deleuze's ontological conception of a world of free differences suggests a defence of the particular against all forms of universalisation or representation. Every time there is representation, he argues, there is an 'unrepresented singularity' which does not recognise itself in the representant (D 1994: 52). However, neither this critique of representation nor the ontological priority of difference establishes a politics of difference. Identities presuppose differences and are inhabited by them, just as differences inevitably presuppose and are inhabited by identities. A politics of difference requires the specification of politically relevant kinds of difference.

Deleuze and Guattari's concept of minority and their support for minoritarian politics provides a novel understanding of the kind of difference which is relevant for democratic political change. They define minority in opposition to majority, but insist that the difference between them is not quantitative since social minorities can be more numerous than the so-called majority. Both minority and majority involve the relationship of a group to the larger collectivity of which it is a part. Suppose there are only two groups and suppose that there is a standard or ideal type of member of the larger collectivity: the majority is defined as the group which most closely approximates the standard, while the minority is defined by the gap which separates its members from that standard. In a social collectivity, majority can take many simultaneous forms:

> Let us suppose that the constant or standard is the average adult-white-heterosexual- European-male speaking a standard language . . . It is obvious that 'man' holds the majority, even if he is less numerous than mosquitoes, children, women, blacks, peasants, homosexuals, etc. That is because he appears twice, once in the constant and again in the variable from which the constant is extracted. Majority assumes a state of power and domination, not the other way around. (D&G 1987: 105, cf. 291)

A liberal politics of difference would simply defend the right of the minorities to be included in the majority. In other words, it would seek to broaden the standard so that it becomes male or female – European or non- European – hetero or homosexual and so on. Social minorities are here conceived as outcasts but potentially able to be included among the majority. Deleuze and Guattari insist upon the importance of such piecemeal changes to the form and content of a given majority. After redescribing the non-coincidence of minority and majority in the language of axiomatic set theory, they assert, 'this is not to say that the struggle on the level of the axioms is without importance; on the contrary, it is determining (at the most diverse levels: women's struggle for the vote, for abortion, for jobs; the struggle of the regions for autonomy; the struggle of the Third World . . .' (D&G 1987: 470–1). At the same time, however, in order to draw attention to the sense in which the reconfiguration of the majority is dependent upon a prior process of differentiation, they introduce a third term in addition to the pair majority-minority, namely 'becoming-minor' or 'minoritarian', by which they mean the creative process of becoming different or diverging from the majority.

This process of becoming-minor, which subjects the standard to a process of continuous variation or deterritorialisation (D&G 1987: 106), is the real focus of Deleuze and Guattari's approach to the politics of difference. They do not deny the importance of the installation of new constants or the attainment of majority status, but they stress the importance of the minoritarian-becoming of everyone, including the recognised bearers of minority status within a given majority. They insist that the power of minorities 'is not measured by their capacity to enter and make themselves felt within the majority system, nor even to reverse the necessarily tautological criterion of the majority, but to bring to bear the force of the non-denumerable sets, however small they may be, against the denumerable sets . . .' (D&G 1987: 471). By this they mean that the limits of the potential for transformation are not determined by the normalising power of the majority but by the transformative potential of becoming-minor, or becoming-revolutionary. They do not mean to suggest that minorities do not enter into and produce effects upon the majority.

Their insistence on the transformative potential of minoritarian becomings does not imply a refusal of democratic politics. Those excluded from the majority as defined by a given set of axioms, no less than those included within it, are the potential bearers of the power to transform that set, whether in the direction of a new set of axioms or an altogether new axiomatic (D&G 1987: 471). Everyone may attain the creative power of minority-becoming that carries with it the potential for new earths and new peoples.

DIFFERENTIATION/DIFFERENCIATION

Adrian Parr

The concepts of 'differentiation' and 'differenciation' are primarily elucidated by Deleuze in *Bergsonism* (D 1988a: 96–8) and *Difference and Repetition* (D 1994: 208–14) and the distinction he forms between the two is an important ingredient of his differential ontology. To begin with he appeals to the mathematical concept of differentiation in order to unlock his understanding of the Whole as a unified system, preferring instead to think of open wholes that continually produce new directions and connections. In effect, what are differentiated are intensities and heterogeneous qualities and this is what makes the virtual real but not actual. In short, differentiation in the way Deleuze intends it happens only in the virtual realm. Continually dividing and combining, differentiation can be likened to a zone of divergence and as such it is fundamentally a creative movement, or flow, that conditions a whole in all its provisional consistency.

Meanwhile, what is differenciated is the heterogeneous series of virtual differentiation. In *Bergsonism* Deleuze points out that differenciation is an actualisation of the virtual. Actualisation can be either conceptual or material such as an 'eye' which Deleuze describes in *Difference and Repetition* as a 'differenciated organ' (D 1994: 211). The problem this poses, given that Deleuze is not a representational thinker, is how difference differenciates without itself turning into a system of representation? That is to say, if differenciation is the process of actualising the virtual how does this avoid the representational trap of similitude and identity? Why isn't differenciation similar to, or a version of, the virtual it differenciates?

For Deleuze, the actualised differences of differenciation do not enjoy a privileged point of view over the differences making up the flow of differentiation, nor is differenciation a process that unifies heterogeneous qualities; rather it simply affirms these qualities and intensities without completely halting the flow in its tracks. The actualisation that differenciation produces is not 'like' differentiation, as this would imply that the differentiation it is like is in itself a fixed subject more than an intensive system continually undergoing change. Put simply, what this means is that the process of differenciation is a question of variation more than identity and resemblance because Deleuze prefers to think of it as a dynamic movement that brings differences into relation with one another.

Overall, Deleuze considers actualisation in terms of creativity, whereby the process does not simply mark a change into what was possible in the first instance. To be truly creative, differenciation needs to be understood as something new instead of something that resembles virtuality. Carrying on from here he outlines that the virtual differenciates itself; without this the virtual could not be actualised because there would be no lines of differenciation that could enable actualisation to happen (D 1988a: 97).

Connectives

Actuality
Individuation
Representation
Virtual/Virtuality

DISJUNCTIVE SYNTHESIS

Claire Colebrook

At its most general, the disjunctive synthesis is the production of a series of differences. The significance of the concept of disjunction in Deleuze's work is threefold. First, whereas structuralism conceives difference negatively, such that an undifferentiated or formless world is then differentiated by a structure. Deleuze regards difference positively, so disjunction is a mode of production. There is a potential *in life* to produce series: a desire can attach to this, or this or this; a vibration of light can be perceived as this, or this, or this. Second, the differences of disjunction are transversal. There is not one point or term (such as consciousness or language) from which differences are unfolded or connected; consciousness can connect with a language, a machine, a colour, a sound, a body, and this means that series may traverse and connect different potentials. Sexual desire, for example, might leave the series of body parts – breast, or mouth, or anus, or phallus – and invest different territories – the desire for sounds, for colour, for movements. Finally, disjunction is not binary. Life should not be reduced to the miserable logic of contradiction or excluded middle – either you want liberalism or you don't; either you're male or female; either you're for the war or for terrorism – for disjunction is open and plural: neither liberalism nor terrorism, but a further extension of the series.

The concept of synthesis is central to both *Difference and Repetition* and *Anti-Oedipus*. In *Difference and Repetition* Deleuze rewrites Immanuel Kant's three syntheses (from the *Critique of Pure Reason*). For Kant, our experienced world of time and space is possible only because there is a subject who experiences and who connects (or synthesises) received impressions into a coherent order. For Deleuze, by contrast, there is not a subject who synthesises. Rather, there are syntheses from which subjects are formed; these subjects are not persons but points of relative stability resulting from connection, what Deleuze refers to as 'larval subjects'. In *Anti-Oedipus* Deleuze and Guattari expand the concept of the three syntheses into political terms: association, disjunction and conjunction. Association is the connection, not just of data (as in Kant's philosophy), but also of bodies or terms into some manifold or experienced thing, an 'assemblage'. Disjunction, the second synthesis, is the subsequent possibility of relations between or among such assembled points of relative stability, while conjunction or the third synthesis is the referral of these terms to the ground or plane across which they range.

The disjunctive synthesis is important for two reasons. First, Deleuze argues that all syntheses (or ways of thinking about the world) have legitimate and illegitimate uses, or an immanent and transcendent employment. Syntheses are immanent when we recognise that there are not subjects *who* synthesise the world; there is not a transcendent or external point beyond the world from which synthesis emerges. Rather, there are connections, syntheses, (desires) from which points or terms are effected. No point or term can be set outside an event of synthesis as its transcendent ground, so there can be no transcendental synthesising subject as there was for Kant. Second, the subjection of modern thought lies in the illegitimate use of the disjunctive synthesis. From relations or syntheses (passions, sympathies) among bodies certain terms are formed, such as the mother, father and child of the modern family. We should, then, see male-female relations or gender as a production, as a way in which bodies have been synthesised or assembled. One can be male *or* female.

The Oedipus complex is the disjunctive synthesis in its transcendent and illegitimate form: either you identify with your father and become a subject (thinking 'man') *or* you desire your mother and remain other than human. An immanent use of the synthesis would refuse this *exclusive* disjunction of 'one must be this *or* that, male *or* female'. Instead of insisting that one must line up beneath the signifier of man or woman and submit to the system of sexual difference, Deleuze and Guattari open the disjunctive synthesis: one can be this or this or this, *and* this *and* this *and* this: neither mother nor father but a becoming-girl, becoming-animal or becoming imperceptible.

Connectives

Becoming
Desire
Kant
Oedipalisation

DURATION (*DURÉE*)

Cliff Stagoll

Henri Bergson interests Deleuze because of his radical departure from philosophy's orthodoxy. Duration (*durée*) is one of several of Bergson's key ideas adopted by Deleuze when developing his philosophy of difference. Typical of Deleuze's usual approach to Bergson, his interpretation and use of the concept is at once almost entirely sympathetic but strikingly idiosyncratic.

According to Deleuze, one can only comprehend the notion of duration by using Bergson's method of philosophical intuition (*intuition philosophique*), a deliberate reflective awareness or willed self-consciousness. Intuition reveals consciousness (or, more generally, mental life) to be essentially temporal; ongoing mental activity that constitutes, in its dynamism and the mutual interpenetration of its states, a time internal to one's self. Mental life is, then, a kind of flowing experience, and duration is the immediate awareness of this flow.

Bergson believes that intuition's findings are best expressed in images, and so explains duration by using analogies with music. Mental states flow together as if parts of a melody, with previous notes lingering and future ones anticipated in the unity of a piece, the permeation of each note by others revealing the extreme closeness of their interconnection. To try and grasp this flow as a complete set of notes is pointless, because the music is always on the verge of ending and always altered by the addition of a new note. To speak of 'mind' or 'consciousness' as a comprehensive system is to ignore an analogous attribute of duration: it is always flowing, overtaking what might be called the 'not yet' and passing away in the 'already'.

Bergson considers quantification of duration to be inconsistent with its immediate, lived reality. It can be contrasted with 'clock time', the time of physics and practical life, which either spatialises time by situating elemental instants end-to-end on a referential grid or uses the digits of a time-piece as a crass and imprecise physical image. When arranged in accordance with these models, time becomes a series of separable instants, consciousness is 'situated' in time as a series of temporally disparate mental states, and movement is conceived in terms of relations between static positions. In other words, clock time abstracts from the notion of duration by distorting its continuity.

But constitutive integration of moments of duration must not be overemphasised. Bergson's intuition confirms also that consciousness is not 'one long thought', as it were, but a flowing together of mental states that are different from one another in important ways. Bergson contends that differences between mental states allow us to mark one kind of thought or one particular thought from another, whilst constituting simultaneously a singular flow, a merging of thoughts as one consciousness. As such, duration is the immediate awareness of the flow of changes that simultaneously constitute differences *and* relationships between particulars.

Several characteristics of duration are critical for Deleuze. In his early works on David Hume, Deleuze used duration as an explicatory tool, rendering anew Hume's accounts of habit, association and time. Subsequently, Deleuze adopts it as a means for exploring difference and becoming as key elements of life. If duration 'includes', as it were, all of the qualitative differences ('differences of kind') of one's lived experience, Deleuze argues, then it also emphasises the productive, liberating potential of these differences. Even in the continuity of one's consciousness, there is a disconnection between events that allows creativity and renewal. For example, one is able to call upon new concepts to reinterpret one's memories or perceive some vista anew in the light of one's exposure to a work of art.

Deleuze uses duration to make some important philosophical points about time and difference. For philosophers such as Immanuel Kant, time is both a form of receptive experience about the world and a necessary condition for any human experience at all. As such, for Kant, time is not an empirical concept but an *a priori* necessity underlying all possible experience. Furthermore, he considers time to comprise a homogeneous series of successive instants, standing in need of synthesis.

In contrast, duration is always present in the 'givenness' of one's experience. It does not transcend experience, and neither must it be derived philosophically. Furthermore, duration, unlike matter, cannot be divided into elements which, when divided or reconstituted, remain the same in aggregate as their unified form. Duration, as lived experience, brings together both unity and difference in a flow of interconnections. For Deleuze, these contrasts represent the difference between a dictatorial philosophy that creates 'superior' concepts that subsume and order the multiplicities and creativity of life and one that creates opportunities for change and variety.

Connectives

Bergson
Intuition
Kant

E

EARTH/LAND (TERRE)

John Protevi

As part of what Deleuze and Guattari come to call a geophilosophy in *What is Philosophy?*, in *A Thousand Plateaus* 'earth' along with 'ground' (*sol*) and 'territory' (*territoire*) express manners of occupying terrestrial space by different social machines: the nomad war machine, the territorial tribe, the overcoding State. Earth can also mean the virtual realm or Body without Organs (BwO), while 'a new earth' (*une nouvelle terre*), called for at points in *A Thousand Plateaus* and made a focal point of *What is Philosophy?*, entails new human relationships to the creative potentials of material systems to form consistencies, war machines, or rhizomes from a variety of means.

In *A Thousand Plateaus*, Brian Massumi uses two English words to translate the French *terre*, which can mean both 'earth' in the astronomical sense of our planet and 'land' in the geographical sense of a cultivated area. There is no consistency in Deleuze and Guattari's use of the majuscule in the French text; both *Terre* and *terre* are used in the sense of 'earth' and 'land'. The anglophone reader should keep in mind the close proximity of *terre* ('earth' and 'land') with *territoire* ('territory').

First, 'earth' is equivalent to the BwO, otherwise understood by

Deleuze and Guattari as the virtual plane of consistency upon which strata are imposed (D&G 1987: 40). Second, 'earth' is part of the earth–territory (*terre–territoire*) system of romanticism, the becoming-intensive of strata. Hence 'earth' is the gathering point, outside all territories, of all selfordering forces ('forces of the earth') for intensive territorial assemblages (the virtual seen from the point of view of territorialising machinic assemblages). Third, the 'new earth' (*nouvelle terre*) is the becoming-virtual of intensive material. Put differently, the 'new earth' is the correlate of absolute deterritorialisation (the leaving of all intensive territorial assemblages to attain the plane of consistency); it is the tapping of 'cosmic forces' (the virtual seen from the point of view of the abstract machines composing it, not the machinic assemblages that actualise a selection of singularities). Hence, it marks new potentials for creation (D&G 1987: 423; 509–10). In this sense, it is unfortunate that Brian Massumi translates *une nouvelle terre* as 'a new land' (D&G 1987: 509).

Land (*terre*) is constituted by the overcoding of territories under the signifying regime and the State apparatus (D&G 1987: 440–1). Land refers exclusively to striated space, and is that terrain that can be owned, held as stock, distributed, rented, made to produce and taxed. Land can be gridded, distributed, classified and categorised without even being physically experienced, and a striking example of this is the township-andrange system of the US that imparted striated space to a vast part of the North American continent ahead of actual settler occupation. The system of stockpiling territories and overcoding them as land for the State does not stop at the farm or even the ranch, but extends to the forest lands (as 'national' forests) and to the unusable spaces that become national parks, biosphere reserves, and so forth. These spaces are held as refuges for State subjects who seek to escape from private property to find some sort of becoming-earth commons.

In *What is Philosophy?*, 'a new earth' becomes the rallying cry in the 'geophilosophy' of Deleuze and Guattari, in which 'stratification' is the process whereby the implantation of codes and territories form dominating bodies. This is opposed to the construction of a 'new earth' that entails new human relationships to the creative potentials of material systems to form consistencies, war machines, or rhizomes from a variety of means. In the construction of the new earth, care must be taken not to confuse the structural difference of strata and consistency with an *a priori* moral categorisation, but rather always to retain the pragmatic and empirical nature of Deleuze and Guattari's work and perform the ethical evaluation of the life-affirming or life-denying character of assemblages.

Strata, along with codes and territories, are always needed, if only in providing resting points for further experiments in forming war machines.

Strata are in fact 'beneficial in many regards' (D&G 1987: 40), though we must be careful not to laud the stability of strata as instantiating the moral virtue of unchanging self-identity espoused by Platonism. The mere fact that an assemblage or body politic is flexible and resilient, however, does not guarantee its ethical choice-worthiness, for what Deleuze and Guattari call 'micro-fascism' is not rigid at all but rather a supple and free-floating body politic. Even if fascists are reterritorialised on the 'black hole' of their subjectivity: 'there is fascism when a *war machine* is installed in each hole, in every niche' (D&G 1987: 214) and not only those practices that 'intend' to produce a life-affirming assemblage will result in such.

Connectives

Black hole
Body without Organs
Deterritorialisation
Plato
Space
Virtual/Virtuality

ETERNAL RETURN

Lee Spinks

The concept of 'eternal return', which Deleuze draws from Friedrich Nietzsche, is crucial to the radical extension of the philosophy of immanence and univocity. In *Difference and Repetition* Deleuze argues that Duns Scotus, Baruch Spinoza and Nietzsche affirmed univocal being. It is only with Nietzsche, according to Deleuze, that the joyful idea of univocity is thought adequately, and this is because Nietzsche imagines a world of 'pre-personal singularities'. That is, there is not a 'who' or 'what' that then has various properties; nor is there someone or something that *is*. Each difference is a power to differ, with no event of difference being the ground or cause of any other. By going through this affirmation of difference, and by abandoning any ground or being before or beyond difference, both Nietzsche and Deleuze arrive at the eternal return. If difference occurred in order to arrive at some proper end – if there were a purpose or proper end to life – then the process of becoming would have some ideal end point (even if this were only imagined or ideal). But difference is an event that is joyful in itself; it is not the difference *of* this being or *for* this end. With each event of difference life is transformed; life becomes other than itself because life is difference. Consequently, the only 'thing' that 'is' is difference, with each repetition of difference being different. Only difference returns, and it returns *eternally*. Time is what follows from difference (time is difference); difference cannot be located in time. Eternal return is therefore the ultimate idea.

This difficult and enigmatic idea, developed most concertedly in Nietzsche's *Thus Spake Zarathustra*, has proved controversial in philosophical circles where it has generally been interpreted as either an existential or inhuman vision of existence. According to the existential reading, the thought of eternal return compels us to consider how we ought properly to live. This thought can be expressed in the following way: were we suddenly to recognise that every aspect of our lives, both painful and joyous, was fated to return in the guise of a potentially infinite repetition, how would we need to live to justify the recurrence of even the most terrible and painful events? Conversely, the inhuman or cosmological reading understands Nietzsche's proposition as the fundamental axiom of a philosophy of forces in which active force separates itself from and supplants reactive force and ultimately locates itself as the motor principle of becoming.

Deleuze's signal contribution to the post-war philosophical revision of Nietzsche was to establish this second reading of eternal return as the return and *selection* of forces at the heart of modern theories of power. He explicitly repudiates the naïve reading of Nietzsche that envisages eternal return as a doctrine proclaiming the infinite recurrence of every historical moment in exactly the same order throughout eternity. The perversity of this naïve reading, Deleuze argues, is that it converts Nietzsche's vision of being as the endless becoming of differential forces into a simple principle of identity. Yet we fail to understand the eternal return if we conceive of it as the ceaseless return of the *same;* instead, eternal return inscribes difference and becoming at the very heart of being. For it is not being that recurs in the eternal return; the principle of return constitutes the one thing shared by diversity and multiplicity. What is at stake is not the repetition of a universal sameness but the movement that produces everything that *differs*. Eternal return is therefore properly understood as a *synthesis* of becoming and the being that is affirmed in becoming. It appears as the fundamental ontological principle of the difference and repetition of forces that will bear the name of Will to Power.

To think the eternal return is to think the becoming-active of forces. The return *selects* forces according to the quantity of Will to Power that they express. Deleuze characterises this process as a *double selection* by the activity of force and the affirmation of the will. In accordance with the principle that whatever we will, we must will it in such a way that we also will its eternal recurrence, the eternal return eliminates reactive states from the becoming of being. This first selection eliminates all but the most powerfully reactive forces – those which go to the active limit of what they can do and form the basis of the nihilistic impulse and the will to nothingness. These strong reactive forces are subsequently *incorporated* into the eternal return in order to effect the overcoming of negation and the transformation of reactive into active force. Such revaluation takes place because the eternal return brings the nihilistic will to completion: the absolute spirit of negation involves a negation of reactive forces themselves. Within this negation of negation reactive forces deny and suppress themselves in the name of a paradoxical affirmation: by destroying the reactive in themselves, the strongest spirits come to embody the becoming-active of reactive force. This movement of affirmation constitutes the second or doubled selection undertaken by the eternal return: the transvaluation of reactive forces by means of an affirmation of negation itself. This second selection transforms a selection of thought into a selection of being: something *new* is now brought into being which appears as the effect of the revaluation of forces. The eternal return 'is' this movement of transvaluation: according to its double selection only action and affirmation return while the negative is willed out of being. The return eliminates every reactive force that resists it; in so doing, it affirms both the being of becoming and the becoming-active of forces.

Connectives

Active/reactive
Becoming
Difference
Kant
Multiplicity
Nietzsche

ETHICS

John Marks

Throughout his work, Deleuze draws a clear distinction between ethics and morality. Morality is a set of constraining rules that judge actions and intentions in relation to transcendent values of good and evil. Morality is a way of judging life, whereas ethics is a way of assessing what we do in terms of ways of existing in the world. Ethics involves a creative commitment to maximising connections, and of maximising the powers that will expand the possibilities of life. In this way, ethics for Deleuze is inextricably linked with the notion of becoming.Morality implies that we judge ourselves and others on the basis of what we *are* and *should be*, whereas ethics implies that we do not yet know what we might become. For Deleuze, there are no transcendent values against which we should measure life. It is rather 'Life' itself that constitutes its own immanent ethics. An ethical approach is, in this way, essentially pragmatic, and it is no surprise that Deleuze admires the American pragmatist model that substitutes experimentation for salvation. Deleuze sets the ideal of this pragmatism – a world which is 'in process' – against the 'European morality' of salvation and charity. It rejects the search for moral consensus and the construction of transcendent values, and it conceives of society as experiment rather than contract: a community of inquirers with an experimental spirit.

Friedrich Nietzsche and Baruch Spinoza are the two main influences on Deleuze's notion of ethics. From them, he takes the idea that ethics is a form of affirmation and evaluation. Such an ethics applies the acceptance that the world is, as Deleuze puts it, neither true nor real, but 'living'. To affirm is to evaluate life in order to set free what lives. Rather than weighing down life with the burden of higher values, it seeks to make life light and active, and to create new values. Both thinkers reorientate philosophy by calling into question the way in which morality conceives of the relationship between mind and body. For the system of morality, mind as consciousness dominates the passions of the body. Spinoza, however, proposes an ethical route that is later taken up by Nietzsche, by rejecting the superiority of mind over body. It is not a case of giving free reign to the passions of the body, since this would be nothing more than a reversal, a licence to act thoughtlessly. Rather in claiming that there is a *parallelism* between mind and body, Spinoza suggests a new, more creative way of conceiving of thought.

For Deleuze, Spinoza is the great ethical thinker who breaks with the Judeo-Christian tradition, and who is followed by four 'disciples' who develop this ethical approach: Nietzsche, D. H. Lawrence, Franz Kafka and Antonin Artaud. They are all opposed to the psychology of the priest, and Nietzsche in particular shows how judgement subjects man to an infinite debt that he cannot pay. This means that the doctrine of judgement is only apparently more moderate than a system of 'cruelty' according to which debt is measured in blood and inscribed directly on the body, since it condemns us to infinite restitution and servitude. Deleuze goes further to show how these four 'disciples' elaborate a whole system of 'cruelty' that is opposed to judgement, and which constitutes the basics for an ethics. The domination of the body in favour of consciousness leads to an impoverishment of our knowledge of the body. We do not fully explore the capacities of the body, and in the same way that the body surpasses the knowledge we have of it, so thought also surpasses the consciousness we have of it. Once we can begin to explore these new dimensions – the *unknown* of the body and the *unconscious* of thought – we are in the domain of ethics. The transcendent categories of Good and Evil can be abandoned in favour of 'good' and 'bad'. A 'good' individual seeks to make connections that increase her power to act, whilst at the same time not diminishing similar powers in others. The 'bad' individual does not organise her encounters in this way and either falls back into guilt and resentment, or relies on guile and violence.

Deleuze's commitment to ethics is closely connected to the concept of becoming, and in particular that of becoming-animal. The ethical drive for the 'great health' that allows life to flourish is all too often channelled into serving the petty 'human' ends of self-consolidation and selfaggrandisement. One way of going beyond this calculation of profit and loss is to 'become' animal. The drive for justice, for example, must overcome itself by learning from the lion who, as Nietzsche says, refuses to rage against the ticks and flies that seek shelter and nourishment on its body. In a more general political sense, it is a question of maintaining our 'belief-in-the-world'. We do this by creating forms of resistance to what we are becoming (Michel Foucault's 'actual') and not simply to what we are in the present. Rather than judging, we need to make something exist.

Connectives

Becoming
Nietzsche
Spinoza

EVENT

Cliff Stagoll

Deleuze introduced the concept of the 'event' in *The Logic of Sense* to describe instantaneous productions intrinsic to interactions between various kinds of forces. Events are changes immanent to a confluence of parts or elements, subsisting as pure virtualities (that is, real inherent possibilities) and distinguishing themselves only in the course of their actualisation in some body or state. Loosely, events might be characterised (as Deleuze does) in terms consonant with the Stoic concept of *lekta*:

as incorporeal transformations that subsist over and above the spatio-temporal world, but are expressible in language nonetheless.

As the *product* of the synthesis of forces, events signify the internal dynamic of their interactions. As such, on Deleuze's interpretation, an event is not a particular state or happening itself, but something made actual in the State or happening. In other words, an event is the potential immanent within a particular confluence of forces. Take as an example a tree's changing colour in the spring. On Deleuze's account, the event is not what evidently occurs (the tree becomes green) because this is merely a passing surface effect or expression of an event's actualisation, and thus of a particular confluence of bodies and other events (such as weather patterns, soil conditions, pigmentation effects and the circumstances of the original planting). Therefore we ought not to say 'the tree became green' or 'the tree is now green' (both of which imply a change in the tree's essence), but rather 'the tree greens'. By using the infinitive form 'to green', we make a dynamic attribution of the predicate, an incorporeality distinct from both the tree and green-ness which captures nonetheless the dynamism of the event's actualisation. The event is not a disruption of some continuous state, but rather the state is constituted by events 'underlying' it that, when actualised, mark every moment of the state as a transformation.

Deleuze's position presents an alternative to traditional philosophies of substance, challenging the notion that reality ought to be understood in terms of the determinate states of things. This notion was expressed clearly by Plato, who established a contrast between fixed and determinate states of things defining the identity of an object on the one hand and, on the other, temporal series of causes and effects having an impact *upon* the object. Deleuze would say that there is no distinct, particular thing without the events that define it as that particular, constituting its potential for change and rate of change. Instead, an event is unrelated to any material content, being without fixed structure, position, temporality or property, and without beginning or end.

Deleuze's event is a sign or indicator of its genesis, and the expression of the productive potential of the forces from which it arose. As such, it highlights the momentary uniqueness of the nexus of forces (whether or not to some obvious effect) whilst preserving a place for discontinuity in terms of some particular concept or plane of consistency. Three characteristics highlighted in Deleuze's texts point to this distinctiveness. First, no event is ever constituted by a preliminary or precedent unity between the forces of its production, being instead the primitive effect or change generated at the moment of their interaction. Second, events are produced neither in the image of some model nor as representative copies or likenesses of a more fundamental reality, being instead wholly immanent, original and creative productions. Third, as pure effect, an event has no goal.

Deleuze is careful to preserve dynamism in his concept. An event is neither a beginning nor an end point, but rather always 'in the middle'. Events themselves have no beginning- or end-point, and their relationship with Deleuze's notion of dynamic change – 'becoming' – is neither one of 'joining moments together' nor one in which an event is the 'end' of one productive process, to be supplanted or supplemented by the next. Rather, becoming 'moves through' an event, with the event representing just a momentary productive intensity.

In his theory of the event, Deleuze is not interested just in the machinations of production, but also in the productive potential inherent in forces of all kinds. Events carry no determinate outcome, but only new possibilities, representing a moment at which new forces might be brought to bear. Specifically, in terms of his model of thinking, he does not mean just that 'one thinks and thus creates' but that thinking and creating are constituted simultaneously. As such, his general theory of the event provides a means for theorising the immanent creativity of thinking, challenging us to think differently and to consider things anew. This is not to say that he means to challenge us to think in *terms* of events, but rather to make thinking its own event by embracing the rich chaos of life and the uniqueness and potential of each moment.

Connectives

Becoming
Plato

EXPERIENCE

Inna Semetsky

Deleuze considered himself an empiricist, yet not in the reductive, *tabula rasa*-like, passive sense. Experience is that milieu which provides the capacity to affect and be affected; it is a-subjective and impersonal. Experience is not an individual property; rather subjects are constituted in relations within experience itself, that is, by means of individuation via haecceity. The exteriority of relations presents 'a vital protest against principles' (D 1987: 55). Experience is rendered meaningful not by grounding empirical particulars in abstract universals but by experimentation. Something in the experiential world forces us to think. This something is an object not of recognition but a fundamental encounter that can be 'grasped in a range of affective tones' (D 1994: 139). In fact, novel concepts are to be invented or created in order to make sense out of singular experiences and, ultimately, to affirm this sense.

Experience is qualitative, multidimensional, and inclusive; it includes 'a draft, a wind, a day, a time of day, a stream, a place, a battle, an illness' (D 1995: 141): yet, an experiential event is subjectless. We are made up of relations, says Deleuze (2000), and experience makes sense to us only if we understand the relations in practice between conflicting schemes of the said experience. The difference embedded in real experience makes thought encounter a shock or crisis, which is embedded in the objective structure of an event per se, thereby transcending the faculties of perception beyond the 'given' data of sense-impressions. Difference is an ontological category, 'the noumenon closest to phenomenon' (D 1994: 222), which, however, is never beyond experience because every phenomenon is in fact conditioned by difference. Transcendental empiricism is what Deleuze called his philosophical method: thinking is not a natural exercise but always a second power of thought, born under the constraint of experience as a material power, a force. The intensity of difference is a function of desire, the latter embedded in experience because its object is 'the entire surrounding which it traverses' (D&G 1987: 30).

If relations are irreducible to their terms, then the whole dualistic split between thought and world, the inside and the outside, becomes invalid, and relational logic is the logic of experimentation not 'subordinate to the verb to be' (D 1987: 57). This logic is inspired by empiricism because 'only empiricism knows how to transcend the experiential dimension of the visible' (D 1990: 20) without recourse to Ideas, moral universals, or value judgements. The experiential world is folded, the fold being 'the inside *of* the outside' (D 1988a: 96), where the outside is virtual yet real by virtue of its pragmatics. It unfolds in an unpredictable manner, and it is impossible to know ahead of time what the body (both physical and mental) can do.

Because the body, acting within experience, is defined by its affective capacity, it is equally impossible to know 'the affects one is capable of' (D 1988b: 125): life becomes an experimental and experiential affair that requires, for Deleuze, practical wisdom in a Spinozian sense by means of immanent evaluations of experience, or modes of existence. As affective, experience is as yet a-conceptual, and Deleuze emphasises the passionate quality of such an experience: 'perhaps passion, the State of passion, is actually what folding the line outside, making it endurable . . . is about' (D 1995: 116).

The Deleuzian object of experience, being un-thought, is presented only in its tendency to exist, or rather to subsist, in a virtual, sub-representative state. It actualises itself through multiple different/ciations. Deleuze's method, compatible with Henri Bergson's intuition, enables the reading of the signs, symbols and symptoms that lay down the dynamical structure of experience. Experience, in contrast to analytic philosophy, is not limited to what is immediately perceived: the line of flight or becoming is real even if 'we don't see it, because it's the least perceptible of things' (D 1995: 45). Thinking, enriched with desire, is experimental and experiential: experience therefore is future-oriented, lengthened and enfolded, representing an experiment with what is new, or coming into being. Experience constitutes a complex place, and our experimentation on ourselves is, for Deleuze, the only reality. By virtue of experimentation, philosophy-becoming, like a witch's flight, escapes the old frame of reference within which this flight seems like an immaterial vanishing through some imaginary event-horizon, and creates its own terms of actualisation thereby leading to the 'intensification of life' (D&G 1994: 74) by revaluating experience.

Connectives

Difference
Force
Power
Spinoza
Transcendental empiricism

EXPERIMENTATION

Bruce Baugh

In French, the word *expérience* means both 'experience' and 'experiment'. To experiment is to try new actions, methods, techniques and combinations, 'without aim or end' (D&G 1983: 371). We experiment when we do not know what the result will be and have no preconceptions concerning what it should be. As an open-ended process that explores what's new and what's coming into being rather than something already experienced and known, experimentation is inseparable from innovation and discovery. The elements with which we experiment are desires, forces, powers and their combinations, not only to 'see what happens', but to determine what different entities (bodies, languages, social groupings, environments and so on) are capable of. Deleuze holds that 'existence itself is a kind of test', an experiment, 'like that whereby workmen test the quality of some material' (D 1992: 317). In literature, politics, painting, cinema, music and living, Deleuze valorises an '*experimentation* that is without interpretation or significance and rests only on tests of experience' (D&G 1986: 7), the crucial experience being the affective one – whether a procedure or combination produces an increase in one's power of acting (joy) or a diminution (sadness).

Experimentation can be an investigative procedure that seeks to explain how assemblages function by analysing the elements that compose them and the links between those elements; an 'assemblage' being any compound in which the parts interact with each other to produce a certain effect. However, experimentation is also a practical dismantling of assemblages and the creative production of new combinations of elements; even when experimentation concerns thoughts or concepts, it is never merely theoretical. Experimentation does not interpret what something, such as a text, an idea or a desire, 'means', but seeks to discover how it works or functions by uncovering an order of causes, namely, the characteristic relations among the parts of an assemblage – their structures, flows and connections – and the resulting tendencies. Effects are demystified by being related to their causes that explain the functions and uses of an assemblage, 'what it does and what is done with it' (D&G 1983: 180).

Experimentation is necessary to reveal 'what a body or mind can do, in a given encounter', arrangement or combination of the affects a body is capable of (D 1988c: 125); and also to reveal the effects of combinations of different bodies and elements, and especially whether these combinations or encounters will increase the powers of acting of the elements combined into a greater whole, or whether the combination will destroy or 'decompose' one or more of the elements. The compatibility or incompatibility of different elements and bodies, and the effect of their combination, can only be ascertained through experience; we have no *a priori* knowledge of them through principles or axioms. An experimental method of discovery through the experience of new combinations of things encountering each other is contrary to any axiomatic-deductive system or any system of judgement using transcendental criteria. Because outcomes cannot be known or predicted in advance, experimentation requires patience and prudence, as certain combinations may be destructive to the experimenter and to others. On the other hand, the knowledge gained through experimentation with different conjunctions and combinations allows for an art of organising 'good encounters', or of constructing assemblages (social, political, artistic) in which powers of acting and the active affects that follow from them are increased.

Life-experimentation, through a set of practices effecting new combinations and relations and forming powers, is biological and political, and often involves experientially discovering how to dissolve the boundaries of the ego or self in order to open flows of intensity, 'continuums and conjunctions of affect' (D&G 1987: 162). Active experimentation involves trying new procedures, combinations and their unpredictable effects to produce a 'Body without Organs' (BwO) or a 'field of immanence' or 'plane of consistency', in which desires, intensities, movements and flows pass unimpeded by the repressive mechanisms of judgement and interpretation. Experimental constructions proceed bit by bit and flow by flow, using different techniques and materials in different circumstances and under different conditions, without any pre-established or set rules or procedures, as similar effects (for example, intoxication) can be produced by different means (ingesting peyote or 'getting soused on water'). 'One never knows in advance' (D 1987: 47), and if one did, it would not be an experiment. Experimentation by its nature breaks free of the past and dismantles old assemblages (social formations, the Self), and constructs lines of flight or movements of deterritorialisation by effecting new and previously untried combinations of persons, forces and things, 'the new, remarkable, and interesting' (D&G 1994: 111). In literature, politics, and in life, experiments are practices that discover and dismantle assemblages, and which look for the lines of flight of individuals or groups, the dangers on these lines, and new combinations that will thwart predictions and allow the new to emerge.

Connectives

Body without Organs
Desire
Immanence
Lines of flight

EXPRESSION

Claire Colebrook

'Expression' is one of Deleuze's most intense concepts. If we take Deleuze's definition of a concept – that it is a philosophical creation that produces an intensive set of ordinates – then expression can be understood as truly conceptual. Indeed, the concept of expression is tied to Deleuze's understanding of conceptuality. It is not that we have a world of set terms and relations, which thought would then have to structure, organise or name – producing organised sets of what exists. Rather, life is an expressive and open whole, nothing more than the possibility for the creation of new relations; and so a concept, or the thought of this life, must try to grasp movements and potential, rather than collections of generalities. A structure is a set of coordinates, a fixed set of points that one might then move among to establish relations, and is extensive, with its points already laid out or set apart from each other. So a simple mechanism takes the form of a structure; if we read a poem as a set of words that might be linked in meaning, with the meaning governing the proper relation and order of the words, then we are governed by a structure. If however, we approach a poem as expressive, we see the words as having unfolded from a potential, a potential that will produce further relations – all the readings or thoughts produced by the poem. Thus, expression is tied to a commitment to the creation of concepts; for expression is the power of life to unfold itself differently, and one would create a concept in trying to grasp these different unfoldings.

Concepts are not structures because although they establish differences, the differences are intensive. An extensive term – such as 'all the cats in the world that are black' – is a closed set, whereas an intensive concept is infinite in its possible movements. In the case of expression, this concept covers the potential for movements; it is not that there are points or potentials in life which *then* undergo an expression. Rather, there are expressions, with the unfolding of life in all its difference being exceeded by expressive and excessive potential. The concept of expression therefore refers to intensity, for it allows us to think a type of relation but not any concluded set of relations. And it is an ordinate field, establishing a temporality rather than a set of terms. The concept of expression is a style or possibility of thinking. We cannot understand this concept of expression without bringing in a new approach to what it is for something to be, and what it is to *think* that being. With expression, we no longer imagine a world of substance – that which remains in itself, remains the same, and then has predicates added to it accidentally. There is not a substance that *then* expresses itself in various different styles. Rather, there are stylistic variations or expressions, and substance is the thought of the open whole of all these expressions. With the concept of expression we begin with a relation, rather than a being that then relates, but the relation is also external: nothing determines in advance how potentiality will be expressed, for it is the nature of expressive substance to unfold itself infinitely, in an open series of productive relations.

In his conclusion to his book on Baruch Spinoza, a book which is avowedly dedicated to expressionism in philosophy, Deleuze distinguishes the expressionism of Spinoza from that of Gottfried Wilhelm von Leibniz.

For Leibniz there is not a world that is then expressed or perceived by separate subjects. Rather, the world is made up of monads or points of perception. A being is just its specific perception of the world, and each perceiving monad is an expression of one being. God is the only being who perceives the world perfectly and completely; each finite being grasps infinite being only dimly. For Spinoza, a more radical and immanent expression is possible, one which allows Deleuze to imagine divergent expressions or planes of life. While there is still not a self-present world that precedes expression, Spinoza's immanence precludes any point of perfect expression that would ground particular expressions. A being just is its expression, its power to act. The world is not an object to be known, observed or represented, so much as a plane of powers to unfold or express different potentials of life.

Connectives

Spinoza

EXTERIORITY/INTERIORITY

Jonathan Roffe

One of the underlying themes of Deleuze's philosophy is a rejection of the value of interiority in its various theoretical guises. In fact, he goes so far as to connect the sentiment of 'the hatred of interiority' to his philosophy. On the other hand, terms like 'outside' and 'exteriority' play a central role.

Deleuze's use of the term 'interiority' refers to the thought, dominant in western philosophy since Plato, that things exist independently, and that their actions derive from the unfolding or embodying of this essential unity. The Cartesian *ego cogito* would be the most familiar example of this thought, whereby the human mind – indivisible and immortal – forms the interior of the self, and where the body and the physical world in general form a contingent exterior. In other words, 'interiority' is a word indexed to transcendent unities, things that have no necessary connection to anything else, and which transcend the external world around them. Deleuze's philosophy is rigorously critical of all forms of transcendence. He wants to come to grips with the world as a generalised exteriority.

In his first book on David Hume (*Empiricism and Subjectvity*, 1953), Deleuze insists that for Hume, there is no natural interiority (conscious willing, for example) involved in human subjectivity. Rather, the subject is formed from pre-subjective parts which are held together by a network of relations. This is part of the Humean philosophy that strikes Deleuze as particularly important, and he comes back to it a number of times. Deleuze considers Hume to be the first to insist that relations are external to their terms – and this presages much of Deleuze's mature philosophy. In other words, in order to understand any state of affairs, we must not look to the internal or intrinsic 'meaning', 'structure' or 'life' of the terms involved (whether they be people, a person and an animal, elements in a biological system, and so on). This will not provide anything relevant, since it is in the relations between (or external to) things that their nature is decided.

Likewise, in his books on Baruch Spinoza, he demonstrates that organised beings are not the embodiment of an essence or an idea, but are the result of enormous numbers of relations between parts which have no significance on their own. In other words, specific beings are produced from within a generalised milieu of exteriority without reference to any guiding interiority.

So, rather than being a philosophy concerned with showing how the interior reason or structure of things is brought about in the world – the interior conscious intentions of a human speaker, or the kernel of social structure hidden within all of its expressions – Deleuze insists on three points. First, that there is no natural interiority whatsoever: the whole philosophical tradition beginning with Plato that wanted to explain things in reference to their essence is mistaken. Second, this means that the interior/exterior division lacks any substantial meaning, and Deleuze sometimes casts the distinction aside. Third – and this describes one of the greatest aspects of Deleuze's philosophical labour – he insists that the interior is rather produced from a general exterior, the immanent world of relations. The nature of this production and its regulation proved to be one of the foci of his philosophy. Hence, human subjectivity as a produced interiority undergoes changes according to its social milieu, its relations, its specific encounters, and so forth: this is a topic that the two volumes of *Capitalism and Schizophrenia* deal with, and can be summed up in the following Deleuzian sentiment: 'The interior is only a selected interior.'

Finally, on the basis of these points, Deleuze's philosophy also embodies an ethics of exteriority. In so far as interiority is a 'caved-in' selection of the external world of relations, it remains separated from the life and movement of this world. The aim of what Deleuze calls ethics is to reconnect with the external world again, and to be caught up in its life.

Connectives

Hume
Immanence

Plato
Spinoza
Subjectivity

F

FABULATION

Ronald Bogue

Fabulation is the artistic practice of fostering the invention of a people to come. The concept of fabulation first appears late in Deleuze's career in *Cinema 2* (D 1989: 150–5; note: the term *fabulation* here is translated as 'story-telling'), where it is linked to the 'powers of the false', but the concept has related antecedents in Deleuze's discussion of the Nietzschean artist as cultural physician (D 1983: 75), his analyses of Sade and Sacher-Masoch as great symptomatologists (D 1971), and the comments in *Kafka* on the writer's relationship to the people (D & G 1986: 84). (See Smith's Introduction to D 1997b for a detailed treatment of this line of development.) Deleuze takes the term from Bergson, who in *The Two Sources of Morality and Religion* (1936) identifies fabulation ('myth-making' in the English translation) as the instinctive tendency of humans to anthropomorphise and attribute intentionality to natural phenomena, such as lightning and earthquakes. This innate tendency, Bergson claims, leads humans to invent the gods, religion, and the social rules that enforce group obedience within traditional societies. For Bergson, fabulation ultimately is a negative faculty, in that it reinforces 'closed societies' of 'us versus them', as opposed to 'open societies', which promote the universal love of humankind. Deleuze finds a positive potential in the concept, however, arguing that we should abandon the notion of 'utopia' and instead 'take up Bergson's notion of fabulation and give it a political meaning' (D 1995: 174).

Modern artists often want to create for 'the people', but no viable collectivity exists. 'It's the greatest artists (rather than populist artists) who invoke a people, and find they "lack a people": Mallarmé, Rimbaud, Klee, Berg' (D 1995: 174). Hence, artists must invent a collectivity that does not yet exist, a 'people to come' (D 1989: 223). Yet they cannot do so alone; they 'can only invoke a people' (D 1995: 174) and work with others to further the task of inventing a people to come. As Deleuze shows in *Cinema 2*, the documentary filmmakers Jean Rouch and Pierre Perrault invite the subjects of their films to collaborate in the construction of the films, in Rouch's case as contributors to 'ethnofictions' that explore creative means of reconceiving community and tradition (D 1989: 151-2), and in Perrault's as participants in an effort to '"legend *in flagrante delicto*"' (D 1989: 150; translation modified). In T. E. Lawrence' *Seven Pillars of Wisdom*, Deleuze finds a similar collaborative process, in this instance one that goes beyond art and directly into political action. Lawrence is often accused of mythomania, but Deleuze insists that Lawrence's effort is not to aggrandise himself but to project 'an image of himself and others so intense *that it takes on a life of its own*' (D 1997b: 118). That image is one of himself and the Bedouin tribes as a people to come, an empowering, larger-than-life image that is a product of 'a machine for manufacturing giants, what Bergson calls a fabulatory function' (D 1997b: 118). Deleuze argues further that even when artists appear to work alone, if their art is genuine, it is collective and oriented toward the invention of a people to come. Hence, when Kafka writes, he does so neither as an isolated individual, nor as the magical, unmediated voice of a 'collectivity that is not yet constituted'; rather, Kafka, as actual writer, and 'the virtual community – both of them real – are the components of a collective assemblage' (D & G 1986: 84), and it is the process of fabulation that brings them together in that collective assemblage.

In *What Is Philosophy?*, Deleuze and Guattari reiterate the notion that 'all fabulation is the fabrication of giants' (D & G 1994: 171), but they also extend the concept of fabulation by tying it to the fundamental aim of the arts – that of capturing the affects and percepts of sensation. Percepts are like landscapes in which the human being as subject no longer exists and yet remains diffused throughout the landscape; affects are intensities that traverse individuals and go beyond ordinary emotions and sensations. Percepts and affects exceed lived experience and our recollections of that experience. Thus, art's domain is 'not memory but fabulation' (D & G 1994: 168). 'Creative fabulation has nothing to do with memory [. . .] In fact, the artist, including the novelist, goes beyond the perceptual states and the affective transitions of the lived. The artist is a seer, a becomer' (D & G 1994: 171). Fabulation, then, is one with the general artistic project of capturing percepts and affects via a general 'becoming'. Fabulation's specific mode of becoming is that of fashioning larger-than-life images that transform and metamorphose conventional representations and conceptions of collectivities, thereby enabling the invention of a people to come.

FACIALITY

Tom Conley

The concept of faciality, theorised in detail in *A Thousand Plateaus* and applied to cinema in the chapters of *Cinema 1: The movement-image* devoted to the close-up, stands at a crossroads of subjectivation and signifiance. The former belongs to the language of psychogenesis (how a living being grows into and negotiates the ambient world) and the latter to semiotics (denoting, contrary to polysemy, signs that disseminate infinite meaning in both conscious and unconscious registers and in directions not under the control of language rules). Subjectivation and signifiance are correlated, respectively, with the 'black hole' or unknown area of the face in which the subject invests his or her affective energies (that can range from fear to passion) and with the 'white wall', a surface on which signs are projected and from which they rebound or are reflected. Faciality is thus constituted by a system of surfaces and holes. The face 'is a surface: traits, lines, wrinkles; a long, square, triangular face; the face is a map' (D 1987: 170). A series of layers or strata, the face becomes a landscape when it is abstracted from the world at large and understood as a deterritorialised space or topography. It is a displacement of what a perceiver makes of the milieu and the faces that he or she discerns.

Deleuze relates faciality to the close-up in film, the cinematic technique that generally uses a lens of long focal length to bring the face forward and soften the edges of the frame, or else, to the contrary, deploys a lens of shorter length to obtain a facial projection or distortion at the centre of the image while the surrounding milieu is seen in sharp focus. In either mode the rotundity of a person's cheeks can resemble hillocks or mesas; the eyes might be reflective pools and ponds; the nostrils lairs and caves, and ears at once quarries and cirques. Yet the landscape or face also looks at its spectators, calling their gaze into question or even psychically 'defacing' them. Such is the effect of close-ups that establish sequences in a good deal of classical cinema (Deleuze's preferred directors being Jean Renoir, Alfred Hitchcock, David Wark Griffith, Georg Wilhelm Pabst, Sergei Mikhailovich Eisenstein, Luis Buñuel). The face emits signs from its surface at the same time that the viewer seeks to fathom meaning from its darker or hidden regions. If the face is a 'white wall' it is connoted to be what resists understanding or semiosis in general.

He further elaborates the concept through reference to literature. For Marcel Proust, describing in *Un amour de Swann* the face of the beloved (but delightfully crass and despicable) Odette de Crécy in the eyes of the awestruck Swann is an abstraction that allows him – aesthete that he is – to wax poetical by recalling infinite expressions, drawn from memories of works of art, musical notes and sculpted surfaces in his fantasies. Yet once she disillusions him the jealous lover discovers that her face is a fetish or even a black hole. Proust meticulously describes Swann's passion for Odette's visage, Deleuze observes, in order to sanctify faciality in the name of art. To counter Proust's reductive turn, he shows that Henry Miller undoes the face by travelling over it with artistic dexterity. The author of *Tropic of Capricorn* (1939) makes it less a goal or an essence than a surface – a white wall or the blank sheet of a future map – on which a creative itinerary can be drawn. In Miller's description of faces a process of deterritorialisation makes the work of art not an end in itself but a process and an adventure that plots the face instead of diving into it.

In *A Thousand Plateaus* faciality is formulated to serve the ends of a political polemic. To discern details of the face without wishing to idealise its aura or charm constitutes a micropolitics that calls into question the power of facial images. Implied is that Deleuze (with Guattari) seeks, first, to be finished with the face where it would be a site of psychological inquiry or of a reassuring human essence or goodness. He and Guattari wish to divest the face of any auratic or seductive power of the kind that contemporary media – cinema, advertising, television – confer upon it. By turning it into an abstraction (but not an idea) and a site of multiple possibilities of affectivity (and neither a hearth nor a site of warmth) they turn it into a zone of intensity. The latter finds a powerful visual correlative in Deleuze's treatment of the paintings of Francis Bacon. The heads of the artist's portraits meld the face into the body and thus confuse the face with its tradition as a 'veil of the soul' with the human animal. In the text of *The Logic of Sensation* that studies Bacon's portraiture Deleuze shows that the head is not what lacks spirit; rather, it is the spirit in a corporeal form, a bodily and vital breath whose end is that of *undoing the face*. In sum, a forceful reconsideration is made of the face work in philosophy, aesthetics and political theory.

Connectives

Bacon
Black hole
Molecular
Subjectivity

FASCISM

John Protevi

In *Anti-Oedipus*, the pole of paranoid desire is opposed to schizophrenic or revolutionary desire. Perhaps we owe the impression that a major focus of *Anti-Oedipus* is fascism to Michel Foucault's preface to the English translation, in which he calls the text 'An Introduction to the Non-Fascist Life' (D&G 1983: xiii). But in fact historical manifestations of fascism – as Foucault acknowledges – are explicitly addressed in *Anti-Oedipus* relatively infrequently. Despite the lack of attention to historical fascism, Deleuze and Guattari's critique of analyses of fascism in terms of ideology is important. Rather than being the result of fooling people by false consciousness, fascist desire has its own proper consistency, and spreads under certain social, economic and political conditions. Roughly speaking, in *Anti-Oedipus* fascist desire is the desire for codes to replace the decoding that frees flows under capitalist axiomatics; such codes would fix subjects to rigid boundaries of thought and action and fix bodies to pre-established patterns of flows, thus attenuating the fascist obsession with erotic perversion.

Deleuze and Guattari discuss both micro- and macro-fascism in *A Thousand Plateaus*. Micro-fascism is a cancerous Body without Organs (BwO). The cancerous BwO is the third type of BwO discussed in *A Thousand Plateaus*, after the 'full' (positively valued in *A Thousand Plateaus*, though not in *Anti-Oedipus*, where the full BwO is catatonia), and the 'empty'. The cancerous BwO is the strangest and most dangerous BwO. It is a BwO that belongs to the organism that resides on a stratum, rather than being the limit of a stratum. It is runaway self-duplication of stratification. Such a cancer can occur even in social formations, not just in the strata named organism, significance and subjectification. The key to tracking down fascism lies here in the cancerous BwO, that forms under conditions of runaway stratification, or more precisely, runaway sedimentation, the first 'pincer' of a stratum. By endlessly repeating the selection of homogenised individuals in a process of 'conformity' the cancerous BwO breaks down the stratum on which it lodges: social cloning and assembly-line personalities.

The cancerous BwO, then, occurs with too much sedimentation, that is, too much content or coding and territorialising, with insufficient over-coding. The result is a cancer of the stratum, a proliferation of points of capture, a proliferation of micro-black holes: thousands of individuals complete unto themselves; legislators and subjects all in one; judge, jury, and executioner – and policeman, private eye, home video operator, the neighbourhood watch organiser. Micro-fascism is then the construction of a 'thousand monomanias' in 'little neighborhood policemen' resulting from 'molecular focuses in interaction . . . rural fascism and city or neighborhood fascism, youth fascism and war veteran's fascism, fascism of the Left and of the Right, fascism of the couple, family, school, and office' (D&G 1987: 214). Such micro-fascisms spread throughout a social fabric prior to the centralising resonance that creates the molar apparatus of the State. In micro-fascism each body is a 'micro-black hole that stands on its own and communicates with the others' (D&G 1987: 228). Although Deleuze and Guattari do not do so, we can call micro-fascism 'molecular molarity': each subjective unit is self-contained, oriented to unity, an individual (molar), but they interact in solely local manner, independently (molecular).

In contrast to *Anti-Oedipus*'s relative neglect of historical fascism, *A Thousand Plateaus* devotes at least a few pages to an analysis of historical manifestations of macro-fascism (in its Nazi form rather than its Italian or Spanish forms). The Nazi regime is characterised, following the analyses of Paul Virilio, as a 'suicide state' rather than a totalitarian one, which is 'quintessentially conservative' (D&G 1987: 230; Stalinist USSR is the target here). Here it is not a State army taking power, but a war machine that takes over the institutions of State power. This triggers the last form of the line of flight, the self-immolating, self-destructive line. This reversion of the line of flight to self-destruction had 'already animated the molecular focuses of fascism, and made them interact in a war machine instead of resonating in a State apparatus' (D&G 1987: 231). Such a runaway war machine, once it reaches a consistency enabling it to take over a State apparatus, forms a 'war machine that no longer had anything but war as its object and would rather annihilate its own servants than stop the destruction' (D&G 1987: 231). In *A Thousand Plateaus*, then, fascism is too fast, a cancer; what we could call, echoing Bataille, a 'solar nihilism', rather than being too slow or the freezing, paranoid, lunar nihilism it is portrayed as in *Anti-Oedipus*.

Connectives

Body without Organs
Desire
Stratification

FAMILY – refer to the entry on 'psychoanalysis'.

FEMINISM

Felicity J. Colman

Deleuze did not advocate 'feminism' as the movement has historically come to be known. Yet in his writings one message that is continually relayed is: Do not ever smugly assume that you have reached the limit edges, or causal origins of knowledge of any form or thought. To do so would be at once to assume and position an organisation of recognition based on prior resemblances, given structures, and relationships that have been coded according to linguistic and economic systems. These systems operate most efficiently through prescribed gender work and leisure roles.

Feminism's theoretical history and legacy have been such that its foundational premises of pointing out the inequalities and restrictions imposed by thinking and practising within given boundaries became principal in activities and theories concerning sexuality, equality, difference, subjectivity, marginalisation, and economics. The concept of a 'limit to be reached' is in itself one of the key critical systematic assumptions that Deleuze and Guattari dismantle.

With the exception of his cinema books, where core conceptual points are made through reference to canonical twentieth-century filmmakers including Marguerite Duras and Chantal Akerman, references to women are few in Deleuze's works. In *A Thousand Plateaus*, Deleuze and Guattari's discussion of 'becoming-woman' focuses on the processes of subjective formation, through the writing of Virginia Woolf. Indicative of the twentieth century's division and demarcation of labour roles according to normative patriarchal gender and biological functions, Deleuze's writings are suffused with examples of published male philosophers, writers, scientists and artists.

However, Deleuze is attentive to the gender biases of western mythology and the patriarchally produced behaviour of both genders. The ethical construction of the body as a constituent/contributor of a pre-configured (and hence gendered) organisation is continually pointed out by Deleuze. In *Anti-Oedipus* Deleuze and Guattari attack and reject the psychoanalytically enframed familial unit and gendered historical zones for its bourgeois hierarchy and assumptions of an Oedipally figured desire. Valuable for feminism is Deleuze and Guattari's discussion of a body in terms of its potentialities and capabilities, once it is conceived of not in terms of its past structure, but in terms of a future modality. Deleuze draws upon Baruch Spinoza to develop the playwright-poet Antonin Artaud's concept of the Body without Organs (BwO). This 'body' is one that affords a creative site for the collection and expression of the formation of desire. Placing the body on a platform of the systems of exchange provides spatial and temporal zones for analysis of gendered categorisations.

Deleuze and Guattari's phrase 'becoming-woman' is a critique of all aspects of anthropocentrism; that is, where man is regarded as the central and most important dynamic in the universe. Becoming-woman refers to every discourse that is not anthropocentric, and is thus coded by all economic, social, cultural, organic, and political circuits as 'minority'. With the concept of a 'minority discourse', and 'becoming woman', Deleuze and Guattari take the body not to be a cultural medium but a composition of socially and politically determined forces.

Deleuze's use of the 'difference' of women undergoes theoretical development in the 1960s, in turn this change influences his later theories of difference and minority groups, as well as public and capitalist generated desire and its effect on things in the world. Deleuze's theories recognise the political and public shaping of an individual's cultural realm and milieu. This philosophical position on the narration of the multiple may appear abstract and antithetical to feminist methodologies that focus on the analysis and identification of the personal. Yet Deleuze's ideas consistently point out how a method that points toward the 'truth' of a particular representation has a universalising tendency and does not refer to the 'forces' that shape beliefs, thoughts or structures.

Deleuze's work demonstrates how, because of its history, subjectivity is a political constitution not the result of an individual community. Individual historical figures are utilised by Deleuze to examine the structuration of bodies via historical organisation, cultural affiliations and social differentiation. The formation and reformation of such bodies and things are questioned in terms of the ways in which relationships and qualities provide identity, reality and virtuality. The economic, ethical, logical and aesthetic constitution of these bodies is also considered by Deleuze in terms of their structural and systematic constitution. Deleuze's system of thinking through concepts of identity given by history, and maintained in capitalism, provides a valuable revolutionary and unorthodox approach for feminism's critique of the surface effects of gender roles, as well as its project of rewriting histories of exclusion.

Connectives

Body
Body without Organs
Desire
Oedipalisation

Psychoanalysis
Woman

FOLD

Simon O'Sullivan

Although appearing throughout Deleuze's work, the 'fold' is particularly mobilised in the books on Michel Foucault and Gottfried Wilhelm von Leibniz. In each case the fold is developed in relation to another's work. We might even say that these books, like others Deleuze has written, involve a folding – or doubling – of Deleuze's own thought into the thought of another. We might go further and say that thought itself, enigmatically, is a kind of fold, an instance of what Deleuze calls the 'forces of the outside' that fold the inside.

Specifically, the concept of the fold allows Deleuze to think creatively about the production of subjectivity, and ultimately about the possibilities for, and production of, non-human forms of subjectivity. In fact, on one level the fold is a critique of typical accounts of subjectivity, that presume a simple interiority and exteriority (appearance and essence, or surface and depth). For the fold announces that the inside is nothing more than a fold of the outside. Deleuze gives us Foucault's vivid illustration of this relation, that being the Renaissance madman, who, in being put to sea in a ship becomes a passenger, or prisoner in the interior of the exterior; the fold of the sea. In Deleuze's account of Foucault this picture becomes increasingly complex. There is a variety of modalities of folds: from the fold of our material selves, our bodies, to the folding of time, or simply memory. Indeed, subjectivity might be understood as precisely a topology of these different kinds of folds.

In this sense, the fold can also be understood as the name for one's relation to oneself (or, the effect of the self *on* the self). The Greeks were the first to discover, and deploy, this technique of folding, or of 'self mastery'. They invented subjectivation taken to mean the self-production of one's subjectivity. Subsequent cultures, such as Christianity, have invented their own forms of subjectivation, or their own kinds of foldings; and of course it might be said that our own time has its own folds, or even that it requires new ones. This imbues the fold with explicitly ethical and political dimensions, for as Deleuze remarks, the emergence of new kinds of struggle inevitably also involves the production of new kinds of subjectivity, or new kinds of fold (here Deleuze has the uprisings of 1968 in mind).

As for Deleuze's use of Foucault and Leibniz, the fold names the relationship – one entailing domination – of oneself to (and 'over') one's 'self '. Indeed, one's subjectivity for Deleuze is a kind of Nietzschean mastery over the swarm of one's being. This can be configured as a question of ownership, or of folding. To 'have' is to fold that which is outside inside. Meanwhile, in the Leibniz book we are offered other diagrams of our subjectivity. One example is the two-floored baroque house. The lower loor, or the regime of matter, is in and of the world, receiving the world's imprint as it were. Here matter is folded in the manner of origami, whereby caverns containing other caverns, in turn contain further caverns. The world is superabundant, like a lake teeming with fish, with smaller fish between these fish, and so on ad infinitum. There is no boundary between the organic and the inorganic here as each is folded into the other in a continuous texturology.

The upper chamber of the baroque house is closed in on itself, without window or opening. It contains innate ideas, the folds of the soul, or if we were to follow Guattari here, this might be described as the incorporeal aspect of our subjectivity. And then there is the fold between these two floors. This fold is like one's style in the world, or indeed the style of a work of art. It is in this sense that the upper chamber paradoxically 'contains' the Whole world folded within itself. This world is one amongst many 'possible worlds' each as different as the beings that express them. The world of a tick, for example, is different from that of a human, involving as it does just the perception of light, the smell of its prey and the tactile sensation of where best to burrow. This is not the tick's representation of the world but the world's expression, or folding in, of the tick.

As with Deleuze's book on Foucault, the later parts of his Leibniz book attend to future foldings. Deleuze calls attention to the possibility of a new kind of harmony, or fold, between the two floors of our subjectivity. This new kind of fold involves an opening up of the closed chamber of the upper floor and the concomitant affirmation of difference, contact and communication. Echoing his book on Foucault, here we might say that these new foldings are simply the name for those new kinds of subjectivity that emerged in the 1960s, in the various experiments in communal living, drug use and sexuality, as well as in the emergence of new prosthetic technologies.

Connectives

Foucault
Leibniz
Nietzsche
Subjectivity

FOLD + ARCHITECTURE

Graham Livesey

In his extended essay *The Fold: Leibniz and the Baroque*, Deleuze draws from architecture, among various disciplines, as he examines the intricacies of the fold. Firstly, he uses the allegory of a two-storied Baroque house to define a relationship between the 'pleats of matter' and the 'fold of the soul'. Secondly, Deleuze references the separating and unifying qualities of Baroque architecture, particularly the relationship between inside and the outside, in the text. Thirdly, the elaborate topographies of Baroque interiors provide a tangible example of material folding and the search for an expression of infinity. Fourthly, the work of the French architect Bernard Cache, subsequently published in his text *Earth Moves: The Furnishing of Territories*, informed some of the key ideas in Deleuze's text, and vice-versa.

While it is often difficult to translate Deleuze's concepts into concrete or material reality, his exploration of the fold as a unifying structure has been widely employed by architects, landscape architects, and urbanists since the publication of the text. The deployment of folded surfaces can create intricate topographic and spatial effects and affects; this means that a singular gesture can achieve great complexity, and has the ability to engage an infinity of folds. The interior created in the Baroque churches, particularly the elaborately sculpted plaster landscapes that often mediate between the architecture and the great ceiling frescoes, come closest to achieving unity and infinity, an endlessly folded condition set off by light and the extensive use of gilding. As Deleuze writes: 'It is not only because the fold affects all materials that it thus becomes expressive matter, with different scales, speeds, and different vectors (mountains and waters, papers, fabrics, living tissues, the brain), but especially because it determines and materializes Form' (D 1993a: 34).

The ability to reconcile opposites, a hallmark of Baroque art and architecture, means that inside and outside (coextensive space), illusion and reality, light and dark, movement and stasis, finite and infinite, and space and mass, interact in complex interplays, both unifying and blurring the distinctions between each. Along with his references to Baroque architecture, Deleuze's description of the Baroque treatment of fabric in painting and sculpture comes closest to a material example of the fold. Commentators, such as the architect Greg Lynn, an important proponent of folded architecture, have extended the concept into cooking, and the folding of ingredients together. He writes: 'If there is a single effect produced in architecture by folding, it will be the ability to integrate unrelated elements within a new continuous mixture' (L 1993: 8).

Against recent postmodern experiments in architecture that have led to historicism, modernist revival, regionalism, or fragmentation (deconstruction), the theories of Deleuze have inspired an architecture based on smoothness and pliancy; this approach strives to generate unpredicted connections. A folded, or pliant, architecture is able to interconnect with a context/site in a seamless manner, and is able to create complexity from a singular gesture. The fold as a concrete possibility leads to architectural maneuvres such as the compliant, supple, adaptable, fluid, responsive, flowing, etc. On the other hand, the architectural critic and theorist Michael Speaks argues that Deleuze's concept of the fold is more useful for defining new kinds of practice, rather than new architectural form (C 1995: xviii). Like the concept of assemblage, the fold brings together architecture, space, and that which occurs in time (expression, social arrangements, etc.); it unifies, produces, and creates connections.

FORCE

Cliff Stagoll

Deleuze's conception of force is clearest in his interpretative readings of Friedrich Nietzsche, but implicit throughout his corpus. Much of what he writes on the subject is borrowed directly from Nietzsche, although the way in which he uses the notion to theorise difference and becoming is Deleuze's own.

For Nietzsche, the world comprises a chaotic web of natural and biological forces without any particular origin or goal, and which never comes to rest at a terminal or equilibrium state. These forces interact ceaselessly, constituting a dynamic world-in-flux rather than a collection of stable entities. The world is always in the process of becoming something that it is not, so that, for Deleuze, the principal (and eternal) characteristic of the world of forces is difference from whatever has gone before and from that which it will become.

Neither Deleuze nor Nietzsche provides a clear definition of 'force'. Deleuze states overtly that he does *not* mean by it 'aggression' or 'pressure' (although Nietzsche is not so clear). For Deleuze, we can only truly *perceive* forces by *intuiting* them; that is, by grasping them without reference to a conceptual understanding of existence. To try and capture in a few words or sentences what is learned through intuition is impossible.

Generally, though, 'force' means *any* capacity to produce a change or 'becoming', whether this capacity and its products are physical, psychological, mystical, artistic, philosophical, conceptual, social, economic, legal or whatever. All of reality is an expression and consequence of interactions between forces, with each interaction revealed as an 'event' (in Deleuze's specific sense of the term). Every event, body or other phenomenon is, then, the *net* result of a hierarchical pattern of interactions between forces, colliding in some particular and unpredictable way.

This enigmatic characterisation of forces is developed in Deleuze's account of their activity. Every force exerts itself upon others. No force can exist apart from its inter-relationships with other forces and, since such associations of struggle are always temporary, forces are always in the process of becoming different or passing out of existence, so that no particular force can be repeated.

Deleuze holds that types of forces are defined in both quantitative *and* qualitative terms, but in special ways. First, the *difference* in quantity *is* the quality of the difference in forces. Second, a force is 'active' if it seeks dominance by self-affirmation, asserting itself over and above another, and 'reactive' if it starts its struggle by first denying or negating the other force. Whereas 'quality' usually refers to a particular complex, or body, that results from interactions between forces, Deleuze uses it to refer instead to tendencies at the *origin* of forces, regardless of the complex that derives from them. On his reading, Nietzsche finds the origin of both quantitative and qualitative characteristics of forces in the Will to Power, and a kind of genealogy should be used to trace qualitative attributes of forces to particular cultures and types of people.

Having no substance, forces can act only upon other forces, even though the interactions between them might result in an apparently substantial reality. 'Things' are merely a temporary outcome, and so ought not to be considered as having an independent existence or essence.Contrary to Immanuel Kant, for example, there are on this view no 'things-in-themselves', and nor are there, contrary to Plato, perfect originals of which all things are but copies. Furthermore, a physical world cannot be considered as an inevitable or permanent consequence of the cognitive equipment of a perceiver or of the nature of whatever is being perceived.

Indeed, for Deleuze, this dichotomous understanding of the perceiver and the perceived is also groundless. In his view, the particularity of a pencil, here and now, involves not simply one 'gazing upon' an object, but a complex set of circumstantial interactions involving a whole 'plane' of events and organising principles ranging from the biology of sight to the circumstances of the pencil's being positioned here, and the physics of carbon structures. As such, the theory of forces challenges the traditional philosophical dualism between essence and appearance, and also draws attention to the contingent and infinitely complex nature of lived reality.

Connectives

Active/Reactive
Body
Event
Nietzsche

FOUCAULT, MICHEL (1926–84)

John Marks

Michel Foucault and Deleuze enjoyed an intense philosophical friendship, and much of Deleuze's writing on Foucault might be located within the tradition of the 'laudatory essay' that characterised a certain strand of intellectual activity in post-war France. Such an essay is not a work of criticism, but rather a gesture of affective intensity. Talking about his writing on Foucault, Deleuze emphasises that it is not necessary to demonstrate a great fidelity to the work of a thinker, nor is it necessary to look for contradictions and blind alleys in a thinker's work: to say that one part works, but another part does not. Approaching a writer's work in the spirit of 'friendship' is the same as a personal friendship. It is about being willing to be carried along by the entirety of the work, accompanying the thinker on a journey. Sometimes, it is about following the work, as one might a person, to the point that the work becomes a little 'crazy', where it breaks down or comes up against apparently insurmountable problems. Friendship in this sense does not mean that one necessarily has the same ideas or opinions as somebody else, but rather that one shares a mode of perception with them. Deleuze explains that it is a matter of perceiving something about somebody and his way of thinking almost before his thought is formulated at the level of signification. It is for this reason that Deleuze talks of remembering something 'metallic', 'strident' and 'dry' in the gestures of Foucault. Deleuze perceives Foucault as an individuation, a singularity, rather than a subject. It is almost as if Deleuze responds to Foucault's thinking at the level of his bodily materiality as much as a set of philosophical propositions. Above all, Deleuze sees Foucault as a writer of great 'passion', and he is particularly struck by the distinction that Foucault draws between love and passion. Love is a relationship between individuals, whereas passion is a state in which the individuals dissolve into an impersonal field of intensities. For these reasons, Deleuze regards his own book on Foucault as an act of 'doubling', a way of bringing out and working with minor differences between himself and Foucault. Both Deleuze and Foucault had a similar conception of the art of 'surfaces', of making visible rather than interpreting, and this is what Deleuze seeks to do with Foucault's work.

As with his other readings of other writers, Deleuze extracts a dynamic *logic* – as opposed to a rational system – from Foucault's work. One of his main aims in *Foucault* is to clear up some of the misunderstandings surrounding the transitions in Foucault's work. For example, Deleuze rejects the notion that Foucault's late work constitutes some sort of return to the subject. Instead he sees this later work as adding the dimension of subjectification to the analyses of power and knowledge that Foucault had previously carried out. The subject that Foucault talks about in his final work is not a retreat or a shelter, but rather one that is produced by a folding of the outside. Deleuze also rejects the simplistic notion that Foucault's formulation of the 'death of man' might preclude political action. The figure of 'man' is simply one historically distinct form of the human. Human forces confront various other forces at different times in history, and it is in this way that a composite human form is constructed.

In a double sense, Deleuze perceives that which is 'vital' in Foucault's work. That is to say, he concentrates on what Foucault thought out of absolute necessity, as well as the ways in which Foucault's work expresses a commitment to life. Foucault may appear to be preoccupied with death, imprisonment and torture, but this is because he is concerned with the ways in which life might be freed from imprisonment. That is not to say that Deleuze and Foucault did not feel there were points of real tension between their approaches. Foucault, for his part, found Deleuze's use of the term 'desire' problematic, since for him desire would always entail some notion of 'lack' or repression. He preferred the term 'pleasure', which was equally problematic for Deleuze, because pleasure seems to be a transcendent category that interrupts the immanence of desire. However, rather than these differences being the basis for a critical interpretation of Foucault's work, they are actually constitutive of the 'tranversal', diagonal line that Deleuze attempts to trace between himself and Foucault. It is in this way that he hopes to bring out what Foucault was striving to do in his work, and it is in this spirit that Deleuze occasionally focuses on one of Foucault's apparently minor concepts, such as that of the 'infamous man'. Deleuze finds this concept particularly resonant and responds to its urgency, since Foucault uses it to attempt to think through difficult problems relating to his own understanding of power.

Connectives

Desire
Transversality

FOUCAULT + FOLD

Tom Conley

The most terse and telling formulation of the fold is found in 'Foldings, or the Inside of Thought (Subjectivation)', the last chapter of Deleuze's *Foucault* that examines Foucault's three-volume study of the history of sexuality. Michel Foucualt, says Deleuze, took sexuality to be a mirror of subjectivity and subjectivation. Deleuze broadens the scope by subsuming sexuality in a matrix of subjectivity. Every human being thinks as a result of an ongoing process of living in the world and by gaining consciousness and agency through a constant give-and-take of perception, affect and cognition. Subjectivity becomes an ongoing negotiation of things perceived, both consciously and unconsciously, within and outside the body. He builds a diagram, principally from *The History of Sexuality: Volume* One (1976) and *The Use of Pleasure* (1984), on the foundation of the earlier writings to sketch a taxonomy and a history of the project. In *The Archaeology of Knowledge* (1972), Foucault had contended that the 'self', the 'I', is always defined by the ways it is doubled by another, not a single or commanding 'other' or *Doppelgänger*, but simply any of a number of possible forces. 'It is I who live my life as the double of the other,' and when I find the other in myself the discovery 'resembles exactly the invagination of a tissue in embryology, or the act of doubling in sewing: twist, fold, stop, and so on' (D 1988b: 105). For Foucault, history was the 'doubling of an emergence' (D 1988b: 98). By that he meant that what was past or in an archive was also passed – as might a speeding car overtaken or doubled by another on a highway – but also mirrored or folded into a diagram. History was shown to be what sums up the past but that can be marshalled for the shaping of configurations that will determine how people live and act in the present and future. Whether forgotten or remembered, history is one of the formative doubles or others vital to the process of subjectivation.

Therein begins Deleuze's rhapsody of folds and foldings. When a doubling produces an inner and an outer surface – a *doublure* in French, meaning at once a lining stitched into a piece of clothing, a stand-in in a cinematic production, and even a double as Antonin Artaud had used the term in his writings on theatre – a new relation with 'being' is born. An inside and an outside and a past (memory) and a present (subjectivity) are two sides of a single surface. A person's relation with his or her body becomes both an archive and a diagram, a collection of subjectivations and a mental map charted on the basis of the past and drawn from events and elements in the ambient world. Deleuze asserts that four folds, 'like the four rivers of Hell' (D 1988b: 104), affect the subject's relation to itself. The first is the fold of the body, what is surrounded or taken within corporeal folds; the second is 'the fold of the relation between forces', or social conflict; the third is the 'fold of knowledge, or the fold of truth in so far as it constitutes a relation of truth to our being' (D 1988b: 104), and viceversa; the fourth is the fold of 'the outside itself, the ultimate' (D 1988b: 104) fold of the limit of life and death. Each of these folds refers to Aristotelian causes (material, efficient, formal and final) of subjectivity and has a variable rhythm of its own. We behoove ourselves, Deleuze reminds us, to inquire of the nature of the four folds before we reflect on how subjectivity in our time is highly internalised, individualised and isolated. The struggle for subjectivity is a battle to win the right to have access to difference, variation and metamorphosis.

The human subject can only be understood under the condition (the formula, it will be shown, is a crucial one) of the fold and through the filters of knowledge, power, and affect. The fold, a form said to obsess Foucault, is shown as something creased between things stated or *said* and things visible or *seen*. The distinction opened between visible and discursive formations is put forward in order to be drawn away from intentionality (as understood in Martin Heidegger and Maurice Merleau-Ponty) that would ally subjectivity with phenomenology. Things spoken do not refer to an original or individual subject but to a 'being-language', and things visible point to a 'being-light' that illuminates 'forms, proportions, perspectives' that would be free of any intentional gaze. Anticipating his work on Leibniz, Deleuze notes that Foucault causes intentionality to be collapsed in the gap between 'the two monads' (D 1988b: 109) of seeing and speaking. Thus, phenomenology is converted into epistemology. To see and to speak is to know, 'but we don't see what we are speaking of, and we don't speak of what we are seeing'. Nothing can precede or antedate knowledge (*savoir*), even though knowledge or knowing is 'irremediably double' – hence folded – as speaking *and* seeing, as language *and* light, which are independent of intending subjects who would be speakers and seers.

At this juncture the fold becomes the very fabric of ontology, the area of philosophy with which Deleuze claims staunch affiliation. The folds of being (as a gerund) and of being (as a noun) are found in Foucault's

Heidegger and that of an outside is twisted, folded and doubled by an inside in the philosopher's reading of Merleau-Ponty. Surely, Deleuze observes, Foucault finds theoretical inspiration in the themes of the fold, the double that haunts the archaeologist of knowledge. As a doubling or a lining the fold separates speech from sight and keeps each register in a state of isolation from the other. The gap finds an analogue in the hermetic difference of the sound and image track of cinema. From such a division knowledge is divided into pieces or 'tracks' and thus can never be recuperated in any intentional form (D 1988b: 111). The divided nature of communication has as its common metaphor the crease or fold between visibility and orality. It is no wonder that in his studies of difference and resemblance Foucault begins at the end of the sixteenth century, at the moment when writing evacuates its force of visual analogy from its printed form. At that point, when print-culture becomes standardised and schematic reasoning replaces memory in manuals of rhetoric, or when words are no longer analogous to the things they seem to embody or resemble, signs begin to *stand in* for their referents and to be autonomous doubles with respect to what they represent.

To demonstrate how the fold is a figure of subjectivation Deleuze calls history into the philosophical arena. He asks in bold and simple language: '*What can I do? What do I know? What am I?*' (D 1988b: 115). The events of May 1968 rehearsed these questions by inquiring of the limits of visibility, of language, and of power. They brought forward thoughts about utopia, and hence about modes of being that would enable resistance in repressive political conditions and foster the birth of ideas vital for new subjectivities. In a historical configuration 'being' is charted along an axis of knowing. 'Being' is determined by what is deemed visible and utterable; by the exercise of power, itself determined by relation of force and singularities at a given moment in time; and by subjectivity, shown to be a process or the places where the fold of the self passes through. A grid or a new diagram makes clear the opposition by setting forward variations of power, knowledge and subjectivity (in French as *savoir*, *pouvoir*, *soi*). The last is conceived as a fold. Foucault, Deleuze advances, does not divide a history of institutions or of subjectivations but of their *conditions* and of their *processes* within creases and foldings that operate in both ontological and social fields.

There is opened a dramatic reflection on the character of thinking which belongs as much to Deleuze as to Foucault. Historical formations are doubled and thus define as such the epistemic traits of knowledge, power and subjectivity: in terms of knowledge, to think is to *see* and to *speak*; in other words, thinking takes place in the interstices of visibility and discourse. When we think we cause lightning bolts to flash and flicker 'in the midst of words, or unleash a cry in the midst of visible things' (D

1988b: 116). Thinking makes seeing and speaking reach their own limits. In what concerns power, thinking is equivalent to 'emitting singularities', to a gambler's act of tossing a pair of dice onto a table, or to a person engaging relations of force or even conflict in order to prepare new mutations and singularities. In terms of subjectivation thinking means 'to fold to double the Outside with a coextensive inside' (D 1988b: 118). Created is a topology by which inner and outer spaces are in contact with each other.

History is taken to be an *archive* or series of *strata* from which thinking, a diagram replete with strategies, draws its force and virtue. To make the point clear Deleuze alludes indirectly to 'A New Cartographer' (D 1988b: 23–47), an earlier chapter that anticipates much of the spatial dynamics of *The Fold*. When we 'think' we cross all kinds of thresholds and strata. Following a fissure in order to reach, as the poet Herman Melville calls it, a 'central room' where we fear no one will be and where 'man's soul will reveal nothing but an immense and terrifying void' (D 1988b: 121). Ultimately, following a line of 1,000 aberrations and moving at molecular speed leads life into the folds and a central room where there is no longer any need to fear emptiness because the self (a fold) is found inside. These ideas arch back to how Deleuze once described the history of forms or an archive as 'doubled' (passed or folded over) by a becoming of forces where any number of diagrams – or folded surfaces of thought – plied over each other. He calls it the torsion of the 'line of the Outside' that Melville described, an oceanic line without beginning or end, an oceanic line that turns and bumps about diagrams. The form of the line was 1968, the line 'with a thousand aberrations' (D 1988b: 44).

FREEDOM

Paul Patton

'Freedom' is not a term that appears often in Deleuze's writings, yet there is a distinctive concept of freedom implicit throughout his ethico-political texts written with Guattari. These describe individual and collective subjects in terms of different kinds of assemblage, line or modes of occupying space. For example, they suggest that we are composed of three kinds of line: firstly, molar lines which correspond to the forms of rigid segmentation found in bureaucratic and hierarchical institutions; secondly, molecular lines which correspond to the fluid or overlapping forms of division characteristic of 'primitive' territoriality; and finally, lines of flight which are the paths along which things change or become transformed into something else. The primacy of lines of flight in this ontology systematically privileges processes of creative transformation and metamorphosis through which assemblages may be transformed. Freedom is manifest in the critical points at which some state or condition of things passes over into a different state or condition. In contrast to the traditional concepts of negative and positive freedom, freedom for Deleuze concerns those moments in a life after which one is no longer the same person as before. This is an impersonal and non-voluntaristic concept of freedom, which refers to the capacity for change or transformation within or between assemblages. In the texts written with Guattari, this concept of freedom appears only in the guise of other concepts such as 'line of flight', 'deterritorialisation' or 'smooth space'.

In *A Thousand Plateaus*, the authors use F. Scott Fitzgerald's novella, *The Crack-Up*, to show how this kind of transformation in a person might be defined in terms of the different kinds of 'line' which characterise an individual life (D&G 1987: 198–200). Fitzgerald distinguishes three different kinds of transition from one state or stage in life to another: firstly, the large breaks such as those between youth and adulthood, between poverty and wealth, between illness and good health, between success or failure in a chosen profession; secondly, the almost imperceptible cracks or subtle shifts of feeling or attitude which involve molecular changes in the affective constitution of a person; and finally, the abrupt and irreversible transitions through which the individual becomes a different person and eventually, Fitzgerald writes, 'the new person finds new things to care about.' The subject of the novella undergoes a particularly severe breakdown involving loss of faith in his former values and the dissipation of all his convictions. He seeks to effect what he calls 'a clean break' with his past self (F 1956: 69–84). Such a break amounts to a redistribution of desire such that 'when something occurs, the Self that awaited it is already dead, or the one that would await it has not yet arrived' (D&G 1987: 198–9).

This kind of sudden shift towards another quality of life or towards a life which is lived at another degree of intensity is one possible outcome of what Deleuze and Guattari call 'a line of flight', and it is on this kind of line that freedom is manifest. The type of freedom that is manifest in a break of this kind cannot be captured in liberal or humanist concepts of negative or positive freedom, since these define freedom in terms of a subject's capacity to act without hindrance in the pursuit of its ends or in terms of its capacity to satisfy its most significant desires. Fitzgerald's character no longer has the same interests nor the same desires and preferences. In the relevant sense of the term, he is no longer the same subject: his goals are not the same, nor are the values which would underpin his strong evaluations.

Whereas the normative status of liberal freedom is unambiguously positive, 'freedom' in this Deleuzian sense is more ambivalent. Freedom in this sense is indifferent to the desires, preferences and goals of the subject in that it may threaten as much as advance any of these. It is not clear by what standards such freedom could be evaluated as good or bad. There is no telling in advance where such processes of mutation and change might lead. Similar comments may also be made about deterritorialisation, lines of flight or smooth space. In the absence of productive connections with other forces, lines of flight may turn destructive or simply lead to new forms of capture. In the conclusion of the discussion of smooth as opposed to striated space at the end of *A Thousand Plateaus*, Deleuze and Guattari reaffirm the normative ambiguity of freedom: 'smooth spaces are not in themselves liberatory. But the struggle is changed or displaced in them, and life reconstitutes its stakes, confronts new obstacles, invents new paces, switches adversaries. Never believe that a smooth space will suffice to save us' (D&G 1987: 500). The presupposition here is that, prima facie, smooth space is the space of freedom. It is the space in which movements or processes of liberation are possible, even if these do not always succeed or even if they are condemned to the reappearance of new forms of capture.

Connectives

Deterritorialisation
Lines of flight
Molar
Molecular
Space

FREUD, SIGMUND (1856–1939) – refer to the entry on 'psychoanalysis'.

G

GENEALOGY

Bruce Baugh

'Genealogy' refers to tracing lines of descent or ancestry. Deleuze's use of the term derives from Friedrich Nietzsche's *On the Genealogy of Morals*, which traces the descent of our moral concepts and practices. One key precept of the genealogical method is that effects need not resemble their causes, as the forces that produce a phenomenon may disguise themselves (for example, a religion of love can arise out of resentment); another is that outwardly similar phenomena may have entirely different meanings because of the difference in the forces that produce them (for example, 'good' as an expression of the affirmative will of 'masters' has an entirely different significance from 'good' as an expression of the negative will of 'slaves', for whom 'good' is merely the negation of 'evil'). In Deleuze's hands, Nietzschean genealogy is allied with the philosophies of immanence (Henri Bergson and Baruch Spinoza), such that the 'past' from which a phenomenon is descended is a set of forces immanent in the phenomenon that expresses those forces, and thus coexistent with the present.

Deleuze distinguishes between force and will. Forces are either 'active', in which case they go to the limit of what they can do by appropriating and dominating, or 'reactive', in which case they are separated from what they can do through a limitation that comes either from external dominating forces or from turning against themselves. Although a force's quality, as active or reactive, is nothing but the difference in quantity between a superior and an inferior force (D 1983: 43), an inferior force can defeat a superior one by 'decomposing' it and making it reactive, so that the genealogist must evaluate whether the forces that prevailed were inferior or superior, active or reactive (D 1983: 59–60). Power or the will is either affirmative or negative, and designates the differential relation of forces which either dominate (active) or are dominated (reactive) according to whether the will affirms its difference from that difference it dominates and enjoys, or whether it negates what differs from it and suffers from that difference (often in the form of resentment). The affirmative will, in affirming itself, wills that it be obeyed; only a subordinate will can obey by converting 'actions' into reactions to an external force, and this becoming-reactive is the expression of a negative will.

Genealogy thus interprets and evaluates the hierarchical difference between active and reactive forces by referring these to the hierarchical 'genetic element' of a 'Will to Power' that is either affirmative or negative. Will to Power differentiates forces as active and reactive, as through it one force dominates or commands another that obeys or is dominated (D 1983: 49–51). However, Will to Power is not external to the forces it qualifies or conditions, but is an immanent principle of forces and the relations of forces, their 'internal genesis' by conditions immanent to the conditioned (D 1983: 91). Genealogy thus connects consequences to premisses, products to the principle of their production, by seeking the sense of phenomena in the forces they express (symptomology), interpreting forces as active or reactive (typology), and evaluating the origin of forces in a quality of will that is either affirmative or negative. For example, reason, rather than being merely a given faculty of the mind, expresses a nihilistic and negative will which negates the senses and the sensory world to produce a 'True world' beyond appearances (D 1983: 91, 125, 145).

Deleuze continues using his genealogical method in later works. In *Anti-Oedipus*, he traces memory and morality to the debtor–creditor relation and the primitive practice of inflicting physical pain for unpaid debts. Originally justice is the assertion of an equivalence between the creditor's pleasure in pain inflicted on the debtor and the injury caused by the unpaid debt; memory is the product of marks inscribed on the body for a debt not paid, living reminders that produce the capacity to remember the future moment at which the promise must be kept. The sovereign individual who can make and keep promises and defines himself by power over himself is thus the product of punishment: how culture trains and selects its members (D 1983: 134–7; D&G 1983: 144–5, 190–2). Deleuze also uses genealogy to show that the reactive forces and negative will expressed by the priest type are also expressed in the figure of the psychoanalyst; both create guilt out of an infinite and unpayable debt, whether that be to a God who sacrifices himself for us, or to the analyst as cure for the condition the analyst produces (D&G 1983: 108–12, 269, 332–3; D&G 1987: 154). Even at the basic ontological level, as when he finds 'the being of the sensible' in 'difference in intensity as the reason behind qualitative diversity' (D 1994: 57), Deleuze remains a genealogist, interpreting phenomena through the hidden relations of forces immanent in them.

Connectives

Active/Reactive
Immanence
Nietzsche

GUATTARI, PIERRE-FÉLIX (1930–92)

Gary Genosko

Pierre-Félix Guattari was fifteen when he met psychoanalyst Jean Oury, founder of Clinique de la Borde, through Jean's brother Fernand, developer of institutional pedagogy in France. By the time he reached twenty years Guattari was taken under Jean's wing. Jean convinced Guattari to abandon his study of commercial pharmacy and, in the early 1950s, he visited Jean at Clinique Saumery, a precursor of La Borde. Saumery was Guattari's initiation into the psychiatric milieu. While a teenager Guattari had met Fernand Oury through the youth hostelling movement (*Fédération Unie des Auberges de Jeunesse*). Fernand Oury was instrumental in getting Guattari involved in the summer caravans he organised in the Paris suburb of La Garenne-Colombes for working-class suburban youth like Guattari himself, who grew up in the same department in nearby Villeneuve.

Guattari assisted in the foundational work at La Borde where he helped write its *Constitution de l'An 1* the year it opened in 1953. Guattari's next task was to organise intra-hospital Therapeutic Clubs for patients. Guattari's involvement increased after 1955.

Guattari's career was also shaped by the friendly tutelage of another master, whom he had met when he was just twenty-three, Jacques Lacan. It was not until 1962 that Guattari graduated to a didactic training analysis with Lacan, joining the École freudienne de Paris as an analyst member in 1969. Guattari's formative intellectual milieu was Lacanian.

By the mid-1960s Guattari had developed a formidable battery of concepts organised around the problem of delivering therapy in institutional settings. *Psychanalyse et transversalité* exposed the limits of the psychoanalytic unconscious by arguing that it was not a concern of specialists treating individuals but rather perfused the social field and history. For Guattari the subject was a group or collective assemblage of heterogeneous components whose formation, delinked from monadic individuals and abstract, universal determinations like the Oedipus myth, structural matheme and part object, could be seen through critical analyses of the actual vicissitudes of collective life in which patients found themselves. A Sartrean-inflected theory of groups emerged distinguishing non-absolutely between subject-groups (actively exploring self-defined projects) and subjugated groups (passively receiving directions), each affecting the relations of their members to social processes and shaping the potential for subject formation.

The foundation of what Guattari called schizoanalysis was laid in *L'inconscient machinique*. Schizoanalysis requires a practical, detailed semiotics as well as a politically progressive and provisional transformation of situational power relations. The analyst's micropolitical task is to discern in a particular assemblage the mutational potential of a given component and explore the effects of its passages in and between assemblages, producing and extracting singularities by undoing impasses, alienating and deadening redundancies: 'Rather than indefinitely tracing the same complexes or the same universal "mathemes", a schizoanalytic cartography will explore and experiment with an unconscious in actuality' (G 1979: 190).

Micropolitical schizoanalysis will map, in a way specific to each passage, delinguistified and mixed semiotic lines flush with matters of expression, rhizomes released from arborescent structures, molecular schizzes on the run from molar bureaucracies, faciality traits loosened from dominant overcodings, and new machinic connections and breaks, regardless of their level of formation, elaborating their becomings and new terms of reference across the social field. This emphasis on molecularity entails a sociopolitical analysis that privileges creative, oppositional flight and eschews so-called professional neutrality. Guattari introduced the machine as a productive connectivity irreducible both to technologies and to foundational substances; machines form assemblages of component parts.

The two editions of *La révolution moléculaire* (1977 and 1980) contained advanced semiotic methods, modified from Hjelmslevian and Peircean roots, adequate to the 'semiotic polycentrism' necessary for engaging in a genuine transversal analysis of the expanded fields of the unconscious, with a less woodenly dichotomous sense of super ego on one side and socius on the other. Guattari's writings on developments in Italy in the 1970s underlined their potential for new molecular forms of collective action, what he called 'generalized revolution'.

Cartographies schizoanalytiques and *Chaosmose* elaborated nonrepresentational maps of the self-engendering processes of subjectification, pragmatically attending to the specific ways in which singularities come together, through four ontological functions of the unconscious, their interfaces, and the character of their components: material fluxes and machinic phylums; existential territories and incorporeal universes. The former are actual and discursive on the plane of expression; the latter virtual and non-discursive on the plane of content. Emergent assemblages of enunciation are ontologically complex because in a given situation a schizoanalyst tries to bridge the virtual and actual by discerning the former and attending to how they actually work themselves out relationally betwixt manifestation and possibility, processually and expressively as subjectivity ever emerges.

Guattari is internationally recognised for his collaborations with Gilles Deleuze on *Anti-Oedipus*, *Kafka*, *A Thousand Plateaus*, and *What is Philosophy?*, yet his key theoretical statements remain virtually unknown.

Connectives

Lacan
Psychoanalysis
Transversality

H

HAECCEITY – refer to the entries on 'experience', 'individuation', 'percept + literature', 'phenomenology + Husserl' and 'post-structuralism + politics'.

HARDY, THOMAS (1840–1928) – refer to the entries on 'art' and 'percept + literature'.

HEGEL, GEORG WILHELM FRIEDRICH (1770–1831) – refer to the entries on 'arborescent schema', 'Bergson', 'capitalism + universal history', 'capture', 'difference', 'immanence', 'phenomenology' and 'Spinoza'.

HEIDEGGER, MARTIN (1889–1976) – refer to the entries on 'Foucault + fold', 'nonbeing', 'ontology', 'phenomenology', 'socius', 'substance' and 'thought'.

HUME, DAVID (1711–76)

Cliff Stagoll

David Hume was a Scottish philosopher, historian, economist and religious theorist, and perhaps the best known of the philosophers commonly designated 'empiricists'. Although Hume's grouping with such thinkers as John Locke and George Berkeley is questionable, mid- to late-twentieth-century histories of philosophy placed them together routinely. In a chapter on Hume, typically one either encounters a naturalist extending and radicalising the work of Locke and/or Berkeley (or René Descartes and Nicolas Malebranche), or a sceptic whose contributions to philosophy are largely or wholly critical. Perhaps his best-known philosophical theory is that ideas not clearly originating from sense impressions ought to be 'committed to flames'. Only in the late 1960s and early 1970s did the focus of Anglo-American Hume studies move away from such strident epistemological assertions towards his analysis of the passions, principles of association, and such features of the mind as instinct, propensity, belief, imagination, feeling and sympathy. Deleuze had adopted this emphasis in 1952 and 1953, focusing mainly upon the naturalism evident in Hume's principles of human nature.

Deleuze's shift in emphasis extended further. Whereas it is commonly held that Hume, finding himself unable to counter his sceptical epistemological conclusions, turned to history, sociology, religion and economics out of frustration, Deleuze considers Hume's entire corpus to comprise various stages in the development of a 'science of human nature'. Just as human life involves ethical, epistemological and aesthetic dimensions, so too it involves economic, religious and historical ones. For Deleuze, one cannot properly understand Hume's philosophy without referring to his work in other disciplines.

In his published works and interviews, Deleuze returns time and again to Hume's empiricism. His most detailed and sustained account of it is *Empiricism and Subjectivity*, his first full book. Deleuze focuses on three aspects of Hume's philosophy in particular. The first is Hume's commitment to a philosophy founded upon direct experience, a position that reappears as a key tenet of Deleuze's 'transcendental empiricism'. On Deleuze's reading, Hume begins his philosophical investigations with straightforward observations about the world: humans see objects, posit the existence of gods, make ethical judgements, plan work to meet economic imperatives, and remain aware of themselves in some sense. Deleuze argues that, because Hume is unable initially to find in thought any element of 'constancy or universality' to which he might refer a psychology per se, he develops instead a 'psychology of the mind's affections', a theory about the regular 'movement' of the mind according to observable social and passional circumstances. Rather than building some philosophical edifice, however, Hume reads the concepts needed to explain such dynamics from out of the reality of experience, treating them as contingent explanatory tools that can always be replaced or supplemented.

The second of Deleuze's emphases is upon Hume's 'atomism'. Hume conceives of the mind as a set of singular ideas, each with a distinct origin or set of origins in experience. Rather than arguing that the mind precedes ideas so that experience is given *to* the mind, Hume holds that the mind just *is* these radically disparate ideas. On this reading, nothing transcends the ideas of the mind, and so the connections between them are in no sense 'pre-programmed'.

Deleuze's third emphasis is upon Hume's 'associationism'. Since ideas are not inherently structured, there are any number of ways that they can be brought together to generate new patterns of understanding, new behaviours and so on. For Deleuze, Hume discounts the possibility of any universal principle or capacity to govern such connections. Rather, such creative potential is realised under the influence of the life of practice (that is, pressures arising from economic and legal structures, family, language patterns, physical requirements and so on). The tendencies evident in human responses to such influences might be called 'general rules', but rather than 'rules' in the usual sense, these are contingent and impermanent.

The epiphenomenon arising from such complex, contingent and changing relationships and tendencies is the human subject, that we call 'I'. This Humean subject is understood by Deleuze as a fiction, sufficiently stable to have identity posited of it and to exist in a social realm, but 'containing' elements of dynamism with the capacity to transcend hierarchical thinking of a human being in favour of rhizomatic thinking of non-human becoming. Whilst portions of the model become targets for Deleuze's subsequent attacks on the ontology of identity and being, others provide him with means of escape to a radical metaphysics of becoming.

Although Deleuze is usually faithful to Hume's writings, his readings are idiosyncratic and go well beyond the original texts. His focus upon general rules, artifice, habit and stabilising fictions carry an inordinate weight in Deleuze's early theorisation of the human individual. Nonetheless, whilst his interpretation of Hume is unusual, it is far less radical than his versions of Gottfried Wilhelm von Leibniz and Friedrich Nietzsche.

Connective

Transcendental empiricism

I

IDENTITY

James Williams

In Deleuze's work, identity is perhaps the most heavily criticised concept from the philosophical tradition. That criticism takes many forms and depends on many different arguments and aesthetic expressions. However, these can be simplified through the claim that Deleuze's opposition to identity is directed at the falsifying power of identity in representation. Identity works against and covers deeper pure differences. It does so because of the dominance of the demand to represent in the history of philosophy. Objects, subjects, faculties, feelings, ideas and thoughts must be represented for them to become a legitimate part of philosophical debate. For this representation to take place they must be identified.

There is a strong description of this historical dominance in *Difference and Repetition*, where Deleuze characterises it according to a series of 'postulates' presupposed by a certain 'image of thought'. When thought is associated by right with truth and with the good, certain unexamined premisses are at work. Most notably, that truths and goods can be represented in thought and most properly by thought.

So what concerns Deleuze is not only the claim that truths and goods must be represented, but also the belief that thought is dependent on representation and on identity for its path to the good and the true. His critiques of other philosophers often depend on showing how this image of thought is operating unconsciously and damagingly in their works. The damage is caused because reality is a process of becoming, which involves pure differences that cannot be represented.

By turning us away from reality, the commitment to identity in representation furthers an illusion that leads us to repress processes of becoming at work in our own existence. The effects of these processes become all the more difficult to work with, once that repression has taken place. In terms of identity, Deleuze's philosophy can be seen as a critical attempt to cure us of the self-destructive dependence on identity.

But what is identity according to Deleuze? In *Difference and Repetition* he gives an account of it in terms of concepts (though in *What is Philosophy?* he and Guattari use the term in a different sense). Identity is opposed to multiplicity, in that multiplicity is both uncountable and not open to a reductive logical or mathematical analysis. Thus, if any concept is defined as a series of identifiable predicates or properties, then to say that all things must be represented through concepts is to further a false image of reality. An identifiable predicate would itself be simple, limited and well-determined, something that could be checked empirically or through reason with certainty.

According to Deleuze nothing can be checked in this way. Concepts and representations do not correspond to anything in reality. This is because all things are connected to multiplicities, that is, to uncountable and unidentifiable processes of becoming, rather than existing as fixed beings with identifiable and limited predicates or essences.

But this shows the extreme difficulty of Deleuze's position, not only in terms of communicability, but also in terms of how it can be understood.

Do we not need to be able to represent something in order to be able to talk about it in an open and effective manner? Do we not need to be able to identify something in order to be able to understand it truthfully?

His answer is that communication is expressive as well as identifying. So though we represent what we think and talk about, a series of unidentifiable processes are always at work behind that representation. There can be no identity without pure differences standing in the background as a condition for the illusory appearance of a pure, well-determined identity.

Connectives

Difference
Multiplicity
Representation
Thought

IMMANENCE

James Williams

The distinction drawn between immanence and transcendence is all-important to Deleuze's philosophy. It characterises his opposition to many metaphysical positions – criticised as philosophies of transcendence. It also aligns his philosophy with philosophies of immanence, most notably Baruch Spinoza.

Immanence and transcendence are terms about the relations that hold at the heart of different metaphysics. Are the privileged relations in a philosophy of the form of a relation 'to' something, or of a relation 'in' something? If it is 'to' then it is philosophy of transcendence. If it is 'in' then it is immanence. Deleuze is radical about immanence, that is, his philosophy is to be thought strictly in terms of relations 'in'.

In the history of philosophy, relations of transcendence can be traced back to theological roots, where a lower realm is related to a higher one: ('Everything down here is related to and acquires values through its relation to God.'). For example, in René Descartes, relations of transcendence hold from body to mind and from created substance to God. Mind is independent of body and yet body is secondary to mind and in its grasp. God is independent of his creation, yet the creation must be referred to God, for example, where he acts a guarantor for the validity of clear and distinct perception.

The objection to relations of transcendence is that they involve founding negations (for example, that mind is completely separate from body).

Such negations are the grounds for negative valuations, both in the sense of a 'lower' realm finding its value or redemption in a 'higher' one, and in the sense of the lower realm depending on the higher one for its definition.

For example, if the human realm is seen as transcended by God, then definitions of human essence may be turned towards that higher realm and away from a purely human one. The human body and mind will be turned away from itself and devalued in the light, for instance, of a transcendent soul. This leads to an interesting concern in Deleuze with notions of eternity that resist definitions in terms of transcendence. We are not immortal in the way we can rise to a different realm (of God or of Platonic Ideas), but in the way we participate in eternal processes.

This explains Deleuze's appeals to, and deep interpretation of, Friedrich Nietzsche's doctrine of eternal return (in *Nietzsche and Philosophy* and *Difference and Repetition*, among others). Eternal return is an immanent process that brings differentiating and identifying processes together. In eternal return, difference returns to transform identities (the same). This is why Deleuze always insists that only difference returns and not the same.

Deleuze's philosophy of immanence emphasises connections over forms of separation. But this connection must itself be a connectivity between relations and not between different identities. This is because an external principle would be needed to ground those identities (for example, identity depended on the human mind – thereby setting it up as transcendent).

In his *Nietzsche and Philosophy*, Deleuze turns on one of the main targets of his philosophy of immanence through a critique of Hegelian dialectics, where a principle of negation itself becomes that which transcends. In contrast, Nietzsche's idea of affirmation emerges out of processes of negation but frees itself from them. A creative relation of affirmation does not depend on negating things, though it may emerge out of past negations.

In *Difference and Repetition*, the philosophy of immanence is set out in ontological terms through a succession of arguments from Duns Scotus, through Spinoza, to Nietzsche. In these arguments, the difficulties in developing a philosophy of pure immanence become apparent, as Scotus then Spinoza are shown still to depend on some forms of transcendence. Only Nietzsche's doctrine of the eternal return of pure differences allows for a full immanent ontology, because all things, whether identifiable or not, are posited as complete only through their relation to an immanent transcendental field of pure differences (Deleuze's 'virtual').

It is important to note that these claims on immanence and the distinction between actual and virtual are a key place for criticisms of Deleuze, notably by Alain Badiou. His critical claim rests on the idea that the virtual itself is a transcendent realm. But this is to miss the necessary interrelation of virtual and actual through a reciprocal determination. Neither is independent of the other and cannot therefore be said to enter into a relation of transcendence.

Connectives

Nietzsche
Spinoza
Virtual/Virtuality

INCORPOREAL

Tamsin Lorraine

In *The Logic of Sense*, Deleuze characterises the distinction made by the Stoics between mixtures of bodies or states of affairs and incorporeal entities that 'frolic' on the surface of occurrences (D 1990: 5). According to Deleuze, this distinction refers to two planes of being, one of which concerns the tensions, physical qualities, actions and passions of bodies; and the other of which concerns 'incorporeal' entities or events that do not exist, but rather 'subsist or inhere' in states of affairs. Although incorporeal entities can never be actually present, they are the effect of mixtures of bodies and can enter into quasi-causal relations with other incorporeals.

The clearest example of the incorporeal is an event of sense. A proposition like 'The sun is shining' expresses a sense that 'inheres' in the proposition, but is never reducible to the state of affairs of either one specific or even an endless series of specific instances of a shining sun (D 1990: cf. 19). Deleuze claims that while states of affairs have the temporality of the living present, the incorporeal events of sense are infinitives (to shine, to be the sun) that constitute pure becomings with the temporality of *aion* – a form of time independent of matter that always eludes the present. Thus, no matter how many times the state of affairs of a shining sun is actualised, the sense of 'The sun is shining' is not exhausted. It is this 'frontier of sense' between what words express and the attributes of bodies that allows language to be distinguished from physical bodies. If the actions and passions of bodies make sense, it is because that sense is not itself either an action or a passion, but is rather an incorporeal effect of a state of affairs that enters into relations of quasi-causality with other incorporeal events of sense. The virtual relations of the events of sense constitute the condition of any given speech-act. Deleuze refers to the work of Lewis Carroll as a revealing example of how these quasi-causal relations can form a 'nonsense' that subsists in 'common sense' language.

In *A Thousand Plateaus*, Deleuze and Guattari characterise a social field in terms of a 'machinic assemblage' and a 'collective assemblage of enunciation' (D&G 1987: 88). In addition to bodies and the actions and passions affecting those bodies (the 'machinic assemblage', for example, the body of the accused or the body of the prison), there is a set of incorporeal transformations current in a given society that are attributed to the bodies of that society (for example, the transformation of the accused into a convict by the judge's sentence) (D&G 1987: cf. 81). We can view the incorporeal effects of states of affairs in terms of either the 'order-words' that designate fixed relations between statements and the incorporeal transformations they express, or the deterritorialising play of Carroll's *Alice in Wonderland* (1865). In *The Logic of Sense*, Deleuze describes the actor or Stoic sage as someone able to evoke an instant with a taut intensity expressive of an unlimited future and past, and thereby embody the incorporeal effects of a state of affairs rather than merely its spatio-temporal actualisation (D 1990: 147). Such actors do more than merely portray a character's hopes or regrets; they attempt to 'represent' a pure instant at the point at which it divides into future and past, thus embodying in their performance an intimation of virtual relations beyond those actualised in the situation portrayed. If one wills to be just in the manner of a Stoic sage, one wills not the repetition of past acts of justice, but a justice that has always been and has yet to be – the incorporeal effect of justice that is never made fully manifest in any concrete situation. When the incorporeal effects of sense are reduced to order-words, we ignore the pure becomings of sense and territorialise the infinite variability of meaning into stale repetitions of the past. When we allow the variables of corporeal bodies and events of sense to be placed into constant variation, even order-words become a passage to the limit. The movement of new connections among these variables pushes language to its limits and bodies to a metamorphic becoming-other (D&G 1987: 108).

Connective

Becoming

INDIVIDUATION

Constantin V. Boundas

Deleuze's concept of 'individuation' is a genetic account of individuals. The concept emerges from a critique of hylomorphism that exposes the error in thinking of an individual as the end point of a progressive specification of the species. Substituting the image of 'the mould' for a processfriendly idea of modulation, this critique also repudiates the idea that an individual is moulded in a specific way. As he develops his theory of individuation, Deleuze borrows and transforms analyses made by Gottfried Wilhelm von Leibniz and Gilbert Simondon.

Deleuze's theory of individuation addresses – in the process of virtual, continuous (intensive) multiplicities becoming (extended) discrete – the apparently contradictory co-existence of the continuum and the discrete. The process of individuation is called 'differentiation' with respect to the continuum, and 'differenciation' with respect to the discrete. Given that Deleuze's concept of becoming is based on the co-imbrication of the virtual real and the actual real, the conception of the virtual is in terms of a differentiated flow of events, singularities and intensities. Meanwhile, the actual is understood as the differenciated realm of bodies, their mixtures, and states of affairs. Actualisation does not mean the death of the virtual. Hence, Deleuze's ontology generates a robust theory of individuation that sustains a creative evolution developed around not just the non-fixity of species but that of individuals as well.

For the elaboration of his theory, Deleuze appeals to Leibniz – first, to Leibniz's concepts, each of which corresponds to an individual; second, to the Leibnizian method of vice-diction that understands an individual as the product of the law of a series and the internal difference that distinguishes one moment of its becoming from another. Ultimately, though, Deleuze moves beyond Leibniz's theory of individuation because of the latter's reliance on *a priori* harmony, the compossibility of the series, and the best possible world.

Finding fresh inspiration in Simondon's theory of individuation Deleuze considers 'modulation' (instead of the mould of the old image of thought) as the process by which metastable (virtual/real) systems explicate the potential energy implicated within them. Populated by singularities and events these systems bring about new (actual/real) metastable systems in the process of their explication. Their metastability is due to the fact that the virtual does not consist only of elements and flows differentiated from one another. Rather the differentiated virtual is difference itself – difference differenciating itself. The modulating process of individuation is the transduction (Simondon's term) of the virtual continuum of intensities to the discrete extended actual, all the while remembering that the actual is never totally devoid of the dynamism of the pre-individual virtual. Thus, the actual is capable of being reabsorbed by the virtual. Intensity is what makes the passage from the virtual to the actual possible.The modulation is in a state of permanent variation – a promise of becomings – disallowing predictions of what an individuation is capable of.

Individuals are not subjects. Deleuze understands 'haecceities' as degrees of intensity (a degree of heat, a certain time of the day) that, in combination with other degrees of intensity, bring about individuals. The individuals they bring about retain the anonymity of the pre-individual realm. First, haecceities consist entirely of movement and rest (longitude) between non-formed molecules and particles. Second, they have the capacity to affect and be affected (latitude). As in Baruch Spinoza's essences, haecceities co-exist on a plane of consistency, each one of which is compossible with, and responsible for, the generation of the others. In order to accentuate their impersonality, Deleuze argues that we need a new language by which to refer to them, one that consists of proper names, verbs in the infinitive, and indefinite articles and pronouns.

Connectives

Actuality
Differentiation/Differenciation
Leibniz
Virtual/Virtuality

INTENSITY

Constantin V. Boundas

'Intensity' is a key notion in Deleuze's philosophical project: it manifests itself as the intensive virtual of his ontology; as the affirmative and creative desire of his ethics and politics; as the affect of his aesthetic theory; as the motivation for his methodological decision to opt for transcendental empiricism; and as the guarantor of a theory of difference (different/ciation).

Deleuze's ontology of becoming denounces the error we commit when we think exclusively in terms of things and their qualities, because by privileging extension and extended magnitudes we bypass the intensive genesis of the extended (transcendental illusion). In an ontology of forces like Deleuze's, force refers to the relation between forces. Forces are experienced only through the results they render; and the results of force-fields are extensive and qualitative. Transcendental empiricism, therefore, demands that the intensities that constitute an extensive being be sensed – the famous Deleuzian '*sentiendum*'. It needs to be noted that this sensing cannot be achieved through the ordinary exercise of our sensibility. Intensity can be remembered, imagined, thought and said. Intensities are not entities, they are virtual yet real events whose mode of existence is to actualise themselves in states of affairs.

The following caveats that punctuate Deleuze's writings must be heeded. First, a virtual intensity exists nowhere else but in the extended that it constitutes. Despite the fact that it is not identical with the extended, a virtual intensity does not entail ontological separation. Second, the imperatives that help us grasp intensity no longer circumscribe the deontology of pure reason alone; they enlarge the scope of this deontology so that it encompasses all faculties: from sensibility, to memory, and to thought. Nevertheless, the encounter of intensity – being the task of sensibility – is the first necessary link in the interaction of all faculties striving to generate the differentiated virtual within thought. Third, intensity is not an Idea/paradigm for particular instantiations or for screening out false pretenders. Intensity is a singularity capable of generating actual cases, none of which will ever come to resemble it.

Deleuze's ontology is built around a notion of difference that is not contained in the 'from' of the 'x is different from y', but rather he aims at difference in itself. Consequently, Deleuze gives weight to intensity because unlike extended magnitudes whose *partes extra partes* permit their division without any corresponding change in their nature, intensities cannot be subdivided without a corresponding change in their nature. Therefore, intensities are incommensurable and their 'distance' from one another makes each one of them a veritable difference in itself. Intensive magnitudes do not add up; instead they average. Placed in the context of the two sides of the Deleuzian ontology – the virtual and the actual – intensities catalyse the actualisation of the virtual, generating extension, linear, successive time, extended bodies and their qualities. The relation of reversibility that obtains between the virtual and actual guarantees intensities will not suffer the fate of negentropic death.

The role of intensity in Deleuze's ethics, politics and aesthetics is also pivotal. Deleuze's ethics revolves around two axes. The first is the Stoic/Nietzschean imperative that we become worthy of the virtual event. The second is the Spinozist admonition to live a life of joy and to multiply powerenhancing 'good encounters'. The ethics of joy and the preference for good encounters increasing our power could belong to a 'feel good', self-help type of psychology if it were not for the intensity of the virtual. Becoming worthy of the event, however, requires the ascesis of the counter-actualisation of the accidents that fill our lives, and as a result, our participation in the intensive, virtual event. Similarly, Deleuze's politics would be a banal celebration of multitudes, if it were not for the fact that the multiple is not the same as 'the many'. In the counter-actualisation of the revolution that befalls us, the revolution that never comes and yet never ceases to pass is grasped as the untimely, virtual, intensive event; the affirmation of which renders us worthy of our fate. Finally, when in his aesthetics Deleuze substitutes sensation for form, intensity is what is given priority. What the artist aims towards is indeed sensation. Sensation is intimately related to the intensity of the forces that it does not represent. Sensation is the affect, which is neither subjective nor objective; rather it is both at once: we become in sensation and at the same time something happens because of it.

Connectives

Differentiation/Differenciation
Nietzsche
Spinoza
Transcendental empiricism

INTERIORITY – refer to the entry on 'exteriority/interiority'.

INTUITION

Cliff Stagoll

Deleuze uses the concept of 'intuition' in two distinct ways. In some of his later works (for example, *What is Philosophy?*, which he co-authored with Guattari), it refers to one of the elements of a plane of immanence. Whereas concepts define the points of intensity on a plane, intuition refers to movements upon it. As such, intuitions can be considered as ideas or even 'lines of thinking' in a general sense, immanent to a particular problem and the circumstances of its consideration.

More frequently, though, Deleuze uses intuition to refer to a kind of philosophical method borrowed from Henri Bergson. This is not to suggest that Deleuze champions any particular philosophical technique. He would oppose consistent adoption of a method because of the tendency for any single approach to limit perspectives on a problem and so to hinder creative thinking. However, when Deleuze *does* refer to method, he often means a modified version of Bergson's philosophical intuition (*intuition philosophique*).

According to Bergson, evolution has resulted in the human mind becoming able to conduct rational investigations and make consequent decisions pertaining to the worlds of science and practice. The mind is not so well adapted to conducting metaphysical inquiries into the dynamics of one's life. Indeed, for Bergson, efforts to turn our analytical intellect to philosophical problems result inevitably in our considering lived reality in terms of some static, material image upon which we 'gaze' and which we then theorise abstractly.

For Bergson, our lived reality comprises a flow of conscious states. Consciousness is essentially temporal: ongoing mental activity constituting the kind of time internal to one's self. The continuity and persistence of this flow makes up our personhood, and its particularity defines our individuality. Once we turn our analytical mind to lived, conscious experience, however, we tend to think instead in terms of successive instants and images situated in space. As such, philosophical precision is lost because reality is no longer theorised on its own terms.

Intuition is the philosophical method that Bergson champions to avoid the analytical mind's tendency to abstraction. He argues that one must enter into an experience *directly*, so as to 'coincide' and 'sympathise' with it. The manner in which one achieves this, though, is notoriously difficult to describe, with as many characterisations as scholarly commentaries. Sometimes Bergson aligns intuition with artistic sensibility and awareness, or a detachment from reality. At other times he associates it with pure instinct.

On Deleuze's interpretation, intuition is somewhat less mysterious but no less problematic. He conceives of intuition as a deliberate reflective awareness or willed selfconsciousness, a concentrated and direct attention to the operations of consciousness (in contrast with mediated 'observations of' consciousness by consciousness in a quest for transparency of thought to itself). This depiction aligns with Bergson's account of the intuition of consciousness as the attention that mind gives itself, continuing its normal functions yet somehow discerning simultaneously the nature of its workings. If our natural tendency is to grasp things in terms of space and quantity, such an effort must be extremely difficult to achieve. (Deleuze and Bergson both suggest at various times that intuition has no limits, and can take us beyond the human condition to 'sympathise' and 'coincide' with animals and even inanimate objects, but the means of doing so remain mysterious.)

Deleuze is particularly attracted to intuition because his desire to move from experience to the contingent conditions of experience in order to rediscover difference demands a means for accessing the particularity of consciousness without metaphysical illusions. If he were to consider reality in terms of concepts supposed to make it (or experience of it) possible, then he would substitute one kind of abstraction for another. Deleuze instead needs to dissociate aspects of the whole that is called 'I' according to natural articulations, and to grasp conscious and material aspects of life *without* recourse to abstract or general concepts. Bergson's intuition enables him to achieve this by creating concepts according to natural articulations of experience. From the lived reality of a flow of consciousness, Deleuze's intuition reveals such articulations as memory, faculties, dreams, wishes, jokes, perceptions and calculations. As such, Deleuze maintains that there is a resemblance between intuition as a method for division and as a means for transcendental analysis.

Interestingly, Bergson sometimes seems to hold more reservations about the precision and general applicability of intuition than Deleuze. He reminds his readers that to express in language the results of an intuitive study of consciousness is to conceptualise and symbolise, and thus to abstract. Yet he means intuition to be free from formal conceptual and symbolic constraints. Accordingly, to communicate about intuition, he argues that we should use metaphor and suggestiveness to point towards what is otherwise inexpressible. Deleuze expresses few such reservations overtly, although his language use hints at his having followed Bergson's suggestion.

Connective

Bergson

K

KAFKA, FRANZ (1883–1924)

John Marks

In *Kafka: Toward a Minor Literature*, Deleuze and Guattari seek to overturn much of the received critical wisdom on Franz Kafka's work by presenting him as a joyful and comic writer, who is positively engaged in the world. Kafka was, Deleuze and Guattari claim, irritated when people saw him as a writer of 'intimacy'. In Deleuze and Guattari's hands he becomes a political author, and the prophet of a future world. It would, they claim, be grotesque to oppose life and writing in Kafka. Kafka seeks to grasp the world rather than extract impressions from it, and if he is fixated on an essential problem, it is that of escape rather than abstract notions of liberty. The tendency towards deterritorialisation in Kafka's work, for example, is evident in his use of animals in his short stories.

Rather than interpretation – saying that this means that – Deleuze and Guattari prefer to look at what they call 'Kafka politics', 'Kafka machines' and 'Kafka experimentation'. Many interpretations of Kafka have concentrated on themes relating to religion and psychoanalysis, whilst others have seen in Kafka's work the expression of his own acute human suffering: his work becomes a tragic *cri de coeur*. In contrast to this, Deleuze and Guattari show how the Kafka machine generates three passions or intensities: fear, flight and dismantling. In *The Trial* (1925) it is less a question of presenting an image of a transcendental and unknowable law, and more a question of an investigation of the functioning of a machine. In contrast to the psychoanalytical approach, which reduces Kafka's particularly intense attachment to the world to a neurotic symptom of his relationship with his own father, they show how Kafka's inaptitude for marriage and obsession with writing have positive libidinal motivations. Kafka's apparently solitary nature – his existence as an unmarried writer – should not be viewed as evidence of a withdrawal into an ivory tower – but rather one component of a 'bachelor machine'. This machine has multiple connections with the social field, and allows the bachelor to exist in a state of desire that is much more intense than the psychoanalytic categories of incestuous or homosexual desire. Kafka's strategy in 'Letter to his Father' is to inflate the father figure to absurd and comic proportions, so that he covers the map of the world. The effect is to provide a way out of the psychoanalytical impasse, a line of flight away from the father and into the world; a new set of connections.

The book on Kafka constitutes Deleuze and Guattari's most detailed reading of literature as *machine*. They claim that Kafka's work is a rhizome or a burrow, in which no entrance is more privileged than another. They also claim that the Kafka-machine, composed as it is of letters, stories and novels, moves in the direction of the unlimited rather than the fragmentary. Kafka's oeuvre is complete yet heterogeneous: it is constructed from components that do not connect but are always in communication with each other. The Kafka machine is, paradoxically, one of continuous contiguity. Such a machinic reading of Kafka is called for by Kafka's own approach, which goes against representation, allegory, symbolism and metaphor. Instead, Deleuze and Guattari show how he works with the components of reality: objects, characters and events. The evolution of Kafka's work is towards a sober 'hyper-realism' that dispenses with impressions and imaginings. Rather than metaphor, Kafka's hyper-reality constructs an immanent assemblage of metamorphosis, a continuum of reversible intensities.

For Deleuze and Guattari,Kafka's work is a 'minor' literature par excellence. A minor literature 'deterritorialises' language and provides an intimate and immediate connection between the individual and the political. It is also a form of literature in which everything is expressed in collective terms and everything takes on a collective value. In short, there is no subject in a minor literature, only collective assemblages of enunciation. In a 'major' literature there are forms of 'individuated enunciation' that belong to literary masters, and individual concerns abound. Minor literature can afford no such luxuries, since it is born out of necessity in restricted conditions. Since major literature is essentially representational in orientation, it moves from content to expression, whereas a minor literature expresses itself out of absolute necessity and only later conceptualises itself. Expression breaks established forms and encourages new directions. This commitment to expression is evident in Kafka's interest in 'musical' sounds that escape any form of signification, composition or song.

Deleuze and Guattari repeatedly emphasise the fact that Kafka's solitude gives him an acutely political, and even prophetic, vision. Kafka the bachelor-machine perceives the 'diabolical powers of the future' – American capitalism, Soviet bureaucracy and European Fascism – that are knocking on the door of his study. The literary machine enables this vision because it functions not like a mirror of the world, but rather like a watch that is running fast. The tendency of Kafka's work towards proliferation opens up a field of immanence that takes his social and political analysis out of the domain of the actual and into the virtual.

Connectives

Desire
Deterritorialisation/Reterritorialisation
Intensity
Lines of flight
Minoritarian
Psychoanalysis
Rhizome

KANT, IMMANUEL (1724–1804)

Alison Ross

Immanuel Kant's critical philosophy marks a turning point in modern thought. Kant distinguishes the 'critical' inquiry he conducts into reason from the 'fanaticism' that afflicts the 'dogmatic' philosophy of his competitors. Against both the excesses of rationalism – which confuses what it is possible to think with what it is possible to know – and empiricism, which scuttle the possibility of systematic knowledge altogether, Kant's self-described Copernican revolution in philosophy follows a language of 'moderation'.

Deleuze rejects the self-conception of Kantian philosophy on two fronts: first, as his own pantheon of selected influences in the history of philosophy indicates, his practice of philosophy undermines Kant's claim to have consigned rationalism and empiricism to history; second, he disputes the style of Kant's philosophy in which thinking is guided by the moderating influence of 'common sense'. The central task of Kantian philosophy is the 'critique' of the faculties of the subject. For Deleuze, Kantian 'critique' does not extend to the orientating moral values of the Kantian philosophy, and it is Friedrich Nietzsche's pursuit of the critique against moral ideals that makes him, in Deleuze's eyes, the truly critical philosopher. At the same time that Deleuze rejects the false limits that Kant places on 'critique' he also adapts the Kantian project of a critique of the faculties of the subject for his own project of 'transcendental empiricism'.

Kant's importance for Deleuze can be described in terms of the way he alters Kant's language of the 'faculties' to cater for the primacy of affect. Deleuze's revision of the language of the 'faculties' calls into question the dualist structure of Kant's thought according to which a juridical conception of reason regulates the field of experience.

In Kantian philosophy the subject occupies the position of an interface between nature and experience. The subject's categories of understanding constitute the organising structure for sensation and form the condition of possibility for experience. According to Kant, the coherence and form of experience are the work of the mind rather than the 'givens' of sensible experience. Further, the condition of possibility for the *cognition* of objects is the mind's own activity. Hence Kant's famous dictum that 'the conditions of the possibility of experience in general are also the conditions of the possibility of the objects of experience.' But if Kant views experience as a compound of the data of impressions and what our faculty of knowledge supplies itself, he also conceives of the task of philosophy as a critique of the categories that redeem experience from the irreducible particularity of sensible perceptions. The adjunct of this critique is the revival of the pursuit of knowledge outside of sensibility and the field of possible experience. Critical philosophy aims to secure the ground of this extension by its investigation into the faculty of reason. In stark contrast, Deleuze uses the language of the faculties to demolish the position of the subject as the pivot between nature and experience and to overturn philosophy's role as a court that adjudicates on the proper limits of reason. Instead of a subject with predetermined faculties ordering the field of experience, Deleuze uses the language of the faculties to describe a register of affect. The Deleuzian force of affect drives the faculties constantly to surpass their accepted limits. This is a transcendental project because, like Kant, Deleuze thinks that philosophy should create concepts that do not merely trace the 'givens' of sensible experience.

Although Deleuze's transcendental empiricism adapts elements of Kant's thought, specifically his conception of the faculties, it does so in order to critique the implacable dualism of Kantian philosophy. Kant's first two Critiques establish a division between freedom and the sensible world. In the *Critique of Pure Reason*, the task of critical philosophy is to restrain reason from the illusory use that consists in confusing what it is possible to think with what may be known according to the sensible conditions of thought (K 1996: 8). The risk of such a confusion of ideas and objects of possible experience is that a fabrication of reason may be confused for something that exists in the domain of experience. The *Critique of Practical Reason*, on the other hand, locates a danger in the influence on moral action of circumstance. Here the sensible world and the subject's feelings do not provide a necessary orientation for ideas of reason, so much as threaten to lead it astray. Accordingly, the formalism of the moral law guards the possibility of a moral action in the world of sensibility, defining such action as a strict adherence to the principles of reason. Whether it is reason's tendency to fanaticism – an error that follows the hubris of limitlessness – or the claim circumstances make upon it and constrain it under a false limitation, critical restraint in either case follows a juridical model.

Kant's texts reinforce the sense of renunciation – of desires or of errant speculation – in the recurrent references to 'the court of reason' which legislates the proper use and safe extension of reason's ideas. Hence the 'revolution' that proceeds by pleas for moderation is fought on two fronts: against the illusions of a reason 'independent of all experience', as well as against the claim of circumstance on action. The final work of the critical trilogy, the *Critique of Judgement*, tries to mediate this split between experience and freedom through the faculty of judgement. It is in this work that Kant's positive influence over Deleuze is strongest. In Deleuze and Guattari's *What is Philosophy?* they argue that Kant's final Critique marks a significant departure from the terms of the first and second Critiques: the *Critique of Judgement* is '. . . an unrestrained work of old age which [Kant's] successors have still not caught up with: all the mind's faculties overcome their limits, the very limits that Kant had so carefully laid down in the works of his prime' (D&G 1994: 2).

The juridical conception of the faculties and the legislative role it gives philosophy to establish the limits of reason unravels, according to Deleuze, in Kant's conception of the sublime. It is important to point out that Deleuze's reading of Kant's appendix on the sublime is an idiosyncratic account. Within Kant's thought the sublime is used to confirm the subject's faculty of reason as that which surpasses any natural form, and is arguably the jewel of Kant's metaphysics. Arguing against Kant's attempt to confine the faculties to their proper limits – to their nth power – Deleuze's account of this appendix argues that in the case of the sublime the faculties enter into unregulated relations and this is what drives the faculties (see D 1983, D 1984, and D 1994).

Aside from these points of direct influence over Deleuze's project, Kant's position within Deleuze's topography of philosophers is highly unusual. Deleuze describes his Kant book as an attempt to know his 'enemy' and this book is the only book that Deleuze devotes to a thinker who is not part of his pantheon of selected influences. Kant's peculiar position needs to be seen as a consequence of Deleuze's description of his own project as 'transcendental empiricism'. Deleuze returns to the very rationalist and empiricist thinkers that Kant believed his critical philosophy had consigned to the past. Deleuze's return, however, is conducted through the Kantian language of 'faculties' and 'transcendental' thinking.

Connectives

Desire
Transcendental empiricism

KLEE, PAUL (1879–1940) – refer to the entries on 'art' and 'utopia'.

L

LACAN, JACQUES (1901–81)

Alison Ross

Jacques Lacan was a French psychoanalyst most famous for his structuralist interpretation of Freudian psychoanalysis. Despite his 'structuralist' fame his work can be divided into many different phases, including an early fascination with surrealism and the avant-garde, an interest in the 1950s and 1960s with Saussurian linguistics and structuralism, as well as his late preoccupation with Borromean knots and his attempt to mathematise his ideas. It is only in this final 'phase' that Lacan poses for the first time the question of what the hitherto distinct elements of the system, real/imaginary/ symbolic (RSI) have in common.

Deleuze's relationship with Lacan is complex. There are places in Deleuze's work, such as his essay on Leopold von Sacher-Masoch, that demonstrate expert familiarity with Lacanian psychoanalysis. Despite this essay's critique of the Freudian category of 'sado-masochism', Deleuze uses elements of Lacanian psychoanalysis as an operative framework for his own analysis of 'masochism'. Similarly, in the two volumes of *Capitalism and Schizophrenia*, Lacan is occasionally a target of the authors' anti-psychiatric polemics, but he can also be cited as an influence on their own attempt to liberate desire from its Oedipal ordering in classical, Freudian psychoanalysis. In this respect the important features of Lacan's thought include his uneven verdicts on the different layers of the subject (RSI) and his interest in psychotic speech.

On the other hand, Lacanian psychoanalysis gives a superb illustration of the general complaint against psychoanalysis in *Anti-Oedipus*, concerning the errors of desire. Lacan exemplifies the 'error' that desire is 'lack'. For Lacan desire is the product of the split between demand and need. Demand is the alienation of 'need' in language. It is the failure of language (demand) adequately to represent 'need' that produces an impotent desire figured around 'lack'. Although Deleuze and Guattari criticise 'lack' as one of the errors of desire they applaud the fact that desire is continuous in Lacan, despite contesting the way it earns this status only on account of its definition as a 'lack' regulated by the law of the symbolic.

The complexity of Lacan's place in the thought of Deleuze and Guattari can be described in relation to the genesis and explanatory scope of their concept of the Body without Organs (BwO). In psychoanalytic doctrine the development of the individual is described in the normative terms of a gradual shift away from the polymorphous perversity of the infant's body to the hierarchical ordering or coding of the body's erogenous zones in an ascending scale from pathways of fore-pleasure (such as kissing) to endpleasure (genital). According to this model, the subject and its sexual identity are not given, but these emerge by ordering the drives that are in turn regulated by Oedipal relations. In the paper Lacan wrote on the 'mirror stage', this process is described as the movement from organs without a clearly defined sense of a body, to the (tenuous and fictional) hold of socio-sexual identity.

In contrast to the 'organs without a body' that precedes the process of acquisition of socio-sexual identity in Lacan, the BwO, a term that Deleuze and Guattari take from Antonin Artaud, is deployed to denaturalise the process of development defined by psychoanalysis. Against the coding of the body's parts according to 'natural' functions and the conception of the organism as a functioning hierarchy of parts on which it depends, this concept aims to explain and to maximise possible connections between the different parts of the body and its 'outside'. In particular, the authors use this concept to de-Oedipalise the description of such connections in classical psychoanalysis. Instead of framing breast-feeding in terms of a primary anaclitic relationship between mother and infant that will need to be broken by the secondary identification with the authority of the father, this connection is described as an assemblage of desire in which 'mouth' and 'breast' replace the terms 'infant' and 'mother'. Despite the genesis of this concept in *Anti-Oedipus* in a polemic against psychoanalysis, a strategic alliance with aspects of Lacanian theory can be discerned in their use of this concept.

According to Lacan the infant's state of physiological fragmentation (the real) is sealed into an illusory formation of unity in the mirror stage. Here the child founds its sense of integrated identity through a visual perception of unity that divides it from its 'real' state of physiological fragmentation. This perception of unity, designated by Lacan as the 'imaginary', establishes the basis of socio-sexual identity as a unity. This unity is paradoxical however, given that the agency of its unity is external. For Lacan, unity only becomes functional when the subject relinquishes its relation with the (M)Other in order to occupy a place in the symbolic order as a speaking subject. The primary sense of unity developed by the subject in the mirror stage, is divided in the subject's secondary identification with the Law of the Father. Deleuze and Guattari disengage the Oedipal narrative that regulates the organisation of socio-sexual unity in psychoanalysis. It is interesting to note that Lacan occasionally sides with the imaginary field of connections prior to symbolic law and sometimes emphasises the unsurpassable force of the real in psychic life. Thus, despite the limitations of his framework, the work of Lacan differs from his precursors in classical psychoanalysis in that he proposes a porous relation between the body and its 'outside'.

Connectives

Desire
Freud

LAMARCK, JEAN-BAPTISTE (1744–1829) – refer to the entry on 'creative transformation'.

LEIBNIZ, GOTTFRIED WILHELM VON (1646–1716)

Brett Nicholls

Gottfried Wilhelm von Leibniz is drawn into Deleuze's engagement with the history of philosophy with a book length study, *The Fold: Leibniz and the Baroque*, and he is present at strategic moments in Deleuze's wider thinking. In *The Fold* Deleuze reinvigorates Leibniz's concept of the monad with the notion that the world is 'a pure emission of singularities' (D 1993a: 60). Leibniz insisted in *Monadology* (written 1714, published 1867) that the universe consists of discrete entities: monads. Monads are simple substances, indivisible and indestructible, with no windows through which anything can pass. The world that we inhabit is constituted by monads that converge in series. And, for Leibniz, varying series converge in a harmonious unity that is preestablished by God.

Existence for Leibniz and Deleuze bursts forth in its various forms from one plane of singularities. This plane can be understood as the inexhaustible and unknowable totality of monads that provide the substance from which subjects and objects in their multifarious manners emerge. It would not be remiss, however, to say that Deleuze seeks to rescue Leibniz from idealism. Leibniz ultimately considered substance as immaterial. For Deleuze the 'pure emission of singularities' is an organic field of life forces. His interest is in what he calls an 'animal monadology' (D 1993a: 109), in which the 'animal in me' is less opposed to the alter ego (as in Edmund Husserl [1859–1938]) and rather, an aggregate of vital forces, monads, that are organised or folded in various ways.

The concept of the fold, expounded as it is via Leibniz's insistence upon one substance, enables Deleuze to think the order of things in ways not determined by dualism. The distinction between the mind and the body, for instance, is produced by a kind of matter that has the capacity to fold in upon itself in order to perceive. Matter outside the mind does not perceive. Enfolding brings the relation of an inner and outer world into being. Unlike the body, the mind is enclosed matter, an interior that does not respond directly to the outside world. This enclosure can be understood as a form of theatre, one in which thinking, imagining and reflecting occur. Deleuze links the form of this theatre to baroque architecture, art and music, which he admires as 'Fold after fold' (D 1993a: 33).

The subject emerges in Deleuze's work upon Leibniz not as an attribute of substance, an essence, but as a point upon which series converge. At one level, the universe as 'pure emission of singularities' is thus reflected in every individual as a virtual predicate, but with a limited point of view (D 1993a: 53). An identity emerges in and through the convergence of a series of singularities. This means that the subject is determined rather than determining, and for Leibniz, writing within a Christian cosmology, the stability of the determined subject is guaranteed by God. This position is outlined in Leibniz's *Theodicy* (1890). He held that the subject is determined in the convergence of what he calls a 'compossible world'. Any series that is bound by the same law, governed by the principle of non-contradiction, belongs to the same world. It is not possible, in this view, for Adam to be both a sinner and not a sinner in the same world. And while we can imagine other realities, say a world in which Adam is not a sinner, the principle of sufficient reason effectively guarantees that this and not that is the best possible world. Leibniz thus claimed to have arrived at a solution to the problem of evil; other worlds would simply be incompossible.

Incompossibility signals the impossibility of the co-existence of worlds that diverge from the law of non-contradiction. Deleuze, however, in all of his engagements with Leibniz, goes to work upon this solution and alters the trajectory of Leibniz's thought. He proposes that incompossibility is a condition of compossibility. Rather than governed by the metaphysical law of non-contradiction, the world is multiple and the subject can be defined in relation to foldable, polychronic temporalities, where incompossibles and compossibles co-exist.We might think, therefore, of the divergence of series not as negation or opposition but as possibility.

This emphasis upon divergence as possibility is sustained in *Difference and Repetition* (D 1994: 123) where Deleuze reads against Leibniz's insistence upon compossibility with the notion that 'basic series are divergent' since they are 'constantly displaced within . . . chaos'. In *The Logic of Sense* (D 1990: 109–17), incompossibility becomes the ground for the overlapping of sense and non-sense. And in *Cinema 2: The Time Image* (D 1989: 130–1), Leibniz figures as a thinker who has unwittingly opened up the problem of time and truth. In each of these works, Deleuze draws Leibniz into his rejection of dualism and his critique of the order of things. He is concerned with pushing Leibniz beyond the limits of the principle of sufficient reason to affirm that incompossibles belong to the same world. Living involves, after Deleuze's Leibniz, not the relation of truth and falsity but the affirmation of possibilities, the work of unfolding and folding compossible and incompossible series.

Connectives

Fold
Force
Substance

LÉVINAS, EMMANUEL (1906–95) – refer to the entries on 'ontology' and 'phenomenology'.

LINES OF FLIGHT

Tamsin Lorraine

Throughout *A Thousand Plateaus*, Deleuze and Guattari develop a vocabulary that emphasises how things connect rather than how they 'are', and tendencies that could evolve in creative mutations rather than a 'reality' that is an inversion of the past. He and Guattari prefer to consider things not as substances, but as assemblages or multiplicities, focusing on things in terms of unfolding forces – bodies and their powers to affect and be affected – rather than static essences. A 'line of flight' is a path of mutation precipitated through the actualisation of connections among bodies that were previously only implicit (or 'virtual') that releases new powers in the capacities of those bodies to act and respond.

Every assemblage is territorial in that it sustains connections that define it, but every assemblage is also composed of lines of deterritorialisation that run through it and carry it away from its current form (D&G 1987: 503–4). Deleuze and Guattari characterise assemblages in terms of three kinds of lines that inform their interactions with the world. There is the 'molar line' that forms a binary, arborescent system of segments, the 'molecular line' that is more fluid although still segmentary, and the line of flight that ruptures the other two lines (D&G 1987: 205). While the supple segmentarity of the molecular line operates by deterritorialisations that may permit reterritorialisations that turn back into rigid lines, the line of flight can evolve into creative metamorphoses of the assemblage and the assemblages it affects. In what they admit is a 'summary' example (since the three lines co-exist and can change into one another), they suggest that the Roman Empire could be said to exemplify rigid segmentarity; the migrant barbarians who come and go across frontiers pillaging, but also reterritorialising by integrating themselves into indigenous communities, supple segmentarity; and the nomads of the steppes who escape all such territorialisation and sow deterritorialisation everywhere they go, a line of flight (D&G 1987: 222–3).

On the one hand an assemblage (for example, an assemblage of the book, *A Thousand Plateaus*, and a reader) is a 'machinic assemblage' of actions, passions and bodies reacting to one another (paper, print, binding, words, feelings and the turning of pages). On the other hand it is a 'collective assemblage of enunciation', of statements and incorporeal transformations attributed to bodies (the meaning of the book's words emerges in a reading assemblage in terms of the implicit presuppositions extant in the social field concerning pragmatic variables in the use of language) (D&G 1987: 88). Both aspects of the book–reader assemblage produce various effects in their engagement with other assemblages (for example, the assemblage of book and hand ripping out pages to feed a fire or the assemblage of a reader plugged into aesthetic assemblages inspired by the notion of 'becomingimperceptible' to create a work of art). Deleuze and Guattari deliberately designed *A Thousand Plateaus* to foster lines of flight in thinking – thought-movements that would creatively evolve in connection with the lines of flight of other thought-movements, producing new ways of thinking rather than territorialising into the recognisable grooves of what 'passes' for philosophical thought. Interpretations, according to Deleuze and Guattari, trace already established patterns of meaning; maps pursue connections or lines of flight not readily perceptible to the majoritarian subjects of dominant reality. Deleuze and Guattari wrote their book as such a map, hoping to elicit further maps, rather than interpretations, from their readers.

Although Deleuze and Guattari clearly value lines of flight that can connect with other lines in creatively productive ways that lead to enlivening transformations of the social field, they also caution against their dangers. A line of flight can become ineffectual, lead to regressive transformations, and even reconstruct highly rigid segments (D&G 1987: 205). And even if it manages to cross the wall and get out of the black hole, it can present the danger of becoming no more than a line of destruction (D&G 1987: 229). Deleuze and Guattari advocate extending lines of flight to the point where they bring variables of machinic assemblages into continuity with assemblages of enunciation, transforming social life in the process; but they never minimise the risks the pursuit of such lines entails.

Connectives

Deterritorialisation/Reterritorialisation
Majoritarian
Molar

LINES OF FLIGHT + ART + POLITICS

Adrian Parr

Understanding the political potential of art has been a concern that goes as far back as the Middle Ages and Renaissance, where political and religious influence often defined the content of art commissions inscribing public space, this being the key concern shaping Richard C. Trexler's *Public Life in Renaissance Florence* (1980). During the early twentieth century, Bertolt Brecht, Georg Lukás, and Ernst Bloch examined German Expressionism, boldly denouncing the aestheticisation of politics; this was a debate that carried enormous influence for both Theodor Adorno and Walter Benjamin's examination of the industries of culture and their subsequent critique of bourgeois culture. In the latter part of the twentieth century Edward Said, and postcolonial theory in general, insisted in *Orientalism* (1978) that the representation of colonised people by their colonisers is inherently political: representing an-other's culture not on their own terms but on the basis of what the occupying culture believes is relevant and important. So what might Deleuze contribute to this longstanding discussion concerning the connection between politics and art?

To begin with, art at its most creative mutates as it experiments, producing new paradigms of subjectivity. What this means is that art has the potential to create the conditions wherein new connections and combinations can be drawn – socially, linguistically, perceptually, economically, conceptually and historically. For example, Antonin Artaud, a favourite of both Deleuze and Guattari, whose animated drawings executed during his confinement in a mental institution, captures a sense of physical and psychic exhaustion, an exhaustion that is intensified by the anarchic language he develops through the combination of colours, words, sounds and forms. Artaud's drawings both document and constitute a process of sensory overload, the lines of which strip away systems of signification. In this way we could use Deleuze and Guattari's concept of a 'line of flight' to consider how Artaud's work prompts us to think differently, to sense anew and be exposed to affects in unpredictable ways. Hence, by generating new percepts and affects, art could be described as an 'affective system' of change.

When considering the political potential of art, we often look to the way in which certain practices are immanent to the social field and the changes these invoke. A practice that dismantles conventional ways of thinking and acting, or one that stimulates upheaval by loosening up some of the rules and orders that organise individuals and social bodies is inherently political. This prompts two key questions to bubble to the surface. First, how can politics condition art? Second, and more pertinently, how do we gauge the political force of art?

Art at its most social exposes the desiring production that organises space, using desire in its most productive sense to bring to life the affective dimension of art. To this extent, the lines of flight emanating out of certain practices, such as Artaud's, result not so much from what an audience can see but more from what they cannot see. That is to say, the movement of lines between primary points of subjectivity – curator, critic, client, artist, madman and spectator – and signification – exotica, erotica, insanity, consumerism, history and value – can locate the majoritarian lines striating space in order to extract the minoritarian forces immanent to a particular space. The reality of such art work is qualitatively different from art that 'represents the real' or even the real of 'reality TV', as this kind of art is determined neither dialectically nor purely as symbolic gesture. This is an art practice that simply makes the coherency and rigidity of social space leak. In the spirit of Deleuze and Guattari the politics of art exposes the very proposition put forward in *A Thousand Plateaus*: 'Lines of flight are realities; they are very dangerous for societies, although they can get by without them, and sometimes manage to keep them to a minimum' (D&G 1987: 204). From this viewpoint, art functions as a line of flight, traversing individual and collective subjectivities and pushing centralised organisations to the limit; it combines a variety of affects and percepts in ways that conjugate one another.

In many respects the connective, expansive and deterritorialising character of lines of flight, when considered in terms of art, draws our attention to the ethical dimension of art. Here the question of ethics in relation to art is primarily taken to be a problem of organisation. Art makes possible, it enables us to broaden our horizons and understanding, sensitising us to our own affective dimension in relation to the world as a whole. It is, therefore, no accident that art often becomes the primary target once repression sinks in, usually setting off alarm bells, and warning us that the social sphere is on the verge of becoming fascistic.

As Deleuze and Guattari insist in *A Thousand Plateaus*, when desire turns repressive it finds investment in fascistic social organisations; at this point the active lines of flight indicative of the political undercurrents of art are susceptible to blockage. This is not to suggest that art is immune to fascistic investment. It, too, can be turned against itself; that is when art is consumed by the black hole that annihilates the innovative radicality of art. For example, although many of the German Expressionists were exemplified as producers of degenerate art by the German Nazis in the 1937 exhibition, *Reflections of Decadence* (in Dresden Town Hall), Lukás insisted that the artists in question in fact participated in the selfsame irrational impulses motivating Nazism. In other words, when positive lines of flight are withdrawn or used to prop up the regulative nature of negative lines of flight, what we are left with is an ethical distinction formed between 'the politics of art' or 'the art of politics'. In effect, then, the politics of art comes from how art engages political subjectivity, sustaining an impersonal reality that allows pre-individual singularities to structure and collectively to orient subjectivity. The politics of art survives along the mutative dimensions positive and creative 'lines of flight' expose; it is not fully apparent and still it exists as a 'yet to come'.

LINES OF FLIGHT + SUICIDE

Rosi Braidotti

The Deleuzian subject is a singular complexity, one that enacts and actualises a radical ethics of transformation. This 'subject' simultaneously rejects individualism and the nihilism of self-destruction. In an ecosophical sense, Deleuze thinks of the subject in terms of a connection, one that takes place between self and others, pushing the subject beyond selfcentred individualism also to include non-humans or the earth itself.

On the issue of suicide, Deleuze is as clear as Baruch Spinoza: the choice for self-destruction is not positive, nor can it be said to be free, because death is the destruction of the *conatus* – defined as the desire to actualise one's power of becoming. Self-preservation, in the sense of a desire for self-expression, constitutes the subject. A *conatus* cannot freely wish its own self-destruction; if it does, this is because some physical or psychical compulsion negates the subject's freedom. As connectivity and mutual implication are the distinguishing features of an intensive understanding of the subject, dying as such means ceasing to partake in this vital flow of life. Hence, the inter-connectedness of entities means that selfpreservation is a commonly shared concern.

Joining forces with others so as to enhance one's enjoyment of life is the key to Deleuzian ethics; it is also the definition of a joyously lived life. The greatest ethical flaw is to succumb to external forces that diminish one's capacity to endure. From this viewpoint, suicide is an unproductive 'black hole'.

Deleuze's view of death is far removed from the metaphysics of finitude. Death is neither a matter of absolute closure, nor a border that defines the difference between existing or not existing. Instead, the Deleuzian subject is produced through a multiplicity of connections that unfold in a process of becoming. This affirmative view of life situates philosophical nomadicism in the logic of positivity, rather than in the redemptive economy common to classical metaphysics. What is more is that this vision of death-as-process, or a Nietzschean vision of the 'eternal return', emerges out of Deleuze's philosophy of time: endurance and sustainability.

Life is the affirmation of radical immanence. What gets affirmed is the intensity and acceleration of existential speed characteristic of desire or the expression of *potentia*. The ethics of nomadic subjects asserts the positivity of *potentia* itself. That is to say, the singularity of the forces that compose the specific spatio-temporal grid of immanence composes one's life. Life is an assemblage, a montage, not a given; it is a set of points in space and time; a quilt of retrieved material. Put simply, for Deleuze what makes one's life unique is the life project, not a deep-seated essence.

Commenting on the suicides of Primo Levi and Virginia Woolf, Deleuze – who also chose to end his own life – stressed that life can be affirmed by suppressing your own life. This he felt was especially true in the case of failing health or when life is spent in degrading social conditions, both of which seriously cripple one's power to affirm and endure life with joy. We do need to exercise some caution here, though, because Deleuze is not proposing a Christian affirmation of life geared toward a transcendent enterprise; rather he is suggesting life is not marked by any signifier or proper noun: Deleuze's vision is of a radically immanent fleshed existence intensively lived.

Deleuze introduces a fundamental distinction between personal and impersonal death. Death is the empty form of time, the perpetual becoming that can be actualised in the present but flows back to the past and seeps into the future. The eternal return of death is 'virtual' in that it has the generative capacity to engender the actual. Consequently, death is the ultimate manifestation of the active principle that drives all living matter, namely the power to express the pre-individual or impersonal power of *potentia*. Death is the becoming-imperceptible of the nomadic subject and as such it is part of the cycle of becoming. Yet, death is still interconnected with the 'outside' and always on the frontiers of incorporeality.

M

MAJORITARIAN

Tamsin Lorraine

Deleuze and Guattari describe a majority as a standard like 'white-man' or 'adult-male' in comparison to which other quantities can be said to be minoritarian (D&G 1987: 291). Human life in a capitalist society operates on the strata of the organism (various corporeal systems organised into the functioning wholes of biological organisms), 'signifiance' (systems of signifiers and signifieds that interpreters interpret), and subjectification (systems that distribute subjects of enunciation and subjects of the statement – that is, subjects who are speakers, and subjects of what is spoken about). Rather than assume that the subject is somehow prior to the society of which it becomes a member, Deleuze and Guattari take the Foucaultian stance that collective systems of enunciation (these could be compared to Michel Foucault's discursive systems, for example legal discourse) and machinic assemblages (these could be compared to Foucault's nondiscursive systems, for example the bodies, lay-out and behaviours related to the court room) are the condition of the subjects they produce. What counts as meaningful speech is dictated not by an individual subject, but by the systems of 'signifiance' that determine what makes sense in a given situation. What counts as a recognisable subject (to oneself as well as others) is dictated by systems of subjectification that determine a subject's position vis-à-vis others.

Deleuze and Guattari insist it is the 'axioms' of capitalist society that constitute majorities (D&G 1987: 469). The axioms of capitalism are primary statements that are not derivable from other statements and which enter into assemblages of production, circulation and consumption (D&G 1987: 461). The functional elements and relations of capitalism are less specified than in other forms of society, allowing them to be simultaneously realised in a wide variety of domains (D&G 1987: 454). Whether you are the worker or businessman or consumer depends more on the function you are performing and the relations into which you enter, than who or what you are. This gives capitalism a peculiar fluidity. Deterritorialising flows can be mastered through the multiplication or withdrawal of axioms (in the latter case, very few axioms regulate the dominant flows, giving other flows only a derivative status) (D&G 1987: 462). The operative statements of various regions of the social field (statements concerning, for example, school and the student, the prison and the convict, or the political system and the citizen) constitute the majoritarian elements of a denumerable set. The majoritarian standard constituted through these statements specifies recognisable positions on points of the arborescent, mnemonic, molar, structural systems of territorialisation and reterritorialisation through which subjects are sorted and significations make sense (cf. D&G 1987: 295). Systems of signifiance and subjectification sort social meaning and individual subjects into binary categories that remain relatively stable and render 'minor' fluctuations invisible or derivative. Minorities are defined by the gaps that separate them from the axioms constituting majorities (D&G 1987: 469). These gaps fluctuate in keeping with shifting lines of flight and the metamorphoses of the assemblages involved. Minorities thus constitute 'fuzzy' sets that are nondenumerable and nonaxiomisable. Deleuze and Guattari characterise such sets as 'multiplicities of escape and flux' (D&G 1987: 470).

From the polyvocal semiotics of the body and its corporeal coordinates, a single substance of expression is produced through the subjection of bodies to discipline by the abstract machine of faciality (a 'black hole/ white wall system'); the fluxes of the organic strata are superseded by the strata of signifiance and subjectification (D&G 1987: 181). The 'white, male, adult, "rational," etc., in short the average European' is the 'central' point by reference to which binary distributions are organised. All the lines defined by points reproducing or resonating with the central point are part of the arborescent system that constitutes 'Man' as a 'gigantic memory' (D&G 1987: 293). The majoritarian standard is thus this 'average' European constituted throughout the social field in its myriad forms through the systems of signifiance and subjectification of various domains.

Connectives

Arborescent schema
Black hole
Deterritorialisation
Foucault

MARX, KARL (1818–83)

Kenneth Surin

Karl Marx does not receive a great deal of explicit attention in the writings of Deleuze and Guattari, though it is clear that the Marxist paradigm is a crucial if tacit framework for many of the conceptions developed in the two volumes of *Capitalism and Schizophrenia*. Especially significant is Marx's dictum in *The German Ideology* (1932) that 'the nature of individuals depends on the material conditions determining their production'. Deleuze, of course, interprets this dictum in a distinctive and even 'post- Marxist' fashion. The necessity for this (Deleuzian) reconstitution of the Marxist project stems from the crisis of utopia represented by the demise of 'actually existing socialism', marked in particular by the events that led to the collapse of the Soviet Union in 1989 (it should, however, be noted that for Deleuze and Guattari this crisis had its beginnings in 1968). Marxism is depicted by them as a set of axioms that governs the field that is capitalism, and so the crisis of utopia poses, as a matter of urgency, the question of the compliance of this field with the axioms that constitute Marxism. To know that capitalism in its current manifestation is congruent with the Marxist axiomatic resort has to be made to a higher-order principle that, necessarily, is not 'Marxist': this metatheoretical specification tells us in virtue of what conditions and principles *this* field (capitalism) is governed by *this* axiomatic (Marxism). Deleuze and Guattari provide this metatheoretical elaboration by resorting to a constitutive ontology of power and political practice. This ontology is influenced by Baruch Spinoza, Friedrich Nietzsche, and Henri Bergson more than Marx, which perhaps accounts for the charge that the authors of *Capitalism and Schizophrenia* are 'post-Marxist'.

Central for the authors of *Capitalism and Schizophrenia* is the delineation of the mode of production, which is of course a crucial notion for Marx, but the analysis of which had fallen somewhat into abeyance as a result of the emphasis on the commodity promoted by the Frankfurt School and cultural studies in recent decades. But Deleuze and Guattari give this notion a novel twist. First, they eschew dialectics, as a matter of philosophical exigency. As they see it, dialectics is a species of the logic of identity which collapses 'difference' into the rational 'same', and so inevitably ensues in a disavowal of multiplicity. Secondly, production is not simply understood by them in terms of such items as investment, manufacturing, business strategies, and so on. Instead, Deleuze and Guattari accord primacy to 'machinic processes', that is, the modes of organisation that link attractions, repulsions, expressions, and so on, which affect the human body. For Deleuze and Guattari the modes of production are therefore expressions of desire, so that it is desire which is truly productive; and the modes of production are merely the outcome of this ceaselessly generative desire. Desire has this generative primacy because it is desire, which is always social and collective, that makes the gun (say) into an instrument of war, or of hunting, or sport, and so forth (as the case may be).

The mode of production is on the same level as any other expressions of the modes of desire, and so for Deleuze and Guattari there is neither base nor superstructure in society, but only stratifications, that is, accumulations or concatenations of ordered functions which are expressions of desire. What enables each mode of production to be created is a specific amalgam of desires, forces and powers, and the mode (of production) emerges from this amalgam. In the process, traditional Marxist conceptions are reversed: it is not the mode that enables production to take place (the gist of these accounts); rather, it is desiring-production itself that makes the mode what it is. *Capitalism and Schizophrenia* is this ontology of desiring-production.

Marx maintained that it is necessary for society and the State to exist before surplus value is realised and capital can be accumulated. Deleuze and Guattari also say that it is the State which gives capital its 'models of realisation'. Before anything can be generated by capital, politics has to exist. The linkage between capital and politics is achieved by an apparatus that transcodes a particular space of accumulation. This transcoding provides a prior realisation or regulated expenditure of labour power and it is the function of the State to organise its members into a particular kind of productive force. Today capital has reached a stage beyond the one prevailing at Marx's time. Capital is now omnipresent, and links the most heterogeneous elements (commerce, religion, art, and so forth). Productive labour is inserted into every component of society. But precisely because capital is ubiquitous, and has a prior social cooperation as its enabling condition, it has its unavoidable limits. Capital needs this prior organisation of cooperation in order to succeed, and it follows from this that collective subjects have a potential power that capitalism itself cannot capture. The question of revolution is thus the question of finding a politics that will use this collective subjectivity so that the productive force of society is subjected to nothing but the desire of its members.

Connectives

Capitalism
Stratification

MARX + ANTONIO NEGRI

Alberto Toscano

Deleuze encountered the work of Antonio Negri and the tradition of Italian workerist Marxism (*operaismo*) via Guattari, who was personally involved with the free radio movement and other political initiatives in the Italy of the late 70s, and who met Negri when the latter was invited by Louis Althusser to lecture on Marx's Grundrisse at the École Normale Supérieure, in lectures later published as *Marx Beyond Marx*. During Negri's imprisonment, Deleuze came to his defence with a public letter. It has been Negri's great merit to emphasise the persistence of Marxist themes in the writings of Deleuze and Guattari, and to appropriate and recast a number of their concepts in his own attempt to transform the vocabulary of Marxism in light of new modes of political subjectivity, new regimes of capital accumulation and new strategies of command and control.

Whilst Deleuze and Guattari's influence can already be felt in Negri's texts of the 80s, it is most evident in *Empire* (with Michael Hardt), where notions of virtuality, deterritorialisation and smooth space feature prominently in the attempt to schematise the changes in the structures of sovereignty and the dynamics of resistance. The influence is by no means unilateral: already in *A Thousand Plateaus*, the work of the Italian communist thinker Mario Tronti and Negri's uptake of it is identified as an important precursor for an understanding of contemporary capitalism that acknowledges the paradoxical centrality of 'marginal' forms of subjectivity (students, women's domestic work, unemployment, etc.). Rather than speaking of influences, it might be preferable to consider the relationship of Deleuze (and Guattari) to Negri in terms of a significant overlap in what they regard as the key problems facing contemporary philosophical and political thought. Among the questions they share are the following: How can we be faithful to the legacy of Spinoza? What are the stakes of contemporary materialism? How can the thought of Marx be rescued from both structuralism and humanism? In what sense can contemporary capitalism be considered as both immanent and transcendent? How can we articulate new models of subjectivation in light of the critiques of Cartesian and Kantian images of the subject?

Deleuze and Negri repeatedly situate their work in terms of a continuation of Spinoza's ontology. Both locate in Spinoza a singular break with the philosophies of transcendence and legitimation, driven by the constitution of a thoroughgoing immanent philosophy. Where Deleuze's writings on Spinoza highlight the manner in which Spinoza's thought provides us with a practical and affirmative extension of Duns Scotus' thesis of univocity, Negri's *The Savage Anomaly*, taking into account the Spinozist studies of Deleuze, Macherey and Matheron points instead to the tensions opened up at the heart of Spinoza's ontology by the emergence of capitalism in seventeenth-century Holland and the formulation in Spinoza's political treatises of a notion of absolute democracy. Though their methodologies diverge, Deleuze preferring a far more internalist reading to Negri's heterodox historical materialist approach, both concur on the need to think the flattening of substance onto its modes, understood as fulcrums of force and composition laid out on a plane of immanence.

It is on the basis of a directly political understanding of ontology as inextricable from practice (whether as communist revolution or ethology) that Negri and Deleuze wish to extract a materialist lineage in the history of philosophy pitted against attempts to legislate over the contingency of being through various forms of representational thought. In this respect, both consider the critique of transcendence as an eminently political matter, linked to the liberation of forces capable of entering into composition without the aid of supplementary dimensions (e.g. sovereignty). Negri and Deleuze's concurrent attempts to move with and beyond Marx in an analysis of contemporary capitalism and political subjectivity can thus be grasped as passages from a transcendental or representational mode of thought to an immanent or constructivist one. Their research programmes converge on the notion of contemporary capital as a very particular admixture of immanence and transcendence, one no longer thinkable in terms of a dialectical totality. This is encapsulated in Deleuze by the concept of the axiomatic and in Negri by that of Empire. In both cases dialectical antagonism is transformed into a figure of conflict that sees forms of subjectivity irreducible to the figures of people or citizenry (i.e. collective assemblages of enunciation, the multitude) faced with a parasitical agency that seeks to capture, control and exploit them. It should be noted that Negri's abiding preoccupation with the Marxian concept of real subsumption and his refashioning of class struggle still differentiate his approach from the definition of capitalism as an axiomatic (which still requires models of realisation) and of resistance in terms of minority (which seems distant from the idea of class composition).

MATERIALISM

John Marks

Deleuze's work is undoubtedly materialist in orientation, but this materialism must be considered in the light of the vitalism and empiricism that also characterises this work. Deleuze draws inspiration for his materialism from a variety of sources, but Baruch Spinoza, Friedrich Nietzsche, Henri Bergson and Gottfried Wilhelm von Leibniz are all extremely important in this respect. Spinoza and Nietzsche challenge the devaluation of the body in favour of consciousness, and in this way propose a materialist reading of thought. They show that thought should no longer be constrained by the consciousness we have of it. Bergson and Leibniz – Deleuze is also influenced by the challenge to the matter-form model put forward by Gilbert Simondon – influence Deleuze in the way he develops a challenge to the hylomorphic model: the metaphysical doctrine that distinguishes between matter and form. In contrast to this, Deleuze claims that matter is in continuous variation, so that we should not think in terms of forms as moulds, but rather in terms of modulations that produce singularities. In *A Thousand Plateaus*, Deleuze and Guattari talk of destratified and deterritorialised 'mattermovement' and 'matter-energy'. Following Spinoza, they challenge the hierarchy of form and matter by conceiving of an immanent 'plane of consistency' on which everything is laid out. The elements of this plane are distinguishable only in terms of movement and velocity. Deleuze and Guattari also talk of the plane being populated by inifinite 'bits' of impalpable and anonymous matter that enter into varying connections. Deleuze's later work on Leibniz develops this theme, again emphasising that matter is not organised as a series of solid and discrete forms, but rather infinitely folded.

In order to grasp the originality of Deleuze's materialism it is necessary to understand what he means when he uses the terms 'machine' and 'machinic'. In his book on Michel Foucault, he speculates on the possibilities for new human forms opened up by the combination of the forces of carbon and silicon. However, this statement should not necessarily be read in terms of the human body being supplemented or altered by means of material prostheses. The sort of machine that Deleuze conceives of is an abstract phenomenon that does not depend entirely upon physical and mechanical modifications of matter. The machine is instead a function of what might be thought of as the 'vital' principle of this plane of consistency, which is that of making new connections, and in this way constructing what Deleuze calls 'machines'. Nor should Deleuze's machinic materialism be seen as a form of cybernetics, according to which the organic and the mechanical share a common *informational* language. The fact that cinema and painting are capable of acting directly upon the nervous system means that they function as analogical languages rather than digital codes. In common with the sort of materialism favoured by cybernetics and theories of artificial intelligence, Deleuze rejects the notion that there is brain behind the brain: an organising consciousness that harnesses and directs the power of the brain. He conceives of the human brain as merely one cerebral crystallisation amongst others: a cerebral fold in matter. Deleuze's particular formulation of materialism depends upon the counterintuitive Bergsonian notion that matter is already 'image': before it is perceived it is 'luminous' in itself; the brain is itself an image. However, he also eschews the reductive molecular materialism upon which artificial intelligence is based. According to such a reductive materialism, all processes and realities can be explained by reducing them down to the most basic components – atoms and molecules – from which they are constructed. Again, the fact that he insists that painting and film can act directly upon the nervous system to create new neural pathways indicates that he is not a reductive materialist.

Ultimately, Deleuze is unwilling to reduce all matter to a single stratum of syntax. Computer technology may well transform the world of the future, but it will not be by means of the development of a computational language that is common to the brain and the computer. It will instead be the result of computers expanding the possibilities for thought in new and perhaps unpredictable ways. In this manner, the brain and the computer will take part in the construction of an abstract machine. In his work on cinema, Deleuze develops the notion of the brain as a fold of the outside or a 'screen'. He considers, for example, Michelangelo Antonioni's films to be an exploration of the way in which the brain is connected to the world, and the necessity of exploring the potential of these connections. Antonioni draws a contrast between the worn-out body, weighed down by the past and modern neuroses, and a 'creative' brain, striving to create connections with the new world around it, and experiencing the potential amplification of its powers by 'artificial' brains. For Deleuze, thinking takes place when the brain as a stratum comes into contact with other strata. In summary, Deleuze thinks in terms of an *expressive* and *intensive* materialism as opposed to a *reductive* and *extensive* materialism.

Connectives

Foucault
Spinoza

MATERIALISM + PHILOSOPHY

Kenneth Surin

For Deleuze and Guattari, traditional philosophy has always functioned on the basis of codes that have effectively turned it into a bureaucracy of the consciousness. Traditional philosophy has never been able to abandon its origins in the codifications of the despotic imperial State. The task of philosophy now is to controvert this traditional philosophy in a way that can be revolutionary only if the new or next philosophy seeks to 'transmit something that does not and will not allow itself to be codified'. This 'transmission' will eschew the drama of interiority that traditional philosophy had perforce to invest in as a condition of being what it is, and will instead involve the creation of concepts that can register and delineate the transmission of forces to bodies, that is, it will be a physics of thought, the thinking of a pure exteriority, in the manner of Deleuze's two great precursors, Baruch Spinoza and Friedrich Nietzsche, and as such will be irreducibly materialist. For Deleuze and Guattari, philosophy that has left behind the codifications of the State will be about bodies and forces, and the concepts designed to bring these to thought. It will therefore have an essential relation to nonphilosophy as well, since it will be rooted in percepts and affects.

This materialism that is philosophy will bring something to life, it will extricate life from the places where it has been trapped, and it will create lines of flight from these stases. The creation of these lines of flight constitutes events and, as events, they are quite distant from the abstractions that constitute the staple diet of traditional philosophy. Deleuze is emphatic that abstractions explain nothing, but rather are themselves in need of explanation. So the new philosophy that will experiment with the real, will eschew such abstractions as universals, unities, subjects, objects, multiples, and put in their place the processes that culminate in the production of the abstractions in question. So in place of universals we have processes of universalisation; in place of subjects and objects we have subjectification and objectification; in place of unities we have unification; in place of the multiple we have multiplication; and so on. These processes take place on the plane of immanence, since experimentation can only take place immanently. In the end a concept is only a singularity ('a child', 'a thinker', 'a musician'), and philosophy is the task of arranging these into assemblages that constitute multiplicities. Deleuze once said that each plateau of *A Thousand Plateaus* was an example of such an assemblage. Philosophy is not so much a form of reflection as a kind of constructionism instituted on the plane of immanence.

At the same time, philosophy is not just a kind of physicalism, insisting on the substantiality of Being, that is set entirely apart from noology, which as an immaterialism insists on the primacy of thought, and in particular the image of thought. For Deleuze, the image of thought is a kind of prephilosophy, and thus is inextricably bound up with philosophy. The image of thought operates on the plane of immanence, and constitutes a prephilosophical presupposition that philosophy has to satisfy. The image of thought, even if it is an immaterialism, is not antithetical to a strict materialism. The plane of immanence reveals the 'unthought' in thought, and its absolute incompatibility with materialism only comes about when philosophers forget that thought and the constitution of matter have the fundamental ontological character of events, and instead identify 'matter' with Body, and 'thought' with Mind, in this way saddling themselves with an impasse that cannot be resolved because Mind and Body are said to possess mutually incompatible properties ('inert' vs 'active', 'material' vs 'spiritual', and so forth). The ontology of events, by contrast, allows the material and immaterial to be interrelated and integrated in a ceaseless dynamism. Thus, the event of 'a house being built' requires many material things to be given functions (windows let in light, doors protect privacy, stairs enable access, and so on), and these functions in turn involve (immaterial) concepts (unless one has the concept of stairs being able to provide access in this rather than that way, a ladder, lift or hoist could serve just effectively as stairs in enabling access to an upper floor). So concepts are returned to material things via functions, and things are integrated with concepts via functions, while functions are immaterial but can only be embodied in things even as they can only be expressed in concepts. All the time a radical immanence is preserved. For Deleuze the materialism of philosophy is compromised only when the immaterial is harnessed to the transcendent: without resort to the transcendent, immaterialism and materialism can be kept on the same plane – immanence – and made to interact productively.

MEMORY

Cliff Stagoll

Deleuze has little time for memory conceived as a means for summoning old perceptions. Such a model lacks creative potential and implies that an object, say, can be re-presented and re-cognised as the *same* one as that experienced in the past. But such a view ignores the fact that today's recollection is quite a different experience temporally and contextually from either the original experience or previous recollections. To theorise away such differences is to discount the productive potential that Deleuze considers inherent in the operation of memory in favour of tying oneself to the past.

Despite proclaiming his lack of enthusiasm for memory as a topic, Deleuze nonetheless reworked his conception of it several times. In early work on David Hume, Deleuze dealt with how the reproductive and representational effects of memory are critical to the fiction of personal identity because of their role in establishing relations of resemblance and causation. In his writings on Henri Bergson, though, and in his own philosophies of difference, Deleuze moved beyond such 'habit memory' to theorise how 'blocks of history' might be brought into productive associations with the present, such that the past might be lived anew and differently.

Deleuze's Bergsonian theories of consciousness outline two kinds of operation. One is the 'line of materiality', upon which he theorises relationships between the mind and the material world (including the body).

Such activity always occurs in the present, understood as a purely theoretical demarcation between past and future. On this line, our relationship with matter is wholly material and unmediated: the world of consciousness is reconciled with the world of matter by means of different kinds of movement. Such activity is always oriented towards the practical life of action rather than pure knowledge. As such, the form of memory at work is 'habit memory', reflex determination of appropriate bodily responses conditioned by whatever has proved useful in the past, but without 'pure recollection'.

Being distinct from consciousness, the line of materiality cannot account for the temporality of lived experience. Consequently, Deleuze invokes Bergson's theory of pure memory on a 'line of pure subjectivity'. Bergson believes that pure memory stores every conscious event in its particularity and detail. The perceptions of actual existence are duplicated in a virtual existence as images with the potential for becoming conscious, actual ones. Thus every lived moment is both actual and virtual, with perception on one side and memory on the other; an ever-growing mass of recollections.

Taking his lead from Bergson, Deleuze contends that the virtual is defined by its potential for becoming conscious. Rather than merely simulating the real (as in 'virtual reality' media), the virtual might be made actual and so have some consequent new effect. How this potential might be realised will be determined by the precise circumstances of its actualisation.

As a collection of purely *virtual* images, memory has no psychological existence, being instead a purely ontological 'past in general' that is preserved neither in time nor space. (As such, loss of memory ought not to be conceived as a loss of 'contents' from pure memory, but merely a breakdown of recall mechanisms.) The virtual images are arranged in various patterns that might be conceived as 'planes' or 'sheets', with every plane containing the totality of the experienced past distributed relative to some particular virtual image, the one from which all others on the plane derive their meaning and history.

Pure memory will be revealed to consciousness when the relevant virtual images are actualised, a matter rarely mentioned in Bergson's texts but central to Deleuze. Such actualisation is the process of recollection in which the virtual differentiates itself by becoming something new – a recalled memory image relevant to some action or circumstance – and thus assuming psychological significance. Deleuze's enigmatic description of the process has two parts. First, memory is accessed by means of a 'leap into the past', enabling the most relevant plane to be located. Second, memory is brought to presence and given a new 'life' or context in terms of current circumstances. In this moment, psychology interacts with ontology in the constitution of the lived present, a special kind of synthesis that Deleuze considers to be essential to the flow of lived time.

Two aspects of Deleuze's Bergsonian theory of memory are critical to his anti-foundationalism. First, it shows that one need not conceive of a transcendent subject 'owning' memory in order for recollection to occur. Indeed, Deleuze argues the opposite: memory helps to give rise to the impression of a consistent and unifying self. Second, it shows that memory, rather than merely redrawing the past, constitutes the past as a new present relative to present interests and circumstances. Thus conceived, memory is a creative power for producing the new rather than a mechanism for reproducing the same.

Connectives

Bergson
Virtual/Virtuality

MERLEAU-PONTY, MAURICE (1908–61) – refer to the entries on 'Foucault + fold' and 'phenomenology'.

MICROPOLITICS

Kenneth Surin

Deleuze and Guattari oppose micropolitics to the politics of molarisation. Where the molar (or 'arborescent', to use their equivalent term) designates structures and principles that are based on rigid stratifications or codings which leave no room for all that is flexible and contingent, the molecular which is the basis of micropolitics allows for connections that are local and singular. A molecular logic of production is basically self-organising or auto-poetic, whereas its molar counterpart finds its generating principle in some feature or entity that is external to what is being produced. The necessity of micropolitics for Deleuze and Guattari stems from the current conjuncture of capitalist production and accumulation. In this conjuncture, capital has become the ever-present condition that ensures the harmonisation of even the most disparate forms (business and finance, the arts, leisure, and so forth). This is the age that Deleuze titles 'the societies of control' and it contrasts with the disciplinary societies of the nineteenth and early twentieth centuries. In this conjuncture, the scope of labour has been amplified exponentially, as capital permeates every interstice of society: the ubiquity of capital coincides with the expansion of everything capable of creating surplus-value, as human consciousness and all that was hitherto considered 'private' is relentlessly incorporated into the latest structures of accumulation. Capitalism has always had as its 'utopia' the capacity to function without the State and in the current conjuncture this disposition has become more profoundly entrenched. On the other hand, for Deleuze and Guattari this is not because State apparatuses have disappeared (clearly they have not); rather the rigid demarcation between State and society is no longer tenable. Society and State now constitute one allencompassing reality, and all capital has become social capital. Hence, the generation of social cooperation, undertaken primarily by the service and informational industries in the advanced economies, has become a crucial one for capitalism.

In a situation of this kind, a molar politics with its emphasis on standardisation and homogeneity becomes increasingly irrelevant, as the traditional dividing line between 'right' and 'left' in politics becomes blurred, and such notions as 'the radical centre' gain credence despite being patently oxymoronic; and as traditional class affiliations dissolve and the social division of labour is radically transformed by the emergence of information and service industries. The enabling conditions of micropolitics derive from this set of developments. The upshot is that the orchestration of affect and desire has now become much more significant for determining lines of affiliation in contemporary politics.

The orchestration of desire in micropolitics will have an oscillating logic, as the desire constrained by the orders of capital is deterritorialised, so that it becomes a desire exterior to capital, and is then reterritorialised or folded back into the social field. When this happens the liberated desire integrates into itself the flows and components of the Socius or social field to form a 'desiring machine'. The heart of micropolitics is the construction of these new desiring machines as well as the creation of new linkages between desiring machines: without a politics to facilitate this construction there can be no productive desire, only the endless repetition of the non-different, as what is repeated is regulated by logics of identity, equivalence and intersubstitutability (this being the underlying logic of the commodity principle as analysed by Karl Marx). In micropolitics the fate of repeating a difference that is only an apparent difference is avoided, and capitalism's negative, wasteful and ultimately non-productive repetition, a repetition of nonbeing, is supplanted by the polytopia of a micropolitics that brings together the strata of minorities, becomings, incorporealities, concepts, 'peoples', in this way launching a thought and practice capable of expressing and instantiating a desire to undo the prevailing world order.

Micropolitics, therefore, creates an 'ethos of permanent becomingrevolutionary', an ethos not constrained by a politics predicated on the now defunct forms of Soviet bureaucratic socialism and a liberal or social democracy. In this ethos, our criteria of belonging and affiliation will always be subject to a kind of chaotic motion, and a new political knowledge is created which dissipates the enabling lie told us by those who now have political power, with their love for nation-states, tribes, clans, political parties, churches, and perhaps everything done up to now in the name of community. At the same time, this ethos will create new collective solidarities not based on these old 'loves'.

Connectives

Affect
Becoming
Control society
Desire
Foucault
Molar
Molecular
Socius

MINORITARIAN

Verena Conley

'Minoritarian' is often used in relation to postcolonial theory and the concept of minor literature. The term is developed in connection with language and the 'order-word', that is, a pass-word that both compels obedience and opens passages. In this sense Deleuze argues that language, because it deals with the art of the possible, is fundamentally political. The scientific undertaking of extracting constants is always coupled with the political enterprise of social control that works by imposing them on speakers and transmitting order-words. In order to cope with this condition Deleuze states that we need to distinguish between a major and minor language, that is, between a power (*pouvoir*) of constants and a power (*puissance*) of variables. In the political sphere where a 'major' language is seen and heard, there also inheres in its form a 'minor' element that does not exist independently or outside of its expression and statements.

The more a language has or acquires the characteristics of a major form, the more likely it is to be affected by continuous variations that can transpose it into a minor language. A language always has internal minorities. No homogeneous system remains unaffected by immanent processes of variation. Constants do not exist side by side with variables; they are drawn from the variables themselves. Major and minor are two different usages of the same language. A minor language opens a passage in the order-word that constitutes any of the operative redundancies of the major language. The problem is not the distinction between major and minor language but one of becoming. A person (a subject, but also a creative and active individual) has to deterritorialise the major language rather than reterritorialise herself within an inherited dialect. Recourse to a minor language puts the major language into flight. Minoritarian authors are those who are foreigners in their own tongue.

A minority is not defined by the paucity of its numbers but by its capacity to become or, in its subjective geography, to draw for itself lines of fluctuation that open up a gap and separate it from the axiom constituting a redundant majority. A majority is linked to a state of power and domination. What defines majorities and minorities are the relations internal to number. For the majority, this relation constitutes a set that is denumerable. The minority is nodenumerable, but it may have many elements. The non-denumerable is characterised by the presence of connections, that is, the additive conjunction 'and' or the mathematical sign '+': a minoritarian language is 'x +y and b + traits a + a and . . .'. It is produced between sets and belongs to neither. It eludes them and constitutes a line of flight. In mathematical terms Deleuze remarks that the axiomatic world of the majority manipulates only denumerable sets. Minorities, by contrast, constitute non-axiomatic (or axiomisable) sets, that is, masses or multiplicities of escape and flux. The majority assumes a standard measure, represented by the integral integer, say, an armed white male or those acting like one. Domination always translates into hegemony. A determination that differs from the constant is considered minoritarian. Majority is an abstract standard that can be said to include no one and thus speak in the name of nobody. A minority is a deviation from the model or a becoming of everybody (*tout le monde*). The majoritarian mode is a constant while its minoritarian counterpart is a subsystem. Minoritarian is seen as potential (*puissance*), creative and in becoming. Blacks, Jews, Arabs or women can only create by making possible a becoming, but never through ownership. Deleuze states clearly that a majority is never a becoming.

Deleuze observes that our age is becoming the age of minorities. Minorities are defined not by number but by becoming and by their lines of fluctuation. Minorities are objectively definable states. One can also think of them as seeds of becoming whose value is to trigger uncontrollable fluctuations and deterritorialisations. A minor language is a major language in the process of becoming minor, and a minority a majority in the process of change. Becoming, as Deleuze states time and again in his work on politics, literature and the arts, is creation. It is the becoming of everybody. In the process of becoming minor, the figure of death (nobody) gives way to life (everybody).

Connectives

Becoming
Deterritorialisation
Majoritarian
Order-word
Power

MINORITARIAN + CINEMA

Constantine Verevis

In *Cinema 2: The time-image*, Deleuze invokes his writing (with Guattari) on Franz Kafka and minor literatures to describe a 'minor cinema' – founded in the Third World and its minorities – that connects immediately to the question of politics. Such a (modern) political cinema is characterised (and opposed to classical cinema) in three ways. First, a minor cinema does not represent (or address) an oppressed and subjected people, but rather anticipates a people yet to be created, a consciousness to be brought into existence. Second, a minor cinema does not maintain a boundary between the private and the public, but rather crosses borders, merging the personal with the social to make it immediately political. And third, recognising that the people exist only in the condition of a minority, political cinema does not identify a new union (a singularity), but rather creates (and recreates) a multiplicity of conditions. Deleuze describes this minor cinema as one that sets out, not to represent the conditions of an oppressed minority, but rather to invent new values and facilitate the creation of a people who have hitherto been missing. Like Kafka's minor literature, a minor cinema is interested neither in representation or interpretation, but in experimentation: it is a creative act of becoming.

Deleuze relates his account of minoritarian cinema to the work of Third World filmmakers (Lino Brocka, Glauber Rocha, Chahine Nasserism) and in doing so implicitly recalls the notion of 'Third Cinema', advanced by Latin American filmmakers in the late 1960s. In their founding manifesto – *Towards a Third Cinema* – Fernando Solanas and Octavio Getino called for a cinema that was militant in its politics and experimental in its approach. The manifesto described 'First Cinema' – the so-called imperial cinema of big capital – as an objective and representational cinema. 'Second Cinema' – the authorial cinema of the petty bourgeoisie – was described as a subjective and symbolic cinema. By contrast, 'Third Cinema' – a political or minoritarian cinema – was an attitude, one concerned neither with representation (a being-whole) nor subjectification (a being-one), but with life-experimentation – the creation and exhibition of local difference. In later writing, Solanas explained that Third Cinema, though initially adapted to conditions prevailing in Latin America, could not be limited to that continent, nor even to the Third World, nor even to a particular category of cultural objects, but rather constituted a kind of virtual geography and conditional objecthood. For Solanas, Third Cinema (as opposed to Third World cinema) was broadly concerned with the expression of new cultures and of social change: Third Cinema is 'an open category, unfinished, and incomplete'.

Third Cinema – minor cinema – is a research category, one that recognises the contingency and multiplicity – the hybridity – of all cultural objects. Paul Willemen, in 'The Third Cinema Question', explains that practitioners of Third Cinema refused to oppose essentialist notions of 'national identity and cultural authenticity' to the values of imperial powers, but rather recognised the multiplicity or 'many-layeredness of their own cultural-historical formations'. That is, a minor cinema (a national cinema) is not singular, but shaped by complex and multiple connections established between local and international forces and conditions. A film such as Tran Anh Hung's *Cyclo* (France–Vietnam, 1995) understands this type of approach. On the one hand, the local (or intranational) multi-layeredness of *Cyclo* is evident in its use of various regional dialects: for instance, the cyclo-driver of the film's title and his sister speak in the vernacular of the North and of the South of Vietnam. On the other hand, the hybridisation of global (or international) forces is evident in the film's use of music (Tranh Lam, Radiohead, Rollins Band) and its expressive vocabulary, one that draws upon influences as diverse as *The Bicycle Thief* (Vittorio De Sica, 1948), *Taxi Driver* (Martin Scorsese, 1976), and *Himatsuri* (Mitsuo Yanagimatchi, 1985).

As in the minor use of language, minoritarian cinema ceases to be representational and moves instead towards its limits. This is evident in *Cyclo*, where the beginning of the film, situated in the streets of neorealism, and in the daily toil and routine of a cyclo driver, soon takes the viewer – through its wayward and *itinerant* movements – in unpredictable and even dangerous directions. The focus of this movement is on becoming, on relations, on what happens between: between actions, between affections, between perceptions. For Deleuze, a minor cinema is situated in a logic and an aesthetics of the 'and'. It is a creative stammering (and . . . and . . . and), a minoritarian use of language that the French- Vietnamese Tran would share with Deleuze's favoured examples (Kafka, Samuel Beckett, Jean-Luc Godard). *Cyclo* can be approached as a kind of living reality, a type of creative understanding between colours, between people, between cinemas – between the red (of the poet) *and* the blue (of the cyclo) *and* the yellow (of the fish-boy); between the First, and the Second, and the Third.

MINORITARIAN + LITERATURE

Ronald Bogue

In a 1912 diary entry, Kafka reflects on the advantages Czech and Yiddish writers enjoy as contributors to minor literatures, in which no towering figures dominate and the life of letters is consumed with collective social and political concerns. Deleuze and Guattari argue that Kafka's characterisation of minor literatures actually maps Kafka's own conception of literature's proper function and guides his practice as a Prague Jew writing in German. The essence of Kafka's minor literature Deleuze and Guattari find in three features: 'the deterritorialization of language, the connection of the individual to a political immediacy, and the collective assemblage of enunciation' (D&G 1986: 18). Kafka discovers in Prague German the instabilities of a deracinated government language subtly deformed through Czech usage, and in his writings he further destabilises that already deterritorialised German in an ascetic impoverishment of diction and syntax. Throughout his stories and novels Kafka directly links psychological and family conflicts to extended social and political relations. And though he necessarily writes as a solitary individual, he treats language as a collective assemblage of enunciation and thereby attempts to articulate the voice of a people to come (since a positive, functioning collectivity is precisely what Kafka finds lacking).

In the concept of minor literature Deleuze and Guattari connect the political struggles of minorities to the formal experimentations typical of the modernist avant-garde. What makes possible this rapprochement of politics and formal innovation is Deleuze and Guattari's view of language as a mode of action in continuous variation. Every language imposes power relations through its grammatical and syntactic regularities, its lexical and semantic codes, yet those relations are inherently unstable, for linguistic constants and invariants are merely enforced restrictions of speech-acts that in fact are in perpetual variation. A major usage of a language limits, organises, controls and regulates linguistic materials in support of a dominant social order, whereas a minor usage of a language induces disequilibrium in its components, taking advantage of the potential for diverse and divergent discursive practices already present within the language.

A minor literature, then, is not necessarily one written in the language of an oppressed minority, and it is not exclusively the literature of a minority engaged in the deformation of the language of a majority. Every language, whether dominant or marginalised, is open to a major or a minor usage, and whatever its linguistic medium, minor literature is defined by a minor treatment of the variables of language. Nor is minor literature simply literature written by minorities. What constitutes minorities is not their statistical number, which may in actuality be greater than that of the majority, but their position within asymmetrical power relationships that are reinforced by and implemented through linguistic codes and binary oppositions. Western white male adult humans may be outnumbered worldwide, but they remain the majority through their position of privilege, and that privilege informs the linguistic oppositions that define, situate and help control non-western and non-white populations, women, children and non-human life forms. Minorities merely reinforce dominant power relations when they accept the categories that define them. Only by undoing such oppositions as western/non-western, white/non-white, male/female, adult/child, or human/animal can minorities change power relations. Only by becoming 'other', by passing between the poles of binary oppositions and blurring clear categories can new possibilities for social interaction be created. Such a process of becoming other is central to minor literature and its minor usage of language and this minor becoming other is that which turns a dominated minority into an active force of transformation. Hence, minor literature is less a product than a process of becoming minor, through which language is deterritorialised immediately social and political issues are engaged, and a collective assemblage of enunciation makes possible the invention of a people to come.

MINORITARIAN + MUSIC

Marcel Swiboda

African-American and Afro-Caribbean cultures, under certain circumstances, constitute instances of 'minor' culture, and in both cases there have been a substantial number of cultural formations that one could describe as being 'minoritarian'. Among these one might number the following: blues, jazz (traditional, be-bop, electric, free, avant-garde), P-funk, techno, hiphop, all largely developed as part of African-American culture; and ska, roots, reggae and dub, all largely developed as part of Afro-Caribbean culture. They constitute instances of minor culture 'under certain circumstances' because their historical development is complex and one cannot locate every development exclusively within minoritarian instances. Sometimes the creative and transformative potential of these formations gives way to the pressures of capitalism or of appropriation as part of the dominant (usually white) cultural formations, pressures which often collectively conspire to exploit or limit this potential. To the extent that any of these cultural developments can be said to constitute instances of the 'minor', it is largely owing to the following reasons.

Where it is a question of language, the various musical developments listed above are subject to linguistic mediation as part of a language that reinforces dominant culture. In each and every case, this language is English. In order to develop a minor use of this language, minor cultural formations, such as those of Black America, the Caribbean or South London, have all had to find ways of altering or recombining elements from the dominant language in order to render them sonorous, as a means to foregrounding their transformative potential. That is to say that minor cultural formations have had to deterritorialise the English language. This indeed is the first characteristic of a minor cultural formation. For example, consider the work of the African-American writer activist Amiri Baraka and his use of the English language. His writing distorts and exposes the normative, exploitative operations of the dominant language through the way in which he recombines its elements, structured according to an aesthetic derived from jazz music. Alternatively, consider the work of the Jamaican-British dub poet, Linton Kwesi Johnson, combining elements from Jamaican Creole and British English in the production of an oral poetry performed over dub music. When written, his poetry deploys portmanteau combinations of words or parts of words in order to politicise the language. In both these instances, the majoritarian, dominant use of the English language is rendered minor in relation to the musics of the writers' respective cultural milieus, and in each case the language becomes musical, or sonorous in its expressions. Consider the title of Linton Kwesi Johnson's poem *Mi Revalueshanary Fren* (Linton Kwesi Johnson, *Mi Revalueshanary Fren: Selected Poems*), written as it is performed with the word 'revolutionary' phonetically rendered in Creole-English as 'revalueshanary' and thereby connoting not only revolution, but also re-evaluation. The manipulation of the relation between the *sound* of the word and its written inscription is purposely developed to challenge the alienation of ethnic groups as embodied in a dominant language, and to address the specific concerns of these groups in ways that provoke or challenge the oppression expressed in the language's dominating operations. This is minor culture's political function.

The third and final criterion for assessing how these musically-derived or oriented cultural formations become minor is the extent to which they move beyond the positions of individual subjects or persons towards collective utterance or enunciation. In order to examine this aspect, it is necessary to recall that – for Deleuze and Guattari – enunciation functions collectively in relation to a machinic assemblage of bodies, both human and non-human, for example geological or technological bodies. What all these different bodies have in common is that they operate through the inscription of surfaces: the layers of rock beneath the surface of the earth, the skin and its markings, the striation of the muscles, or the grooves of a record . . . Consider early hiphop culture or 'wildstyle', and its characteristics such as 'bombing' (graffiti) or the isolation of a musical passage ('break' or 'breakdown') by scratching vinyl records, or even the bodies of breakdancers whose moves are only legible in relation to the surfaces on which they dance. These inscriptions and their interacting surfaces at least partially constitute the machinic assemblage of early hiphop. To the extent that these bodies produce utterances or enunciations it is via the MC whose rappin' skills ostensibly mark her out as an individual, and yet their function remains completely tied into the hiphop *collective*, comprising all the other aspects of the hiphop assemblage. Furthermore, rappin' provides another instance of a strategic or minor deployment of the (American) English language as part of an urban cultural formation.

MINORITARIAN + REVOLUTION

Janell Watson

Deleuze and Guattari were deeply marked by the events of May 1968, and made frequent references back to Lenin and the Bolshevik revolution, but always with an eye to possible revolutions to come. Today it is becoming increasingly plausible that, as they intuited, future revolutions will arise out of the world's marginalised minorities rather than out of class struggle (D&G 1987: 469-73). Guattari, as political activist, was sympathetic to minority nationalitarian movements, including those of the Palestinians, Armenians, Basques, Irish, Corsicans, Lithuanians, Uyghurs, Roma, Indians, and Aboriginal Australians, and he supported homosexual and women's movements; whilst Deleuze wrote several supportive articles about the Palestinian cause.

However, despite the history of revolutionary movements evoked in *Capitalism and Schizophrenia* (the Bolsheviks in 1917, French students in 1968, minorities today), according to Deleuze and Guattari, revolution itself is not historical, nor are the minoritarian groups which incite them. Paradoxically, history is made only by those who oppose history. Revolution is untimely, in Nietzsche's sense (D&G 1987: 292-6). Minorities lie outside of history because they operate at the margins of the state, which excludes them. To explain in Deleuzo-Guattarian terms, revolution is a-historical because it is a molecular minoritarian becoming, whereas history is a molar majoritarian state apparatus. Minority and revolution are both becomings. Unlike the more static concepts of being or identity, becoming emphasises transformation on the molecular level. Deleuze has described May 1968 as a becoming (D 1995: 171-2). Revolutions entail becoming because revolution is by nature molecular, as reflected in the title of Guattari's book *Molecular Revolution*.

This outsider relation to history is one of many similarities between Deleuze and Guattari's minorities and their nomads, who simply have no history (D&G 1987: 393-4). Like the nomads who also operate in opposition to the State, minorities are undenumerable multiplicities which are capable of following lines of flight and of forming war machines. Although Deleuze and Guattari do not explicitly say so, minorities could be understood as the nomads of the current epoch, the global capitalist counterpart to the ancient nomadic peoples in the time of the Roman Empire. One difference between the ancient and current periods would be their respective forms of territoriality: according to *A Thousand Plateaus*, territories organised into empires dominated in the earlier era, while radically deterritorialised capital dominates now. Whereas the term nomad originally designated a particular way of occupying territory, the term minority derives from mathematics. This distinction blurs with Deleuze and Guattari's peculiar adaptations of the two terms, since they associate nomads with a way of counting, and in their usage minority does not refer to a quantity but to a relation to power. However, the concept of minority is much better suited to the deterritorialised capitalist landscape because it is much less tied to a territorial context. Sedentary, the opposite of nomadic, hardly applies to the most powerful state formations today, whereas majority, the opposite of minority, does apply to capitalist states.

Deleuze and Guattari championed minorities not only in the political sphere, but also within philosophy and science, repeatedly arguing that all creativity and mutation necessarily come from a minoritarian position. They claim that revolutionary innovation always comes from nomad or minor science rather than from state science. Nomad thought aligns itself with a singular race, a specific minority, unlike classical thought that posits a universal subject (D&G 1987: 361-9). Deleuze associates philosophy itself with a 'revolutionary becoming' which, he says, has nothing to do with historical revolutions, although philosophy is always profoundly interconnected with the geopolitics of its time (D 2006: 379). Deleuze and Guattari locate thought between territory and the earth, as evidenced by Greek philosophy's relation to the city and modern philosophy's relation to capitalism – the city and capitalism understood as two different configurations of territory in relation to the earth. They recount a history of philosophy marked by nationalitarianisms: there are English, French, German philosophies. Whereas nationalism excludes based on a single criterion (such as race, ethnicity, or language) and legitimates itself by claims based on linear history, nationalitarianism fosters complex heterogeneous subjectivities and opposes the standardization imposed by capitalism and the state (G 1986 55-70). Philosophy is nationalitarian because even though it thrives only amidst deterritorialisation and even though philosophers are always strangers or immigrants, philosophical concepts always belong to a territory. Art and philosophy summon a minor race. Philosophy takes capitalist territorialisation to the absolute, pushing toward revolution defined as an absolute deterritorialisation which calls forth a new earth and a new people. This new people and new earth will not come from democracies, which are majorities (D&G 1994: 85-113).

Unfortunately, it is not enough to become minoritarian to launch a revolution. Although revolution is by definition minoritarian, minoritarian logic is not necessarily revolutionary. Races are always minoritarian by definition (Deleuze and Guattari insist there is no dominant race), but race can always morph into racism, fascism, or microfascism, which also operate on a molecular level (D&G 1987: 379, 214-15). The state cannot function without its outside, without its minorities, despite their constant exertion of potentially revolutionary resistance. Capitalism is particularly adept at capturing whatever is unleashed by the revolutionary creativity of minorities.

MOLAR

Tom Conley

The adjective 'molar' belongs to a chemical idiolect that Deleuze uses to inform his work on aesthetics and politics. In a strict sense things molar relate to aggregates of matter and not to either their molecular or atomic properties, or their motion. In a geological sense, 'molar' is understood to be what pertains to mass, ground, continence or telluric substance. It also pertains to the general patterns of behaviour taken by an organ or an organism, and thus the term can describe a trait of personality or the character of the ego. Deleuze tends to jettison the psychological inflections in order to correlate molarity with his different ways of describing the world; this is especially the case in his treatment of 'wholes' (*Tout* and *touts*) that he describes as being composed of a compact and firm terrestrial oceanic mass. A molar form can either rise up and command a great deal of earthly space or be seen either afloat or drifting in great bodies of water (a point developed in a very early piece of writing called 'Causes and Reasons of the Desert Island').

Broadening the biological definitions to include philosophy, geology and aesthetics, Deleuze conceives landscapes as masses of greater or lesser molarity. He draws Lucretian and pre-Socratic philosophy through the human sciences and into an aesthetic domain such that he can detect difference, vibration, disaggregation, deterritorialisation and metamorphosis in terms of molecular activities taking place in and about molar masses. The term assists him in studying *perception* in its range from 'macro' or totalising process to 'micro' or keen detection of infinitesimal differences in the physical and biological world.

In his work on cinema, the dyad of molar/molecular is used to discern effects of convection and atmosphere. When contrasting the four great schools of montage – American, French, German, Soviet – that grew in the first thirty years of cinema, he notes that the signature of poetic realism in directors ranging from René Clair to Jean Vigo and Jean Renoir is marked by emphasising the 'molar' (and not moral) aspect of the physical world: social contradiction is conveyed through imposing and massive monuments of Paris that humble the lost citizens in *The Crazy Ray* (1924); in Vigo's *L'Atalante* (1934) the cobblestone streets on the edges of the Seine make obdurate and unyielding stone the antithesis of fluidity; the inert piles of old editions and lithographs cluttering the walls in the bookseller's apartment in *Boudu Saved from Drowning* (1932) attest to a molarity against and with which atmosphere – fog, drizzle, mist – defines a general mood or state of things in the time of the Great Depression.

In *A Thousand Plateaus* Deleuze and Guattari apply the 'molar' and 'molecular' to political bodies. Molar entities belong to the State or the civic world. They are well defined, often massive, and are affiliated with a governing apparatus. Their molecular counterparts are micro-entities, politics that transpire in areas where they are rarely perceived: in the perception of affectivity, where beings share ineffable sensations; in the twists and turns of conversation having nothing to do with the state of the world at large; in the manner, too, that a pedestrian in a city park sees how the leaves of a linden tree might flicker in the afternoon light. The shifting to and from molar and molecular forms can be associated not only with deterritorialisation but also the very substance and effect of *events* that begin and end with swarms and masses of micro-perceptions.

Molecules often aggregate and swarm into active masses of molar aspect and vice versa. In *The Fold* Deleuze suggests that *events*, the very product of philosophy and determining features of perception, depend on the prehension of the textures of elements in terms of their wholes and the parts that swirl and toss within them or on their very surfaces. The process entails grasping a 'chaosmos' that becomes discernible through the categories of the molar and molecular. Deleuze is in turn enabled to study matter as a function of mass, hardness, and of 'coherence, cohesion' (D 1993a: 6). He projects the distinction onto the body in so far as it can be appreciated in its elasticity and fluidity. Thus, with the 'molar' the philosopher correlates surfaces with structures, masses with territories, and vibrations or waves with landscapes.

Connectives

Body
Deterritorialisation/Reterritorialisation
Event
Molecular

MOLECULAR

Tom Conley

Deleuze pairs the adjective 'molecular' with 'molar'. Informed by atomistic philosophy and biology that runs from Lucretius to Gabriel Tarde, Deleuze studies objects not as they seem to be before the naked eye but as dynamic masses of molecules. The chemical definition is broadened to include subjectivity. In a psychoanalytical sense molecularity relates to individual (as opposed to collective) responses to phenomena or types of behaviour. Hence any perceived object, organic or inorganic, has a life of its own and is felt through the tension of its moral mass and molecular parts and pieces. Deleuze uses molecularity to counter the orthogonal and massive pensive – seemingly heavy and unwieldy – system of Cartesian philosophy to arrive, by way of Leibniz, at a sensibility touching on the chemical animism of all things, 'the action of fire, those of waters and winds on the earth,' in various systems 'of complex interactions' (D 1993a: 9).

Molecular action becomes a vital element in what Deleuze uses to describe the processes of things and of creation. At a decisive moment in his presentation of Bergson's theses on movement in relation to cinema, Deleuze uses molecularity to illustrate how wholes (worlds or spatial aggregates) are related to duration. When a teaspoon of sugar is dissolved in a glass of water the 'whole' is *not* the container and its contents but the action of creation taking place in the ionisation of the molecules of sugar, a sort of 'pure ceaseless becoming which passes through states' (D 1986: 10). Molecularity goes with the perception of wholes (such as molar masses) that are open and disperse themselves in a continuum of duration. Surely the most compelling correlative to the Bergsonian thesis, not mentioned in either of the books on cinema, is the sequence in Jean-Luc Godard's *2 or 3 Things I Know About Her* (1965), a film in which a man in a Parisian café, in the midst of the clatter of porcelain and glasses striking the zinc surface of the bar in the background, contemplates a cup of coffee. He drops a cube of sugar into the brown liquid, stirs it with a teaspoon, and watches. In an extreme close-up galaxies seem to grow from the swirl of bubbles just as Godard's own voice-off speaks in the name of the man's thoughts about the end of the world and time. Before a puff of cigarette smoke wafts over the cup, an endless moment of pure duration is felt in the sight of a cosmos becoming molecular.

The molecular sensibility is found in Deleuze's appreciation of microscopic things, in the tiny perceptions or inclinations that destabilise perception as a whole. They function, he says, to 'pulverize the world' and, in the same blow, 'to spiritualize dust' (D 1993a: 87). The microscopic perspective has a political dimension as well. All societies are rent through by molar and molecular segmentarities. They are interrelated to the degree that all action is conceivably political if politics are understood to be of both molar and molecular orders. The former, a governmental superstructure, does not disallow the presence of the latter, 'a whole world of unconscious micropercepts, unconscious affects, rarefied divisions' that operate differently from civic and political arenas. Molecularity is tied to a 'micropolitics' of perception, affect, and even errant conversation (D&G 1987: 220).

The molecular enables Deleuze to move from philosophy of relation (or difference and repetition) to chemistries of being, and then on to delicate issues of perception in cinema, music, literature and painting. As in the dyad of the 'root' and the 'rhizome', that of molar and molecular forms bears no privileged term. In Deleuze's reading of subjectivation and predication in Leibniz, both terms are in and of each other. Each is used heuristically to test and to determine sensation beyond and within the limits of perception and cognition. The molecular attests to a creative process at work in Deleuze's concepts, and it also indicates the manner in which he uses concepts in the context of philosophy, science and aesthetics.

Connectives

Deterritorialisation/Reterritorialisation
Leibniz
Molar
Rhizome
Sensation

MOVEMENT-IMAGE

Tom Conley

The movement-image is the title of the first panel of a historical diptych, *Cinema 1* and *Cinema 2*, that classifies modes of perception and production of film from its beginnings in 1895 up to 1985. In this work and its complement, *The Time Image*, Deleuze uses cinema to show how philosophy is not constrained to a canon or an academic world but to life at large. Cinema is a surface on which viewers reflect their thinking, and in itself it is a medium or a machine that thinks with autonomy with respect to its viewers and creators. The movement-image defines and describes the quality of cinematic images that prevail in the medium over its first fifty years. From 1895 to 1945 cinema became the seventh art by embodying images not in movement but *as* movement. Motion was at that time the essence of cinema. By way of Henri Bergson Deleuze shows that cinema does not furnish the spectator with 'an image to which it adds movement', but rather, 'it immediately gives us a movement-image' (D 1986: 2). A cut between two shots is part of the image, and thus a temporal gap that allows the eye to perceive an effect of movement. The latter is gained by a succession not of static photographic poses but of 'instants of any kind whatsoever' (D 1986: 7–8), that is, of instants equidistant from one another. The event of the moving image thus owes to a 'distribution of the points of a space or of the moments of an event,' a moment seen as a 'translation in space' (D 1986: 7–8). The two components of the movement-image are found in what happens *between* parts or objects, and in what expresses the duration of a whole or a sum, that which might be indeed the world in the field of the image.

The cinema most characteristic of the movement-image is based on action and its intervals. It is seen in the comedies of Charlie Chaplin and Buster Keaton, to be sure, but also in the molecular agitation of wind, dust or smoke in the films of Louis Lumière.Movement-images tend to attach to the sensori-motor reflexes of the viewer who is drawn to them. The movement-image is made of moments in a given whole, such as a single shot or a *plan-séquence*, and it can be felt in the panoramic or tracking shots that confer motion upon the field of the image.

At a crucial point in his treatment Deleuze delineates and redefines three kinds of movement-images that renew and energise the traditional lexicon of cinema. The 'action-image', generally a medium shot or a *plan américain*, organises and distributes movement in space and time. Characterised by a hold-up or a heist, it abounds in *film noir*. The 'perception-image', often a long shot and a long take, conveys a 'drama of the visible and invisible' within the staging of action. The spectator perceives the origins and limits of visibility in images that are common to the classical western. The 'affection-image' is best seen in close-ups in which faces tend to occupy the greater area of the screen. Each of these types of movement-image constitutes 'a point of view on the Whole of the film, a way of grasping this whole, which becomes affective in the close-up, active in the medium shot, and perceptive in the long shot' (D 1986: 70). Other types of images that he takes up – the memory-image, the mental-image, the relation-image – derive from these three principal categories.

The movement-image reaches the end of its tenure at the time of World War II, concludes Deleuze, for five reasons. It no longer refers to a totalising or synthetic situation, but a dispersive one. Characters begin to multiply and become interchangeable. It loses its definition as either action, affection or perception when it cannot be affiliated with a genre. An art of wandering – the camera seems to move on its own – replaces the storyline, and plots become saturated with clichés. Finally, narratives are driven by a need to denounce conspiracy. Reality itself becomes 'lacunary and dispersive'. At this point, generally at the end of World War II, the time-image begins to mark cinema. Yet, as in most of Deleuze's dyads, the one term is always a function of the other that is tied to it. Movement-images tend to be the substance of narrative cinema while time-images are especially evident in experimental film. A study of genres and styles could be based on the relation of movement and time and the types of images that define their traits and qualities.

Connectives

Cinema
Faciality
Time-image

MULTIPLICITY

Jonathan Roffe

'Multiplicity' is arguably Deleuze's most important concept. It is found throughout his work, and is the basis for other important concepts such as rhizome, assemblage, and 'concept' itself. It is also one of Deleuze's most difficult concepts to grasp because of the many different ways and contexts in which he puts it to work. Yet, there are some essential traits to be noted.

A multiplicity is, in the most basic sense, a complex structure that does not reference a prior unity. Multiplicities are not parts of a greater whole that have been fragmented, and they cannot be considered manifold expressions of a single concept or transcendent unity. On these grounds, Deleuze opposes the dyad One/Many, in all of its forms, with multiplicity. Further, he insists that the crucial point is to consider multiplicity in its substantive form – a multiplicity – rather than as an adjective – as multiplicity of something. Everything for Deleuze is a multiplicity in this fashion.

The two people whom Deleuze regularly associates with the development of the concept of multiplicity are the mathematician Georg Riemann, and the French philosopher Henri Bergson. From Riemann, Deleuze takes the idea that any situation is composed of different multiplicities that form a kind of patchwork or ensemble without becoming a totality or whole. For example, a house is a patchwork of concrete structures and habits. Even though we can list these things, there is finally no way of determining what the essence of a particular house is, because we cannot point to anything outside of the house itself to explain or to sum it up – it is simply a patchwork. This can also be taken as a good description of multiplicities themselves.

Deleuze's debt to Bergson here is more profound. It is in *Bergsonism* (1966) that Deleuze first discusses multiplicity, which receives an extended elaboration in Bergson's philosophy. Deleuze notes first of all that there are two kinds of multiplicity in Bergson: extensive numerical multiplicities and continuous intensive multiplicities. The first of these characterises space for Bergson; and the second, time. The difference between extensive and intensive is perhaps the most important point here. In contrast to space, which can be divided up into parts (this is why it is called numerical), intensive multiplicity cannot be divided up without changing in nature. In other words, any alteration to an intensive multiplicity means a total change in its nature – a change in its intensive state. This is important for Deleuze because it means that there is no essence of particular multiplicities which can remain unaffected by encounters with others.

Deleuze also makes the important link between the concept of the virtual and that of multiplicity in the context of his reading of Bergson, and it is in connection with the theme of virtual intensive multiplicity that Deleuze most palpably remains a Bergsonian. Frequently when discussing the virtual, Deleuze quotes Marcel Proust's adage in relation to memory: 'Real without being actual, ideal without being abstract'. Virtual multiplicity, then, is real without being necessarily embodied in the world. And, rather than expressing abstract alternative possibilities, virtual multiplicity forms something like the real openness to change that inheres in every particular situation.

This is perhaps the most difficult point to grasp in Deleuze's doctrine of virtual multiplicities. While virtual multiplicities are embodied in particular states of affairs, they must not be considered to be somehow transcendent or essentially immutable. As Deleuze shows in his discussion of Gottfried Wilhelm von Leibniz in *Difference and Repetition*, the virtual and the actual are interrelated, and effect changes in each other. So, while the virtual is embodied in actual situations, the changes in actual situations also effect changes in the virtual multiplicity. Existence, then, is a combination of actual multiplicities – states of affairs – and virtual multiplicities – particular intensive movements of change.

While these concepts seem particularly abstract, they offer Deleuze grounds upon which to develop a very practical picture of the world. The concept of multiplicity makes no reference to a transcendent realm of the world that contains the structures or laws of existence. Since we live among actual multiplicities (and are ourselves multiplicities), we are always elements and actors within the world. In this sense, both philosophy and human existence are eminently practical. The virtual counterparts of our actual multiplicities also make possible continued movement and change, even at the points where the world of actuality seems most rigid and oppressive.

Connectives

Bergson
Concepts
Rhizome
Virtual/Virtuality

N

NIETZSCHE, FRIEDRICH (1844–1900)

Lee Spinks

The importance of Deleuze's reading of Friedrich Nietzsche cannot be over-estimated. Although Deleuze engages continually with the work of Baruch Spinoza, Gottfried Wilhelm von Leibniz, David Hume and Henri Bergson (and wrote books on all these philosophers and what they enabled), his approach to the philosophical tradition is marked fundamentally by the Nietzschean goal of an affirmative philosophy. When Deleuze reads a philosopher, he follows Nietzsche in examining what their work enables, what concepts they create, the positive effects of the questions they ask and how their philosophies respond to life. While Deleuze is careful to locate the idea of a practical philosophy in the work of Spinoza, he glimpses the radical potential of this tradition for modern thought in Nietzsche's development of a number of Spinozist ideas.

One way in which Nietzsche's work becomes central to Deleuze is through Nietzsche's reworking of the Spinozist idea of expressivism. Expressivism demands that we no longer conceive of an event as a predicate attached to a prior substance; there is not a matter or uniform substance which *then* becomes or takes on a form or quality. On the contrary, expressivism suggests that there is nothing other than the becoming of specific and singular qualities; and these qualities or events do not need to be related back to some neutral ground or substance. Deleuze argues that Nietzsche is the first philosopher actually to consider a world composed of these 'pre-personal singularities'. As Nietzsche argues, we do not need to relate actions back to a subject or 'doer', nor do we need to see events as effects or as having a pre-existing cause. These ideas provided Deleuze with a way of developing a philosophy of immanence and an understanding of being as univocity. If there is not a substance which *then* becomes, or a substance which *then* takes on qualities, it follows that there is no dualist distinction between being and becoming, or identity and difference. There is no prior ground, unity or substance which *then* differentiates itself and becomes; instead there is only a univocal field of differences. Difference conceived in this way is not *difference from* some original unity; if there is only one univocal being, then differences themselves become primary and constitutive forces. There is not a hierarchy in which an original unity or being then becomes; there is an original becoming which expresses itself in the multiplicity of events. The apprehension of immanent and univocal being demands that we account for the events of existence from existence itself without positing a transcendental condition (such as God, the subject or being). Deleuze's stress on Nietzsche as a *philosopher* whose significance lies in the tradition of univocity differs from the dominant Anglo- American interpretation of Nietzsche as a more literary writer who avoided arguments and principles.

Alongside the development of the concept of immanent and univocal being, Nietzsche also presented a vision of life seen as a conflict between singular and antagonistic forces. Deleuze's use of the concept of 'life' in his reading of Nietzsche is neither biological nor humanist. Life is neither matter (as in biologism) nor the proper form or end of matter (as in humanism or vitalism). Life is a power of singularisation; a power to create differences. For Nietzsche, phenomena, organisms, societies and States are nothing other than the expression of particular configurations of forces. One of his most influential contributions to the understanding of life, consciousness and moral thought was to conceive of each of them as the effect of a primary distinction between *active* and *reactive* forces. Nietzsche's diagnosis, in particular, of the connection between reactive formations such as ressentiment, bad conscience and the ascetic ideal on one hand, and modes of subjectivity and forms of life on the other had a profound impression upon Deleuze's political thought. Similarly, Nietzsche's identification of Will to Power as the basis for a positive vision of life influenced Deleuze's elaboration of an immanent and anti-humanist mode of philosophy. The postulation of such an immanent principle – a principle that accepts nothing other than life – enables thought to focus upon the production and legitimation of divisions between different forms of life. Life, in Nietzsche's view, is constituted by a common and inexhaustible striving for power; human life (with its regulative norms, moral judgements and social truths) is merely a form through which life *passes*. This Nietzschean philosophy, which envisaged a plurality of forces acting upon and being affected by each other, and in which the quantity of power constituted the differential element between forces, remained of lasting importance to Deleuze's own philosophy of life.

Following Nietzsche, Deleuze sought to move beyond the human investment in transcendence: the ascription of ideas beyond life that determine the goal and value of life.His work is marked by the attempt to engage with the broader movements of becoming from which our idea of life is constituted. This led him to concentrate upon a number of *different* forms of difference (such as language, genetic developments and mutations, social forms, historical events and so on) that bring the image of the human into focus. Deleuze also develops Nietzsche's genealogical reinterpretation of moral ideas while taking it in a wholly new direction. Where Nietzsche exposed the origins of morality in the manipulation of affect by regimes of cruelty and force, Deleuze developed the concept of affect to rethink the meaning and function of ideology and politics. Working against a vision of the 'political' that conferred privilege upon the ideological determination of social codes, Deleuze explored the production of 'politics' and 'ideology' through a series of pre-subjective or 'inhuman' styles and intensities. Before there is a political or ideological decision, Deleuze claimed, there is first an unconscious and affective investment in an image of life and a style of morality that is subsequently reconceived as the moral ground of life itself.

Connectives

Active/Reactive
Becoming
Difference
Eternal return
Plato
Will to Power

NOMADICISM

Claire Colebrook

The concepts of 'nomad', 'nomadology' and 'nomadicism' are spelled out most explicitly in *A Thousand Plateaus*, but the concept does have a significant philosophical heritage. In 1781, in the preface to the *Critique of Pure Reason*, Immanuel Kant lamented that whereas dogmatists had maintained a certain despotism of reason – giving reason fixed but unjustifiable rules – a certain barbarism had allowed for 'a kind of nomads who abhor all permanent cultivation of the soil' (K 1998: 99). Deleuze is anything but a Kantian philosopher, for Kant's aim of limiting the principles of reason to a legitimate and harmonious use is countered by Deleuze's nomadic aim of allowing principles to be pushed to their maximum power (D 1984).

Kant's dismissal of the nomadicism that would be precipitated by a loss of dogmatic law – a law that is fixed and determines space in advance – is warded off in the *Critique of Pure Reason* by an appeal to the proper domain of any principle; while reason, for example, has a tendency to think beyond its own domain (trying to know the unknowable) it ought to be contained within its principle – it should only act according to what it can do in terms of good and common sense. Reason has a proper domain, just as the power to feel has a proper domain (art) which should not be carried over into morality. Deleuze, by contrast, rejects the idea that a principle, or a power or tendency to think, should be limited by some notion of common sense and sound distribution. Nomadicism allows the maximum extension of principles and powers; if something can be thought, then no law outside thinking, no containment of thought within the mind of man should limit thinking's power (D 1994: 37).

In *Difference and Repetition*, Deleuze begins a definition of nomadic distribution from the opposition between *nomos* and *logos*. If, as Deleuze insists, we cannot have a hierarchy of *beings* – such as the dominance of mind over matter, or actuality over potentiality, or the present over the future – this is because being is univocal, which does not mean that it is always the same, but that each of its differences has as much being as any other. You do not have some ideal 'whiteness' or essence, which is primary, and then varying derivative degrees of white; for degrees, differences and intensities are all real, are all differences of one being. Nevertheless, there are still individuations and hierarchies, but these can be regarded in two ways.

The first, the point of view of *logos*, works by analogy: some beings are truly real (the actual, what is present, what remains the same), while others are only real in relation, or by analogy. And this subordination of some differences to others is, even in this early work of Deleuze's, related to territories and the agrarian question; a space is divided, distributed and hierarchised by some law, logic or voice (*logos*) that is outside or above what is distributed.

The second point of view of *nomos* or nomadic law has its principle of distribution within itself. That is, there are still hierarchies but these are not determined by a separate principle; rather by the power of the principle itself. This is extremely important for Deleuze's philosophy. Deleuze wants to get rid of transcendent and external criteria – say, judging philosophy according to whether it will help us to acquire transferable life skills, or judging art according to whether it will make us more moral – but he does not want to get rid of distribution and hierarchy altogether.

Nomadic distribution judges immanently (D 1994: 37). A philosophy would be a great philosophy, not if it could be placed *within* a specific and delimited territory of reason (such as a correct and consistent logic) but if it maximised what philosophy could do, and created a territory: creating concepts and styles of thought that opened new differences and paths for thinking. An artwork would be great not if it fulfilled already existing criteria for what counts as beautiful, but if it took the power for creating beauty – the power to prompt us to bathe in the sensible – and produced new and different ways of confronting sensibility.

Even as early as *Difference and Repetition* Deleuze's reference to the 'agrarian question' marks a politics of nomadicism: the difference between immanent and transcendent criteria. If we subject difference to a logical distribution then we have a principle that determines life in advance, just as land would be distributed according to some external law (say, its most efficient economic use, or its history of ownership according to a general law of property). This is sedentary space; the space remains what it is and is then divided and distributed. Nomadic space, however, is produced through its distribution.

So we can consider nomadic space, not as a space with intrinsic properties that then determine relations (in the way chess pieces determine how movements might be enacted), but as a space with extrinsic properties; the space is produced from the movements that then give that space its peculiar quality (just as in the game of Go the pieces are not coded as kings or queens but enter into relations that produce a field of hierarchies). Nomadic space is, in this sense, smooth – not because it is undifferentiated, but because its differences are not those of a chessboard (cut up in advance, with prescribed moves); the differences create positions and lines through movement. A tribe dreams about, crosses and dances upon a space and in so doing fills the space from within; the actual space – the material extension owned by this tribe that might then be measured and quantified by a State structure – would be different from (and dependent upon) virtual, nomadic space, for if the tribe moved on, danced and dreamed elsewhere, then the original space would already have been transformed, given a different depth and extension, now part of a whole new series of desires, movements and relations. And if other tribes crossed that first space, the space would be traversed by different maps. On nomadic distribution there is not one law that stands outside and determines space; law is produced in the traversal of space.

With Guattari, in *A Thousand Plateaus*, Deleuze writes a manifesto for 'nomadology', which is here tied far more explicitly to the 'war machine'. The idea of the war machine does have a clear relation to Deleuze's earlier rejection of *logos*. It is not that there are proper beings, each with their identity, that must then be distributed according to their essence and definition, and that then enter into relation. It is not, for example, that there are masters who then dominate and govern the slaves or slavish; rather, one becomes a master through an exercise of force and in so doing the master-slave relation is effected, a certain distribution occurs in and through the act. Everything begins with forces or the war machine; States do not have an existence or power outside their warring power. The distribution of land or territory – its use, seizure, occupation and measurement – produces distinct hierarchies and identities. In this sense, the war machine is not something exercised by the State, for the State's sovereignty and law, or the power to distribute space, has to be carved out from a radical exteriority of war, of forces and dominations which the State may or may not harness as its own.

Connectives

Desire
Kant
Nomos
Smooth space
Space

NOMADICISM + CITIZENSHIP

Eugene Holland

The concept of 'nomadicism' that Deleuze and Guattari develop refers less to placeless, itinerant tribes-people than to groups whose organisation is immanent to the relations composing them. Put differently, the organisation of a nomadic group is not imposed from above by a transcendent command. An improvisational jazz band forms a nomadic group, in contrast with a symphony orchestra: in the former, group coherence arises immanently from the activity of improvising itself, whereas in the symphony orchestra, it is imposed from above by a conductor performing a composer's pre-established score.

Until recently, citizenship has been thought and practised mostly in relation to the nation-state. Social groups considered on this scale have of course always included a rich entanglement of heterogeneous groupings of various sizes and kinds, involving varying degrees of allegiance to families; neighbourhoods; professional organisations; ethnic, sexual, and other affinity groups; religious denominations, and so on. But State citizenship commands allegiance of a qualitatively different and homogenising kind, largely because it can declare war and thereby legitimate killing in its name and demand the sacrifice of citizens' lives for its own sake (as formulated in Carl Schmitt's *magnum opus*, *The Concept of the Political*). This 'vertical' master-allegiance to the State transcends all other 'horizontal' allegiances within the State, making State citizenship literally a matter of life and death.

Nomad citizenship is a utopian concept created to re-articulate and suggest solutions to the problem posed by the lethal nature of modern nation-state citizenship. Terrorised citizens – citizens terrorised in large part by their own State governments by the hyped spectre of some enemy or other – are all too easily mobilised to give their lives and take others' lives in war; in fact, little else States do inspire in citizens the kind of devotion that war does. At the same time, war waged in the name of the State gives capitalism a longer and longer lease on life by forestalling its perennial crises of overproduction: nothing addresses over-production and keeps the wheels of industry turning like a good war – especially today's high-tech wars in which each guided missile strike or smart bomb explosion means instant millions of dollars in replacement costs. In this context, the concept of nomad citizenship is created in order to break the monopoly exercised by the State over conceptions and practices of citizenship, and to add or substitute alternative forms of belonging and allegiance.

Of course, all kinds of heterogeneous groups and allegiances already exist, some of which were listed above; to the degree that these groups self-organise more or less spontaneously or immanently rather than under command from above, they could imply nomadic forms of citizenship. Yet most of these groups involve or require some degree of face-to-face contact and are hence understood to take place *among friends* in a *shared space*. But there is another, properly placeless dimension to nomad citizenship which is linked to the burgeoning world market and exemplified in the fair trade movement. We might call this the economic or market component of nomad citizenship, for it depends on the capacity of market exchange to link far-flung groups or individuals together in a social bond that defines them *neither* as *friends nor* as *enemies*, but simply as temporary partners in exchange. In this way, the market is able to capitalise on differences without turning them into enmities. For the virtue of market exchange – provided of course that it is voluntary and fair; that it is a *post-capitalist* market – is that it enriches the lives of nomad citizens by making regional, ethnic, religious, cultural (and many other) differences available to everyone, regardless of who or where they are.

NOMOS

Jonathan Roffe

'Nomos' is the name that Deleuze gives to the way of arranging elements – whether they are people, thoughts or space itself – that does not rely upon an organisation or permanent structure. It indicates a free distribution, rather than structured organisation, of certain elements.

The Greek word *nomos* is normally translated as law. Deleuze notes, however, in one of the few instances of etymological consideration in his work, that it is derived from the root word *nem*, which means 'to distribute'. He gives the example of the related word *nemô*, which in ancient Greek meant to 'pasture livestock' – in other words, to send out the animals to an unbounded pasture according to no particular pattern or structure. Deleuze opposes *nomos* as distribution to another Greek work, *logos*. While difficult to translate well, it means 'word' or 'reason'. However, for Deleuze, it can also be understood as 'law'. This is because the picture of the world indicated by *logos* is one in which everything has its right place: it is a structured and ordered conception of existence. *Logos* also implies, then, a conception of distribution, but one that is founded on a previous structure and is well-organised. To this well-organised legal distribution of the *logos*, Deleuze will oppose the anarchic distribution of the *nomos*.

The sense of *nomos* as anarchic distribution can be understood in reference to the nomad. Rather than existing within a hierarchical structure like a city, nomadic life takes place in a non-structured environment where movement is primary. In this context, Deleuze makes a link between *logos* and *polis*, where the political ordering of states draws its main coordinates from a prior structured idea of existence (this is Plato's procedure in the *Republic*, for example). Fixed points like dwellings are subordinated to this fundamental and lawless movement. In other words, while there may be points of significance in nomadic life, they do not form fixed references which divide up the movement of life into discrete elements (inside/outside, the city/the wilds). As Deleuze goes on to suggest with Guattari in *A Thousand Plateaus*, life itself is nomadic.

Deleuze first employs the figure of *nomos* in *Difference and Repetition*. Here, it is a matter of considering the nature of Being itself in terms of non-ordered distribution rather than the fixed coordinates of a logically and hierarchically structured universe, such as we find in Plato and Aristotle.

The most elaborate developments of *nomos*, in contrast to *logos*, take place in *A Thousand Plateaus*. Here, Deleuze and Guattari use the distinction to discuss opposing models of science, mathematics and space. In terms of science, *logos* as the structured and 'good' distribution of elements leads to what they call 'royal' science, one based upon universal values. It is also a scientific method that naturally leads to truth, and is at once based on the values of the State and supposed to be unrelated to the concrete practices of life. Science undertaken in the name of *nomos*, on the other hand, is an ambulant or minor science. It does not proceed from universals, but rather keeps close to the movement of events themselves – it 'follows' rather than 'copies'. Only the practice of science as *nomos* can be said to have attained a true experimental method, since the *logos* presumes the results in advance in the form of global presuppositions. Ambulant science is thus profoundly engaged with life rather than examining it from a supposed neutral outside.

The two conceptions of mathematics are closely related to this. On the one hand, there is the geometric conception that presumes universal structures: straight line, uniform field and parallel lines. This mathematics is underwritten by the ordered distribution of the *logos*. On the other hand, *nomos* supports mathematics in the form of arithmetics proceeding by local operations, without presupposing general structures. In this context, Deleuze also privileges differential calculus in so far as it takes the local operation of numerical values and determines their movement, one that is unbounded by any one point and cannot be understood in terms of the absolute fixity presumed by geometric mathematics.

In keeping with the two poles of distribution indicated by *nomos* and *logos*, Deleuze and Guattari also distinguish two types of space. *Logos*, the ordered conception of existence, offers a picture of space that is primordially cut up in various ways, one that includes intrinsic boundaries. This space is termed 'striated'. On the contrary, not only does *nomos* indicate that space does not have any intrinsic organisation, and must be considered to be open, or what Deleuze and Guattari call 'smooth space', but this space itself is something that must be created. The political radicality of *nomos*, and of nomadic distribution, is that it proposes the dissolution of the imposed structures of *logos* as lawful structure, and a creation of smooth space in which encounters outside of the ordered conception of existence can become possible.

Connectives

Event
Plato
Space

NONBEING

Claire Colebrook

Perhaps the most profound challenge of Deleuze's work today is its rejection of nonbeing. The question of nonbeing goes back to the very origins of western philosophy – in Parmenides – and the twentieth-century critique of western metaphysics. Traditionally, and this is the problem opened by Parmenides, if we try to speak of nonbeing, or say what *is not,* then we have already said that nonbeing *is*. Negativity, negation and nonbeing have been subordinated to the thought of what is, not only because in speaking we attribute being to nonbeing, but also – as Martin Heidegger insisted in his readings of Parmenides and Plato – we pass over nonbeing because we have always begun thinking from the simple beings before us, those things which are present and remain the same. The challenge which Heidegger put to this tradition, and one which is continued in different ways by Jacques Derrida and Jacques Lacan, is that before we can have beings – things that are or are not – and before we see nonbeing as the simple absence of being, there is a nonbeing at the heart of being. First, any experience of something that *is* must come into presence or be revealed through time; being is never fully and finally revealed for there are always further experiences. Second, we experience something *as something* only by bringing it into the open, and thereby disclosing it; it was, therefore, not always fully present, but must come to presence or come *into being*. This emphasis on the nonbeing in being or presence is intensified by Derrida, who argues that presence, or the possibility for experience, depends on a process of tracing which *is not*. And for Lacan, while we live and desire in a world of structured and meaningful beings, we are nevertheless oriented towards that which is other than or beyond being, that inarticulable desired fullness, *jouissance* or plenitude that is not a being, not a thing, nothing.

Now Deleuze will have none of this death, nonbeing, or negativity in life; in effect this is the main affirmative thrust of his work and the inspiration for all his philosophy. There may be effects of nonbeing, but these are *productions* from the fullness of life. If I experience my life as governed by 'lack' – that I am forced to decide among things but never arrive at *the* thing – then this is only because of a structure of desire (such as the Oedipal fantasy) which has produced this negative beyond. And Deleuze and Guattari spend much time in showing how this nonbeing beyond desired things is produced; from all the beings of life we imagine some ultimate nonbeing or beyond, but this is only because we have a far too miserable and limited conception of being. From the orders of speech, structure and culture, we assume that what cannot be named or given extended existence is nothing, or nonbeing. Against this paltry opposition between being and nonbeing Deleuze, in *Difference and Repeition*, refers to '?being'. That is, being cannot be reduced to the world of present beings or things, or what we can say *is*, but this does not mean we should posit some negative beyond being or nonbeing. Rather, being (as ?being) is life understood as the potential for creation, variation and production in excess of what we already know to have existence (or being in its traditional sense).

Deleuze tends to read the history of philosophy as though it is always the production and affirmation of life, but he draws particularly upon Friedrich Nietzsche and Henri Bergson in his criticism of nonbeing. For Nietzsche, all philosophy, even the most moral and ascetic, needs to be understood as flowing from life. Those philosophers who attend to nonbeing are suffering from reactive nihilism; they posit some ultimate good or being, and when this cannot be found their piety merely directs itself to nonbeing, the absence, lack or negation of values. For Bergson, similarly, nonbeing is formed from a failure to think life in due order. We may perceive an absence or 'lack' and assume that something like nonbeing has torn a hole in life; but we are really perceiving *more* rather than less life. If I go into an untidy room I do not see an absence of order. I see the room, and then *add* to it my expectation of how it ought to be. Following Bergson, who insisted on the fullness and positivity of life (and who argued that negation was secondary and illusory), Deleuze rejects the negative idea of nonbeing which has been at the heart of western metaphysics. Deleuze wants to reject the strong idea of negativity or nonbeing, so he does not attribute a *lack* of being or reality to error, destruction, the assertion that something is not, or even change and development. But Deleuze also wants to affirm a positive nonbeing, which he also writes as ?being. On this understanding, nonbeing is not the lack of presence, such as when we say that something is missing or lacking or not the case. Nonbeing (as ?being) is the positive power of life to pose problems, to say 'no' to the commonsensical, self-evident or universally accepted. This nonbeing is fully real and positive.

Connective

Bergson

NOOLOGY

Claire Colebrook

The concept of 'noology' can be set against phenomenology, or the grounding of thought in what appears to consciousness, and ideology, or the idea that there are systems or structures of ideas that are imposed upon thinking. Deleuze's early work *The Logic of Sense*, while critical of phenomenology, nevertheless drew upon Edmund Husserl's 'noeisis/noema' distinction: the noeisis is the act or subjective aspect – remembering, imagining, desiring, perceiving – while the noema is the objective pole – the remembered, imagined, desired and perceived. Even in *The Logic of Sense* Deleuze criticised Husserl for restricting the noema to being an *object* of consciousness and argued that there were pure noematic predicates – colour itself, for example, which is still a relation – between light and eye – but a relation liberated from any specific observer. Noology would, then, be a study or science not of appearances (phenomenology) nor ideas (ideology) but noology. If there are pure noema – or 'thinkables' – we can also imagine approaching life, not as grounded in personal consciousness, but as a history of various images of thought, or what counts as thinking. Ideology, for example, is the image of a mind that can think only through an imposed or external structure; phenomenology is the image of a mind that forms its world and whose ideas and experiences are structured by a subject oriented towards truth.

In general, noology can be opposed to ideology. Instead of arguing that we, as proper subjects, are subjected to *ideas* that are false and that might be demystified, Deleuze argues that it is the idea of a proper 'we' and assumption of the good self or 'mind' which precludes us from actualising our potential. Noology, as it is defined in *A Thousand Plateaus*, is not only the study of images of thought, but also claims a 'historicity' for images. The modern subject who is subjected to a system of signifiers is therefore produced and has its genesis in previous relations of subjection. In addition to its critical function, noology therefore assumes that if images of thought have been created they can always be recreated, with the ideal of liberation from some proper image of thought being the ultimate aim. In *Difference and Repetition*, Deleuze argues that we have failed to think truly precisely because we assume or presuppose an 'image of thought'. Not only philosophy, but everyday notions of common sense and good sense fail to question just what it is to think. In this regard, the concept of mind (or, in Greek, *nous*) has been an unargued, implicit and restrictive postulate of our thinking. Noology does not only study what it might mean for human subjects to think; it also strives to imagine thought carried to its infinite power, beyond the human.

Connective

Thought

O

OEDIPALISATION

Tamsin Lorraine

In *Anti-Oedipus*, Deleuze and Guattari describe human beings as unfolding processes of individuation in constant interaction with their surroundings, and they characterise three syntheses of the unconscious: connective syntheses that join elements into series ('desiring-machines', for example, mouth and breast), disjunctive syntheses that resonate series in metastable states ('Bodies without Organs' (BwO), for example, mouth and breast or head and arm or milk and stomach resonating in a state of bliss), and conjunctive syntheses that gather metastable states into the continuous experience of conscious awareness. They propose that Oedipal subjectivity is but one form that human sentience can take. The syntheses they describe have anoedipal as well as Oedipal forms. 'Oedipalisation' is a contemporary form of social repression that reduces the forms desire takes – and thus the connections desire makes – to those that sustain the social formation of capitalism.

Capitalism's emphasis on the abstract quantification of money and labour (what matters is how capital and labour circulates – not the specific form wealth takes or who in particular does what) encourages desire to permute across the social field in unpredictable ways. Oedipalisation reduces the anarchic productivity of unconscious desire to familial forms of desire. Productive desire that flows according to immanent principles becomes organised in terms of 'lack', thus reducing the multiple forms desire can take to those forms that can be referred to the personal identities of the Oedipal triangle. On the BwO, desire is the only subject. It passes from one body to another, producing partial objects, creating breaks and flows, and making connections that destroy the unity of a 'possessive or proprietary' ego (D&G 1983: 72). Oedipalisation makes it appear that partial objects are possessed by a person and that it is the person who desires. Productive desire that would fragment personal identity is reduced to the desire of a person who wants to fill in a lack. Oedipalisation thus ensures that the innovations of deterritorialising capital are constrained by the tightly bound parameters of personal identity and familial life (or the triangulated authority relationships that mimic Oedipus in the public realm).

According to Deleuze and Guattari, Oedipalisation constitutes an illegitimate restriction on the productive syntheses of the unconscious because it emphasises global persons (thus excluding all partial objects of desire), exclusive disjunctions (thus relegating the subject to a chronological series of moments that can be given a coherent narrative account), and a segregative and biunivocal use of the conjunctive syntheses (thus reducing the identity of the subject to a coherent or static set of one side of a set of oppositions). The subjection of desire to a phallic paradigm results in a subject who experiences himself as 'having' an identity that is fixed on either one side or the other of various oppositional divides (male *or* female, white *or* black), and who designates the various pleasurable and painful states through which he passes in terms of the attributes of a fundamentally unchanging identity.

Capitalism's drive for ever-new sources of profit fosters innovating flows of desire that, if left to themselves, could so alter capitalist formations that the latter would evolve into something else. Oedipalisation is a form of social repression that funnels the productive capacity of the unconscious back into the constricting channels of Oedipal desire. Following Oedipal subjectivity to its limits and beyond entails liberating unconscious production so that desire can create new realities. Whereas Oedipal desire constitutes the subject as lacking the object desired, the goal of anoedipal desire is immanent to its process: it seeks not what it lacks but what allows it to continue to flow. In order to flow, anoedipal desire must mutate and transform in a self-differentiating unfolding implicated with the social field of forces of which it is a part. Deleuze and Guattari reject the psychoanalytic contention that the only alternative to Oedipal subjectivity is psychosis and instead explore anoedipal flows of desire and the schizo who is a functioning subject of such desire. Their notion of the unconscious suggests ways of approaching its 'symptoms' that point to possibilities for creative transformation inevitably linked with social change.

Connectives

Body without Organs
Capitalism
Desire
Deterritorialisation/Reterritorialisation
Psychoanalysis
Subjectivity

ONTOLOGY

Constantin V. Boundas

For Deleuze, philosophy is ontology. In this sense, he is one of only two philosophers (the other being Emmanuel Lévinas) of the generation we call 'poststructuralists' not to demur in the face of ontology and metaphysics. Deleuze's ontology is a rigorous attempt to think of process and metamorphosis – becoming – not as a transition or transformation from one substance to another or a movement from one point to another, but rather as an attempt to think of the real as a process. It presupposes, therefore, an initial substitution of forces for substances and things, and of (transversal) lines for points. The real bifurcates in two inextricably interlinked processes – the virtual and the actual – neither one of which can be without the other. Present states of affairs, or bodies with their qualities and mixtures, make up the actual real. Meanwhile, incorporeal events constitute the virtual real. The nature of the latter is to actualise itself without ever becoming depleted in actual states of affairs. This bifurcation of the real does not enshrine transcendence and univocity: becoming is said in one and the same sense of both the virtual and the actual. It should be noted here that there is no separation or ontological difference between the virtual and actual. Deleuze claims the virtual is in the actual; it is conserved in the past in itself. Meditating on temporality, Deleuze retrieves the Bergsonian *durée*, working it into three interrelated syntheses. First, the time of habit; second, the time of memory; and third, the empty time of the future.

Substituting force for substance, and thinking of processes in terms of series, requires an ontology of multiplicities. This is because force exists only in the plural – in the differential relation between forces. Series diverge, converge and conjoin only in the deterritorialisation of themselves and other series. In the Deleuzian ontology, multiplicities, unlike the 'many' of traditional metaphysics, are not opposed to the one because they are not discrete (they are not multiplicities of discrete units or elements), with divisions and subdivisions leaving their natures unaffected. They are intensive multiplicities with subdivisions affecting their nature. As such, multiplicities have no need for a superimposed unity to be what they become. Forces determining their becoming operate from within – they do not need transcendent forces in order to function. It is in the virtual that intensive multiplicities of singularities, series and time subsist. It is the virtual that is differentiated in terms of its intensive multiplicities. As the virtual actualises and differenciates itself the series it generates become discrete, without ever erasing the traces of the virtual inside the actual.

Hence, the ontology of Deleuze is firmly anchored by difference, rather than being. This is difference in itself, not a difference established *post quo* between two identities. The ontological primacy Deleuze gives difference can no longer be sublated or eliminated by either resemblance, analogy or the labour of the negative. In the space inscribed by Martin Heidegger with his *Being and Time*, Deleuze erects his ontology of *Difference and Repetition*. Being is the *different/ciation* at work in the dynamic relationship between the virtual and the actual. Actualisation occurs in a presence that can never be sufficient unto itself for three reasons. First, the actual carries the trace of the virtual difference that brought it about. Second, actualisation differs from the 'originary' difference. Third, actualisation is pregnant with all the differences that the never-before-actualised virtual is capable of precipitating at any (and all) time(s).

Connectives

Actuality
Becoming
Differentiation/Differenciation
Force
Post-structuralism
Virtual/Virtuality

ORDER-WORD

Verena Conley

The 'order-word' is a function immanent to language that compels obedience. The fundamental form of speech is not the statement (*énoncé*) of a judgement or the expression (*énonciation*) of a feeling, but the command. Language gives life-orders, and as a result humans only transmit what has been communicated to them. All language is expressed in indirect discourse; thus the transmission of order-words is not the communication of a sign in so far as it is understood to contain information.

Order-words are not restricted to commands. They are also the relation of every statement with implicit presuppositions and speech-acts that are realised in statements themselves. The relation between a statement and speech-act is internal. It is one of redundancy, not of identity. Newspapers use redundancy to order their statements; they tell people what to think. Seen thus, the redundancy of the order-word is its most pertinent trait. Information is only the minimal condition for the transmission of order-words. An expression always contains collective assemblages; statements are individuated only to the degree that a collective assemblage requires them to be transmitted as they are.

Order-words transform bodies. It is the judge's sentence that transforms the accused into a convict. What takes place beforehand (the alleged crime the accused is said to have committed), or afterwards (the enactment of the penalty) are actions and passions affecting bodies (that of victim, convict or prison) in the largest sense. The instantaneous transformation from the suspect into the convict is a pure incorporeal attribute that takes the form of content in a judge's sentence. Order-words are thus always dated. History recounts the actions and passions of bodies that develop in a social field. Yet, history also transmits order-words from one generation to another. Performative statements are nothing outside of the circumstances that qualify them to be as such. Transformations apply to bodies but are, themselves, incorporeal. In the political sphere language mobilises the order-word, causing vocabulary and sentences to vary and change as also do the order-words.

Order-words function as explicit commands or implicit presuppositions. They lead to immanent acts and the incorporeal transformations expressed in their form. They also lead to assemblages of expressions. At a certain moment these variables combine into a regime of signs. New order-words arise and modify the variables without being part of a known régime. The scientific enterprise that claims to extract constants is coupled with a political enterprise that transmits order-words. Constants, however, are always drawn from variables so that certain linguistic categories – such as language and speech, competence and performance – become inapplicable. Language consists of a major and a minor mode. The former extracts constants while the latter places them in continuous variation. The order-word is the variable that defines the usage of language according to one of these two treatments. As the only metalanguage, it is capable of accounting for a double direction: it is a 'little' (or simulated) death, but it is also a warning cry or a message to take flight. Through death the body reaches completion in time and space. As a warning cry or harbinger of death the order-word produces flight. All of a sudden variables find themselves in a new state and in continuous metamorphosis. Incorporeal transformations are again attributed to bodies, but now in a passage to a limit-degree. The question is less how to elude the order-word than how to avoid its impact as a death-sentence and, in turn, to develop a power of escape from within the scope (expression and statement) of the order-word.

It is thus imperative that life answer the order-word of death not by fleeing but by making flight, in order to accentuate active and creative attributes. Beneath order-words, Deleuze adds, there exist pass-words, what he otherwise describes as words that pass and are components of passage. In strong contrast, order-words mark stoppages, they are arrestive, and in massive shape they organise stratified compositions. Yet, every single thing or word has this twofold nature, a capacity to impose order and to inspire creative passage. For the benefit of life and flight it is necessary to extract the one from the other, that is, to transform the compositions of order into components of passage.

Connectives

Body
Death

ORGANISM

John Protevi

An 'organism' in the way that Deleuze and Guattari intend it is a centralised, hierarchised, self-directed body. It is akin to the 'judgement of God' (He who provides the model of such self-sufficiency); it is also a molarised and stratified life form. The organism is an emergent effect of organising organs in a particular way, a 'One' added to the multiplicity of organs in a 'supplementary dimension' (D&G 1987: 21, 265). Also important to note is that an organ is a 'desiring-machine', that is, an emitter and breaker of flows, of which part is siphoned off to flow in the economy of the body. Organs are a body's way of negotiating with the exterior milieu, appropriating and regulating a bit of matter-energy flow.

The organism is the unifying emergent effect of interlocking homeostatic mechanisms that quickly compensate for any non-average fluctuations below certain thresholds to return a body to its 'normal' condition (as measured by species-wide norms; hence Deleuze and Guattari's sense of 'molar'). The organism as unifying emergent effect is a stratum on the Body without Organs (BwO), it is hence a construction, a certain selection from the virtual multiplicity of what a body can be, and therefore a constraint imposed on the BwO: 'The BwO howls: "They've made me an organism! They've wrongfully folded me! They've stolen my body!"' (D&G 1987: 159).

While all actual or intensive bodies are 'ordered', that is, contain some probability structure to the passage of flows among their organs (only the virtual BwO, at 'intensity = 0', has removed all patterning among its organs), the organism is 'organised', that is, its habitual connections are centralised and hierarchical. The organs of an organism are patterned by 'exclusive disjunctions', that is, series of virtual singularities actualised in such a way as to preclude the actualisation of other, alternative, patterns; in complexity theory terms, an organism is locked into a basin of attraction, or stereotyped set of such basins. As such a fixed habitual pattern locked onto normal functioning as determined by species-wide average values, the organism deadens the creativity of life; it is 'that which life sets against itself in order to limit itself' (D&G 1987: 503). Like all stratification, however, the organism has a certain value: 'staying stratified – organized, signified, subjected – is not the worst that can happen' (D&G 1987: 161), although this utility is primarily as a resting point for further experimentation.

Constructing an organism out of a body (centralising or molarising the body) is one of the three principle strata separating humans from the plane of consistency (along with signifiance and subjectivity). As a stratum, we can use the terminology of form substance and content-expression with regard to organisms, though we must remember that on the organic stratum, content and expression must be specified at many different scales: genes and proteins, cells, tissues, organs, systems, organism, reproductive community, species, biosphere. At the level of genes and proteins the substance of content consists of amino acids. Meanwhile, the form of content or coding of these acids can be understood as amino acid sequences or proteins. Expression, as we recall, is the putting of content to work, so the form of expression at this scale is composed of nucleotide base sequences that specify amino acids, while the substance of expression, the emergent functional unit, is the gene, which determines protein shape and function. It is important to note that in this treatment we are overlooking the DNA/RNA relation, the dependence of genes on cellular metabolism, and the role of genes in intervening in the self-organising processes of morphogenesis. Skipping over several scales (cell, tissue and organ) for simplicity's sake, we arrive at the level of organic systems (for example the nervous, endocrine and digestive systems), where the substance of content is composed of organs and the form of content is coding or regulation of flows within the body and between the body and the outside. The form of expression at this level is homeostatic regulation (overcoding of the regulation of flows provided by organs), while the substance of expression is the organism, conceived as a process binding the functions of a body into a whole through coordination of multiple systems of homeostatic regulation.

Contemporary treatment of Deleuze's biophilosophy begins with Keith Ansell Pearson's *Germinal Life*. Other treatments include Manuel DeLanda, *A Thousand Years of Nonlinear History* and *Intensive Science and Virtual Philosophy*. While DeLanda interprets Deleuze and complexity theory side by side, Mark Hansen sees Deleuze and Guattari's biophilosophy as incompatible with complexity theory. For Hansen, Deleuze and Guattari's devalorisation of the organism, while resonating with the 'molecular revolution' in twentieth-century biology, is in marked contrast to the treatment of the organism as irreducible in the autopoietic theory of Humberto Maturana and Francisco Varela, as well as the valorisation of species as 'natural kinds' found in the complexity theory biology of Stuart Kauffman and Brian Goodwin.

Connectives

Body without Organs
Molar

Stratification
Virtual/Virtuality

P

PARTIAL OBJECTS

Kenneth Surin

Sigmund Freud's metapsychology was in essence a theory of drives, in that it invoked the concepts of energy and structure to show that every human action has its basis in a fundamental and irreducible instinctual ground. Two drives were pre-eminent: the sexual drive and the drive for selfpreservation. Connected with the concept of drive was the notion of an object – the psychic economy was populated by a plethora of such objects, with the objects in question being related to the 'discharge' of an underlying drive. Interestingly, Freud himself was not always clear or consistent on the relation between drive and object, and changed his position in subsequent writings or sometimes said incompatible things about objects in different parts of the same text. Yet, the fundamental point remained: the psychic object is a result of the drive, and the relation to an object is the function of a drive's discharge. Freud and his followers construed successful psychic development, then, as the capacity an individual psyche has to form relations with whole objects. Subsequent thinkers in the psychoanalytical tradition criticised this emphasis on the individual psyche, and charged Freud with de-emphasising social relations and group ties, despite his attempts to deal with such issues in, for example, *Totem and Taboo* and *Moses and Monotheism*. Freud was said to have failed to consider adequately the mechanisms that link objects to drives and objects to each other. These mechanisms – introjection and projection – are highly flexible in their operation, and blend objects with each other, as well as decomposing objects into 'partial' or 'part' objects. Object creation can also be enhanced by the particular dealings an individual has with the external world.

The positions taken by Deleuze and Guattari on psychoanalysis belong to this deviant or post-Freudian tradition. Perhaps the most significant figure in this post-Freudian movement was Klein. Klein differed from Freud in her insistence that the drives are not mere streams of energy, but possess from the beginning a direction and structure, that is, they are object-focused. For Deleuze and Guattari, though, Klein remained within the psychoanalytic tradition: while Klein acknowledged the centrality and power of partial objects, with their changes of intensity, their variable flows, and having the capacity to ebb or explode, she still located the task of interpreting these objects in a contractual relation between analyst and patient. The analyst provided an interpretation of these psychic objects in the context of the contract that existed between her and the patient. Even Winnicott, who moved further from Freudianism than Klein because he dispensed with the contractual relation between analyst and patient, was said by Deleuze to have remained within the psychoanalytic paradigm. For Deleuze, the analyst and patient have to share something beyond law, contract or institution. But the primary disagreement that Deleuze and Guattari had with the psychoanalytic tradition arose from the latter's insistence that psychic well-being resides ultimately in a relationship with a whole object, thereby consigning partial objects (the mother's breast, the penis, a whisper, a pain, a piece of cake, and so on) to a necessarily inferior or proleptic position in the psychoanalytic scheme of things – partial objects were always something that one moved on from, a stage that one went though, in attaining psychic maturity.

For Deleuze and Guattari, however, partial objects (and even drives) are not mere structural phenomena or stages on a developmental trajectory, but, as they put it in *A Thousand Plateaus*, 'entryways and exits, impasses the child lives out politically, in other words, with all the force of his or her desire' (D&G 1987: 13). Psychoanalysis forces the desire of the patient into a grid that can then be traced by the analyst, whereas this desire needs to be kept away from any pre-traced identity or destiny. Only in this way can the patient (and the analyst) experiment with the real. But to undertake this experimentation it is necessary to treat psychic objects as political options and just as significantly, to refrain from relegating partial objects to a merely secondary or provisional status in relation to whole objects.

Partial objects are invariably something 'menacing, explosive, bursting, toxic, or poisonous', and it is this flexible and plastic quality which makes them inherently political. For parts follow a specific course when they are detached from a whole or from other parts, or when they are collected into other wholes along with one or more other parts, and so the question of the specific processes that underlie this detachment or reattachment is absolutely crucial: is a particular attachment, detachment or reattachment menacing, reassuring, painful, pleasurable, tranquillising, alluring, and so on? What makes it any one (or more) of these things? For Deleuze and Guattari it is absolutely essential that we see these processes and their meanings as inherently political, as phenomena that move people on, or hold them back, in the courses taken by their lives. As they see it, psychoanalysis, by privileging the whole psychic object, can never do justice to politics.

Connectives

Psychoanalysis
Real

PERCEPT + LITERATURE

John Marks

Deleuze is particularly struck by the way in which the great English and American novelists write in percepts, claiming by comparison that authors such as Heinrich von Kleist and Franz Kafka write in affects. The 'percept' is at the heart of Deleuze's *impersonal* conception of literature, whereby conventional literary categories like character, milieu and landscape are read in new ways. In order to explore how the percept works in literature it is necessary to understand how Deleuze is preoccupied with all that leads to the dissolution of the ego in art. This might manifest itself in the capacity of Virginia Woolf 's characters to merge with the world, in T. E. Lawrence's devastation of his own ego, or even Bartleby's persistent refusal to be 'particular'. The percept also has something of childhood perception in it, given that small children are unable to distinguish between themselves and the outside world. By means of the percept, literature becomes a way of exploring not how we exist in the world, but rather how we become with the world. It has the capacity to explore our existence as haecceities on the plane of consistency; to remind us that we ourselves are part of these compounds of sensation. The percept makes visible the invisible forces of the world, and it is the literary expression of the things that the writer has seen and heard that overwhelm her or him. Consequently, it has a visionary potential. The percept challenges conventional notions of forms and subjects. It also has a political significance, in that it enables us to explore an impersonal and pre-individual collectivity that might be the basis for a particular sort of ethical community.

The authors that Deleuze initially refers to in order to illustrate the function of the percept in literature are Herman Melville and Virgina Woolf. *Moby Dick* is a particularly important reference point for Deleuze. Through his perceptions of the whale, Ahab passes into the landscape, which in turn becomes a plane of pure expression that escapes form. Ahab enters into a relationship of becoming with the whale, and the ocean emerges as a pure percept, a compound of sensations. Another important reference point is Virginia Woolf, who talks of 'moments of the world', in which a character such as Mrs Dalloway 'passes into' the town. Similarly, Deleuze alludes to the way in which the moor functions as a percept for Thomas Hardy, as does the steppe for Anton Chekhov and the desert for T. E. Lawrence. It can be seen, then, that the percept implies a particular relationship between character and landscape. Essentially, the landscape is no longer an environment that either mirrors, mocks or forms the character. Nor is it the case that the character perceives the landscape by directing a gaze at it. Rather, Deleuze feels that the percept in literature shows us how the mind is a sort of membrane that is both in contact with, and is actually part of, the external world. The self is not a thing that is distinct from the external world, but something more like a 'fold' of the external world, a membrane that captures other things. The intimate contact between the outside and inside means that literature can explore the 'private desert' (T. E. Lawrence), or the 'private ocean' (Melville) that results from this contact. As Deleuze puts it, every bomb that T. E. Lawrence explodes is a bomb that explodes in himself. He cannot stop himself from projecting intense images of himself and others into the desert, with the result that these images take on a life of their own.

Given this emphasis on impersonality and the dissolution of the ego, it is not surprising that the literary hero of the percept is the 'man without qualities'. This sort of character – closely related to what Deleuze calls the 'seer' (*le voyeur*) in his books on cinema – ultimately has the tendency, at once modest but also crazy, to 'become' everyone and everything. He might be a character who is literally 'on the road', and an obvious example from popular literature would be the openness to experience of Jack Kerouac's narrator in *On the Road*. In 'taking to the road' and being open to all contacts, Deleuze talks about how a particular, pragmatic notion of democracy is expressed in the way the soul in American literature seeks fulfilment, rather than salvation. The percept is primarily a literary form of experimentation, but it has something to contribute to politics. In simple terms, the percept has the effect of drawing us out of ourselves and into the world, and of challenging the individualising and infantilising tendency of much contemporary culture. It is not enough, Deleuze and Guattari argue, to turn our own perceptions and affections into a novel, to embark upon a journey in search of the father who ultimately turns out to be oneself.

PHENOMENOLOGY

Tamsin Lorraine

Phenomenology as a philosophical movement was founded by Edmund Husserl. René Descartes, Immanuel Kant and Georg Wilhelm Friedrich Hegel are important precursors to this movement that insists upon returning to 'the things themselves', or phenomena as they appear to us, in order to ground knowledge in the apodictic certainty of self-evident truth. Husserl instituted a method of 'bracketing' that suspends metaphysical questions about what is 'out there', and instead focuses on phenomenological descriptions of experience itself. Husserl took from Franz Brentano the notion that consciousness is intentional – that is, that it is always conscious *of* something. To investigate what lies outside of consciousness is fruitless. Instead, we should investigate the structure and contents of our conscious experiences. By suspending the 'natural attitude' (that is, the assumption that our experience is caused by something 'out there') with its reifying prejudices, we can discover and describe the 'eidetic essences' that structure consciousness. This, in turn, will reveal how our knowledge is constituted and will give us a new method for grounding knowledge in our 'pre-predicative experience' (that is, experience that has not yet been posited from the perspective of the natural attitude).

Martin Heidegger, Emmanuel Lévinas, Jean-Paul Sartre, and Maurice Merleau Ponty were some of those inspired by Husserl to develop various responses to versions of phenomenology. But whereas Husserl thought of phenomenology as a rigorous science of consciousness, these philosophers emphasise the notion (created by Heidegger) of 'being-in-the-world' and direct their attention toward the lived experience of an embodied subject always already immersed in a world from which she cannot separate herself. Phenomenology's insistence on describing phenomena as they appear thus opened up to philosophical reflection the realm of experience as it is experienced by ordinary individuals in everyday life prior to the theoretical attitude of 'objective' thought. It was embraced by many as a revitalising alternative to forms of philosophical thought such as positivism (another important philosophical movement prominent in the early twentieth century) that took the methods of natural science as their paradigm.

On Deleuze's view, phenomenology's emphasis on lived experience territorialises philosophy onto habitual forms of perception and conception (perception formed from the point of view of the self or thought in keeping with the form of the 'I'). Deleuze sought to determine an 'impersonal and pre-individual transcendental field' that is the condition of any actual conscious experience (D 1990: 102). In *Foucault*, Deleuze lauds Michel Foucault for converting phenomenology into epistemology. There is a gap between what we perceive and what we say 'as though intentionality denied itself' (D 1988b: 109). There is no such thing as a pure or 'savage' experience prior to or underlying knowledge. The gap between what we say and what we feel and perceive (as well as the Bergsonian gap Deleuze characterises in his *Cinema* books that can open up between perception and action) indicates implicit tendencies or forces that insist in what we say and do. The conscious experiences of an individual are the emergent effects of virtual, as well as actually unfolding, forces of which the individual is, for the most part, unaware. The singularities or events defining these forces constitute a transcendental field of the virtual that may never be actualised in individual bodies. Events of sense (for example, the concepts of philosophy), as well as events of physical processes (for example, the capacity to fall, to run, to sweat) and their virtual relations 'insist' in concrete states of affairs, whether or not they actually unfold in specific speech-acts or physical states.

Philosophy as 'genuine thinking' does not attempt to represent or describe, but rather to make things happen by creating concepts in response to the problems of life that actualise the virtual relations of the transcendental field in novel ways. Phenomenology's invocation of the 'primordial lived' renders immanence in terms of what is immanent to a subject's experience rather than processes unfolding at levels below as well as above the threshold of consciousness, thus grounding its investigations in what are, in Deleuze and Guattari's view, opinions that are already clichés extracted from experience (D&G 1994: 150). The notion of a world 'teaming' with anonymous, nomadic, impersonal and pre individual singularities opens up the field of the transcendental and allows thinking of individuals in terms of the singularities that are their condition, rather than in terms of the synthetic and analytic unities of conscious experience (D 1990: 103).

Connectives

Bergson
Experience
Foucault
Singularity

PLATEAU

Tamsin Lorraine

Rather than plotting points or fixing an order, Deleuze and Guattari wrote their book, *A Thousand Plateaus*, as a rhizome composed of 'plateaus'. They claim that the circular form they gave it was 'only for laughs' (D&G 1987: 22). The plateaus are meant to be read in any order and each plateau can be related to any other plateau. Deleuze and Guattari cite Gregory Bateson's use of the word 'plateau' to designate a 'continuous, self-vibrating region of intensities' that does not develop in terms of a point of culmination or an external goal. Plateaus are constituted when the elements of a region (for example, the microsensations of a sexual practice or the microperceptions of a manner of attending) are not subjected to an external plan of organisation. An external plan imposes the selection of some connections rather than others from the virtual relations among the elements that could be actualised, actualising varying capacities to affect and be affected in the process. A plateau emerges when the singularities of an individual or a plane that previously only 'insisted' in a concrete state of affairs are put into play through the actualisation of connections that defy the imposition of external constraints (for example, tantric sexual practices in which orgasm is not the goal or meditative states that deliberately avoid goal-oriented thinking).

Deleuze and Guattari deliberately avoided writing *A Thousand Plateaus* in a style that moves the reader from one argument to the next, until all the arguments can be gathered together into the culminating argument of the book as a whole. Instead they present fifteen plateaus that are meant to instigate productive connections with a world they refuse to represent. Throughout Deleuze's work and his work with Guattari, he and Guattari create philosophical concepts that they do not want to pin down to any one meaning. Instead they let their concepts reverberate, expressing some of the variations in their sense through the shifting contexts in which they are put to use. In *A Thousand Plateaus*, they characterise such concepts as fragmentary wholes that can resonate in a powerful, open Whole that includes all the concepts on one and the same plane. This plane they call a 'plane of consistency' or 'the plane of immanence of concepts, the planomenon' (D&G 1987: 35).

Deleuze and Guattari advocate constructing a Body without Organs (BwO) and 'abstract machines' (with a 'diagrammatic' function D&G 1987: cf. 189–90) that put into play forces that are not constrained by the habitual forms of a personal self or other 'molar' forms of existence. A BwO is a plateau constructed in terms of intensities that reverberate in keeping with a logic immanent to their own unfolding rather than conventional boundaries of self and other. An abstract machine 'places variables of content and expression in continuity' (D&G 1987: 511). It (for example, the Galileo abstract machine) emerges when variables of actions and passions (the telescope, the movement of a pendulum, the desire to understand) are put into continuous variation with incorporeal events of sense (Aristotelian mechanics and cosmology, Copernican heliocentrism), creating effects that reverberate throughout the social field (D&G 1987: cf. 511). There are various ways in which an assemblage's capacity to increase its number of connections into a plane of consistency can be impeded; creative connections can be replaced with blockages, strata, 'black holes', or 'lines of death'. An assemblage that multiplies connections approaches the 'living abstract machine' (D&G 1987: 513).

Connectives

Actuality
Black hole
Rhizome
Whole

PLATO (c. 428–c. 348 BC)

Alison Ross

Plato's philosophy exerts a profound influence over modern thought. Immanuel Kant's 'Copernican revolution' in philosophy was styled as an inverted Platonism in which the dependence of a finite consciousness on sensible forms to think ideas reversed the Platonic hierarchy between the intelligible and the sensible. Friedrich Nietzsche, who found Kant's critical philosophy inadequate for such a reversal on account of the primacy in Kant of the moral idea, defined the task of the philosophy of the future as the 'reversal of Platonism' in which the distinction between the real and the apparent worlds would be abolished. Deleuze follows Nietzsche in this task of a reversal of Platonism, but also refines the 'abstract' Nietzschean formula of this task by asking about the motivation of Platonism. In his analysis of this motivation Deleuze finds in Plato, unlike Nietzsche's 'external' critique, the conditions for the reversal of Platonism. For this reason, Deleuze's reversal of Platonism is also better equipped to critique the dualist ontology of Platonism that continues to operate in Kant.

The motive of Plato's theory of the Ideas needs to 'be sought in a will to select and to choose' lineages and 'to distinguish pretenders' (D 1990: 253–4). In Plato, the hierarchy that distinguishes Ideas from models and copies describes a degradation of use and knowledge. According to Plato, the sensible world is derived from and modelled as a 'copy' on the realm of the Ideas. 'Copies', that comprise the sensible world, mark a graded descent away from the realm of the Ideas to the merely 'apparent' world of the senses. The copying of these copies in art marks a further decline in ontology (use) and epistemology (knowledge). In the *Republic*, the mimetic mechanism of art leads to Plato's hostility to art as a 'copy of a copy' and to the dramatic arts in particular which dissimulate their status as a copy of a copy. The Idea of 'a bed' is a model untrammelled by sensibility and contains only those features that are the necessary conditions for any bed (that it is a structure able to support the weight of a person). A sensible 'copy' of this Idea necessarily places certain limitations on this form by making it a certain height and colour. However, the painter who paints a copy of this bed copies all the things about the bed that are inessential to its use (that it is a particular colour, a particular height, in a particular setting), but is unable to copy any of those features of the bed that relate to its function (that it has a structure able to support the weight of a person). The restriction of painting to the copying of the mere appearance of the object shows, for Plato, that the artist produces things whose internal mechanisms they are ignorant of. This degradation of use and knowledge in the fabricated object makes art a futile, but harmless activity.Dramatic poetry, however, is dangerous because it produces a spectacle able to suspend disbelief.The spectators of dramatic poetry are inducted into the world of the performance where an actor playing the role of a statesman or a philosopher 'is' this role. For Plato this dissimulation of its status as a copy renders dramatic poetry dangerous to the proper order of the State because it trains in the souls of its citizens a disregard for the distinction between the true and false copy. This distinction in Plato between a harmless copy and the malevolent copy, that itself becomes a model, is the key to Deleuze's project of a 'reversal of Platonism'.

According to Deleuze the pertinent distinction for the reversal of Platonism is not model-copy but copy-simulacra. The simulacra are those false copies that place 'in question the very notations of copy and model' and the 'motivation' of Plato's philosophy is transcribed by Deleuze as the repression of the simulacra in favour of the copies (D 1990: 256–7). Simulacra are images without resemblance to the Idea. As such they undermine the dualism between Idea and image in Platonic thought, which regulates and grades terms according to a presupposed relation of resemblance to the Ideas. It is because the simulacra are not modelled on the Idea that their pretension, their merely external resemblance to the

Idea, is without foundation. But it is also because of this merely external resemblance that the simulacra suggest a conception of the world in which identity follows 'deep disparity', and contest the conception of the world in which difference is regulated according to a prior similitude (D 1990: 261). Thus, Deleuze's 'reversal of Platonism' asserts the rights of the simulacra over the copy. He argues for a pop art able to 'be pushed to the point where it changes its nature' as a copy of a copy (Platonism) to be 'reversed into the simulacrum' (anti-Platonism) (D 1990: 265). In this way, the essence-appearance or model-copy distinctions used by modern philosophers to tackle Plato are shown by Deleuze's genealogy of Plato to be ineffective in reversing Platonism.

Connectives

Kant
Nietzsche
Thought

POLITICS + ECOLOGY

Rosi Braidotti

Adapting Baruch Spinoza's monism to an ecosophy of transcendental empiricism, Deleuze constructs the concept of 'immanence': incorporating strains of vitalism and yet still bypassing essentialism. Choosing to move beyond the dualism of human/non-human, Deleuze's ecosophy rejects liberal individualism as much as it does the holism of 'deep ecology'. Primarily, the ecosophy of Deleuze aspires to express the rhizomatic structure of subjectivity. The subject's mind is 'part of nature' – embedded and embodied – that is to say immanent and dynamic. As the structure of the Deleuzian subject is interactive, it is inherently ethical. In this manner, when Deleuze imbues ethical agency with an anti-essentialist vision of 'commitment' he accordingly displaces the anthropocentric bias of communitarianism.

The ecosophical ethics of Deleuze incorporates the physics and biology of bodies that together produce ethological forces. Instead of the essentialist question – 'What is a body?' – Deleuze prefers to inflect his questions slightly differently. He asks: 'What can a body can do?' and 'How much can a body can take?'. We are therefore invited to think about the problem of ecosophy in terms of affectivity: How is affectivity enhanced or impoverished? In this way, ethical virtue, empowerment, joy and understanding are implied. However, an act of understanding does not merely entail the mental acquisition of certain ideas, but it also coincides with bodily processes. It is thus an activity that actualises what is good for the subject, for example *potentia*. Mind and body act in unison and are synchronised by what Spinoza calls *conatus*, that is to say the desire to become and to increase the intensity of one's becoming.

The selection of composite positive passions, that constitute processes of becoming,works as a matter of affective and corporeal affinity. An ethical relation is conducive to joyful and empowering encounters that express one's *potentia* and increase the subject's capacity to enter into further relations. This expansion is bound both spatially (environmental) and temporally (endurance). By entering into ethical relations, nomadic becomings engender possible futures in that, as they produce connections, they in turn produce the affective possibility of the world as a whole.

Vitalist ecosophy also functions to critique advanced capitalism; more specifically capitalist consumerism and the over-indulgent consumption of resources. As a temporal sequence, capitalism engenders the schizophrenic simultaneity of opposite effects and therefore it short-circuits the present. Thus, it immobilises as it saturates the social space with commodities. The temporal disjunction induced by the speedy turnover of available commodities is not different from the jet-lag one suffers after flying from London to Sydney. Capitalism induces a perverse logic of desire based on the deferral of pleasure fulfilment, deferring the gratification onto the 'next generation' of technological commodities and gadgets: the piecemeal instalments of popular culture in the form of 'info-tainment' that become obsolete at the speed of light. These legal addictions titillate without release, inducing dependency without any sense of responsibility. This mixture of dependency and dissatisfaction constitutes power as a nucleus of negative passions, such as resentment, frustration, envy and bitterness.

Deleuze's ecosophy of radical immanence and intensive subjects responds to the unsustainable logic and internal contradictions of advanced capitalism. This Deleuzian body is in fact an ecological unit. Through a structure of mutual flows and data-transfer, one that probably is best understood in reference to viral contamination or intensive interconnection, this body is environmentally interdependent. This environmentally-bound intensive subject is a collective entity; it is an embodied, affective and intelligent entity that captures, processes and transforms energies and forces. Being environmentally-bound and territorially-based it is immersed in fields that constantly flow and transform.

All in all, Deleuze expands the notion of universalism to be more inclusive. He does this in two ways. First, by affirming biocentred and transspecies egalitarianism as an ethical principle, he opens up the possibility of conceptualising a post-humanity. Second, a new sense of global interconnection is established as the ethics for non-unitary subjects, emphasising a commitment to others (including the non-human, non-organic and 'earth' others). By removing the obstacle of self-centred individualism, the politics of Deleuzian ecosophy implies a new way of combining interests with an enlarged sense of community. Deleuze insists that it is the task of philosophy to create forms of ethical and political activities that respond to the complex and multilayered nature of 'belonging'. In other words, philosophy in the hands of Deleuze becomes a nomadic ecosophy of multiple beings.

POST-STRUCTURALISM + POLITICS

Alberto Toscano

The post-structuralist, or even anti-structuralist, character of Deleuze's writings following his encounter with Guattari can be said to rest on four elements: a theory of subjectivation, a critique of the notion of ideology, an ontology of control and an analysis of capitalism. Deleuze's post-structuralism is best gauged, not only by his attack on structuralism in the 70s, but by considering his earlier appropriation of structuralist themes, especially his formulation of the fundamental criteria for structuralism in the essay 'How Do We Recognize Structuralism?'. This text stands out for its attention to how structuralism articulates the empty place at the heart of the symbolic, the accidents of structure (or spatio-temporal dynamisms) and an instance of subjectivity. It indicates what is perhaps the key political problem for Deleuze, the problem of novelty (or becoming). By portraying the structuralist subject (or hero) as comprising impersonal individuations and pre-individual singularities, affected by events immanent to the structure, Deleuze, in 1967, formulated one of the few consistent definitions of post-structuralism – otherwise a vague and faddish designation.

By emphasising the importance of praxis in the mutation of structures, Deleuze lay the ground for a conception of politics that would leave structuralism behind. Treating the unconscious, with Guattari, as a factory driven by flows of desire, rather than as a theatre of representation, Deleuze broke with the whole thematic of ideology (and its critique) which defined the Freudo-Marxism of the 60s (and thus continued his earlier empiricist concern with institutions and jurisprudence). The emphasis on a sub-representational, libidinal dimension to social and psychic (re) production heralded a move from a focus on structures to what might be called a constructivist or ethological approach, aimed at discerning the modalities of synthesis at work in the collective production of subjectivity. Accompanying this shift was one from an earlier concern with problems of organisation and genesis (see the discussion of the idea of revolution in *Difference and Repetition*), to a focus on evental forms of individuation (haecceities) populating a plane of immanence that cannot be captured by any structure of places and differences.

By shifting the focus of an analysis of capitalism from labour and exploitation to codification and desire, whilst retaining many elements of the Marxian problematic, Deleuze and Guattari aimed to evade a dialectical correlation of political subjectivity and systemic change, preferring an inventory of the types of operations (or syntheses) whereby desiring subjectivity is produced, along with an outline of how capitalism and its states are able to axiomatise and capture subjectivity, in order to bend it to the imperatives of surplus-value. It is the material effects of the axiomatic on subjects, and not their placement in a structure through ideological interpellation, which are at stake. It is not only from the side of command that the systemic correlation (whether structural or dialectical) between power (or domination) and subjectivation is undermined.

In their formulations of the concept of minority and of the war machine, Deleuze and Guattari also delineate the constructive autonomy or externality of certain forms of subjectivation to the mechanisms of control and exploitation. Rather than identifying the subject with an instance that accompanies the structure and appropriates it 'heroically', the minoritarian subject (or the subject of the war machine) is defined by a line of flight, which signals both its capacity for independent ontological creativity and the manner in which it affects the society that perpetually seeks to capture or identify it. This attack on symbolic and dialectical understandings of politics is both a matter of principle and of conjuncture.

On the one hand, Deleuze and Guattari's philosophy is determined by an anti-dialectical impetus to think the independence of becoming, and the possibility of an ethics outside any framework of legitimation or regulation. Consider their separation of becoming and history, such that becoming-revolutionary is a trans-temporal event that can detach itself from the fate of an actual revolution. In conjunctural terms, Deleuze's definition of the society of control, following Burroughs and Foucault, argues that we are no longer in a situation where, even at the formal level, we could speak of a correlation or transitivity between the system and its individual subjects. As mechanisms of discipline come to be superseded by technologies of control, politics is more and more a matter of 'dividuality', where the impersonal and the preindividual become the very material of control, but also of minoritarian subjectivation and the construction of effective alternatives. Whence Deleuze's preference for notions of combat or guerrilla over the martial ideas of antagonism or (class) struggle: for Deleuze, the combat between and within individuals, as becoming, is the precondition of the combat against or resistance. This is what differentiates combat from war, which takes the confrontation of subjects as primary.

POWER

Claire Colebrook

Although the concept of power in French philosophy is usually associated with Michel Foucault, and although Deleuze and Guattari in *A Thousand Plateaus* are explicitly critical of Foucault's use of the word 'power' (rather than their own 'desire' which they see as *creating* relations through which power might operate), it makes a great deal of sense to locate Deleuze within a tradition of the philosophy of power. This is not power in the political sense – a power exercised by one body over another body – but is closer to the positive idea of *power to*. Deleuze's antecedents in this tradition are Baruch Spinoza and Friedrich Nietzsche. For Spinoza a being is defined by its power, its striving or its potential to maintain itself. Rather than seeing human life as having a proper form which it then ought to realise, so that potential would be properly oriented towards actualisation, Spinoza regards potentiality as creative and expressive; if *all* life is the striving to express substance in all its different potentials then the fulfilment or *joy* of human life is the expansion of power. Joy, as the realisation of power, is therefore different from the moral opposition of good and evil, an opposition that impedes power by constraining it within some already given norm.

Nietzsche, whose 'Will to Power' for Deleuze is also an affirmation of life (and not the assertion or imposition of power), extended Spinoza's expressive philosophy. Instead of there being bodies or entities that have a certain power or potential, Nietzsche begins with powers or forces, from which beings are effected. A master does not have power because he is a master; rather, it is the exercise of a certain power which produces masters and slaves. Deleuze's reading of Nietzsche is concerned primarily with Nietzsche as a philosopher of power and forces, where force has a strict metaphysical function. There are powers (or quanta of force) that in their encounter or connection with other powers produce relations, but nothing in the power itself determines how it will be actualised, and any power has the potential to be actualised differently.

Deleuze's repeated insistence that relations are external to terms has a twofold significance. First, in line with a philosophy of power, Deleuze does not begin from beings that then enter into relations; rather, there are powers *to be*, powers that are actualised only in their relation to other powers. So what a power *is* is secondary to its potential; the virtual precedes the actual. Second, if powers are, in this world, actualised in a certain way, through the particular relations that have been effected, it is also possible for different relations to produce different worlds; powers might be actualised through other relations.

For Deleuze, power is positive; there are not beings who then have the power to act, or who then suffer from power (where power would be the corruption of, or fall from, some passive state). Rather, a being is its power or what it can do. For Deleuze, then, power poses a problem: How is it that beings can be separated from their power? Why does power appear to be something from which we suffer; why does power seem to be repressive? For Deleuze, this is because we rest too easily with the effects of power – its manifestations, what we already are – without intuiting power's force – how points of power emerge, what we might be, and what we can do. More importantly, and following Nietzsche, Deleuze makes an ethical distinction between active and reactive powers. An active power maximises its potential, pushes itself to its limit and affirms the life of which it is but one expression. A reactive power, by contrast, turns back upon itself. The usual concept of political power is reactive. We imagine – from the image of individuals who exist together in a possible community – that we then need to form some form of political relation or system (so power in this sense is power between or among beings). But there can only be a polity or individual beings if there has already been an active power that has created such a community or assemblage of persons; once we realise this then we might think of politics as the recreation or reactivation of power, not as the redistribution or management of power.

Connectives

Active/Reactive
Force

PROUST, MARCEL (1871–1922) – refer to the entries on 'art', 'faciality', 'multiplicity', 'semiotics' and 'thought'.

PSYCHOANALYSIS – FAMILY, FREUD, AND UNCONSCIOUS

Alison Ross

Family

The 'family' has a pivotal conceptual role within psychoanalytic theory; its primacy in psychoanalysis is neither limited to the bourgeois nuclear family nor the therapeutic practice of analysis that deals with it. Rather, through the organising role given by Sigmund Freud to the Oedipus complex, the 'family' acts as an explanatory model for the organisation of desire in the individual – as seen in his therapeutic practice – but extends as well to the historical forces involved in the shaping of instinct described in his meta-psychological writings on civilisation.

The Oedipus complex introduces the sense of an external prohibition under which infantile libido is definitively shaped. The significance of this complex is that unlike the other forces shaping the libido, which Freud describes as standing in a relation of psychical opposition to unrestrained expenditure and which appear to be internally generated, the Oedipus complex takes the form of an external prohibition and presupposes the triangular relation between the child and its parents. The universality of this complex is used by Freud to explain the agency against incest that sets up the necessary division for civilisation between wishes and the law. Its universality is also indicative of the primacy of the family unit as an explanatory category in psychoanalysis.

The libidinal relations within the family have a crucial role to play as the prototype for adult relations, in which an external prohibition organises attempts at instinctual satisfaction. It is important to remember, however, that these libidinal ties are not dependent upon an actual nuclear family and thus an Oedipus complex can be formed with a paternal figure or structure of authority, or, in the work of Jacques Lacan, an institutional force such as language, rather than an actual father. Here, as in Freud's writings on phylogenesis, the important theme in the negotiation of libidinous relations within the family is the credence of the threat of the prohibition placed on incestuous relations. The writings on the topic of phylogenesis examine a similar theme in the prohibitive force of the 'primal father' over the 'primal horde'.

In Deleuze's writing on psychoanalysis, he attacks the use of the model of the Oedipal family because he sees it as justifying a particular conception of desire. In the *Anti-Oedipus*, for instance, he and Guattari complain not only about the unhistorical projection of the familial structure across cultures and history, so that some psychoanalysts locate the figure of the 'primal father' in Neo- and Paleolithic times, but also, that the psychoanalytic use of a familial structure contains desire to sexual relations within the family. These relations do not simply constitute desire in relation to the shaping force of an external prohibition but also mark out intellectual, political and cultural formations as substitutes that compensate for the prohibition placed on desire by the incest taboo. Against the 'daddy-mummy-me' formation of desire described in Freud's case study of little Hans, or the explanation of Leonardo da Vinci's curiosity in terms of his infantile memories, they propose a defamilialisation of desire and consecrate those writers, such as D. H. Lawrence, who write against the trap of familialism. In particular, Deleuze and Guattari are critical of the interpretative licence given to psychoanalysis by its postulate of the familial organisation of desire: through this postulate, psychoanalysis neither explains desire nor renders cultural formations legible but, on their view, justifies the misinterpretation of desire as a libidinal force captured within and shaped by familial dynamics.

This critique of the psychoanalytic account of the family derives its force from Deleuze and Guattari's analysis of the reterritorialising function of capitalism in the two volumes of *Capitalism and Schizophrenia*. Capital operates according to a logic of deterritorialisation in which the flows of capital are no longer extracted from agricultural labour, but, rather than being tied to the produce of the land, are transnational or global. Although capital tends toward a deterritorialisation of geographical, familial and social ties, it defers this limit by reiterating artificial territorialities. In this context psychoanalysis, but particularly its use of the family as an explanatory unit for desire, is criticised as one of the paradigmatic movements by which the family is reiterated and the logic of deterritorialising flows is captured by a function of reterritorialisation.

Freud, Sigmund (1856–1939)

Sigmund Freud wrote conventional medical case histories; studies in the particular categories of psychoanalytic research: the unconscious, narcissism, dreams and infantile sexuality; as well as analyses of cultural institutions and practices such as art and religion. His postulate of a repressed infantile sexuality at the core of the pathologies of civilised life led to his isolation from the medical establishment. This postulate, which formed the basis for the interpretative posture taken by psychoanalysis toward cultural and therapeutic material, also underpinned its counter-cultural status. Freud's approach to art and religion was, for instance, a radically demystifying one, which held that religious belief was an infantile desire for an irreproachable father figure and that the products of high culture were financed by, and legible as, displaced libidinal drives. Deleuze, however, is sceptical of the radical status claimed by Freudian psychoanalysis. His criticisms of Freud relate to the way he insists on the Oedipal ordering of desire, even despite the questions raised against it by clinical evidence and the researches of other psychoanalysts.

Nonetheless, important points of departure for some of Deleuze's ideas can be found in Freud's thought. In the two volumes of *Capitalism and Schizophrenia*, Deleuze and Guattari try to marry Freud's conception of libidinal flows with Karl Marx's conception of capital. This project, which refuses the dualism between psychic and material reality, involves a recuperation of some of the elements in Freudian thought. Hence they reject the way desire's productivity is confined to a psychical reality, but in so doing they develop and radicalise the Freudian insight that wrests desire from pre-ordained functions such as reproduction.

Aside from rejecting the impotent, psychical confinement of desire, the constant complaint of the authors in this study against Freud concerns his willingness to accept Eugene Bleuler's negative account of schizophrenics as autistic figures who are cut off from reality. Even here, however, Freud also provides an important point of departure for their defence of schizophrenia. They argue against confusing, as Freud does, the 'clinical' schizophrenic who is rendered ill and autistic with the connective practice of desire, which fuses conventionally segregated states and produces assemblages that they believe are modelled in schizophrenia. In this project, they follow the practice in some of Freud's writing in which literary and cultural productions become the diagnostic source able to correct and develop 'clinical' terms. Hence, the evidence of the schizo pole of desire is found in Antonin Artaud and Henry Miller, rather than the clinical context that pathologises and renders impotent connective desires.

This strategy, which formed the basis for Deleuze's unfinished 'critique and clinical' project, calls into question some of the central diagnostic categories of Freudian psychoanalysis. Freud's conception of 'sadomasochism' as a couplet, for instance, is refuted by Deleuze's examination of the writing of Leopold von Sacher-Masoch in which he shows sadism and masochism to be completely distinct, rather than inverse and complementary disorders.

Finally, Deleuze's critical relation to Freud can be summarised in terms of the Freudian drive to teleology. In his meta-psychology and therapeutic practice, what was of interest to Freud was an account of the 'origins' underpinning current circumstances. For the psychoanalyst 'origins' play a role in two distinct senses: as an explanatory model that the analyst, blocked from direct access, had to fathom – in this sense finding the origin for the symptoms of neurosis also has a curative function. But Freud's mode of access to these origins, the interpretative frame he used to locate the events that had become pathogens in an individuals' life, ought not to obscure the fact that the interpretative force he gave to these originating events came to be used as a predictor for development and a theory, therefore, of the different courses it was possible for psychic life to follow. It is this teleological orientation and its installation of a dualism between 'nature' and 'civilisation' that Deleuze rejects and that underpins his critical reworking of key Freudian ideas.

Unconscious

The 'unconscious' in psychoanalytic terminology refers to the accretion of instinctual drives that are repressed by the individual in the process of adaptation to social demands. Nonetheless, these drives remain active forces on the psyche and behaviour of individuals. Dreams, parapraxis and somatic displacements of instincts in cases of hysteria provide Freud with the proof of the unconscious not as a sealed off locality, but as processes and laws belonging to a system. In Freud's first topography of the psychical apparatus (unconscious, pre-conscious, conscious), the unconscious designates those contents banished by repression from the pre-conscious–conscious system. In his second, dynamic conception of the psyche (id, ego, superego) the unconscious is replaced by the id or instinctual pole of the psyche. Here instincts have the status of agencies in the psychical apparatus. In both cases, the dynamic role of the unconscious or instincts takes psychoanalysis away from a descriptive, phenomenological approach to the 'facts' of psychic life, and designates the active role of the analyst in the interpretation of the work of systematisation performed by the unconscious.

In Deleuze's thought, he uses aspects of this psychoanalytic account of the unconscious to argue against both the conception of desire as configured in psychoanalysis in relation to a transcendent principle of 'lack', and the interpretative relation to psychic life that this relation licenses. In *Anti-Oedipus* the 'desiring machine' is modelled on a conception of the unconscious, which is without the regulating function of a limit that contains it to an individual subject. The processes ascribed by Freud to the unconscious – that it operates without conceding to the demands of social acceptability – dovetail with the features that Deleuze and Guattari ascribe to the desiring machines – these machines form, for instance, conjunctive syntheses that operate according to an expansive sense of possibility. However, instead of an impotent manifestation of unrealisable wishes, interpretable by psychoanalysis in the form of their distorted manifestation in conscious life, the desiring machines are defined in terms of their capacity to forge links to an outside and therefore in terms of their capacity to surpass the regulating force of a higher principle (such as the superego) or natural limit. Reinterpreted in these terms, the unconscious is not an interior locale only able to be interpreted in its impotent and distorted formations, but is the logic according to which anarchic connections are assembled or made.

Although desiring machines give a positive account of the psychoanalytic category of the unconscious, the term 'unconscious' is not directly transposable to that of the 'desiring machine', or the term 'assemblage' used in *A Thousand Plateaus*. This is because the unconscious designates what gets left over in the process of the construction or shift from one machine/assemblage to another. In such uses, however, the unconscious is not reconcilable to the Freudian conception of a register of submerged affects, but refers to prior, fractal, material components of desiring machines/assemblages.

Connectives

Desire
Lacan
Partial Objects
Schizoanalysis

PSYCHOANALYSIS + POLITICAL THEORY

Janell Watson

As its title implies, *Capitalism and Schizophrenia* simultaneously engages radical political theory and psychoanalytic theory. A disciplinary combination of this kind is not unusual, Freud too used his own concepts and paradigms to analyse social and political life. In addition, psychoanalysis informs the political theories of Louis Althusser, Herbert Marcuse, Wilhelm Reich, and, more recently, Slavoj Žižek and Wendy Brown. Many less famous authors have attempted to synthesise Freud and Marx, comparing the libidinal economy to the political economy. Deleuze and Guattari differentiate themselves from the typical Freudo-Marxian synthesis by critiquing psychoanalysis just as vehemently as they denounce capitalism. They replace psychoanalysis with their own schizoanalysis, which is as much a political project as it is a clinical practice or analytic paradigm. For them there is only one economy, and it is both political and libidinal.

According to schizoanalysis, politics revolves around desire, while madness is deeply political, as is the clinical treatment of madness. The result is a political theory which does not confine itself to questions of agency, subjectivation or inter-subjective relations. Deleuze and Guattari instead use desire and madness to theorise socio-political organisation, from militant cells to vast civilizations, especially that of contemporary capitalism. Rejecting Freud's classical thermodynamics of a finite quantity of libido bound up in a closed system, they describe the binding and unbinding of flows which have a propensity to leak in all directions.

As both practising psychoanalyst and political activist, Guattari always understood psychoanalytic concepts to be deeply political. He developed the idea of transversality to describe the degree of hierarchisation within a clinic or organisation. The La Borde psychiatric clinic where he worked was an experiment in transversalising relations among patients, staff, and doctors. He was also involved in efforts to secure rights and benefits for mental health workers, and in anti-psychiatry movements across Europe even though he did not always agree with their aims or tactics.

Deleuze and Guattari contend that psychoanalytic politics far exceed the bounds of the mental health sector. They argue that by reinforcing the Oedipal structures which characterise neurosis, psychoanalysis aids the capitalist state by taming the desires of its subjects. Oedipus thus serves as an instrument not only of psychic repression but also of social repression. Schizoanalysis consists in shifting the emphasis from neurosis to psychosis, which is to say from Oedipal paradigms to the non-Oedipal world of psychosis. Psychoanalysis defines psychosis negatively, in terms of what the psychotic lacks. The psychotic's biggest problem, in this view, is her inability to function within society's standard familial and social structures. Schizoanalysis redefines psychosis in positive terms, as a process of desiring production which operates outside the confines of the family and of the state. This does not, however, mean that schizophrenics are disengaged from politics, for as Deleuze and Guattari note, delusional psychotics rave universal history, evoking tribes, races, nations, classes, ethnicities, civilisations, continents. Moreover, each type of political regime is characterised by a specific form of madness. Primitive and despotic regimes correspond to various forms of paranoia, understood as types of investment in social formations. Although bourgeois society is grounded in neurosis, capitalism itself corresponds to schizophrenia, understood as a way of organising desire. It is a matter of, on the one hand, blocking, capturing, organising, encoding, or axiomatising flows, or, of liberating flows.

Schizophrenia organises desires outside of mainstream Oedipal models, whose purpose is to block the flows of desire. When Deleuze and Guattari deploy the term in the political context, schizophrenia refers to both the system of liquidated flows on which capitalist deterritorialisation depends, as well as the tendency of these flows to leak from all sides even when they are blocked or captured by the analyst or the state. Schizophrenia provides a path toward liberation and it is the operative mode of capitalism, which now dominates the planet because it has understood, captured, and channeled desire more thoroughly than any other regime ever has.

R

REACTIVE – refer to the entry on 'active/reactive'.

REAL

James Williams

Deleuze subverts the concept 'real' through his distinction drawn between the 'actual' and the 'virtual'. For him, the actual is more like what we would ordinarily understand as the real, that is, a realm of things that exist independently of our ways of thinking about them and perceiving them. Whereas the virtual is the realm of transcendental conditions for the actual, that is, things that we have to presuppose for there to be actual things at all.

More seriously, with respect to any discussion of his work in terms of realism, Deleuze denies any priority accorded to human subjects, to their minds, ideas, perceptual apparatuses or linguistic capacities. If we traditionally frame the opposition between real and unreal through the distinction drawn between a thing that is dependent on us (the chair I dream of, or imagine) and an independent existent (the real chair), then we shall have started with a conceptual framework that does not fit Deleuze's philosophy well at all.

Rather, Deleuze provides us with critical angles against traditional realism and a new metaphysical framework for developing a concept of the real. According to this concept the real is the virtual and the actual.

It is hence better to think of real things in terms more of complete things rather than independent ones. Note that this commits Deleuze to degrees of reality and unreality or illusion.We should not say real or unreal, but more or less real, meaning a more or less complete expression of the thing.

It is questionable whether we can say that a thing is completely real, in Deleuze's work, other than the metaphysical statement that the real is all of the actual and of the virtual. Whenever we give an expression of a thing it will be under an individual form of expression that allows for further completion. More importantly, that completion will involve a synthetic alteration of the components of any earlier reality, to the point where no component can be claimed to be finally real or complete.

For example, for Deleuze, a mountain exists as real with all the ways it has been painted, sensed, written about and walked over. It also exists with all the virtual conditions for them, such as ideas and different intensities of sensations. The real mountain changes completely when it is painted and sensed anew: when its name changes, when it is mined, or moved through differently.

This means that traditional forms of realism are completely at odds with Deleuze's philosophy, since the notion that the real stands in opposition to something unreal or imaginary already sets the real as something incomplete. So to speak of the real chair as if it could be identified independently of our ideas about it is a mistake concerning the significance of things. Reality goes hand in hand with ideal and emotional effects, rather than being free of them.

Does this mean that Deleuze is an idealist, denying the existence of an independent external reality and bringing all things into the mind? Deleuze's philosophy is beyond the idealist and realist distinction. There are actual things and we should pay attention to them. Without them it does not make sense to speak of virtual ideas or intensities. But, reciprocally, it makes no sense to speak of real or actual things as if they could be abstracted from the ideal and emotional fields that make them live for us.

Connectives

Actuality
Virtual/Virtuality

REICH, WILHELM (1897–1957) – refer to the entry on 'schizoanalysis'.

REPETITION

Adrian Parr

The concept of 'repetition', as it appears in the Deleuzian corpus, encompasses a variety of other concepts such as 'difference', 'differentiation', 'deterritorialisation', and 'becoming'. To begin with, it should be noted that for Deleuze, repetition is not a matter of the same thing occurring over and over again. That is to say, repetition is connected to the power of difference in terms of a productive process that produces variation in and through every repetition. In this way, repetition is best understood in terms of discovery and experimentation; it allows new experiences, affects and expressions to emerge. To repeat is to begin again; to affirm the power of the new and the unforeseeable. In so far as life itself is described as a dynamic and active force of repetition producing difference, the force of which Deleuze encourages us to think of in terms of 'becoming', forces incorporate difference as they repeat giving rise to mutation.

The first question that arises is: How is repetition produced? For Deleuze, repetition is produced via difference, not mimesis. It is a process of ungrounding that resists turning into an inert system of replication. In fact, the whole Platonist idea of repeating in order to produce copies is completely undermined by Deleuze. For Deleuze maintains this approach is deeply flawed because it subsumes the creative nature of difference under an immobile system of resemblance. Deleuze refuses to seek an originary point out of which repetition can cyclically reproduce itself. He insists that the process does not depend upon a subject or object that repeats, rather it is self-sustainable. Whilst repetition is potentially infinite, consisting of new beginnings, it is crucial we do not mistake this to be a linear sequence: the end of one cycle marking the beginning of the next.

In his innovative discussions of Friedrich Nietzsche's concept of the eternal return, Deleuze turns his back on a teleological understanding of repetition condemning such interpretations to be flawed. Instead, he insists that the process Nietzsche outlines is considerably more complicated than that: the return is an active affirmation that intensifies as it returns. Put differently, heterogeneity arises out of intensity. In addition, the return points to a whole that emerges through difference and variation: one and the multiple in combination. In his reading of Nietzsche, Deleuze explains in his 1968 work *Difference and Repetition* that this is the 'power of beginning and beginning again' (D 1994: 136).

This now leads us on to the second question: What is repeated? First, it is important to note that repetition is not unidirectional, there is no object of repetition, no final goal toward which everything that repeats can be said to direct itself. What repeats, then, is not models, styles or identities but the full force of difference in and of itself, those pre-individual singularities that radically maximise difference on a plane of immanence. In an early essay from 1956 on Henri Bergson, Deleuze insists repetition is more a matter of coexistence than succession, which is to say, repetition is virtual more than it is actual. It is this innovative understanding of the process of difference and differentiation that mutates the context through which repetition occurs.

Thus, in a very real sense, repetition is a creative activity of transformation. When Deleuze speaks of the 'new' that repetition invokes, he is likewise pointing to creativity, whereby habit and convention are both destabilised. The 'new', for Deleuze, is filled with innovation and actually prevents the trap of routines and clichés; the latter characterise habitual ways of living. As a power of the new, repetition calls forth a *terra incognita* filled with a sense of novelty and unfamiliarity. For instance, this is a far cry from Sigmund Freud who posited that we compulsively repeat the past, where all the material of our repressed unconscious pushes us to reiterate the past in all its discomfort and pain. Actually, psychoanalysis limits repetition to representation, and what therapy aims to do is stop the process entirely along with the disorders it gives rise to. Deleuze, on the other hand, encourages us to repeat because he sees in it the possibility of reinvention, that is to say, repetition dissolves identities as it changes them, giving rise to something unrecognisable and productive. It is for this reason that he maintains repetition is a positive power (*puissance*) of transformation.

Connectives

Active/Reactive
Becoming
Difference
Eternal return
Psychoanalysis

REPETITION + CINEMA

Constantine Verevis

Deleuze's books on cinema – *Cinema 1: The movement-image* and *Cinema 2: The time-image* – are about the possibility of 'repeating' a film (or films) within the institution of cinema studies. As in Roland Barthes' account of re-reading, this repetition would not be the re-presentation of identity (a re-discovery of the same), but the re-production – the creation and the exhibition – of the difference that lies at the heart of repetition (B 1974). For film studies, Deleuze's *Cinema* books can be seen as an attempt to negotiate the tension between (film) theory and history via a non-totalising concept of difference, one which can attend to the heterogeneity – the local and specific repetitions – of historical material.

In *Difference and Repetition*, Deleuze puts forward two alternative theories of repetition. The first, a 'Platonic' theory of repetition, posits a world of difference based upon some pre-established similitude or identity; it defines a world of copies (representations). The second, a 'Nietzschean' theory of repetition suggests that similitude and identity is the product of some fundamental disparity or difference; it defines a world of simulacra (phantasms). Taking these formulations as distinct interpretations of the world, Deleuze describes simulacra as intensive systems constituted by the placing together of disparate elements. Within these differential series, a third virtual object (dark precursor, eternal return, abstract machine) plays the role of differenciator, the in-itself of difference which relates different to different, and allows divergent series to return as diversity and its re-production. As systems that include within themselves this differential point of view, simulacra evade the limit of representation (the model of recognition) to effect the intensity of an encounter with difference and its repetition, *a* pure becoming-in-the-world.

The idea of the intensive system, and its frustration of any attempt to establish an order of succession, a hierarchy of identity and resemblance between original and copy, is nowhere more evident than in the serial repetition of new Hollywood cinema, especially the film remake. The majority of critical accounts of cinematic remaking understand it as a one-way process: a movement from authenticity to imitation, from the superior selfidentity of the original to the debased resemblance of the remake. For instance, much of the discussion around the 1998 release of Gus Van Sant's close remake ('replica') of Alfred Hitchcock's *Psycho* (1960) was an expression of outrage and confusion at the defilement of a revered classic. Reviewers and 'Hitchcockians' agreed that Van Sant made two fundamental mistakes: the first, to have undertaken to remake a landmark of cinematic history; and the second, to have followed the Hitchcock original (almost) shot by shot, line by line. Even for those who noted that the remake differed in its detail from the Hitchcock film, the revisions added nothing to what remained an intact and undeniable classic, a semantic fixity (identity) against which the new version was evaluated and dismissed as a degraded copy.

Rather than follow these essentialist trajectories, Deleuze's account of repetition suggests that cinematic remaking in its most general application might – more productively – be regarded as a specific aspect of a broader and more open-ended intertextuality. A modern classic, *Psycho* has been retrospectively coded as the forerunner to a cycle of slasher movies initiated by *Halloween* (1978) and celebrated in the sequels and series that followed. More particularly, the 1970s interest in the slasher movie subgenre saw the character of Norman Bates revived for a number of *Psycho* sequels (*II–IV*), and the Hitchcock original quoted in a host of *homages*, notably the films of Brian De Palma. Each of these repetitions can be understood as a limited form of remaking, suggesting that the precursor text is never singular, and that Van Sant's *Psycho* remake differs textually from these other examples not *in kind*, but only *in degree*.

While the above approach establishes a *large circuit* between *Psycho-60* and *Psycho-98*, there is another position: namely, that Van Sant's *Psycho* is not close enough to the Hitchcock version. This suggestion – that an irreducible difference plays simultaneously between the most mechanical of repetitions – is best demonstrated by an earlier remake of *Psycho*, Douglas Gordon's *24 Hour Psycho* (1993). So named because it takes twenty-four hours to run its course, Gordon's version is a video installation that re-runs *Psycho-60* at approximately two frames per second, just fast enough for each image to be pulled forward into the next. Gordon's strategy demonstrates that each and every film is remade – dispersed and transformed – in its every new context or configuration. Gordon does not set out to imitate *Psycho* but to repeat it – to change nothing, but at the same time allow an absolute difference to emerge. Understood in this way, *Psycho-98* is not a perversion of an original identity, but the production of a new event, one that adds to (rather than corrupts) the seriality of the former version.

REPRESENTATION

John Marks

'Representation', for Deleuze, entails an essentially moral view of the world, explicitly or implicitly drawing on what 'everybody knows', and he conceives of philosophy as an antidote to this view. Representation cannot help us to encounter the world as it appears in the flow of time and becoming. It constitutes a particularly restricted form of thinking and acting, working according to fixed norms, and which is unable to acknowledge difference 'in itself'. In *Difference and Repetition* Deleuze challenges the representational conception of philosophy. Here, he contrasts the 'poet' to the 'politician'. The poet speaks in the name of a creative power, and seeks to affirm difference as a state of permanent revolution: he is willing to be destructive in the search for the 'new'. The new, in this sense, remains forever new, since it has the power of beginning anew every time. It enables forces in thought which are not the forces of recognition, but the powers of an unrecognisable *terra incognita*. The politician, on the other hand, seeks to deny that which differs in order to establish or maintain a particular historical order. In philosophical terms, Deleuze proposes to 'overturn' Platonism, which distinguishes between the original – the thing that most resembles itself, characterised by exemplary self-identity – and the copy, which is always deficient in relation to the original. Platonism is incapable of thinking difference in itself, preferring to conceive of it in relation to 'the thing itself '. In order to go beyond representation, it is necessary, therefore, to undermine the primacy of the original over the copy and to promote the simulacrum, the copy for which there is no original.

A key influence on Deleuze as far as the anti-representational orientation of his thought is concerned, is Friedrich Nietzsche. Nietzsche's speculations on metaphor show that there is no 'truth' behind the mask of appearances, but rather only more masks, more metaphors. Deleuze elevates this insight into something like a general metaphysical principle. For him, the world is composed of simulacra: it is a 'swarm' of appearances. Deleuze's Bergsonism, which emphasises a radical analysis of time, is an important element of his challenge to representation. In his books on cinema in particular, Deleuze draws on Henri Bergson's very particular materialism in order to claim that life is composed of images. Rather than human consciousness illuminating the world like a searchlight, it is the case that the world is 'luminous' in itself. Bergson's critique of the problematics of perception and action, and matter and thought, springs from the claim that we tend to think in terms of space rather than time. This tendency immobilises intuition, and to counter this Bergson conceives of materiality in terms of images that transmit movement. This has important consequences for perception, which can no longer be conceived of as knowledge that is rooted in consciousness. All life perceives and is necessarily open to the 'outside' and distinctions between automatism and voluntary acts are only differences of degree, rather than differences in kind. This alternative, non-psychological metaphysics, according to which the world is 'luminous in itself ', rather than being illuminated by a beam of consciousness, is at the heart of Deleuze's non-representational project, and is explored at length in his books on cinema. Following Bergson's materialist ontology, according to which our body is merely an image among images, Deleuze opens the self to the outside, the pure form of time. The self comes into contact with a virtual, non-psychological memory, a domain of diversity, *difference*, and with potentially anarchic associations, that jeopardise the sense selfhood.

Such forms of anti-representational thought are threatening and potentially disorientating. As Bergson argues, human beings choose on the basis of what is the most useful. As such they tend to *spatialise* the fluidity of duration, reducing it to a static and impersonal public form. We separate duration into dissociated elements and reconfigure these elements in a homogeneous spatial form organised around the conventions of 'public' language that conveys widely recognised notions. We like 'simple thoughts', Bergson remarks, and we prefer to rely on custom and habit, replacing diversity with simplicity, foregoing the novelty of new situations. In short, we prefer the comforts and conventions of representation. This helps to explain why art – literature, painting and cinema – plays such an important part in Deleuze's work. For Deleuze, art is not a way of representing experiences and memories that we might 'recognise': it does not show us what the world *is*, but rather imagines a possible world. Similarly, art is concerned with 'sensation', with creating 'sensible aggregates', rather than making the world intelligible and recognisable. In order to challenge representational views of art, Deleuze talks of 'affects' and 'percepts'. These are artistic forces that have been freed from the organising representational framework of perceiving individuals. Instead, they give us access to a pre-individual world of singularities. In this way, Deleuze sees art as a way of challenging the interpretative tendency of representation to trace becomings back to origins.

Connectives

Affect
Art
Becoming
Difference
Sensation

REPRESSION

Claire Colebrook

On the one hand, Deleuze might appear to be a philosopher set against the dominant image of repression, that being repression in its everyday sense and in its technical psychoanalytic sense. At its most general the concept of 'repression' would seem to imply a natural self or subject who precedes the operation of power of socialisation (so that all we would have to do is lift the strictures of repression to arrive at who we really are). The concept of repression seems, then, to be associated with the idea of a pre-social self who must then undergo socialisation or structuration. Deleuze wants to avoid this naïvety, and so to a certain extent he accepts the productive nature of repression as it was put forward by Sigmund Freud and then Jacques Lacan. It is only because of our existence within a symbolic order, or perceived system, that we imagine that there must have been a real 'me' prior to the net of repression. For psychoanalysis, then, it is not the self who is repressed, for the self – the fantasy of that which exists before speech, relations and sociality – is an effect of the idea of repression. Repression is primary and produces its own ' before'. Deleuze accepts this Lacanian/Freudian picture up to a point. With Guattari he argues that there are Oedipal structures of repression. Living in a modern age, we are indeed submitted to a system of signification. We then imagine that there must have been a moment of plenitude and *jouissance* prior to Oedipal repression, and that we must therefore have desired the maternal incest prohibited by the structures of the family. But Deleuze and Guattari regard repression – or the internalisation of subjection – as a modern phenomenon that nevertheless draws upon archaic structures and images.

Deleuze and Guattari's main attack on what Michel Foucault (in *The History of Sexuality: Volume One*) referred to as 'the repressive hypothesis' occurs in *Anti-Oedipus*. Whereas Freud's Oedipus complex seeks to explain why and how we are repressed – how it is that we submit to law and renounce our enjoyment – Deleuze and Guattari argue that we suffer from the idea of repression itself, the idea that there is some ultimate object that we have abandoned. Psychoanalysis supposedly explains our repression by arguing that we all desired our mothers but had to abandon incest for the sake of social and cultural development. Deleuze and Guattari argue that this repressive idea of renunciation and submission is a historical and political development. Desire, they insist, is not the desire for some forbidden object, a desire that we must necessarily repress. Rather, all life is positive desire – expansion, connection, creation. It is not that we must repress our desire for incest. Rather, the idea of incest – that we are inevitably familial and desire only the impossible maternal object – is itself repressive. What it represses is not a personal desire, but the impersonality of desire or the intense germinal influx. To imagine ourselves as rational individuals, engaged in negotiation and the management of our drives – this idea of ourselves as bourgeois, selfgoverning, commonsensical agents – represses the desire for non-familial, impersonal, chaotic and singular configurations of life. We are repressed, then, not by a social order that prohibits the natural desire for incest, but by the image that our desires 'naturally' take the form of Oedipal and familial images.

The late modern understanding of the self or subject as necessarily subjected to law is the outcome of a history of political development that has covered over the originally expansive, excessive and constructive movements of desire. A number of philosophical movements, including psychoanalysis, have explained life from the point of view of the already repressed subject, the bourgeois individual who has submitted his desires to the system of the polity and the market. Against this, Deleuze and Guattari aim to reveal the positive desire behind repression. In the case of Oedipal repression, it is the desire of the father – the desire of white, modern, bourgeois man – that lies at the heart of the idea of all selves as necessarily subjected to repressive power.

Connectives

Desire
Foucault
Freud
Oedipalisation
Psychoanalysis
Woman

RETERRITORIALISATION – refer to the entry on 'deterritorialisation/reterritorialisation'.

RHIZOME

Felicity J. Colman

'Rhizome' describes the connections that occur between the most disparate and the most similar of objects, places and people; the strange chains of events that link people: the feeling of 'six degrees of separation', the sense of 'having been here before' and assemblages of bodies. Deleuze and Guattari's concept of the 'rhizome' draws from its etymological meaning, where 'rhizo' means combining form and the biological term 'rhizome' describes a form of plant that can extend itself through its underground horizontal tuber-like root system and develop new plants. In Deleuze and Guattari's use of the term, the rhizome is a concept that 'maps' a process of networked, relational and transversal thought, and a way of being without 'tracing' the construction of that map as a fixed entity (D&G 1987: 12). Ordered lineages of bodies and ideas that trace their originary and individual bases are considered as forms of 'aborescent thought', and this metaphor of a tree-like structure that orders epistemologies and forms historical frames and homogeneous schemata, is invoked by Deleuze and Guattari to describe everything that rhizomatic thought is not.

In addition, Deleuze and Guattari describe the rhizome as an action of many abstract entities in the world, including music, mathematics, economics, politics, science, art, the ecology and the cosmos. The rhizome conceives how every thing and every body – all aspects of concrete, abstract and virtual entities and activities – can be seen as multiple in their interrelational movements with other things and bodies. The nature of the rhizome is that of a moving matrix, composed of organic and non-organic parts forming symbiotic and aparallel connections, according to transitory and as yet undetermined routes (D & G 1987: 10). Such a reconceptualisation constitutes a revolutionary philosophy for the reassessment of any form of hierarchical thought, history or activity.

In a world that builds structures from economic circuits of difference and desire, Deleuze responds by reconsidering how bodies are constructed. He and Guattari argue that such structures constrain creativity and position things and people into regulatory orders. In *A Thousand Plateaus*, Deleuze and Guattari staged the entire book as a series of networked rhizomatic 'plateaus' that operate to counter historical and philosophical positions pitched toward the system of representation that fix the flow of thought. Instead, through a virtuoso demonstration of the relational energies able to be configured through often disparate forms and systems of knowledge, they offer the reader an open system of thought. Rhizomatic formations can serve to overcome, overturn and transform structures of rigid, fixed or binary thought and judgement – the rhizome is 'anti-genealogy' (D&G 1987: 11). A rhizome contributes to the formation of a plateau through its lines of becoming, which form aggregate connections. There are no singular positions on the networked lines of a rhizome, only connected points which form connections between things. A rhizomatic plateau of thought, Deleuze and Guattari suggest, may be reached through the consideration of the potential of multiple and relational ideas and bodies. The rhizome is any network of things brought into contact with one another, functioning as an assemblage machine for new affects, new concepts, new bodies, new thoughts; the rhizomatic network is a mapping of the forces that move and/or immobilise bodies.

Deleuze and Guattari insist bodies and things ceaselessly take on new dimensions through their contact with different and divergent entities over time; in this way the concept of the 'rhizome' marks a divergent way of conceptualising the world that is indicative of Deleuzian philosophy as a whole. Rather than reality being thought of and written as an ordered series of structural wholes, where semiotic connections or taxonomies can be compiled from complete root to tree-like structure, the story of the world and its components, Deleuze and Guattari propose, can be communicated through the rhizomatic operations of things – movements, intensities and polymorphous formations. In opposition to descendent evolutionary models of classification, rhizomes have no hierarchical order to their compounding networks. Instead, Deleuzian rhizomatic thinking functions as an open-ended productive configuration, where random associations and connections propel, sidetrack and abstract relations between components. Any part within a rhizome may be connected to another part, forming a milieu that is decentred, with no distinctive end or entry point.

Deleuze's apparatus for describing affective change is the 'rhizome'. Deleuze viewed every operation in the world as the affective exchange of rhizomatically-produced intensities that create bodies: systems, economies, machines and thoughts. Each and every body is propelled and perpetuated by innumerable levels of the affective forces of desire and its resonating materialisations. Variations to any given system can occur because of interventions within cyclical, systematic repetition. As the rhizome may be constituted with an existing body – including existing thoughts one might bring to bear upon another body – the rhizome is necessarily subject to the principles of diversity and difference through repetition, which Deleuze discussed in his books *Nietzsche and Philosophy* and *Difference and Repetition*.

Deleuze acknowledges Friedrich Nietzsche's concept of the eternal return as the constitution of things through repeated elements (existing bodies, modes of thought) that form a 'synthesis' of difference through the repetition of elements (D 1983: 46). 'Synthesis' is also described by Deleuze and Guattari as an assemblage of variable relations produced by the movement, surfaces, elusions and relations of rhizomes that form bodies (desiring machines) through composite chains of previously unattached links (D&G 1983: 39, 327). As a non-homogeneous sequence, then, the rhizome describes a series that may be composed of causal, chance, and/or random links. Rhizomatic connections between bodies and forces produce an affective energy or entropy. As Deleuze describes in his work on David Hume, the interaction of a socially, politically, or culturally determined force and any given body both produces and uses associations of ideas (D 1991: ix, 103). The discontinuous chain is the medium for the rhizome's expanding network, just as it is also the contextual circumstance for the chain's production.

Rhizomatic writing, being, and/or becoming is not simply a process that assimilates things, rather it is a milieu of perpetual transformation. The relational milieu that the rhizome creates gives form to evolutionary environments where relations alter the course of how flows and collective desire develop. There is no stabilising function produced by the rhizomatic medium; there is no creation of a whole out of virtual and dispersed parts. Rather, through the rhizome, points form assemblages, multiple journey systems associate into possibly disconnected or broken topologies; in turn, such assemblages and typologies change, divide, and multiply through disparate and complex encounters and gestures. The rhizome is a powerful way of thinking without recourse to analogy or binary constructions. To think in terms of the rhizome is to reveal the multiple ways that you might approach any thought, activity, or a concept – what you always bring with you are the many and various ways of entering any body, of assembling thought and action through the world.

Connectives

Affect
Becoming
Desire
Hume
Intensity
Lines of Flight

RHIZOME + ARCHITECTURE

Graham Livesey

Deleuze and Guattari's concept of the rhizome as a continuously reorganising network, or web, has application to both architecture and urbanism. Deleuze and Guattari describe the principles of rhizomatic structures as involving connection, heterogeneity, multiplicity, asignifying rupture, cartography, and decalcomania. Applying Deleuze and Guattari is always challenging, nevertheless rhizomatics provides a useful model for examining the internal relationships within buildings, the inter-connections between buildings and their surroundings, and most specifically the structure of cities. In fact Deleuze and Guattari describe Amsterdam as a 'rhizome-city' (D&G 1987: 15). Elsewhere, Deleuze describes the city as a labyrinth in terms that strongly invoke the rhizome (D 1993a: 24).

The notion that a point or site (building, space, location, etc.) is connected to an infinitude of other points or sites is a productive concept. This results in structures and relationships that are 'acentered, nonhierarchical, nonsignifying' (D&G 1987: 21). The concentration on the line inherent to the rhizome places emphasis on connectivity and movement. This invokes both communication systems and the movement of people, goods, and services; architecture and cities are widely engaged in these functions.

Various examples can be cited for a rhizomatic architecture and urbanism. Drawing from the plant and animal derivation of the term, the concept of architecture behaving like a rhizomatic weed was invoked by R.E. Somol when describing architect Peter Eisenman's Wexner Center for the Visual Arts in Ohio. Somol suggests that the building rises up in-between other structures, much like a weed, and that it makes rhizomatic connections to various existing structures and conditions (S 1989: 48–51). Another example of a rhizomatic architecture draws from the work of the post-war Team 10 movement, which generally invoked arborescent structures in their design of buildings and city. However, they also developed the 'mat-building' typology, derived from open-ended urban structures. Mat-buildings such as the Berlin Free University project, by the architects Candilis-Josic-Woods, employed a web and matrix of spaces and movement systems. Describing mat-buildings, the British architect, and Team 10 member, Alison Smithson writes: '. . .the functions come to enrich the fabric, and the individual gains new freedoms of action through a new and shuffled order, based on interconnection, close-knit patterns of association, and possibilities of growth, diminution, and change' (S 1974: 573). The emphasis placed by Deleuze and Guattari on cartography, in their definition of the rhizome, also resonates with architectural and urban practices. However, the mapping they describe, and it is a powerful formulation, 'pertains to a map that must be produced, constructed, a map that is always detachable, connectable, reversible, modifiable, and has multiple entryways and exits and its own lines of flight' (D&G 1987: 21). This implies that cartography is most productive when it captures complexity and temporality; the mapping of non-conventional qualities and quantities has become an important aspect of architecture and urbanism influenced by Deleuze and Guattari.

Architecture tends to focus on the material and formal aspects of buildings, however buildings are spatial, functional, and social environments. Deleuze and Guattari's concept of the rhizome is a vital concept for shifting the emphasis of architecture to the complex networks of movement, social connections, and communications that buildings and urban environments encompass.

RHIZOME + TECHNOLOGY

Verena Conley

The 'rhizome' replaces an arborescent structure that has been dominating the west and the world for centuries. The rhizome carries images of the natural world, of pliable grasses, of weightlessness, and of landscapes of the east. It is horizontal and flat, bearing what the mathematician in Deleuze calls 'n-1 dimensions'. It is always a multiplicity; it has no genealogy; it could be taken from different contexts (including Freudian psychoanalysis); and is neither genesis nor childhood. The rhizome does away with hierarchies. It augments its valences through hybrid connections that consist by virtue of addition, of one thing 'and' another. The rhizome operates in a space without boundaries and defies established categories such as binaries or points that would mark-off and be used to fix positions in extensive space. It ceaselessly connects and reconnects over fissures and gaps, deterritorialising and reterritorialising itself at once. It works toward abstract machines and produces lines of flight.

The rhizome does not imitate or represent, rather it connects through the middle and invents hybrids with viruses that become part of the cells that scramble the dominant lines of genealogical trees. The rhizome creates a web or a network; through capture of code, it increases its valences and is always in a state of becoming. It creates and recreates the world through connections. A rhizome has no structure or centre, no graph or regulation. Models are both in construction and collapse. In a rhizome, movement is more intensive than extensive. Unlike graphic arts, the rhizome makes a map and not a tracing of lines (that would belong to a representation of an object). It is a war machine: rhizomatic or nomadic writing operates as a mobile war machine that moves at top speed to form lines, making alliances that form a temporary plateau. The rhizome is in a constant process of making active, but always temporary, selections. The selections can be good or bad. Good or bad ideas, states Deleuze in consort with Gregory Bateson, can lead to good or bad connections.

The proximity of the rhizome to digital technology and the computer is evident. The connection with Donna Haraway's cyborg has often been made. Yet Deleuze and Guattari do not write much about computers. They derive some of their ideas on rhizomes from Bateson's *Steps to an Ecology of Mind*. They connect with the anthropologist's pronouncements in which biology and information theory are conjoined. Bateson argues that a person is not limited to her or his visible body. Of importance is the person's brain that transmits information as discrete differences. The brain fires electrons that move along circuits. Through the transmission of differences, the person connects and reconnects with other humans, animals and the world.

Deleuze and Guattari see the potential in Bateson's work for rhizomatic thinking. The nervous system is said to be a rhizome, web or network. The terminology is the same as for computers though it does not pertain to them exclusively. Clearly, computers do offer possibilities. Not only the brain, but humans and the world consist of circuits in which differences are transmitted along pathways. Through computerassisted subjectivity, humans can increase their valences. Deleuze and Guattari write about a 'becoming-radio' or 'becoming-television' that can yield good or bad connections; productive or nefarious becomings. Computers and the internet have great potential as rhizomatic war machines. The way they are being captured by capitalism, that deploys order-words, consumer codes, and their multifarious redundancies makes them too often become ends in and for themselves, in a sphere of what Deleuze calls a generalised 'techno-narcissism'. The science of technology takes over with its order-words. Yet, in Deleuze's practical utopia, just as every major language is worked through by minor languages, so the capitalist war machine is always being threatened by mobile nomadic war machines that use technologies to form new rhizomes and open up to becoming.

S

SACHER-MASOCH, LEOPOLD VON (1835–95) – refer to the entries on 'art', 'Lacan' and 'psychoanalysis'.

SARTRE, JEAN PAUL (1905–80) – refer to the entries on 'Guattari' and 'phenomenology'.

SAUSSURE, FERDINAND DE (1857–1913) – refer to the entries on 'semiotics' and 'signifier, signified'.

SCHIZOANALYSIS

Eugene Holland

Schizoanalysis is the revolutionary 'materialist psychiatry' derived primarily from the critique of psychoanalysis. As the concept 'schizoanalysis' indicates, Sigmund Freud's theory of the Oedipus complex is the principle object of critique: schizoanalysis, drawing substantially on Karl Marx, transforms psychoanalysis so as to include the full scope of social and historical factors in its explanations of cognition and behaviour. Yet psychoanalysis is not rejected wholesale: schizoanalysis also draws substantially on Freud and especially on Jacques Lacan to transform historical materialism so as to include the full scope of libidinal and semiotic factors in its explanations of social structure and development. Ultimately, though perhaps least obviously, both structuralist psychoanalysis and historical materialism are transformed by Friedrich Nietzsche's critique of nihilism and asceticism and his transvaluation of difference, which inform both the libidinal and the social economies mapped by schizoanalysis. Ultimately, universal history for schizoanalysis offers the hope and the chance that the development of productive forces beyond capitalism and the expansion of Will to Power beyond nihilism will lead to greater freedom rather than enduring servitude.

The basic question posed by schizoanalysis (following Baruch Spinoza and Wilhelm Reich) is: Why do people fight for their own servitude as stubbornly as if it were their salvation? The answer is that people have been trained since birth in asceticism by the Oedipus complex, which relays social oppression into the heart of the nuclear family. Social oppression and psychic repression, thus, are for schizoanalysis two sides of the same coin, except that schizoanalysis reverses the direction of causality, making psychic repression depend on social oppression. It is not the child who is father to the man, as the psychoanalytic saying goes, rather it is the boss who is father to the man, who is in turn father to the child: the nuclear family imprints capitalist social relations on the infant psyche. Just as capital denies (through primitive accumulation) direct access to the means of production and the means of life, and mediates between the worker, work, consumer goods and eventual retirement, so the father denies (through the threat of castration enforcing the incest taboo) direct access to the mother (the means of life), and mediates between the child, other family members and eventual marriage with a mother-substitute. By denying the child all the people closest to her, the nuclear family programmes people from birth for asceticism and self-denial.

The critique of Oedipus is mounted on two fronts. Internally, schizoanalysis models the psyche on schizophrenia rather than neurosis, thereby revealing the immanent operations of the unconscious at work beneath the level of representation. The Oedipus complex is shown to be a systematic betrayal of unconscious processes, an illegitimate metaphysics of the psyche. But it is a metaphysics that derives directly from the reality of capitalist society. For in the external critique of the Oedipus, through a comparison of the capitalist mode of production with two other libidinal modes of production, schizoanalysis shows capitalism to be the only social formation organised by quantitative rather than qualitative relations. Capitalism organises the social by the cash nexus of the market rather than by codes and representation. Furthermore, this is the only social formation where social reproduction is isolated from social production at large, through the privatisation of reproduction in the nuclear family: the nuclear family, but also Oedipal psychoanalysis itself, are thus revealed to be strictly capitalist institutions. Yet at the same time that the nuclear family is capturing and programming desire in the Oedipus complex, the market is subverting codes and freeing desire from capture in representation throughout society at large, thereby producing schizophrenia as the radically free form of semiosis and the potential hope of universal history.

Connectives

Desire
Freud
Marx
Oedipalisation

SCHIZOPHRENIA

Rosi Braidotti

The touchstone of Deleuze and Guattari's conceptual critique of psychoanalysis is their emphasis on the positivity of schizophrenic language. Refusing to interpret desire as symptomatic of 'lack' or to use a linguistic paradigm that interprets desire through the system of metaphor and metonymy, they insist we understand desire in terms of affectivity, as a rhizomic mode of interconnection.

Although Sigmund Freud recognises the structure of affectivity and the heterogeneous and complex pleasures of 'polymorphous perversity', he ends up policing desire when he captures it in a normative theory of the drives. The Freudian theory of drives codes and concentrates desiring affects into erotogeneous zones. Thus, psychoanalysis implements a functional vision of the body that simply turns schizoid language and expression into a disorder. This is in stark contrast to the schizoanalytic vision both Deleuze and Guattari offer us.

Building on Georges Canguilhem and Michel Foucault, Deleuze and Guattari blur the distinction drawn between normal/pathological and all the negative connotations that this model of desire implies. Casting affectivity, the passions and sexuality along the axes of either normative or pathological behaviour, they say, is complicit with those selfsame political forces of biopower that discipline and control the expressive potentialities of a body. The double burden that comes from medicalising emotions and affects, in conjunction with reducing sexual expression to genitalia, leaves bodily affects and intensities in an impoverished state.Their theory of the Body without Organs (BwO) not only critiques psychoanalysis' complicity in repression but the functionalist approach to human affectivity as well. Instead, Deleuze and Guattari assert the positive nature of unruly desire in terms of schizoid flows.

For Deleuze, the distinction between proper and abject objects of desire is implemented as a normative index to police and civilise behaviour. The more unmanageable aspects of affectivity have either to come under the disciplinary mechanism of representation or be swiftly discarded. Deviance, insanity and transgression are commonly regarded as unacceptable for they point to an uncontrollable force of wild intensity. These tend to be negatively represented: impersonal, uncaring and dangerous forces. Concomitantly, such forces are both criminalised and rendered pathological. The schizophrenic body is emblematic of this violent 'outside', one that is beyond propriety and normality.

Deleuze's efforts to depathologise mental and somatic deviancy, unconventional sexual behaviour and clinical conditions – like anorexia, depression, suicide, and so forth – is not a celebration of transgression for its own sake. Instead, it is integral to his intensive reading of the subject as a structure of affectivity. That is, Deleuze maps out alternative modes of experimentation on the level of sensation, perception and affects. The intensity of these states and their criminalised and pathological social status often makes them implode into the black hole of ego-indexed negative forces. Deleuze is interested in experimenting with the positive potential of these practices. What is at stake in this reappraisal of schizophrenia is how other modes of assemblage and variations of intensity for non-unitary subjects are gestured to.

A subject is a genealogical entity, possessing a minoritarian, or countermemory, which in turn is an expression of degrees of affectivity.

Genealogical ties create a discontinuous sense of time, closer to Friedrich Nietzsche's Dionysiac mode. Hence, spatially, a subject may seem fragmented and disunited; temporally, however, a subject develops a certain amount of consistency that comes from the continuing power of recollection. Here Deleuze borrows the distinction between the molar sense of linear, recorded time (*chronos*) and the molecular sense of cyclical, discontinuous time (*aion*) that the Greeks once described. Simply put, the former is related to being/the molar/the masculine; the latter to becoming/the molecular/the feminine. The co-occurrence of past and future in a continuous present may appear schizophrenic to those who uphold a vision of the subject as rational and self-contained, however, we need to have some caution here as Deleuze's philosophy of immanence rests on the idea of a transformative and dynamic subject who inhabits the active present tense of continuous 'becoming'. Using Henri Bergson's concept of 'duration' to guide him, Deleuze proposes a subject as an enduring entity, one that changes as much as it is changed through the connections it forms with a collectivity.

Also important to note is that Deleuze disengages the notion of 'endurance' from the metaphysical tradition that associates it with an essence or permanence. Hence, the potency of the Deleuzian subject comes from how it displaces the phallogocentric vision of consciousness, one that hinges on the sovereignty of the 'I'. It can no longer be safely assumed that consciousness coincides with subjectivity, or that either consciousness or subjectivity charges the course of events. Thus, the image of thought implied by liberal individualism and classical humanism is disrupted in favour of a multi-layered dynamic subject. On this level, schizophrenia acts as an alternative to how the art of thinking can be practised.

Together with paranoia, schizoid loops and double-binds mark the political economy of affectivity in advanced capitalism. These enact the double imperative of consumer consumption and its inherent deferral of pleasure. With capitalism the deferral of pleasure concomitantly turned into a commodity. The saturation of social space, by fast-changing commodities, short-circuits the present inducing a disjunction in time.

Like the insatiable appetite of the vampire, the capitalist theft of 'the present' expresses a system that not only immobilises in the process of commodity over-accumulation, but also suspends active desiringproduction in favour of an addictive pursuit of commodity goods. In response, Deleuze posits 'becoming' as an antidote: flows of empowering desire that introduce mobility and thus destabilise the sedentary gravitational pull of molar formations. This involves experimenting with nonunitary or schizoid modes of becoming.

Connectives

Becoming
Bergson
Black hole
Body
Body without Organs
Duration
Molar
Nietzsche
Representation

SEMIOTICS

Inna Semetsky

'Semiotics' is, in general, the study of signs and their signification. Deleuze and Guattari's semiotics present a conceptual mix of Charles S. Peirce's logic of relatives and Louis Hjelmslev's linguistics; both frameworks are taken to oppose Saussurean semiology. In *A Thousand Plateaus*, Deleuze and Guattari assert that content is not a signified, neither is expression a signifier: instead both are variables in common assemblage. An a-signifying rupture ensures transfer from the form of expression to the form of content. Dyadic, or binary signification gives way to triadic, a-signifying semiotics, and the authors employ the Peircean notion of a 'diagram' as a constructive part of sign-dynamics. A diagram is a bridge, a diagonal connection that, by means of double articulations, connects planes of expression and content leading to the emergence of new forms. Fixed and rigid signifieds give way to the production of new meanings in accord with the logic of sense (D 1990). Concepts that exist in a triadic relationship with both percepts and affects express events rather than essences and should be understood not in the traditional representational manner of analytic philosophy, which would submit a line to a point, but as a pluralistic, a-signifying distribution of lines and planes. Ontologically, 'being-as-fold' (D 1988a; 1993a) defies signification. The transformational pragmatics consists of destratification, or opening up to a new, diagrammatic and creative function. According to the logic of multiplicities, a diagram serves as a mediatory in-between symbol, 'a third' (D 1987: 131) that disturbs the fatal binarity of the signifier/signified distinction. It forms part of the cartographic approach, which is Deleuze and Guattari's semiotics par excellence, that replaces logical copulas with the radical conjunction 'and'.

For Deleuze, the theory of signs is meaningless without the relation between signs and the corresponding apprenticeship in practice. Reading Marcel Proust from the perspective of triadic semiotics, Deleuze notices the dynamic character of signs, that is, their having an 'increasingly intimate' (D 2000: 88) relation with their enfolded and involuted meanings so that truth becomes contingent and subordinate to interpretation. Meanings are not given but depend on signs entering 'into the surface organization which ensures the resonance of two series' (D 1990: 104), the latter converging on a paradoxical differentiator, which becomes 'both word and object at once' (D 1990: 51). Yet, semiotics cannot be reduced to just linguistic signs. There are extra-linguistic semiotic categories too, such as memories, images or immaterial artistic signs, which are apprehended in terms of neither objective nor subjective criteria but learned in practice in terms of immanent problematic instances and their practical effects. Analogously, a formal abstract machine exceeds its application to (Chomskian) philosophy of language; instead semiotics is applied to psychological, biological, social, technological, aesthetic and incorporeal codings. Semiotically, discursive and non-discursive formations are connected by virtue of transversal communication, 'transversality' being a concept that encompasses psychic, social and even ontological dimensions. As a semiotic category, transversality exceeds verbal communication and applies to diverse regimes of signs; by the same token, Deleuze and Guattari's schizoanalysis and cartographies of the unconscious presuppose a different semiotic theory from the one appropriated in Lacanian psychoanalysis. The semiotic process, based on the logic of included middle, is the basis for the production of subjectivity. The line of flight or becoming is a third between subject and object and is to be understood 'not so much . . . in their opposition as in their complementarity' (D 1987: 131). The relationship between subject and object is of the nature of reciprocal presupposition.

Brian Massumi points out that Deleuze reinvents the concept of semiotics in his various books: in *Proust and Signs,* Deleuze refers to four differently organised semiotic worlds (M 1992). In *Cinema 1* he presents sixteen different types of cinematic signs. For Deleuze, philosophers, writers and artists are first and foremost semioticians and symptomatologists: they read, interpret and create signs, which are 'the symptoms of life . . . There is a profound link between signs, events, life and vitalism' (D 1995: 143). The task of philosophy is the creation of concepts, and a concept, in accord with a-signifying semiotics, has no reference; it is autoreferential, positing itself together with its object at the moment of its own creation. A map, or a diagram, engenders the territory to which it is supposed to refer; a static representation of the order of references giving way to a relational dynamics of the order of meanings.

Connectives

Lacan
Schizoanalysis
Signifier/Signified

SEMIOTICS + NEW MEDIA

Janell Watson

The distinction between old media (such as the printing press, or analogue recording and broadcast) and new media (such as the internet, HD television, and high-tech multi-media art) is generally made on the basis of digitisation, networking, interactivity, and pervasiveness. These new qualities seem to call for new theoretical tools beyond those of literary, film, music, and art criticism, even though both old and new media carry word, sound, and image. Unprecedented is the globally networked unrelenting sensory bombardment made possible by the way new technologies deliver torrents of words, sounds, and images. With their assemblages and rhizomes composed of multiplicities, intensities, flows, speeds and slownesses, chronos and aion, Deleuze and Guattari offer numerous insights into the workings and effects of new media. Their machinic semiotics focuses less on language and symbols than on image, data, sensation, movement, subjectivity, and global political economics. Like the interactive networks of new media, this machinic semiotics brings together a diverse array of elements operating at many registers and affecting multiple senses, often below the level of conscious cognition.

Deleuze and Guattari extend semiotics well beyond the realm of human interactions in order to take into account animals, machines, bio-chemistry, and physics. They were avid readers of cybernetics, information theory, and communication studies, which they incorporate into their semiotics. They recognise signs and signals everywhere, and understand their role in the functioning of social, organic, and even inorganic processes. Most of these signs and signals are neither linguistic nor symbolic, and involve no human perceiver. Such signs have no meaning, and need none. No signification is conveyed by the body's endocrine and hormonal signals. No one wrote the genetic code (D&G 1983: 248). These signals and codes create, but they do not signify. For example, as Marshall McLuhan put it, electric light is pure information, a medium without a message (D&G 1983: 241). For Deleuze, *sens* (which in French designates both sense and meaning) does not necessarily involve Saussurean signification. In *Logic of*

Sense he accounts for the convergence of heterogeneous series by way of internal resonance, a concept from information theory which explains why two tuning forks brought together begin to oscillate at the same frequency (D 1990). He borrows this idea from Gilbert Simondon, who posits that internal resonance conveys information exchanges necessary to sustain life. Deleuze and Guattari's semiotic category of the diagrammatic likewise creates and produces real effects without recourse to meaning. Unlike the sign or symbol, the diagram does not signify or represent, but instead operates in the real to produce something new. Music, mathematics, and computer coding are examples of the diagrammatic at work (D&G 1987: 142). Accordingly, it is misleading to speak of computer 'languages' or to describe musical notation as an alphabet. New media relies heavily on these non-linguistic semiotic elements.

Given the predominance of moving images in video games and art installations, as well as the spread of new media technologies into cinema itself, the Deleuzian concepts of movement-image and time-image have been used in the study of new media. Interestingly, despite his emphasis on images, Deleuze describes cinema as a pure semiotics, although he maintains that it is not a language. He thereby distances himself from the theory of cinematic language associated with Christian Metz (D 1986, ix; 1989: 25, 262). Deleuze reverses the relation between word and image, grounding narration in the image itself, and not the other way around (D 1986: 69). However, this does not mean that images signify, for he argues that even when they include verbal elements, cinematic images form a plastic mass of diverse types of elements – sensory (visual, sonorous), kinetic, intensive, affective, rhythmic, tonal, and even verbal (D 1989: 29-30). This semiotics of material flows takes into account physical sensation and perception, in a way that no theory of language or the signifier ever could.

Signs combine with material flows to form what Deleuze and Guattari call rhizomes and assemblages, web-like agglomerations which are heterogeneous, fragmented, meta-stable, and open to interactions of all kinds – an apt description of the new media landscape. Rhizomes and assemblages may include both desiring machines (not to be confused with human individuals) and technological machines, as, for example, when an ear is connected to an iPod in order to produce a sensation machine. Such biological-technological couplings necessarily result in profound changes in the constitution of the self, and its relations to its environment. Personal electronic devices become integral components of a polyphonic, machinic subjectivity (G 1995: 16-17, 24).

Old media technologies were controlled by the mass media industry, whereas the new media often seem more democratic because they allow for user input. However, corporations see profit-making potential in user interactivity. This changing relationship to the consumer can also be analysed using Deleuze and Guattari's semiotics, which is inherently political. For them, any type of social organisation corresponds to a regime of signs dominated by a particular medium of expression (D&G 1987: 111-48). For example, the despotic regime invents writing, but in the imperial formation writing dominates all other forms of expression (D&G 1983: 202). Capitalism, in contrast, is illiterate, preferring flows, codes, and networks to speech and writing (D&G 1983: 240). It is therefore not daunted by the seemingly chaotic freedom implied by the de-centred, deterritorialised mode of production of new media. Guattari foresaw this potential empowerment of the user, which he described as a post-media era to come (G 1995: 97). This optimistic view of the liberation through new media must, however, be tempered by attentiveness to capitalism's ability to capture and axiomatise any flow, through processes which are themselves deterritorialised. Wall Street, which itself consists primarily in networked data flows, is determined to profit from user-generated content of social-networking sites, even as the culture industry, after a slow start, is making rapid progress not only in adapting to new media, but especially in harnessing the money-making potential of their production and distribution technologies.

SENSATION

Tom Conley

Biology infuses much of Deleuze's philosophy, especially in the domain of sensation. It remains at the basis of perception, perception in turn being what brings about the creation of events, the very matter common to philosophy, art, and science. Sensation opens at the threshold of sense, at those moments prior to when a subject discovers the meaning of something or enters into a process of reasoned cognition. Sensation takes place before cognition and thus pertains to signifiance. In film it is grasped in what takes place before words and images are grasped, as in Jean-Luc Godard's title, *Prénom: Carmen*, in which the field of sensation inheres in what comes prior to the name, *before* the naming of 'Carmen', in what is felt and experienced before the name is understood in a common way (D 1989: 154). In aesthetics, which Deleuze takes up through his study of Francis Bacon in *The Logic of Sensation*, sensation is what strikes a viewer of a painting or the reader of a poem before meaning is discerned in figuration or a thematic design. It has the productively deformative power of defacing the representations that cause it to be felt. It is also what vibrates at the threshold of a given form; in other words, what causes the 'appleness' of the painter Paul Cézanne's apples to be felt as the geometric and painterly abstractions that they become in the field of his still lifes.

One of Deleuze's most famous figures, the Body without Organs (BwO), is conceived as a surface of sensations, of a texture and elasticity of equal force and intensity over the entirety of its mass. Sensation passes over and through the body in waves and rhythms that meld its perceptible sites or organisation of parts into vibrations and spasms. Borrowing from Wilhelm Wörringer's writings on the generativity of 'gothic' linearity, Deleuze and Guattari's concept of BwO is in continuous and autonomous movement, endlessly emanating sensation less in its design than in its process. The line is continually becoming of itself, exuding force; what Deleuze calls the 'condition of sensation'. Of animal and vegetal character, it has the capacity of turning inward and outward, into the body and along different trajectories, making palpable what otherwise could be sensed in sensation itself. Deleuze explains the point through Cézanne, whom he champions for having made visible the folding character of the Mont-Saint-Victoire, the germinating forces within seeds, or the convection and heat transpiring in a landscape. These elements are within sensation prior to becoming felt or visualised.

Deleuze uses Bacon's distinction between two types of violence to refine his 'logic' of sensation. A violence of public spectacle, seen in athletic and political arenas and in traditional 'theatres of torture' must be refused in order to reach a kind of sensation that the British painter calls a 'declaration of faith in life'. Many of the paintings place deformed bodies in arenas so that their abstraction can embody invisible forces; forces that accordingly condition the uncanny sensation the spectator feels in view of both familiar and monstrous human forms. When seen in series (many are diptychs and triptychs), the paintings exude rhythms that are tied to what Bacon calls 'figures', which are neither figurative nor beyond figuration but accumulations and coagulations of sensation. In another context he links composite units of percepts and affects to blocks of sensation, in themselves beings that exist autonomously, as much in paintings as in the spectators who look at them. The artist finds in the area between the perceiver and the work a field of sensation, one that is 'sculpting, composing, writing sensations. As percepts, sensations are not perceptions referring to an object' (D&G 1994: 166) but something that inheres in its being and its duration. The task of the artist, as he shows with Bacon and Cézanne, is to extract from a 'block of sensations, a pure being of sensation' (D&G 1994: 167).

In this respect, in his unique gallery of natural history, two of Deleuze's totems of sensation are the tick and the dog. The tick is a creature that feels rhythmic sensations that inspire it to fall onto the skin of the animal it covets. A melody or 'block' of sensation causes it to leap. The dog that is eating at its food bowl senses the arrival of the master that will flog it, prior to the flogging, with thousands of sensations that anticipate the event itself: a hostile odour, the sound of footsteps, or the sight of a raised stick, that 'subtend the conversion of pleasure into pain'. Sensations are mixed with 'tiny perceptions' that are 'the passage from one perception to another', and they constitute 'the animal condition par excellence' (D 1993a: 87).

Readers of Deleuze note that sensation acquires increasing resonance in the works written after 1980. It becomes a common term of speculation on aesthetics, biology and philosophy at the same time as it retrieves the vitalism and intuition of Henri Bergson's formative work written from the early 1950s. Sensation becomes a decisive element in the style and texture of Deleuze's writing, for in its rhythms, its 'blocks' of reflection and its own conceptual figures, conceived in a manner akin to those of his favourite painters, the writing exudes the forces that it describes.

Connectives

Art
Bacon
Bergson
Body without Organs
Faciality

SENSATION + CINEMA

Constantine Verevis

In *Difference and Repetition*, Deleuze states that the modern work of art leaves the domain of representation in order to become pure experience: 'a transcendental empiricism or science of the sensible' (D 1994: 56). Deleuze develops this idea in *Francis Bacon: The Logic of Sensation*, suggesting that modern painting transcends the representation of both illustrative and narrative figuration by moving either toward a pure form of abstraction (as exemplified by, say, Piet Mondrian or Wassily Kandinsky) or toward what Deleuze calls (following Jean-François Lyotard) the purely *figural.* For Deleuze (as for Bacon, who refuses both straight abstraction and figurative illustration), the preferred option is the latter, for the abstract painting, like the figurative artwork, is ultimately directed toward ordinary thought or to the *brain*, whereas the figure is the sensible form related to sensation, to the *nervous system* or to 'vital movement'. Citing Paul Cézanne, Deleuze describes a 'logic of the senses' that is neither rational, nor cerebral, but a bodily sensation – an unequal difference between forces – that overflows and traverses all domains.

Sensation (figure) shifts attention from the form of the artwork, be it representational or abstract, to the nature of its encounter with other bodies, and the becomings – becoming-other, becoming-unlimited, becoming-intense – that they bring about. Deleuze says: 'I *become* in sensation, and something *happens* through sensation, one through the other and one in the other' (D 1993b: 187). In the case of cinema, narrativerepresentational film can be understood as a machine assemblage – a potentiality of intensities or sensations – that, on the one hand, is organised (*re*presented) by an activity of figuration, and on the other, is reproduced – multiplied and intensified – as a creative figure of sensation. The first describes a habitual recognition where the film is familiar and banal because it is represented in terms of its identity and sameness. The latter describes a moment of attentive recognition (of *dis*-figuration) in which the object does not remain on the one and the same plane, but passes through different planes. This is the moment of the crystal, where past and future collide; the moment where repetition is the eternal return: difference repeating.

Sensation can be related to the concept of 'cinephilia', an obsessive passion for cinema – in particular the Hollywood films of 1940s and 1950s – that developed in the front rows of the Paris *cinémathèques* in the 1950s and 1960s. Paul Willemen suggests that the phenomenon of cinephilia, influenced by still active residues of surrealism in post-war French culture, involves a sublime moment of defamiliarisation, an encounter with the unpresentable sublime. Willemen links cinephilia to Jean Epstein's notion of *photogénie*, a fleeting moment of experience or emotional intensity – a sensation – that the viewer cannot describe verbally or rationalise cognitively (W 1994). As in the case of Deleuze's time-image, *photogénie* is a direct representation of time, a 'crystal-image', or direct sensation of a present presence. Focusing upon that aspect of cinephilia which escapes existing networks of critical discourse,Willemen describes an encounter – a 'dangerous moment' that points to a 'beyond of cinema' (241). In a brief example, one can find this potential dislocation in the films of David Lynch: the anamorphic deformity of the dream in *The Elephant Man* (1980), Ben's lip-synching of 'In Dreams' in *Blue Velvet* (1986), the lighting of a cigarette in *Wild at Heart* (1990).

Contemporary cinephilia – which embraces not only the Hollywood films of classical cinephilia and the work of the *nouvelle vague*, but also Hollywood's delayed *nouvelle vague* (Francis Ford Coppola, Brian De Palma, Martin Scorsese), the *new* French new wave (Jean-Jacques Beineix, Luc Besson, Leos Carax), and international art cinema (Pedro Almodovar, Takeshi Kitano, Abbas Kiarostami) – can be seen as one of the many diverse reading strategies encouraged by recent cultural technologies. The developments include not only new storage and information technologies (television, video, internet) and agencies of promotion and commodification (reviews, advertisements, merchandise) but an associated increase in film and media literacy and a mode of viewing imbricated with an intertextual network of mass cultural discourses. Understood in this way, the reproduction of the cinephile is a type of infinite representation, an extensive function of a standardised, serial product designed to be consumed within globalised and/or specialised niche markets. But equally, the intensive experience of cinephilia, the resonance created within the proliferating, differential series, can be described as a moment of sensation, a glimpse over the edge of cinematic representation. Contemporary cinephilia thus becomes both a general economy of viewing, one which guarantees the endless circulation (sameness) of the cinematic institution, and also a point of resistance to these forms of re-presentation – the moment at which the founding principle (Idea) breaks down to become a positive event, *a* universal un-founding. The serial repetition of the (global Hollywood) film product, and the reproduction of the new cinephile, become both the confirmation of identity and the affirmation of multiple sensation, the return of the absolutely different.

SIGNIFIER/SIGNIFIED

Claire Colebrook

According to the structuralist linguist, Ferdinand de Saussure, a language is made up of signifiers or differential marks, which then organise or structure, not only our language, but also the very conceptualisation of our world. The revolution of structuralist linguistics lay in the insistence on both the arbitrary nature of the signifier and on the highly contingent production of the system of signification. Whereas linguistics prior to structuralism might have studied a word diachronically by looking at the way the Latin word *ratio* comes to form a common root (and meaningful cause) for the modern words, 'reason', 'rational', 'rationalise', 'irrational' and so on, structuralist linguistics is synchronic. One should not study the emergence or genesis of signs, for this is vague, but only signs as they form a system. So it would be significant that one language might mark a difference between grey and blue, or like and love, while another language would not mark out such a difference. The consequences of this supposed primacy of the signifier extended well beyond linguistics. If it is the case that we think only within a system of differences, then thought depends upon a prior structure *and* that structure can only be studied or criticised as a whole. There can be no intuition of any term or thing in itself, for we only know and think within a system of differences without positive terms.

Not only does Deleuze favour the linguistics of Louis Hjelmslev over Saussure so that there are already forms or differentiations that are not the effect of a language or conceptual scheme, he also (with Guattari) conducted an intense political assault on the ideology or despotism of the signifier. How is it that we come to think of thought as reducible to a system of linguistic signs? Not only do Deleuze and Guattari insist, positively, that there are régimes of signs beyond language, ranging from music and the visual arts to the signs of the inhuman world – smoke being a sign of fire, light being a sign for a heliotrope or a bird's refrain being the sign of its territory, they also conduct a critique of the modern concept of signification, the idea that we are submitted to a system of signs beyond which we cannot think. On the structuralist understanding of the signifier, all thought takes place in a system of signs and all differences are mediated through this system such that nothing can be considered in itself. Structuralism is often, therefore, considered to be a 'break' in this history of western metaphysics, for it concedes that there can be no knowledge of pure presence, only knowledge of the world as mediated through signs. According to Deleuze and Guattari, however, the signifier is yet one more way in which we fail to think difference positively; one more way in which we mistake already structured experience for the positive structuring power of life to differ. Signifiers, Deleuze and Guattari argue, are just examples of the ways in which life is expressed or differentiated. Deleuze's argument for positive difference is in direct contrast with the idea that there is *a* system of relations that determines life in advance. On the contrary, Deleuze says that while language can overcode other systems of difference, for we can speak about other systems of signs, it is also possible for language to be deterritorialised through the positive power of difference. If, for example, our régime of visual signs is overturned by an event in cinema, then we might be forced to think differently and create new concepts. In such a case thinking would not be governed by a preceding system, but would be violated by the shock or encounter with life, a life that emits signs well beyond those of the system of signification.

Connectives

Deterritorialisation/Reterritorialisation
Difference

SIMONDON, GILBERT (1926–87) – refer to the entries on 'individuation' and 'materialism'.

SIMULACRUM

Jonathan Roffe

In his 1990 'Preface' to Clet-Martin's book on his work, Deleuze states that the concept of 'simulacrum' was never an essential part of his philosophy. However, it does offer one of the strongest forms of his critique of identity, and the affirmation of a world populated by differences-in-themselves which are not copies of any prior model.

Simply put, 'simulacrum' means 'copy'. It is in Deleuze's discussion of Plato in *The Logic of Sense* that simulacra are most closely discussed. Plato offers a three-level hierarchy of the model, the copy, and the copy of the copy which is the simulacrum. The real concern for Plato is that, being a step removed from the model, the simulacrum is inaccurate and betrays the model. He uses this hierarchy in a number of places, and in each case it is a matter of distinguishing the 'false pretender' or simulacrum. For example, in the *Sophist*, Socrates discusses the means with which we might distinguish between the philosopher (the good copy), who is in search of the Good (the model), and the sophist (the simulacrum of the philosopher – the bad copy), who uses the same skills as the philosopher in search of profit or fame.

Deleuze notes that while the distinction between the model and the copy seems the most important one for Plato, it is rather the distinction between the true and the false copies which is at the heart of Platonism. The copy of the copy, cut off from reference to a model, puts into question the modelcopy system as a whole, and confronts it with a world of pure simulacrum. This reveals, for Deleuze, the moral nature of Plato's system, which fundamentally values identity, order, and the stable reference to a model over the groundless movements of simulacra. This does not mean that Deleuze considers the world to be made up of appearances, 'simulations' of a real world that has now vanished. It is the sense of the word 'appearances' itself that is in question. Simulacra do not refer to anything behind or beyond the world – they make up the world. So what is being undermined by Deleuze here is a representational understanding of existence, and the moral interpretation of existence that goes along with it. Furthermore, this understanding embodies a certain negativity that is also problematic. For a copy to be a copy of any kind it must have reference to something it is not – a copy stands in for something that is not present. It requires this other thing (what linguistics would call the 'referent') to give it sense and importance.

The simulacrum, on the other hand, breaking with this picture, does not rely upon something beyond it for its force, but is itself force or power; able to do things and not merely represent. It is as a result of this positive power that simulacra can produce identities from within the world, and without reference to a model, by entering into concrete relations – in this case, the philosopher is not the one searching for the Good, but the one who is able to create new concepts from the material available in the world; concepts which will do something. We can see here a hint of the understanding of the world as a productive-machine that will emerge in *Anti-Oedipus* and *A Thousand Plateaus*.

Deleuze also connects the thought of the simulacrum to that of the eternal return. As Deleuze frequently argues, we must understand the eternal return in terms of the return and affirmation of the different, and not of the Same. Rather than distinguishing between good and bad copies, the eternal return rejects the whole model/copy picture – which is grounded on the value of the Same and infuses negativity into the world – in favour of the productive power of the simulacra themselves.

Connectives

Difference
Eternal return
Plato
Representation

SINGULARITY

Tom Conley

In the histories of cartography and of the cognition of terrestrial space, 'singularity' is a term that replaces that of the mirror. It is first seen in the early modern period. In the Middle Ages the 'mirror of human salvation' (*speculum humane salvationis*) charted a typology of events in human and divine time that made clear the order of the world on the basis of events in the Old Testament that also have analogues in the New Testament. The mirror was that which assured a reflection of a totality and the presence of God, a reflective surface, resembling perhaps the pupil of an eye on which were gathered and assembled the variety and wealth of divine creation. When, in the later fifteenth century, oceanic travellers ventured south and east from Europe to the Indies by way of Africa or west to the Caribbean or eastern coast of South America, most representations of the world could no long conform to the figure of the *speculum mundi*. Discovery and encounter prompted cosmographers to register new, often conflicting, and sometimes unthinkable things into works of open form. As singularities these works were subject to change and revision – indeed what Deleuze often calls 'open totalities'. For a brief time, the world itself was taken to be a mass of islands and continents, of insular shapes that contained a possibly infinite measure of singularities. Thus are born works such as *Les singularités de la France antarctique* (by André Thevet) or *isolarii* ('island-books', by Benedetto Bordone, Tomasso Porcacchi and others). They are conceived to account for, record and cope with new shapes of alterity and difference coming from distant spaces.

Wherever Deleuze invokes singularity, it can be understood against this historical background. As a philosopher he embraces the idea of virtual travel, along infinite trajectories or lines of flight that lead the thinker anywhere about the world, but first and foremost among and between conceptual islands or points of singularity. As islands, they are also points that can be seen in series, as inflexions or emissions of events. A singularity, also insularity, is a decisive point and a place where perception is felt in movement. In Leibniz's concept of the monad, Deleuze notes how a 'singularity' is frequently associated with condensed events. Singularities are the 'zone of clear expression' of the monad. Less abstractly, in terms of civic geography, a singularity would be a county, a regional department, or even a topography.

The singularities of the monad are what assure the presence of a body in or through which they vibrate. They are the events that make it both unique and common, both an entity of its own perceptual data and a ground for the relation that the monad holds with its environs. They are the places where the 'singularities belonging to each . . . are extended up to the singularities of others' (D 1993a: 86). The world as a whole is perceived infinitesimally in microperceptions and gigantically, in macroperceptions. Singularity allows the subject to perceive the world in both ways, infinitesimally and infinitely, in hearing the whir of a familiar watermill, in being aware of waves of water striking the hull of a boat, or even in sensing music that accompanies a 'dance of dust' (D 1993a: 86). These formulations about singularity inflect Deleuze's work on style and the creative imagination. With the same vocabulary he notes that great writers possess 'singular conditions of perception' (D 1997b: 116). Indeed singularities allow great writers to turn aesthetic percepts into veritable visions; in other words, to move from a unique site of consciousness to an oceanic one. Such is what makes the writer change the world at large through microperceptions that become translated into a *style*, a series of singularities and differences that estrange common usages of language and make the world of both the writer and those in which the reader lives vibrate in unforeseen and compelling ways.

Were singularity associated with the 'Causes and Reasons of the Desert Island', (one of Deleuze's first pieces of philosophical writing) it would be connected with difference and repetition, one of the bases of his work on duration, identity and ideation in *Difference and Repetition*. A singularity is a unique point but it is also a point of perpetual recommencement and of variation. Like other keywords in his personal dictionary, singularity shifts and bears different inflections in different contexts but is always related to perception, subjectivity, affectivity and creation.

Connectives

Event
Leibniz
Lines of flight

SMOOTH SPACE

Tamsin Lorraine

In *A Thousand Plateaus*, Deleuze and Guattari characterise living organisms in terms of 'interior milieus' (cellular formation, organic functions) and 'exterior milieus' (food to eat, water to drink, ground to walk on). Milieus are vibratory blocks of space-time constituted by the periodic repetition of the configurations of forces that makes them what they are (D&G 1987: 313). All the milieus of the organism have their own patterns and these patterns interact with the patterns of other milieus with which they communicate. The rhythm of the interactions between these different milieus operates in terms of heterogeneous blocks rather than one homogeneous space-time. Thus, an organism emerges from chaos ('the milieu of all milieus') as vibratory milieus or blocks of space-time that create rhythms within the organism as well as with the milieus exterior to the organism. Territorial animals (including human beings) are natural artists who establish relations to imperceptible as well as perceptible forces through the refrains of song (birds) or movements and markings (wolves, rabbits) that create the rhythms of life-sustaining regularities from cosmic chaos. The various rhythms of the human subject's components and their relations to interior and exterior blocks of space-time become territorialised into the sentient awareness of one organism living in the 'striated' space of social life, cancelling out anomalous interactions among milieus in the process. The conventional notion of space as a homogeneous whole within which movement unfolds is thus, for Deleuze and Guattari, a totalised construct of space that emerges from heterogeneous blocks of space-time. They contrast their concept of 'smooth space' to the more conventional notion of space; 'smooth space' haunts and can disrupt the striations of conventional space, and it unfolds through 'an infinite succession of linkages and changes in direction' that creates shifting mosaics of space-times out of the heterogeneous blocks of different milieus (D&G 1987: 494). Deleuze and Guattari are interested not in substituting one conception of space with another, but rather in how forces striate space and how at the same time it develops other forces that emit smooth spaces (D&G 1987: 500).

In a discussion of the concept of the 'movement-image' inspired by Henri Bergson, Deleuze distinguishes movement from space: 'space covered is past, movement is present, the act of covering' (D 1986: 1). Spaces covered by movement are divisible and belong to a single, homogeneous space while movement changes qualitatively when it is divided. Movements, of what Deleuze and Guattari in *A Thousand Plateaus* call 'deterritorialization', are acts of covering that are not referred to space conceived as a uniform area of measurable units within which changes occur. A subject who orients himself with respect to movements, rather than a retrospectively created construct of space, experiences space not in terms of a totality to which it is connected (I walk across the snow five miles from the centre of town), but rather in terms of pure relations of speed and slowness (snow under moving feet as wind lifts hair) that evoke powers to affect and be affected, both actual and potential (pushing feet against ground, could also jump or run). A person on a trip to another city might orient himself by following the road mapped out through social convention from one point to another. A nomad of the desert in search of food might orient himself differently, travelling not from one point to a predesignated destination, but rather travelling from one indication of food to the next as the need arises. In the former case, local movements are charted with respect to already specified points (thus imposing a plane of organisation upon the movements that unfold). In the latter case, space shifts with each movement in keeping with shifts in meeting the need for food. These shifts do not occur *in* space; rather they establish different configurations of nomad and vegetation and landscape that unfold *as* the smooth space of the search for food. The smooth space shared with others emerges not with reference to an 'immobile outside observer', but rather through the tactile relations of any number of observers (D&G 1987: 493). It is thus a space – like that of the steppes, the desert or polar landscapes – occupied by intensities, forces and tactile qualities, with no fixed reference point (D&G 1987: 479).

Connectives

Deterritorialisation/Reterritorialisation
Nomadicism
Space
Subjectivity

SOCIUS

Kenneth Surin

Traditional philosophy relied overwhelmingly on the operation of transcendental principles which were required to make claims possible, as well as moral aesthetic judgements. There are also transcendental principles, perhaps less widely acknowledged than the ones that underlie traditional philosophy, which subtend the constitution of the social order. These principles are embodied in what Deleuze and Guattari call the 'socius'. The well-known philosophical counter-tradition inaugurated by Friedrich Nietzsche, and continued by Martin Heidegger, undertook a dismantling of the transcendental basis of traditional philosophy, and the work of Deleuze is to be located in this tradition. For Deleuze, as for Nietzsche, an entire tradition extends from Plato to Kant, in which it is declared that the yardstick of knowledge is verisimilitude. In Plato's case verisimilitude derives from an ideal 'world of Forms' (the transcendent), whereas for Immanuel Kant this world of the transcendent was banished to the realm of the 'noumenal absolute'. Kant, though, insisted that the counterpart to the noumenal world, for example the world of phenomena, was constituted by the activity of the transcendental (or non-empirically given) subject of possible experience. In their reflection on the socius, conducted throughout the two volumes of *Capitalism and Schizophrenia*,

Deleuze and Guattari seek what amounts to a comprehensive undoing of the transcendental basis of the constitution of the social order. In so doing, they adhere to the 'transcendental empiricism', in which the basis for the constitution of real (as opposed to possible) experience is sought. This project is 'transcendental' in so far as the conditions for real experience require a nonempirical organisation of the objects of experience, though the source of this organisation is not a transcendental subject à la Kant, but rather the very form in which real objects are experienced as active and dynamic.

In *Anti-Oedipus*, the socius is said to be necessary because desiring-production is coterminous with social production and reproduction, and for the latter to take place desire has to be coded and recoded, so that subjects can be prepared for their social roles and functions. The socius is the terrain of this coding and recoding. Another rationale for the socius stems from the part it plays in consolidating the capitalist order. Desire is simultaneously enabled and limited by capital, which frees it from its previous embodiments or codings so that it can be placed at the disposal of capitalist expansion; and desire, after this decoding by capital, is reined in or recoded so that it can subserve the novel requirements of capitalist production.

Coding or 'inscription' are thus central to the constitution of the socius, and Deleuze and Guattari respond to the crucial question of the surface on which inscription takes place by invoking the notion of the earth. The earth precedes the constitution of the socius, and is the primordial unity or ground of desire and production. As such the earth is the precondition of production while also being the object of desire. The first form of the socius has therefore to involve a territorialisation, undertaken by a 'territorial machine', which parcels out the earth into segments of social meaning.

Once territorialisation has occurred, it becomes possible for social machines (the core of the socius) to operate. Social machines have humans as their parts and are essential to the generation of cultural forms, these forms being needed to link humans to their (technical) machines. Social machines organise flows of power and desire by coding them. There are all kinds of flows: different kinds of humans, vegetation, non-human animals, agricultural implements, flows that involve bodily functions and organs, and so on. Nothing escapes coding, and so nothing can escape the purview of the socius.

If the socius is a megamachine, the fuel that drives this machine is desire, though desire is shaped and orchestrated by its insertion into this megamachine. In modern societies, the nature of this insertion of desire into the social megamachine has been significantly transformed. To facilitate the functioning of capitalism, flows have had to become more abstract, since capital requires intersubstitutibility, homogeneity, relentless quantification, and exchange mechanisms to work. Hand in hand with this abstraction goes a privatisation of the social, since an over-valuation of the individual is required to compensate for the massive collective disinvestment that takes place in the social as a result of the inexorable growth of the processes of abstraction. The vehicles of this privatisation are ruled by the Oedipus principle, which functions as a kind of transcendental regime for the investment of social desire. Other principles, primarily concerned with morality and punishment, but also with death and cruelty, are effective in this domain too.

Dispensing with psychoanalysis as the ontology for how a socius is constituted, Deleuze and Guattari find it necessary to replace Freudianism with a different ontology. The alternative – called 'schizoanalysis' or 'nomadology' – begins by refusing any kind of transcendental principle purporting to serve as the ground of the socius. In place of the logic of necessity and continuity that characterised previous social ontologies, Deleuze and Guattari opt for one that is marked by ruptures, limits, singularities, ironies and contingencies. Traditional logic displaces desire as the motor driving the social megamachine. Schizoanalysis or nomadology provide a new conception of experience and desiring-production, emphasising forms of experimentation not constrained by the ego or Oedipal structures, as well as the need to create new forms of collective (as opposed to merely individual) liberation. Importantly, this kind of liberation cannot be sponsored either by the State or capital.

Connectives

Capitalism
Desire
Earth/Land
Guattari
Psychoanalysis
Schizoanalysis

SPACE

Tom Conley

In a view of a port seen at night at the beginning of Jean-Luc Godard's *Pierrot le fou* (1965), one of Deleuze's model films in his work on the timeimage, a voice quotes a passage from Elie Faure on Velasquez: 'Space reigns'. The remark could apply to all of Deleuze's writings. For the philosopher, space is what is at once created and exhausted or annihilated in the creation of an event. Wherever philosophy creates events, it recoups literature and the arts in general. In an important essay on Samuel Beckett, Deleuze notes that space is rich in potentiality because it makes possible the realisation of events. A given image or concept, when it is seen or engaged, creates and dissipates space in the time of its perception. Space is something that is at the edges of language. Deleuze calls the apprehension of space an 'exhaustion' of meaning. The artist dissipates meaning in order to make space palpable at the moment it is both created and annihilated. For both Godard and Beckett it could be said that the stakes are those of 'exhausting space' (D 1997b: 163). Only then can it be seen and felt in an event, in a sudden disjunction, that scatters what we take to be the reality in which we live.

The almost mystical tenor of Deleuze's work on space and the event (especially in 'The Exhausted' in *Essays Critical and Clinical*) is explained by what the historian of religion Michel de Certeau writes in a 1984 study of the invention of everyday life: Space is a discursive practice of a place. A place is a given area, named and mapped, that can be measured in terms of surface or volume. It becomes space only when it becomes a site of existential engagement among living agents who mark it with their activities or affiliate with dialogue and active perception. Place in this sense is equivalent to Deleuze's concept of an *espace quelconque*, 'any-space-whatsoever', that is determined and given to be what it is without being inflected by a user or a traveller. The task of the philosopher and artist is to take the most innocuous or ineffectual of all places and to fragment (even atomise or molecularise) or strip them of their potential. The task of the film-maker is to make visible these non-places before fracturing and dispersing them through creative manipulation. Roberto Rossellini, in *Paisan* (1947) or *Germany, Year Zero* (1948) extends before the eyes of the spectator proliferations of any-spaces-whatsoever, 'an urban cancer, an indifferent surface, a wasteland' (D 1986: 212) that have as their counterparts the clichés of everyday life, that his camera makes untenable and inhuman. Accordingly, the task of the philosopher is to turn 'commonplaces' into matter for more exhaustive speculation. Therein are engendered other spaces that can be hypothetical and utopian or even virtual.

Space is elsewhere measured in Deleuze's political writings according to degrees of smoothness and striation. A 'smooth space' is one that is boundless and possibly oceanic, a space that is without border or distinction that would privilege one site or place over another. It does not belong to a prelapsarian world from which humans have fallen (as Rousseau might argue), nor is it utopian unless it can be thought of in conjunction with its 'striated' counterpart, a space drawn and riddled with lines of divide and demarcation that name, measure, appropriate and distribute space according to inherited political designs, history or economic conflict. Without boundaries or measure, smooth space is frequently affiliated with the unconscious. It is 'occupied by events or haecceities more than by formed and perceived things', and thus it is more a space of affects or sensations than properties (D&G 1987: 479). It is defined by a flow of forces and hence is perceived haptically instead of optically. It is 'intensive' where striated space is 'extensive'. A Body without Organs (BwO) bears a surface of smooth space that lacks zones or organs that have affective privilege over others. Striated space is one where lines and points designate itineraries and trajectories. Smooth space can be perceived in and through striated space, indeed what is seen and experienced in the world at large, in order to deterritorialise given places. In Deleuze's lexicon that pertains to space and place, deterritorialisation and reterritorialisation are at the basis of most biological and philosophical activity. In this respect the nomad is the person or thinker who constantly creates space by moving from place to place. The nomad, the philosopher, and the scientist and artist alike are capable of creating spaces through the trajectories of their passages that move from one territory to another and from given striations on the surface of the world to smooth and intensive areas, areas that are tantamount to the folds and creases of events that vibrate in the body, itself a place that can be affectively spatialised in infinite ways.

Connectives

Body without Organs
Deterritorialisation/Reterritorialisation
Nomadicism
Smooth space
Utopia
Virtual/Virtuality

SPACE + ARCHITECTURE

Graham Livesey

From Deleuze and Guattari's extended discussion of smooth and striated space in *A Thousand Plateaus*, one would typically determine that architecture is highly striated: rectilinear, measured, controlled, centered, extensive, constructed, and regulated. As an example they identify the city has an exemplar of striated space (D&G 1987: 481). Smooth space, as the space of nomadicism, displays opposite tendencies to those of striated space. However, as they point out, space is always a mixture of the smooth and striated, and a given space (or territory) can reverse its dominant tendencies or qualities. Examples of smooth and striated space reversals drawn Deleuze and Guattari include their description of Henry Miller walking through a city effectively converting striated space to smooth space (D&G 1987: 482), and the smooth spaces found in the shantytowns, or 'informal cities', that surround many large global cities (D&G 1987: 481).

The striated qualities of architectural space are evident across much of the history of architecture, as architecture emerges with settled or sedentary cultures, in opposition to the nomadic cultures that urbanisation displaces. Here architectural space is precisely delineated, the rectilinear room being the most enduring example. Like cities, most urbanised cultures have produced buildings that respond to the spatial and functional patterns of the State (or the dominant religion). Nevertheless, even within State organisations there have been cultures that have produced architecture that moves away from the highly striated. Buildings, under certain circumstances, can act as smooth space structures; notably, traditional Japanese residential architecture, the architecture of the European Baroque (see D 1993a), and some examples of twentieth-century architecture, particularly recent experiments in folded architecture. In contradistinction to the architecture of urbanised cultures, the structures of nomadic cultures (tents, huts, yurts, etc.) operate in smooth space.

Ultimately Deleuze and Guattari have no generalised concept of space, they tend to foreground localised concepts of territoriality over spatiality. These localised conditions are most precisely defined by modes of movement and navigation, and are continuously remade by the forces of deterritorialisation and reterritorialisation. The concept of assemblage can be useful for architects in that it signals how bodies, actions, expressions, and territorialities (spatialities) productively combine.

Beyond his concepts of smooth and striated space, Deleuze examines folded and pliant space in *The Fold: Leibniz and the Baroque*. Consistent with his emphasis of smooth and folded space, Deleuze is always more interested in the intensive qualities of space over the extensive. Spatiality is continuously created and is part of the productivity inherent to assemblages, space is the effect of inter-connections. In this sense, territoriality is a more productive concept for Deleuze and Guattari than spatiality. Therefore, Deleuze and Guattari's spatial and territorial concepts do lend themselves to examining existing architecture and creating new architecture, and they stress the idea that buildings and cities can allow for the continuous production of new spatial, or territorial, arrangements.

SPINOZA, BARUCH (1632–77)

Kenneth Surin

In the last few decades the writings of Louis Althusser, Etienne Balibar, Pierre Macherey, Antonio Negri, Deleuze and others, have marked a resurgence of interest in the thought of Baruch Spinoza, in which Spinoza's materialist ontology has been used as a framework for constructing a matrix of thought and practice not regimented by the axioms of Platonic metaphysics, the epistemology of René Descartes, and the transcendental rationalism of Immanuel Kant and Georg Wilhelm Friedrich Hegel. Also important for these thinkers has been the use of Spinoza as a resource to reconceptualise some of Karl Marx's more important categories and principles. Coupled with this resurgence has been a parallel development in the area of more technical commentary on Spinoza, associated primarily with the massive works of Martial Gueroult and Alexandre Matheron. Deleuze himself dealt with Spinoza in two texts: his 1968 doctoral thesis *Spinoza et le problème de l'expression* (D 1992) and the 1970 shorter text *Spinoza: Philosophie pratique* (D 1988c), though the thought of Spinoza permeates all his works, including the texts co-written with Guattari.

Deleuze views Spinoza as the first thinker to make judgements about truth and virtue inescapably social. Hence, for Spinoza, notions of moral culpability, responsibility, good and evil have no reality except in so far as they stem from the disposition to obey or disobey those in authority. The State cannot compel the individual as long as she is seen to obey, and so Deleuze credits Spinoza with being the first philosopher to place thought outside the purview of the State and its functions: Spinoza, says Deleuze in *Spinoza: Practical Philosophy*, 'solicits forces in thought that elude obedience as well as blame, and fashions the image of a life beyond good and evil, a rigorous innocence without merit or culpability' (D 1988c: 4). Life for Spinoza, since it cannot be constrained by the state or milieu from which it emerges, is irreducibly positive: life cannot be enhanced if it is trammelled by the interdictions of priests, judges, and generals whose own lives are marked by an internal sado-masochism. Needless to say, Deleuze's use of Spinoza is inevitably selective. There are many Spinozas, just as there are many Platos and Hegels, and Deleuze's Spinoza is a Spinoza read through the eyes of Friedrich

Nietzsche, and especially Nietzsche's doctrine of the eternal return. For Nietzsche, according to Deleuze, the eternal return means that one will be willing to experience life over and over again in exactly the same way. Similarly, where Spinoza is concerned, the person who will not be a victim of the sad passions, the aspirant for beatitude, will be someone whose actions cannot be an occasion for regret. In both cases, therefore, the individual concerned will not want the terms under which she lives life to be any different.

For Spinoza, there are two primary kinds of forces which diminish life – hatred, which is turned towards the other; and the bad conscience, which is turned inwards. Only a new kind of life, capable of sustaining experimentation and a new appetite for living, can overcome these negative and reactive passions. Spinoza's works, primarily the *Ethics*, delineate an intellectual framework (going under the name of an 'ethics') for leading this new life. In this new ontology, a body is defined by its speeds and slownesses, not its forms and functions, as it was in the age-old Aristotelian metaphysics that dominated philosophy until the Enlightenment. Also important in this ontology are the linkages between different bodies, culminating in the forming of a nexus of connections, each connection or set of connections proceeding with its own speed and slowness. Knowledge understood in this way is essentially material and contingent, since no individual knows ahead of time what their bodily affects are and what they are likely to involve in relation to other individuals and forces.

Deleuze and Guattari's kinship with Spinoza stems from their perception that philosophy today has to come to terms with the emergence of new knowledges that have been accompanied by the explosive rise of a whole range of new sciences, based on the creation of 'nonstandard' logics and topologies of change and relation, and typically devised to deal with situations that have the character of the irregular or the arbitrary (what Deleuze and Guattari call 'nomad thought', 'rhizomatics', 'schizoanalysis'). These new logics and topologies concern themselves not only with the structural principles of change and process, but also with surfaces, textures, rhythms, connections and so on, all of which can be analysed in terms of such notions as those of strings, knots, flows, labyrinths, intensities and becomings. Spinoza is viewed by Deleuze as the pre-eminent precursor of this 'nomad thought', though clearly for them Leibniz, Nietzsche and Bergson are also exemplary predecessors.

The appropriation of Spinoza's thought by Deleuze (and Guattari) is undeniably selective. There is a rationalism in Spinoza that is downplayed in Deleuze's interpretation of him, and while Spinoza was critical of State power, he cannot easily be made to share the same theoretical premisses as the anarcho-Marxism of Deleuze and Guattari. All this notwithstanding, Spinoza's rigorous immanentism and materialism, mediated in complex ways by the thought of several other thinkers, are very much in evidence in Deleuze's oeuvre.

Connectives

Eternal return
Immanence
Materialism

SPINOZA + ETHICS OF JOY

Constantin V. Boundas

Deleuze has often been praised for his (Stoic) commitment to the ethics of the event – our becoming worthy of the event through the process of counter-actualisation of that which is happening to us. But Deleuze has also laid claim to an ethic of joy, the articulation of which is the result of his many encounters with Baruch Spinoza. The nodal point that represents the linkage of this commitment is the Nietzschean affirmation of the 'eternal return' – the lynchpin of Deleuze's ontology and the indispensable imperative of his ethics.

Deleuze thinks of desire as an affirmative, non-intentional intensity, producing connections – real in their function and revolutionary in their multiplicity. Deleuze's desire is modelled after Spinoza's *conatus*; it is neither a 'want' nor 'lack' but the effort of an individual entity to persevere in its own existence. Spinoza always thinks of *conatus* as being determined by its capacity to affect and to be affected; it is not, therefore, difficult to think of *conatus* as desire. Provided that we do not separate essence from action, a *conatus* can be understood as the essence of an entity or its degree of power. Actions themselves constitute a person's affirmation of life and his will to exist.

Spinoza speaks of an order of essences, that is, of an order of intensities, within which all singular essences cohere and are mutually responsible for each other's production. In Deleuze's work, this order helps him articulate the virtual/real. But in Spinoza, there is also an order of organisation, with its own laws eternally determining the conditions for the coming into being and the endurance of singular entities. On this plane, arrangements are made ad infinitum, but not every arrangement is compatible with the others. Spinoza recognises an order of fortuitous encounters: bodies encounter other bodies and in some cases the singular arrangements of one body are such that they 'fit' the singular arrangements of the bodies they encounter; together they increase each other's power of affectivity. Sometimes however, some bodies are incompatible with others' arrangements, thus when they meet they decrease the power of one another.

In an effort to think about desire as joy, Deleuze borrows from Spinoza's schema of intensities. To the extent that desire is not phantasmatic, desire is the power that one has, which allows one to go as far as this power permits: the power to annex being. Here the distinction between progressive and regressive annexation becomes the urgent task of the ethicist. Deleuze's allegiance to Spinoza permits him to argue that the question of the effort of the individual to maintain and prolong his existence is also a question of how to enable the maximum experience of active affects. The order of fortuitous encounters does not give us an edge because it leads to the formation of inadequate ideas – an inadequate idea being the idea whose cause is not in our own power to understand. Nevertheless, even an inadequate idea causes an affect, and an affect, whose adequate cause we are not, is a passion. Conversely, an adequate idea finds its formal cause in our power to think and to understand, and also generates an affect in us, an affect whose adequate cause is our own power to think and is, therefore, an action. In this case, we no longer count on accidental encounters to multiply joyful passions.

An entire genetic phenomenology of the becoming-active of human beings can be found in Spinoza's *Ethics*, and this is what inspires Deleuze's ethics of joy.We begin with passive desires/joys that increase our power to act despite the fact that they are at the mercy of inadequate ideas. But, then, thanks to these desires and passions, we begin to form common notions, or adequate ideas. Active desire/joy accompanies the common notions as our power to act increases. Finally, active joy replaces passions, filling us with new capacities to be affected; this combination constitutes the active life of the individual. In turn our capacity to understand sadness and contrariety is enhanced, and as we develop a better understanding of these affections our active joy increases.

At this time, the influence of Friedrich Nietzsche in Deleuze's ethics of joy is revealed: the pedagogy for the formulation of adequate ideas becomes the process of the counter-actualisation of that which happens to us. It is no longer the generality of the common notion that stands for the *cogitandum* of practical reason; it is the event that must be grasped through the process of counter-actualisation. The sadness in the state of affairs passively affecting us is transformed into a joyful affirmation of the event. Passive affections are turned into active ones that are capable of transvaluing and transforming states of affairs.

STATE

Kenneth Surin

Deleuze and Guattari have a conception of the State that is indebted to the work of the anthropologist and anarchist Pierre Clastres. Clastres had argued against the conventional evolutionist account of the emergence of the State as a form of political and social organisation. According to this traditional account, the State can develop only when a society reaches a certain degree of complexity, evidenced primarily by its capacity to create and sustain a more sophisticated division of labour. Against this view, Clastres argued the State is the condition for undertaking significant economic and political projects and the division of labour that ensues from these projects, and so logically and empirically the division of labour does not condition economic and political projects. Deleuze and Guattari follow Clastres in repudiating this evolutionist theory.

In *Capitalism and Schizophrenia*, Deleuze and Guattari view the State as an overarching power that brings together labour power and the prior conditions for the constitution of labour power, enabling the creation of surplus-value. As a result, there is a constitutive antagonistic relation between the State and labour, especially since the State supplies capital with its models of realisation, and so there is also necessarily an antagonism between capital and labour. Capital exists and perpetuates itself by organising itself to orchestrate and contain this proletarian antagonism. The necessary concomitant of the State's apparatuses' capacity to engage in this task of organisation is the production of surplus-value and facilitating accumulation. As a result, capital and the State are under unceasing internal pressure to neutralise and contain the antagonism that, paradoxically, is the very thing that enables it to exist. The assemblages created and maintained by the State and capital create a collective subjectivity which establishes the material aspects of the productive forces that generate surplus-value and by so doing make production and accumulation possible. Along with the formation of collective subjectivity goes the (State's) power of subjection.

The State's capacity to engage in the formation of a collective subjectivity, needed to constitute labour as a productive force, does not remain the same throughout history. The despotic State in early historical times used slavery and serfdom with their accompanying forms of subjectivity for this task; industrial capitalism used the figure of the mass worker and disciplinary social formations; and today, in the age of a globalised and worldintegrated capitalism, the State is still needed to regulate the flows of production and to reproduce the forms of accumulation. But this power of domination is no longer mediatory, as was the case with the previous economic dispensations, in as much as the State is no longer needed to create and maintain classes and other social and economic subgroupings. Instead, the function of the State/capital in the current phase of capitalist accumulation is to engage in the work of disaggregation, to segment, through administrative procedures and the use of media and informational systems, the countervailing power that the proletariat has developed. Capital/State has a negative relationship to the forces and forms that oppose it.

In the present capitalist conjuncture, the authors of *Capitalism and Schizophrenia* say that capitalism is an independent, worldwide axiomatic that is like a single City,megalopolis, or 'megamachine' of which the States are parts, or neighbourhoods. Towards this end, capitalism will even create States that are not viable, like Somalia and Rwanda, for its own purposes: subjugating minorities through forced integration and extermination. In the present conjuncture, that is, the age of the societies of control (as opposed to the disciplinary societies of the previous epoch), capital has become the ubiquitous milieu that secures the isomorphism of even the most disparate forms (commercial, religious, artistic, and so forth). In this milieu, productive labour is inserted into every section of society: the universality of capital is simultaneous with the omnipresence of everything that creates surplus-value, as human subjectivity, leisure and play, and so on, are incorporated into the latest regimes of accumulation. Capitalism has always striven to create an economic order that is able to function without the State, and in its current phase this propensity has become more marked than ever. However, for Deleuze and Guattari this is not because the State itself has been abolished, but rather because the separation between State and society can now no longer be maintained. Society and State now constitute a single and unified nexus, and all capital has become social capital. Hence the production of social cooperation, undertaken primarily by the service and informational industries in developed countries, has become crucial for capitalism. Deleuze and Guattari insist that the deterritorialising effect of State/Capital merely produces an even more powerful reterritorialisation, that is, State/Capital only breaches limits in order to impose its own limits.

Connective

Capitalism

STATE + GEOGRAPHY

John Protevi

In *A Thousand Plateaus* the state's production of striated space has complex relations to numerous other spatialising processes. Among them we find two familiar forms: the territories operated by primitive societies and the smooth spaces of nomads, as well as two less well-known forms; the networking of cities and the burrowing producing the holey space of itinerant metallurgists. In this entry we will concentrate on the relation of the spatialising processes of the state and the war machine, that is, on striating and smoothing, with some preliminary attention paid to territorialisation as practised by primitive social machines. We should stress that such spaces are never finished and isolated products, but are the results of processes in constant interchange with each other, so that, for example, we should speak of the 'smoothing of striated space' and the 'striating of smoothed space', that is, the interchange of smoothing and striating processes (D&G 1987: 474-5).

The most straightforward relation is that between the state and striation. Given that the state apparatus must operate to transform the earth [*terre*] of primitive society and the ground [*sol*] of nomads into land [*terre*], striation is one of the fundamental tasks of state, presignifying, or primitive territories that allow for the free movements of bodies, regimes produce territories to tie production to the earth. Primitive territorialising practices continually ward off being striated from their exterior as long as they are able to challenge states. State striation results from the overcoding, centralisation and hierarchisation of primitive territories. Although primitive social machines operate by territories, they also can be said to operate a smooth space insofar as they allow for the free movement of bodies. Striation fastens upon the territorialised earth of primitive societies and transforms it into gridded plots so that people then occupy precisely located parcels of land. In thus fixing the land into comparable parcels, striation enables rent (D&G 1987: 440-1).

Let us now consider the relation of the state to the nomad war machine, the cutting edge that smoothes striated space. In this sense, smooth space is the substance of expression of which the nomad war machine is the form of expression. The war machine was however long ago appropriated by states as their armies, yet this defeat is the moment of the war machine's non-geographical, that is, entirely social, proliferation: 'Could it be that it is at the moment the war machine ceases to exist, conquered by the State, that it displays to the utmost its irreducibility, that it scatters into thinking, loving, dying, or creating machines that have at their disposal vital or revolutionary powers capable of challenging the conquering State?' (D&G 1987: 356). This is no dialectics, or romanticism; the creativity the war machine effectuates is not the opposite of state capture. The war machine is that which effectuates non-organic life. In the contemporary world the war machine is taken up by its own process of material creativity which is both social and technological. As Deleuze and Guattari write: 'the war machine's form of exteriority is such that it exists only in its own metamorphoses; it exists in an industrial innovation as well as in a technological innovation, in a commercial circuit as well as in a religious creation, in all flows and currents that only secondarily allow themselves to be appropriated by the State' (D&G 1987: 360). Because of the emphasis on creativity, 'war is like the fall or failure of the war machine, the only object left for the war machine after it has lost its power to change' (D&G 1987: 230). The worst case for the failed war machine occurs when it 'has constructed itself a State apparatus capable only of destruction. When this happens, the war machine no longer draws mutant lines of flight, but a pure, cold line of abolition' (D&G 1987: 230). Here Deleuze and Guattari are referring to the Nazi regime.

In a fascinating inversion correlative with the military aspect of what is commonly called globalisation, smooth space has become the regime of state security forces that can descend on the land at any point after gathering surveillance information. Along with the construction of a global smooth space of thorough security intervention, terrorist enemies are discovered everywhere. This results in 'a macropolitics of society by and for a micropolitics of insecurity' (D&G 1987: 216). The production of smooth space by state security forces also operates on a local scale; a case in point is in urban warfare. For instance, Weizman has drawn attention to the way in which the Israel Defense Forces used Deleuze and Guattari's concept of smooth space as a military strategy (W 2007).

To conclude, we should note that it's not just states in their political-military aspect that produce smooth spaces. Contemporary capitalism, with its multinational corporations, produces a type of machinic enslavement, that is, 'a complex qualitative process bringing into play modes of transportation, urban models, the media, the entertainment industries, ways of perceiving and feeling'. The result: the creation of a new smooth space (D&G 1987: 492).

Taking into account how security procedures operate, smoothing as a military strategy, and the machinic enslavement of contemporary capitalism, we can understand why Deleuze and Guattari warn: 'never believe that a smooth space will suffice to save us' (HD 2000: 500).

STRATIFICATION

Kylie Message

Deleuze and Guattari explain 'stratification' is an ongoing, rhizomatic process that contributes to the line of emergence or becoming. This process may (or may not) lead to our rejection of a unifying subjectivity and embrace instead the forever-formative Body without Organs (BwO). However, the process/term 'stratification' also refers to what is essentially an organising principle of sorts, whereby it assists writers in their attempt actively to apply – or put into practice – their ideas (*A Thousand Plateaus* aims to put forth a series of 'pragmatics' rather than abstract theories). As such, the term provides both an organising form for discussion, as well as the subject matter or content contained by that form.

The processes (rather than just the effects) of everyday experience are invoked by Deleuze and Guattari in order to show interweaving journeys between states of consciousness and unconsciousness that we both take and make routinely and repetitively. These often forgotten journeys and the non-cognitive decisions that accompany our movements are precisely where a potential line of flight or becoming may be located, and in evoking largely taken-for-granted State systems, all processes of becoming occur – at least initially – within these systems.

In what is perhaps the most useful and accessible paradox of Plateau 3 of *A Thousand Plateaus*, a primary point of discussion emerges as the relationship between the production and reception of language (via theories of semiotics). As paradoxical meta-narrative forms, the chaotic principles motivating maintenance of the concepts of the earth and God function to destabilise the claims for truth or universality that are often associated with somehow more seamless semiotic theories that attempt to provide a generalising explanation for all aspects of reality. Instead, Deleuze and Guattari show that language, like all systems and all aspects of life, is constituted by a series of strata that have been traditionally contained by physiochemical, organic or anthropomorphic categories. Straddling these fields, language affects every aspect of the universe by contextualising them within a single sphere of interaction. For Deleuze and Guattari, every articulation (or stratum) consists of abstract and discrete components. In accord with this, language (and semiotics as the science of language) can clearly be seen as an organising principle that presumes to make sense of our experience of these components that, when combined, produce reality. However, while acknowledging that they need to invoke the system they aim to critique (language must be used for general communication to occur between writers and readers), Deleuze and Guattari also show that linguistic terms or signifiers tend to be used in such generalising and structural ways that they cease to function linguistically in relation to a specific idea or field of content. As such, the signifier comes to adopt instead a kind of physical or distinct independence and objecthood, whereby the relationship between signifier and signified is further obliterated.

Deleuze and Guattari contend that all articulations are always already a double articulation because they are constituted by the dual components of content and expression. We can understand this to mean that strata come in pairs and are themselves made up of a double articulation that can then be recognised as molar and molecular (and bound by the third even more variable term/line of nomadic), or which we may alternatively consider through the terms of 'expression' and 'content' (these replace the Saussurian concepts of 'signifier' and 'signified'). However, as indicated by the more generally accepted breakdown in referential relations between the signifier and signified, it is important to note that the layers, planes or discrete strata of content or expression are arbitrary. There is no referential, signifier-signified, or cause-and-effect relationship regulating their production or existence, despite the fact that the layers may cooperate with each other or bleed into one another in order to produce new strata or lines of deterritorialisation.

The concept of 'stratification' is an attempt to promote a new kind of thinking about the way language produces an image of reality (and is itself reframed as a product of this same activity). Language is an important point of focus because it is both a grand and minor narrative, and an organising as well as organised principle through which our subjectivity is only ever provisionally contained.

Connectives

Becoming
Body without Organs
Lines of flight
Rhizome
Semiotics

Signifier/signified
Subjectivity

SUBJECTIVITY

Constantin V. Boundas

Deleuze abandons the old image of the subject as a fixed substance or foundation stone, in favour of a subject that is the provisional outcome of a process of subjectivation. The Deleuzian subject is an assemblage of heterogeneous elements whose source is not the interiority of the traditional image of thought. Deleuze insists that subjectivity is not given; it is always under construction.

At first glance, Deleuze's shifting attitudes about subjectivity seem to defy reconciliation. First, in *Empiricism and Subjectivity* he outlines that 'a subject is defined by the movement through which it is developed' (D 1991: 85, 86). Second, in the *Dialogues* he explains that there are 'no more subjects, but dynamic individuations without subjects, which constitute collective assemblages. . . Nothing becomes subjective but haecceities take shape according to the compositions of non-subjective powers and effects' (D 1987: 93). Last, in *Foucault* he writes that 'the struggle for [modern] subjectivity presents itself, therefore, as the right to difference, variation and metamorphosis' (D 1988b: 106). The reconciliation of these positions hinges on our ability to read each one of them as a separate answer to a distinct question.

In *Empiricism and Subjectivity,* Deleuze outlines that the intensive, integrative act of our practical interest (extension of an initially intensive – yet narrow – moral sympathy over those who are not our kin), together with the associative rules of our speculative interest, make the organisation of subjectivity possible. Far from establishing the seamless identity of the subject, this organisation shows us that the subject's constitution is a fiction, for the subject is an entity out of joint (cracked). There would be no belief in the subject without the (illegitimate and fictitious) belief in God and the World – illegitimate, because neither God nor World can ever be objects of knowledge. Yet, these fictions act as the horizons of all possible beliefs, including the (illegitimate and fictitious) belief in the subject and its unity.

For Deleuze in *Difference and Repetition*, the subject is the tensive arrangement of many larval subjects. A self exists as long as a contracting machine, capable of drawing a difference from repetition, functions somewhere. There is a self lurking in the eye; another in the liver; a third in the stomach. A subject is the inclusive disjunction borne from the contraction of all these selves.

In *Capitalism and Schizophrenia*, the subject's recognition of itself as subject is described by Deleuze and Guattari as 'retrospective'. It emerges not as the agent of selection but as an after-effect of desiring-production. Capitalism and the isolation of the nuclear family from society that capitalism facilitates provide a perfect training ground for the ascetic subjectivity that capitalism requires. It also reproduces patriarchy by producing hierarchically gendered subjects in accordance with specific values and imperatives that thrive within the nuclear family.

Meanwhile, in *The Fold* a subject is that which comes to a point of view, or rather that which remains at the point of view, provided that the point of view is one of variation. It is not the point of view that varies within the subject; on the contrary it is the condition through which an eventual subject apprehends variation. A subject is a monad that includes in itself – and also conveys – the entire World obscurely, by expressing clearly only a small region of the world.

Deleuze and Guattari propose in *Foucault* that the inside is an operation *of* the outside or a doubling up of the outside. Here, the subject is the result of a process of subjectivation in accordance with four foldings. These are as follows: first, the material part of ourselves; second, the folding of force; third, the folding of knowledge; and fourth, the folding of the outside. A person does not fold the forces composing them, without the outside itself also being folded, hence forming a self within a person. Folding is the memory of the outside.

Further, the 'other' as it is discussed in *The Logic of Sense* makes possible the categories of 'subject' and 'object'. The other is the structure of all possible worlds: it inhabits the transitions from one object to another; it relativises distances and differences; it forms the background from which forms rise up; and the other spatialises and temporalises. The intensive bracketing of 'the other', therefore, is tantamount to the intensive bracketing of 'the Self'. The familiar world and the subjects that inhabit it, in the presence of others, release and molecularise the elements and singularities that were previously sedimented and stratified inside them. The ideology of 'lack' and negation that kept the subject's desire captive is now shown to be the result of socio-historical processes of subjectivation, rather than the irreducible datum of subjectivity. What emerges after the bracketing of the other as structure of all possible worlds is the 'otherwise other' – *l'autrement qu'autre*.

Connectives

Capitalism
Desire
Fold
Memory

SUBJECTIVITY + ART

Simon O'Sullivan

Deleuze has been portrayed as a philosopher of dissolution, as a thinker of flows and intensities somehow 'outside' of, or 'beyond', the human. Indeed a cursory reading of *A Thousand Plateaus* might lead one to suppose that Deleuze and Guattari are interested in 'escaping' lived life. Certainly this trajectory is there, perhaps most infamously in the notion of the Body without Organs (BwO), understood as a strategy that helps free us from the strata that constitutes us *as* human (that is to say, in a particular configuration). However Deleuze's philosophy is also very much one of caution, for it is never a question of wildly destratifying but of dosages, of finding *creative* lines of flight that lead somewhere and from which one can 'return'. Deterritorialisation always ends in a reterritorialisation and in fact needs a territory from which to operate.

It is in this sense that Deleuze might also be understood as a constructive philosopher. Certainly he is involved in the prodigious construction of concepts, as evidenced by this dictionary. However, we might also see him, specifically in his collaborations, as being involved in the parallel project of the construction, or *production*, of subjectivity. This is even more the case with Guattari's own work, which was always involved in thinking through what Guattari called 'resingularisation': the potentiality for, and practicalities of, reconfiguring our subjectivities. For Guattari, as for Deleuze, this is a pragmatic and specifically materialist project. Through involvement with certain materials of expression, with groups and individuals, and always with an 'outside' we can open up new universes of reference: new ways of seeing and being in the world. For Guattari La Borde clinic operated as just such a site of transformation. It encouraged new relationships and new experiences. At stake here was not the reintegration of a 'cured' individual into society, but an encouragement to become involved, to participate, in one's own processual self-creation. Whatever the successes or failures of the clinic, we have here an interesting framework for thinking those collaborative and collective art practices of today that might be seen as producing communities and subjectivities in precisely this sense. This field of expanded practice, or 'relational aesthetics' as it has become known does not require spectators as such, but participants who are 'transformed' through their interaction with the practice.

We might recognise Deleuze's Spinozism here. Indeed Baruch Spinoza's ethics involves a similar mapping to the above: the organisation of one's world so as to produce productive – that is *joyful* – encounters. Involving the coming together of two 'bodies' that essentially agree with one another, such encounters have the concomitant result of increasing our capacity to act in the world. We might call this a 'rhizomatics of friendship', the latter understood in its broadest sense. For Spinoza, ethics involves exploring what a body, in both the individual and collective sense, is capable of that begins with ethical principles or guidelines, but ultimately it produces an understanding of one's self and world – and in fact a certain overcoming of one's separation from the world.

Perhaps the key factor preventing these transformations is habit. Here 'habit' is taken to mean not just our daily routines but also our dominant refrains and typical reactions to the world. In this sense aesthetics becomes important. For naming as it does a 'disinterested' response to the world, aesthetics can operate as a rupture in otherwise dominant régimes of signification and expression (the clichés of our being and indeed of our consumer culture). Aesthetics here need not be a transcendent category, rather we can think of it simply as the generation of unexpected affects in and on the body. This rupture can and does produce possibilities for resingularisation.

Another way of thinking this 'immanent aesthetic' is as involving a kind of hesitation or gap between stimulus and response. In his use of Henri Bergson, Deleuze attends to this: the pause between action and reaction is what constitutes the human as a particularly complex brain-body assemblage. This pause allows a certain amount of freedom and the possibility for a more creative response to the world. Put differently, in today's world it is important to change speed, to slow down sometimes and even at times to remain still. Art, in fact the *contemplation* of art, might have a role to play here (this is also the sense in which meditation can be understood as a creative technology of self production). In some senses such an 'aesthetic' is 'beyond' subjectivity.

Throughout his work, Deleuze attends to those experiences that are atypical and 'non-ordinary'. For example, what happens to an individual in a 'world without others'? Here the interaction with the world takes on an idiosyncratic and perverted character. The individual harnesses cosmic forces and 'becomes world' as it were.Again this might be a name for certain art practices from prehistory to today, those that allow access to a kind of immanent beyond to the everyday, and to everyday consciousness. We might say, then, that this is the aesthetic – and *ritualistic* – function of art that always accompanies the latter's ethical or indeed political character.

SUBSTANCE

Claire Colebrook

Deleuze might appear to be a purely inventive philosopher, avowedly creating concepts and vocabularies while rejecting the constraints of already formed metaphysical systems. Certainly, he would seem to be a far cry from the project of Martin Heidegger that approached Being through its philosophical history. Central to Heidegger's destruction of the history of philosophy was the way in which the concept and grammar of 'substance' had dominated thinking. In *Difference and Repetition*, Deleuze repeatedly refers to Heidegger's project of re-activating thinking, and part of this reactivation depends upon avoiding the logic of a certain understanding of substance. However, it is not only in his early works on the history of philosophy but also in his later work with Guattari that Deleuze engages with the concept of 'substance'. There are two reasons for the importance of this concept. Philosophically, the concept of susbstance goes back to the Greek term, *hypokeimenon,* or that which underlies, and to the concept of *ousia,* or that which remains present through a series of changes. We can think of a substance that *then* has various accidental qualities or predicates. The history of metaphysics has therefore debated just what counts as a substance, or that upon which all other properties depend. Deleuze takes part in, at the same time as he overturns this debate. For Deleuze, part of this overturning is to think of substance, not as a noun – something that is – but as an infinitive: not, 'The tree *is* green,' but a power 'to green'. So, Deleuze accepts the function of substance – that from which differentiated beings are expressed – but he does not see substance as some ultimate being or entity, but as a power of creation and expression.

If we think of substance (as it is traditionally defined) as what exists in itself before all relations, requiring no other being in order to be, then this has two resonances in Deleuze's philosophy. First, following Baruch Spinoza, Deleuze argues that substance cannot be numerically several. This is because Spinoza adopts the traditional definition of something that exists *in itself,* but also says that substance is conceived *through itself.*

We do not need more than one substance – say, the substance of mind that will represent or know the substance of matter. Substance – or what is – unfolds in two modes: the mode of extension (or spatial matter) and the mode of thought or mind. So there is just one substance that is then expressed both in thought and in body. If there were more than one substance – say mind and body (which is the Cartesian answer) – then we would have to explain a relation between the two. But it is the very nature of substance to be independent of its relation to anything else. Substance must then be one, but it must also express itself differently. Indeed, real difference is only possible on such an account. We should not, for example, think of different minds as different substances. What is numerically several – all the different minds in the world – is substantially univocal; each mind is an expression of the one power of life to express itself in the attribute of mind; each is a different mode of the one attribute. Because there is only one substance we cannot say that mind is the origin or author of matter, or vice versa; all dualisms are invalid and arise from mistaking the expressions of substance – the relations unfolded from substance – for relations between substance. No substance is the cause or ground of any other; there is just one univocal substance that expresses itself infinitely, and cannot be reduced to any of its expressions, effects or accidents. This allows Deleuze to think of substance in terms of powers or potentials. We cannot reduce life to already effected relations, for there is *also* a power or potential to produce relations. In this sense, then, the metaphysical function of substance, as that which exists in itself before relations, and through itself, forms a vital role in Deleuze's work.

In traditional metaphysics, a substance is whatever can exist without requiring any other being in order to be. For instance, there cannot be whiteness without some thing that is white; substance is the bearer of predicates or properties. Deleuze's philosophy is concerned with the *problem* of substance, for the usual commitment to substance allows philosophers to establish an ultimate reality or ground – what really is – before its different expressions or perceptions. Even more importantly, God was established as the only true substance, while all other beings were said to 'be' only by analogy. Against ontology and the notion of substance as a preceding ground, Deleuze argues that all beings possess full reality – whiteness, a memory, a smile, a potentiality – and are equally real and are formally distinct while numerically one (that is, are truly different only because there is only one substance and so nothing is a lesser being in relation to any other).

Connectives

Memory
Real
Spinoza

T

TERRITORY

Kylie Message

In *A Thousand Plateaus*, Deleuze and Guattari privilege ideas of spatiality (evidenced by the privileged term of 'plateau') and the geographies and cartographies of movement, presenting these as an informal antidote to history (here they can be distinguished from Michel Foucault). Even in their geological discussions, history is presented as being subsumed within the constitution of space; it is significant for the role that time plays in movement across fields (in, for example, its relations of speed and slowness), but not for its institutionalised mode of categorical dating. Rather than denying the affectivity of history, Deleuze and Guattari reject the universalising chronological grand narrative strategies that are frequently associated with it. In their preference for lines of flight and becoming, they critique history for being a tool of the unitary State apparatus. These lines are understood not only as a deterritorialising impulse, but they also contribute to the spatial, material and psychological components that constitute or deconstitute a society, group, or individual (those apparatuses that comprise history as a lived, experiential assemblage of events and circumstances). All these components help produce the concept of a 'territory' that concomitantly accompanies the concepts of 'deterritorialisation' and 'reterritorialisation'.

The concept of 'territory' evades easy categorisation because rather than being a sedentary place maintaining firm borders against outside threat, the territory itself is a malleable site of passage. As an assemblage, it exists in a state of process whereby it continually passes into something else. However, it also maintains an internal organisation. A territory is also an assemblage that, as a necessary component of deterritorialisation, accompanies the concept of 'nomadology'. A territory refers to a mobile and shifting centre that is localisable as a specific point in space and time.

It does not privilege or maintain the nostalgic or xenophobic protection of any particular homeland; instead, this centre (that may be more correctly called a 'vector' because it can reside outside of the assemblage/territory) expresses an experiential concept that has no fixed subject or object. It is neither symbolic nor representational, and does not signify. As an assemblage, a territory manifests a series of constantly changing heterogeneous elements and circumstances that come together for various reasons at particular times. Although a territory establishes connections from the areas of representation, subject, concept and being, it is distinct from a fixed image, signification or subjectivity. Through this, we can see that a territory is primarily marked by the ways movement occurs over the earth, rather than by State borders. A territory is necessarily lived and produced as a vague entity because of this desire to avoid categorisation by language or other State apparatuses. Hence, it is closely connected to molecular – cognitive and non-cognitive – modes of movement.

A territory does not simply hold back the process of deterritorialisation, nor does it provide it with an opposing or dichotomous term (Deleuze and Guattari contend that there is no need to leave the territory to follow a line of deterritorialisation). Neither does a territory provide a base or originary term (home) from which deterritorialisation may occur. Instead, it is a constant accompaniment to (and even proponent facilitating) the lines of flight deterritorialisation proposes.

In addressing the idea of territory, Deleuze and Guattari discuss many examples, from the refrain of the birdcall (which they describe as a mode of expression that both draws a territory and envelops into territorial motifs and landscapes) to the role played by the artist's signature, that equates with placing a flag on a piece of land. However, they frequently return to the relationship between territory and the earth in order to show that the territory does not escape from maintaining its own organising principle and structure. This example is used to illustrate that such a relationship is not dichotomous simply in the sense that one term can be differentiated in a straightforward manner from the other. Instead, taken together, these terms show the magnetic pull that often works toward accumulating a synthesis of apparently disjunctive terms. As such, territories cannot contain or encompass the earth, but neither can the earth be fixed to a single territory. On the other hand, even though the earth embraces all territories (as a series of molecular or nomadic moments collected by the conjoining '. . . and . . . and . . . and' logic that motivates it), it is also the force of deterritorialisation and reterritorialisation since its continuous movements of development and variation unfold new relations of materials and forces (predicated on a relationship of speed and slowness). So, in contrast to the specific or localisable time and place offered by territories, the earth offers up an alternative complex assemblage (and various productive lines of becoming or flight) – the Body without Organs.

Connectives

Body without Organs
Deterritorialisation/Reterritorialisation
Earth/Land
Lines of flight
Nomadicism

THEORY

Bruce Baugh

Deleuze's most interesting thoughts on theory come in a discussion with Michel Foucault, where he puts forward the following idea: 'A theory is exactly like a box of tools . . . It must be useful. It must function' (D&F 1977: 208). A theory is something that we must construct as a response to a problem, and if it ceases to be useful, then 'we have no choice but to construct others'. This approach to theory is inherently practical, although Deleuze distinguishes between theoretical and practical activity, while at the same time arguing that theory is neither a foundation for practices that would merely apply universal theories to particular cases, nor the result of a reflection on particular practices that extract universal norms from particular cases. Rather than being universal, a 'theory is always local and related to a limited field'. Extending theory to practice is not merely the application of universal rules or theorems to particular cases, but a 'relay' to a 'more or less distant field of practice' in response to 'obstacles, walls and blockages' within the theory's own immanent domain. By 'relaying' to practice as 'another type of discourse' with a different domain, theory uses practice as a way of overcoming its internal difficulties, making practice serve as 'a set of relays between one theoretical point and another' (D&F 1977: 206). Conversely, theory can serve as a relay from one practice to another, connecting one practical field to a different one in order to overcome a practical impasse. In the latter case, theory does not represent or 'speak for' practice, any more than practice 'applies' theory: 'there's only action – theoretical and practical action' connected in networks and relays. As an example, Deleuze refers to his and Foucault's work with prisoners as a way of connecting 'official discourses of confinement' to the discourse of the confined themselves, a move that is simultaneously theoretical and practical. As

Foucault puts it in the same dialogue, 'Theory does not express, translate, or serve to apply practice: it is practice' (D&F 1977: 208).

Nowhere else does Deleuze offer such a positive appreciation of theory, which he usually downgrades in contrast with thought: 'Thinking's never just a theoretical matter. It has to do with vital problems' (D 1995: 105). Yet thought shares many characteristics with what he said about 'theory' in the dialogue with Foucault. Thought is a practical activity, work; philosophy, specifically, is thought-experimentation through the creation of concepts, each concept being a response to a problem whose conditions and scope the concept helps define, and each concept being created in the midst of already existing concepts which encounter impasses or blockages that require new concepts as 'bridges or crossroads' enabling them to join up with other concepts responding to problems subject to the same conditions (D&G 1994: 27). 'A concept lacks meaning to the extent that it is not connected to other concepts and is not linked to a problem that it resolves or helps resolve' (D&G 1994: 79). Problems necessarily change along with the changing conditions of thought and action. Thought, then, is a strategy in the face of problems, and seeks solutions through creating concepts, ways of thinking, and a system of coordinates that dynamically relates thoughts and problems to one another. On this conception, the 'practice' that serves as a relay between one theoretical point and another is thought itself, and the singular theoretical points are concepts in the case of philosophy, affects and percepts in the case of art, and functions in the case of science.

Deleuze's pragmatic conception of theory also extends to his explanation of Foucault's distinction between the 'classic' intellectual, who 'could lay claim to universality' in virtue of the writer's social position being on a par with jurists and lawyers who represent the universality of law, and the 'specific intellectual' who 'tends to move from one specific place or point to another', 'producing effects not of universality but of transversality, and functioning as an exchanger' between different theoretical fields, but in the context of practical and political struggles (D 1988b: 91). The specific intellectual's expertise or theory is always local, expressing a fragmentary totality that is necessarily limited and necessarily runs up against impasses or 'walls' that can be breached by a strategic relay or detour through other theoretical fields. No intellectual, and no theory, can totalise the entire field of knowledge and action. A theory multiplies and erupts in a totally different area by finding 'lateral affiliations and entire system of networks', or else it loses its efficacy (D&F 1977: 212). Transversal connections between theory and practice on the part of specific intellectuals would include nuclear physicists using their expertise to speak against nuclear weapons; a transversal relay from one theoretical domain to another would be Deleuze and Guattari's strategic shift of Friedrich Nietzsche from philosophy to ethnology in their own theoretical-political *Anti-Oedipus* (D&G 1983: 190–1).

Connectives

Concepts
Foucault

THOUGHT

John Marks

In his earlier work, and in particular *Difference and Repetition*, Deleuze talks of a dominant 'Image of thought' that he sets out to challenge, exploring the possibility of a 'thought without image'. The image that Deleuze challenges is essentially dogmatic and moral. In this sense, it is representational in nature, in that it presupposes that 'everyone knows' what it means to think, and that the only prerequisite for 'thought' is an individual in possession of goodwill and a 'natural capacity' for thought. René Descartes, for example, presumes that everybody knows what is meant by self, thinking and being. For Deleuze, this image of thought as *cognito natura* is extraordinarily complacent. Instead, he claims that we think rarely and more often under the impulse of a shock than in the excitement of a taste for thinking. Genuine thinking is necessarily antagonistic towards the combination of good sense and common sense that form the *doxa* of received wisdom, and it frequently requires something more than the formulations of common language. In general terms, Deleuze challenges the assumption that thought has a natural affinity with the 'true'. Instead, he claims that thought is an act of problematisation. Thought may, in this way, have a prophetic role in anticipating the forces of the future. It is, moreover, able to bring out the 'new', as opposed to established values. Deleuze also argues that there is something that he calls an 'image of thought' that changes through history. Works such as *The Logic of Sense*, *Proust and Signs* and *A Thousand Plateaus* all contribute to the study of images of thought, or 'noology' as Deleuze calls it. Noology is different from a history of thought, in that it does not subscribe to the notion that there is a narrative development in thought. It is not the case that there is a sort of long-term debate in the course of which either some ideas and concepts win the day, or disagreements are eventually turned into consensus. This would be a history of thought as the uncovering or construction of universals. Deleuze talks instead in terms of 'geophilosophy'; the superimposition of layers of thought. Drawing on Friedrich Nietzsche's concept of the 'untimely', Deleuze suggests that what is new in a philosopher's work remains new, and the reactivation of these untimely elements is an important component of Deleuze's work.

As far as noology is concerned, an image of thought is a system of coordinates or dynamics: a sort of map that shows how we orientate ourselves within thought. One of Deleuze's influences here is Martin Heidegger, who claims that to think is to be under way, to be on a path that one must clear for oneself, although one can have no certain destination in mind. For Deleuze, we must initially make a decision as to our orientation in relation to the vertical and horizontal axes. Should we stretch out, and follow the 'line of flight' on the horizontal axis, or should we erect vertical axes? In other words, this constitutes a choice between immanence and transcendence. If we choose transcendence, this entails a further choice to be made between three types of 'universal': contemplation, reflection and communication. Immanuel Kant seemed equipped to overturn the Image of thought, but ultimately he was committed to an orientation in which thought would have an upright nature.

Deleuze claims that philosophers tend to invent 'conceptual personae' who will help the philosopher in question to negotiate and establish a new image of thought that springs from a series of intuitions. The conceptual persona functions something like the detective in crime fiction. He is the everyman who must orientate himself within the image of thought. So, for example, Deleuze shows how the 'rational' man of scholastic thought is replaced by the Cartesian 'idiot', who is later replaced by the Russian 'idiot'. This 'underground man' has what Deleuze calls in a characteristically wry statement, the 'necessary modesty' *not* to manage to know what everybody knows. He is like a character in a Russian novel, paralysed and stupefied by the coordinates of problems that do not correspond to representational presuppositions. Thought may not have a history, but it does have a dramatis personae.

This approach to thought leads Deleuze to value and promote the 'private thinker', as opposed to the 'public professor'. The model for this sort of thinker is Baruch Spinoza, who pursues a frugal and itinerant lifestyle, and is in this way able to avoid the pitfall of confusing his purpose with that of the State or religion. Rather than a model of opinion and consensus, Deleuze prefers what he calls a 'nomadic' or 'clandestine' form of thinking. The only form of 'communication' that is suitable to the contemporary world is the Nietzschean arrow or Adorno's 'message in a bottle'. Thought is fired like an arrow, in the hope that another thinker – a 'friend' – may pick up the arrow and fire it in turn.

Connectives

Lines of flight
Nomadicism
Noology
Spinoza

TIME-IMAGE

Tom Conley

The time-image is what tends to govern cinema from the end of World War II until the present. It is the title of the second or dexter panel of Deleuze's historical taxonomy of film. It designates images that Henri Bergson qualified as imbued with duration: a component of time that is neither successive nor chronological. Seen less as matter than felt as pure duration time-images relate a change in the configuration of the world. They draw attention to the qualities of their own optical and aural properties as much as the signs or matter they represent. They tend not to favour narrative or beg the spectator to identify with their content. For Deleuze the time image is apt to be read – it is a *legible* image – as much as it is seen or given to visibility. It prompts the spectator to think through the signs with which it articulates narrative matter.

In the régime of the movement-image, intervals are vital to the perception of motion, sensation, affection and change; in the time-image, perception becomes a 'perception of perception', offering a shift of emphasis that is witnessed in the image itself rather than the linkages (or cuts) between images. What this means is that when montage, the foundation of classical cinema, loses its hold time begins to be increasingly spatialised. For instance, in *film noir* the past or narratives that tell a person's life-story through his or her point of view is shown in flashbacks. This classical device gives way, in the era of the time-image, to a perpetual duration that cannot be located in one moment or another. Memory elides temporal distinction in ways such that only 'is it in the present that we make memory, in order to make use of it in the future when the present will be past' (D 1989: 52). The time-image frequently becomes a site of amnesia where waves of action turn the world at large into a matrix in which personages seem to float indiscriminately. Certain films, such as Jean Renoir's *La règle du jeu* (1939) or Orson Welles' *The Lady from Shanghai* (1946), suggest that subjectivity can only be felt through the perception of time: humans, be they spectators or characters in film are determined by the environs of time in which they are held. Deleuze calls the effect that of a 'time-crystal', a way of being that is discovered in a time inside of the event that allows it to be perceived. In *La règle du jeu* the time-crystal might be the illuminated greenhouse or the chateau in which the characters are held. In Welles' film it would be the hall of mirrors in which the characters shatter the narrative to pieces.

The time-image (and its crystals) is often discerned in deep focus photography, the model par excellence for Renoir and Welles, for whom montage is folded into the spatial dynamics given in a single take. Yet it acquires legibility in Godard's cinema, such as *Pierrot le fou* (1965) in which a 'depth of surface' is created by patterns of writing or abstract forms painted on walls against which human players seem flattened. Timeimages are seen in *nappes* or 'sheets' in what Deleuze calls 'mental cartographies' of cinema (D 1989: 121). In Alain Resnais' *Hiroshima mon amour* (1959) the past is a matte surface on which traumatic memoryimages are reflected and meld into one another. Time is bereft of dates, thus inhering in the body and soul of the two lovers estranged in the places where they happen to meet.

In this continuum, cinema becomes a site where thought itself acquires a force of becoming unknown to historical time. It is a power of the irrational or unthought that is essential to all thinking: something incommunicable, something that cannot be uttered, something undecided or undecidable. Where the movement-image *represented* time, the time-image is 'no longer empirical, nor metaphysical; it is "transcendental" in the sense that Kant gives the word: time is out of joint and presents itself in the pure state' (D 1989: 271). Through the concept of the time-image Deleuze (with Guattari) notes that the question at the basis of all film theory – 'What is cinema?' – that André Bazin posed turns into the question 'What is philosophy?'. The time-image demonstrates that cinema is a new practice of images and signs for which philosophy is summoned to construct a theory and a conceptual practice. Thus, with the corresponding concept of the movement-image an enduring inquiry into the nature of cinema is set in place.

Connectives

Becoming
Cinema
Duration
Event
Memory
Movement-image

TRANSCENDENTAL EMPIRICISM

Cliff Stagoll

Empiricism refers to the view that the intelligible derives always from the sensible, whilst transcendentalism assumes that experience must rest upon some logically necessary foundation. The former position is typified by the work of David Hume, who argued that ideas of consciousness are derived just from sensory impressions, and that any test of sound reasoning should refer to the nature of the connection between the two. On this view, ideas and philosophical concepts can never found or logically precede sense perceptions.

In theorising the human subject, Immanuel Kant developed perhaps the best known form of transcendentalism. He sought to identify all of the conditions of the *possibility* of attaining distinctively human knowledge. It is only because humans possess particular cognitive capabilities, he argues, that we experience the world as we do and are able to make claims about the world as it appears *a priori*. This set of capabilities – the 'forms' of sensibility, understanding and reason – is universal and logically necessary for human knowledge. On Kant's account, without time and space, a range of basic concepts of reason (such as modality, quantity and quality), and 'Ideas' founding a kind of rational faith, there would be no knowledge of the kind evident in the human experience of the world. As such, the categories and conditions uncovered by Kant are claimed to be true of *all* selves.

According to Deleuze, this argument fails on two counts. First, it does not account for differences between whatever one knows of a phenomenon in advance and what one learns about it *a posteriori*. Second, Kant conceives of experience only in terms of re-presentation and consistencies in mental functioning from time to time and person to person. As such, Deleuze argues, transcendental deduction reproduces the empirical in transcendental form and then shields it from further critique. The Kantian subject, for instance, is constructed as an explanation for how diverse experiences are synthesised and unified, and then employed as the essential precondition for any human experience whatsoever.

Deleuze's description of his philosophy as a transcendental empiricism is a challenge to these positions rather than a unified counter-theory. In contrast to transcendentalism, Deleuze seeks after the conditions of *actual* rather than all possible experience. These conditions are not logically necessary, but contingent upon the nature of experience as it is lived. Therefore, for Deleuze as for Hume, philosophy must begin with the immediate given – real conscious awareness – without presupposing any categories, concepts or axioms. Only then should it begin to develop concepts that might refer to objects and their relations, perceptions and their causes, or any of a range of psychological or physiological relations evident in consciousness. It is precisely the actuality of the empirical and the priority accorded real experience that, for Deleuze, are ways of avoiding transcendentalism's imprecision and universalising abstractions.

Deleuze's approach is a *transcendental* empiricism because it is an attempt to deduce the conditions of the possibility of conscious experience (such as the apparent conscious immediacy to which one refers when saying 'I'). Reality as it is experienced does not reveal the preconditions of experience and, because such elements are inaccessible to consciousness, they necessitate transcendental, deductive study of their implicit conditions. Unlike Kant, Deleuze does not conceive of these unthought conditions as abstract or necessary philosophical entities, but as contingent tendencies beyond the reach of empirical consciousness. As such, he presumes no being or subject *who* experiences. Deleuze finds that the 'I' only ever refers to contingent effects of interactions between events, responses, memory functions, social forces, chance happenings, belief systems, economic conditions, and so on that together make up a life. By taking a different approach to the transcendental philosophers and moving beyond a view of empiricism based upon just the epistemological relationship between ideas and sense impressions, Deleuze shifts the philosophical focus from determining a foundation of likeness amongst humans to revealing and celebrating the contingency, dissimilarity and variety of each individual life.

Connectives

Actuality
Hume
Kant
Real
Virtual/Virtuality

TRANSCENDENTAL EMPIRICISM + POLITICS

Bruce Baugh

Deleuze often quoted Alfred North Whitehead's dictum that the abstract does not explain, but needs to be explained. This thought stands at the basis of both Deleuze's transcendental empiricism that searches for the real conditions of actual experience rather than for the abstract conditions of any possible experience, and of his politics. Empiricism wants to hold onto the concrete richness of experience, and to resist abstract universals by insisting on the situated and historical nature of the conditions of experience. Deleuzian politics likewise insists on the singularity of experiences and practices, rather than merely seeing these as either instances of some universal rule or exceptions to the rule. Yet, in contrast with classical empiricism and liberalism, transcendental empiricism holds that the empirical is not composed of discrete givens, but of concrete particulars (individuals, groups) defined by the history of their contingent and actual relations with other beings. Against idealism and Marxism, transcendental empiricism sees all supposedly necessary universals and structures as being either causally or logically dependent on contingent particulars, and thus as themselves contingent.

Classical empiricism (John Locke, George Berkeley, David Hume) holds that universal class terms, predicates and relations ('dog', 'black', 'next to') are derived through abstraction from particular experiences, and linked together through habits of association based on the 'constant conjunction' of those experiences; unlike in Plato, universals have no independent standing, and particulars do not depend on universals. Classical liberalism (Thomas Hobbes, John Stuart Mill and John Locke) similarly holds that aggregates such as 'society' and 'the State' are nothing over and above the individuals which compose them, and so are dependent on individuals, rather than the reverse. The 'independence' of individuals in classical liberal theory is the basis of its demand for individual rights and liberty, understood as freedom from the coercion of society or the State.

Although Deleuze agrees that the universal depends on the particular, he rejects the 'atomism' of experiences and of individuals. For Deleuze, sensations are not 'givens', but must be explained by conditions involving a complex and mostly unconscious set of relations among different bodies' powers of acting and reacting. Similarly, individuals are conditioned not just by other individuals with whom they interact, but by factors common to all of them (language, social relations, biological structures, technology). Liberalism's 'individual' is superseded by what Deleuze calls an 'assemblage' (*agencement*): a conjunction of a number of persons, forces and circumstances, capable of its own collective experiences and actions. Rather than the rights and liberties of individuals, power or agency is the prime concern of Deleuzian politics. Rather than universal principles being the criteria by which practices are evaluated, practices are judged entirely with respect to whether their effects increase or decrease someone's or something's power of acting. Principles emerge as a reflection on how much certain practices increase or decrease agency, as an *a posteriori* generalisation, rather than an *a priori* necessary condition.

Like Deleuze, Marxism also argues that social relations – particularly economic relations – condition individual experience and agency. Yet, unlike classical Marxism, Deleuze does not believe that 'classes' are basic units of analysis, or that the economic base is more fundamental than the ideological superstructure. Social and economic structures, forms of thought, norms of action, are all produced through particular and contingent conjunctions of desires, actions and affects, and are all part of an assemblage in which each element is conditioned by all the others. 'Classes' are abstract in relation to assemblages that are not just subdivisions within classes, but can cut across different socio-economic classes. To some extent, classical Marxism retains the precedence of abstract universals over singular assemblages that – whether the universal be a class, a party, the State or history – suppresses creativity and blocks the emergence of the new. Subjection to higher universals cuts off assemblages from their power and is always reactive.

Transcendental empiricism would be the basis of a politics of positive individuality and difference, valorising agency and creative power, but mindful of the oppressive conditioning of individuals and our voluntary servitude to universal norms.

TRANSVERSALITY

Adam Bryx and Gary Genosko

A critical concept for literary criticism, 'transversality' is introduced by Deleuze in the second edition of *Proust and Signs*. The concept concerns the kind of communication proper to the transversal dimension of machinic literary production. Transversality defines a modern way of writing that departs from the transcendent and dialectic presuppositions of the Platonic model of reminiscence, and envisions an immanent and singularising version instead.

Also termed an 'anti-*logos* style', transversality assembles heterogeneous components under a unifying viewpoint, which is far from totalising. Unlike the Platonic counterpart that strives to imitate the Idea and thus reproduce what is both stable and transcendent, Proust's reminiscence departs from subjective associations and culminates in an originating viewpoint. The critique of Plato centres on the issue of intelligence always *coming before*, where the disjunctive use of faculties merely serves as a prelude for the unifying dialectic found in a single *logos*. The disjunctive use of faculties in Proust is unhinged from this transcendent and dialectic model, and works on an immanent principle where intelligence always *comes after.*

The transversal dimension of fiction fundamentally counters the principles of the world of attributes, *logos*, analytic expression, and rational thought with the characteristics of the world of signs and symptoms, pathos, hieroglyphs, ideograms and phonetic writing. Where order has collapsed in states of the world, the viewpoint provides a formula by which fiction can constitute and reconstitute a beginning to the world. Such a beginning is necessarily singularising; the transversal dimension or the never-viewed viewpoint draws a line of communication through the heterogeneous pieces and fragments that refuse to belong to a whole, that are parts of different wholes, or that have no whole other than style. The ephemeral images, memories and signs of the odours, flavours and drafts of particular settings are swept along at various rhythms and velocities in the creation of the nontotalising transversal dimension of fiction that is not reproductive, imitative or representative, but depends solely on its functioning.

Deleuze finds third parties that will communicate aberrantly between partitioned partial objects of hermaphroditic bodies and plants. The famous apiarian bestiary of Deleuze shows itself here. But the pollinating transversal insect is not simply natural or organic, for that is a trope of the *logos.* Rather, it is a line of passage, a zig-zagging flight, or even the narration of involuntary memory, that productively transverses. Transversality is machinic. The literary machine produces partial objects and resonances between them. The fore-mentioned viewpoint, understood as an essential singularity, is superior to the partitioned objects, yet not beyond them, for the self-engendering literary machine works in and upon itself.

Connectives

Guattari
Psychoanalysis

TRUTH

James Williams

Deleuze's work is opposed to the coherence theory of truth and to the correspondence theory of truth. The first claims that the truth of a proposition depends on its coherence with some other propositions. The second claims that the truth of a proposition depends on its correspondence to some objective facts. So a proposition is either true due to certain logical relations or due to a relation to things in the world.

For Deleuze, both theories are wrong-headed from their very premisses. That is, propositions are false simplifications of reality and cannot be bearers of truth in any significant sense. Objective facts do not exist and cannot be identified or shown, because real things are limitless and always caught in endless processes of becoming. To abstract from these processes is to give a false image of reality.

So, in contrast to the two traditional and dominant theories of truth, Deleuze defines truth in terms of creativity and construction. We create truth in complex constructions of propositions and sensations that express the conditions for the genesis and development of events. Truth then would not be a property of single propositions in a book or in a paper. It would be a property of a series of them through a work as it captured and changed our relation to the events expressed in the work.

Deleuze is apt to mock philosophical theories based on simple propositions that say little of the world. According to him, it is a mistake to begin an enquiry about truth with abstracted propositions such as 'The cat is on the mat'. Instead, truth only appears in more complex works such as a series of paintings or literary and philosophical works. It is a mistake to think that the truth of such works depends on the truth of their components because the significance of the components only appears when they are in context.

It is not so much that simple propositions have no relation to truth at all. It is rather that truth is a matter of degrees. The more a work, or a proposition in a work, expresses about reality and the inter-relation of all things, and the more a work creates with that inter-relation in order to be able to express it, the more truth it will carry. This carrying is itself a matter of the transference of significance and intensity in the event, rather than a representation of it.

Thus, to say something is true is not to say something verifiable in some way, but to say something that vivifies and alters a situation. A poem about World War I that makes us sense it and live through and with it in a different way is truthful. A statistic about the war that is not accompanied by sensations and transformations is not truthful. The less statistics transform and give us signs of the deeper ideas and intense sensations at work in the war, the less truthful they are.

This means that Deleuze is caught in a difficult position of opposing concepts of truth, but without being able to say that we can somehow move beyond truth or stop using the concept at all. In *Nietzsche and Philosophy*, he notes how truth and the search for truth fixes worlds, in the sense of setting down truths that become immutable and settled representations of states of things. Instead, truth should be a destructive and transforming process. Similarly, traditional concepts of truth turn us away from the world, in the sense of searching for truths that are not here or missing; whereas, for Deleuze, truths are always latent and it is a matter of dramatising them, of bringing them out and allowing them to transform us, rather than a matter of projecting ourselves into an identifiable truthful future.

Again following Friedrich Nietzsche, Deleuze sees truth as necessarily involved in moral presuppositions. Truth is associated with the morally good and it is assumed that through truth we arrive at the moral good. For Deleuze this cannot be the case because both the moral good and truth are part of a struggle between different values with no external way of dividing them into true and false, good and evil. Instead, the good and the true are relative to different attitudes to life – where Deleuze and Nietzsche seek those that affirm becoming over being, transformation (or transvaluation) over identity and sameness.

In *Cinema 2*, Deleuze extends this view of truth as becoming and part of the complex struggle for life, by pointing out that there are no simple oppositions of the true and of the false. This is already an idea from his *Difference and Repetition*, where the false can have an affirmative power and where the deep opponent of both the true and the false (and life) is stupidity – defined as the desire for simple oppositions, for common sense and for transcendent life-denying values. Thus, in *Cinema 2*, Deleuze emphasises the variation of truth over time and hence the power of falsehoods to vary those truths (any given settled series of truths must be challenged by falsehoods from their angle, but truths from a different one). Falsehoods, for example in cinematic narration, have the power to reveal different and more affirmative views of life.

It could be objected that when Deleuze moves away from truth as an arbiter of propositions, it is as if he does not care about facts and logical necessity. That is not the case. He believes that facts and logical necessity have roles to play, but these are secondary to a much higher vocation for truth; which is to reveal deep connections between all things and to allow us to live up to the events that make and transform us. In this respect, a temperature reading has some importance but a film capturing the significance of the cracking ice-caps is more truthful.

Connectives

Difference
Nietzsche

U

UEXKÜLL, JACOB VON (1864–1944) – refer to the entries on 'becoming + music' and 'deterritorialisation/reterritorialisation'.

UNCONSCIOUS – refer to the entry on 'psychoanalysis'.

UNIVOCAL

Claire Colebrook

According to one of Deleuze's most important critics, Alain Badiou, 'univocity' is the central concept of Deleuze's project. In *Difference and Repetition*, Deleuze describes an alternative history of philosophy comprising those philosophers daring enough to think of being as univocal: John Duns Scotus, Baruch Spinoza and Friedrich Nietzsche. If philosophy has been dominated by Platonism, this is because being has been deemed to be equivocal: only one being truly is, while other beings are dependent, secondary, either not truly substances or different types of substance. Mind is elevated above matter; original is elevated above copy; the actual is the privileged and proper locus of the potential; only the actual is real or proper being, while the potential cannot be said to be in the same sense. Against this equivocity, Deleuze argues for univocity: no event or phenomenon is more real than any other. There is only one being: perceptions, anticipations, memories and fictions are as real as atoms, universals, concepts or bodies. From his history of univocal philosophers, Deleuze emphasises three revolutionary ideas.

From Duns Scotus, Deleuze insists that only with univocity can there be real difference. If there is only one being then we cannot relate differences – say, differences of colour – as differences *of* some grounding neutral being, a being which is, and which then has secondary or less real qualities. Rather, each difference is fully real: each shade of a colour, each fleck of light, each sound or affect is fully real and therefore different in itself, not merely a different way in which some other subtending being is grasped. From Spinoza's univocity, Deleuze articulates the concept of immanence. If there is only one substance then there cannot be a creating God outside creation; the divine is nothing outside its expression.

Mind and matter are, accordingly, not two distinct substances; nor does one depend on or derive from the other. Mind and matter are attributes of the one divine substance and each body – such as a human body – is just one expression or mode of the attribute of mind and the attribute of matter.

There is not some transcendent being which *then* creates or grounds different beings, beings that can be said to be only by analogy. Each being is fully real and is so because it just is the expression of the divine substance, which is nothing outside its expressions. Immanence follows from univocity precisely because the commitment to one substance precludes any point outside being; everything that is *is* equally, possessing full reality.

From Nietzsche, Deleuze's favoured philosopher of univocity, Deleuze affirms the concept of 'eternal return'. There is only one being but this does not mean that there cannot be radically new events and futures. On the contrary, eternal return and univocity preclude the idea that a state of completion or rest will ever come about.We should neither wait nor hope for a better world, nor should we imagine an apocalyptic break with this world in order to achieve a radical future. If there is only one being then all life, all futures, all events, will be actualisations of this immanent life, which in all its virtual power can continually create and differentiate new experiences. Eternal return describes a future that is positive because it repeats and affirms this life. There are two ways in which this one immanent life can be affirmed univocally. The first would be a biologist or vitalist account, whereby life could be identified with the actual, material being that already exists – nature as it is commonly understood; if this were so then futures, events and becomings would already exist in potential and would then unfold. So we could say, for example, that the potential that created William Shakespeare would, eventually, produce another Shakespeare. After all, there is only one life, and all potential would eventually be repeated. But this is where Deleuze's conception of life differs from a grounding on *actual* life. Imagine that we were to find some of Shakespeare's DNA and were to clone Shakespeare; we would not have a Renaissance bard who would then write *Hamlet*. Why? Because this would only be possible in an equivocal life, one where life in all its becoming and difference was submitted to pre-given forms, 'a Shakespeare' would have had to emerge. But because life is univocal, because there is no form, idea or principle that governs or grounds life, all we have is the potential for difference and variation. Cloning would not produce life's effects; indeed really to repeat life is to repeat creation, difference. By life Deleuze refers not to what actually is, but the virtual power from which life is unfolded. The potential that produced Shakespeare would, if it were repeated, produce as much difference and variation as the 'original'. And this is because the original life was not an actuality – something that simply was, and then had to go through time and alteration – but a 'pre-personal singularity', a power of variation that is *singular* because it is radically different from the stable, definable and general forms it effects. Only if we see repetition as a pale copy or resemblance do we need to think of the radically new as other than this already full life. If, however, we grasp each repetition of the world's virtual power as thoroughly new we will recognise that univocity – one life, one being yielding infinite difference – is also difference and futurity.

Connectives

Eternal return
Immanence
Nietzsche
Spinoza

UTOPIA

Jonathan Roffe

The term 'utopia' designates for Deleuze the political vocation of philosophy: the attempt to bring about different ways of existing and new contexts for our existence through the creation of concepts. The word 'utopia', however, has been associated with many different conceptions of political thought and action in ways that would seem antithetical to the philosophy of Deleuze. On the one hand, there is the real naïvety with which doctrines of utopia are often propounded. On the other, as the word itself indicates (u-topia, no-place) the idea of utopia seem to refer to a world totally disconnected from the real social engagements that characterise life here and now, as if we could leap outside of our concrete existence into a fundamentally different kind of society, free of any kind of strife. Despite these concerns, Deleuze makes pivotal use of the concept (while noting these potential problems), even if these uses are few in number.

The primary location of the use of utopia in his philosophy is in *What is Philosophy?*, written with Guattari. Utopia names the point of contact between the present state of affairs and the activity of philosophy. No ideal future is involved, but rather the view that the present can always be negotiated with philosophically in order to bring about more freedom. Philosophy therefore has two temporal loci: the present and the future.

While engaging with the concrete present situation as it in fact is, philosophy's aim ought to be the breaking with or resisting of the present for the future. We can think here of Friedrich Nietzsche's statement in his *Untimely Meditations*, that philosophy acts on the present, and therefore against it, for the benefit of a time to come. This task is undertaken by philosophy because it is, according to Deleuze and Guattari, the creation of concepts. Unlike many other ideas of philosophy, concepts are not to be thought of as representations of reality, or tools for uncovering the truth. Rather, concepts are true creations, and philosophy as the creation of concepts makes possible new ways of existing through them. Art and science also undertake the same creative task, but through their own ways of thinking that do not include the concept. In the context of discussions about the creation of concepts, Deleuze often brings up the artist Paul Klee's claim that the audience for a work of art does not preexist the artwork itself – the people are lacking, as he says – but is called into being by it. For Deleuze, all creative thought calls for a new people and a new earth.

So utopia is what links philosophy with its own time, but is also that which gives it the forum for its critical political activity that has its focus in the future (D&G 1994: 99). This conception of politics clearly does not concern statements about the ideal nature of social existence (unlike many utopian philosophies), but sees politics as those acts that offer resistance to the norms and values of the present. Finally, for Deleuze, we cannot claim in advance that certain concepts will necessarily lead to a better future. While resisting the present and opening up the future for us, there is no guarantee that the world thus opened will be freer. These decisions can only be made on the difficult path of practical, empirical learning and careful attention.

Connectives

Art
Concepts
Freedom

V

VAN GOGH, VINCENT (1853–90) – refer to the entry on 'art'.

VARIATION

Jonathan Roffe

Deleuze mobilises the concept of variation in order to insist on what is perhaps his most fundamental theme, that existence is not characterised primarily by unities, but rather by a continual sense of movement and change. That is, to recall the philosopher Heraclitus as Deleuze does on occasion, being is becoming. In turn, the unities and structures that we find in life are therefore the result of organising this fundamental movement, and not the other way around.

Deleuze offers a number of examples for the concept of 'variation' in his work, one of which is music. Music is traditionally understood on the basis of scales that are fixed moments of pitch extracted from the whole range of frequencies. In western music, there is also the concept of the octave that divides sound up into repeatable scalar units. For Deleuze, we must consider these structures to be secondary in relation to the movement of sound itself, which has no intrinsic notes or scales. There is, fundamentally, only the continuous variation of pitch – a pure movement of difference without identity. Likewise, for Deleuze, if we examine language use, we do not find the fixed categories of a logical grammar or innate structure. Rather, the use of words is always shifting around, depending on the context of its use. In *A Thousand Plateaus*, Deleuze and Guattari describe this as the inherent variability of language. The fact that language use does not remain fixed but is fluid is the very nature of language itself.We can also consider the important example of space. Deleuze and Guattari offer the opposition between smooth and striated space. Smooth space is the type of space in which there are no fixed points or boundaries, and in which movement is uninhibited. In smooth space,movement is therefore continuous variation. In contrast, striated space is structured and organised, creating fixed points and limits between what movements can be undertaken. As a result, there is a sense as a result that the nature and construction of certain spaces forms one of the primary concerns of politics, since smooth space is by definition the space of freedom. On a more fundamental level, nature itself for Deleuze is continuous variation. Even animal species must be understood in terms of a movement of life which has been structured into localised patterns of stability.

Perhaps the fundamental point with regard to variation in Deleuze's work comes in connection to the theme of difference-in-itself, pursued most systematically in *Difference and Repetition*. Rather than seeing difference as a difference between two things, difference must be thought of as the continual movement of self-differing, like the continual variation of a sound rising and lowering in pitch without stopping at notes in a scale. In other words, difference is continuous variation. This is in contrast to the bulk of the western tradition of philosophy since *Parmenides* that from the outset postulates a primary identity. The whole of Deleuze's thought is in this sense based upon the primary value he gives to continuous variation. As a result, Deleuze's books and concepts must also be considered according to the principle of continuous variation. No one on its own can be considered to be definitive, but each works best when placed alongside his other texts and concepts, that vary from each other, outlining the movement of his thought rather than the doctrines that he espouses along the way.

Connectives

Difference
Freedom
Space

VIRTUAL/VIRTUALITY

Constantin V. Boundas

In Deleuze's ontology, the virtual and the actual are two mutually exclusive, yet jointly sufficient, characterisations of the real. The actual/real are states of affairs, bodies, bodily mixtures and individuals. The virtual/real are incorporeal events and singularities on a plane of consistency, belonging to the pure past – the past that can never be fully present. Without being or resembling the actual, the virtual nonetheless has the capacity to bring about actualisation and yet the virtual never coincides or can be identified with its actualisation. Deleuze leans upon Duns Scotus when he insists that the virtual is not a potential. Other philosophical influences for his concept of the virtual include Henri Bergson and his critique of the possible, Baruch Spinoza's idea of one substance that is differentiated in its infinite attributes and always in the process of being further differenciated in its modes, and finally Friedrich Nietzsche's concept of the 'eternal return'.

One way of characterising becoming is with the following schema: virtual/real↔actual/real↔virtual/real. What such a diagram points to is that becoming is not a linear process from one actual to another; rather it is the movement from an actualised state of affairs, through a dynamic field of virtual/real tendencies, to the actualisation of this field in a new state of affairs. This schema safeguards the reversible nature of virtual and actual relations.

Meanwhile in different contexts Deleuze has characterised the virtual as the *durée* and *élan vital* in his studies of Bergson; as Ideas/structures and the realm of problems in *Difference and Repetition* whereby the diverse actualisations of the virtual are understood as solutions; and finally throughout many of his texts he referred to the virtual as an event. The variety of characterisations given the virtual by Deleuze raises the question of how the virtual ought to be understood and the extent to which each characterisation is complicit in the next. That the virtual is the Bergsonian *durée* and *élan vital* stems from the basic agreement between Deleuze and Bergson regarding the structure of temporality. Any actual present passes only because all presents are constituted both as present and as past. In all past presents the entire past is conserved in itself, and this includes the past that has never been present (the virtual).

The idea of a past that has never been present (the immemorial past) can also be found in the writings of Jacques Derrida and Emmanuel Lévinas. The reasons for its postulation vary from one thinker to another, but there is one thing that they have in common: any philosophy that puts a premium on the de-actualisation of the present, in order to tap the resources of the past or the future, runs the risk of reifying the past (as in Plato's recollection) and the future (as in some apocalyptic eschatologies). To prevent this reification, the notions of the immemorial past and the messianic future (Deleuze prefers to talk of the pure past and of the eternal repetition of the different) succeed in safeguarding the idea of a process that presupposes non-determining tendencies. The past is called 'pure' in order to emphasise that it is the site of problems and the source of actualisations; that the realm of solutions is limited in numbers and, unlike the virtual past, it is rich in extention and poor in intensity; and that, occasionally, a great artist may assist something past to reveal its real being as if in a time that has been nobody's present. To the extent that both Deleuze and Bergson agree *durée* is not empty; rather it is an immanently differentiated dynamic process of the real whose nature is always to actualise itself in novel differenciations. Hence, the appropriate name '*élan vital*'.

Boldly transforming Kantianism in *Difference and Repetition*, Deleuze begins to identify the virtual with Ideas. An Idea, for Immanuel Kant, has no instantiations in the empirical world, yet at the same time *it must be thought*. Deleuze retains this imperative when he thinks of the virtual (for example, the *cogitandum*) but he moves beyond pure Kantianism when he multiplies Ideas by making them the gerundives of all faculties (the *memorandum*, the *loquendum*, and so on). The claim that Ideas are structures in large part comes from the prevailing structuralist vocabulary Deleuze uses throughout *Difference and Repetition.* In later work, Deleuze elaborates upon this claim that Ideas are structures when he describes the nature of the virtual in terms of a plane of consistency. Most important for Deleuze is that the virtual is not to be understood as duplicating or resembling the actual, nor should it be taken to mean transcendence. Simply put, problems do not resemble or represent their solutions.

Were we to understand the relationship between virtual singularities and actual individuals in terms of resemblance or analogy, we would reduce the notion of repetition that Deleuze advances simply to a repetition of the same. To understand how the virtual may be characterised as an event we need to recall Deleuze's theory of *sense*, which is given in the infinitive of verbs (a verb, unlike a noun or an adjective, is better suited for an ontology of becoming). In their infinitival modes, verbs best introduce the *untimely* nature of the virtual, and the absence of subjects or objects; yet they also introduce the strange combination: the impassive and dynamic aspects of multiplicities in the process of actualisation.

Connectives

Becoming
Bergson
Differentiation/Differenciation
Duration
Eternal return
Event
Spinoza

W

WHITEHEAD, ALFRED NORTH (1861–1947)

Roland Faber

Alfred North Whitehead is one of the more hidden but influential sources of Deleuze's thought. Unlike philosophers on whom Deleuze wrote books, Whitehead appears only in scattered remarks but, nevertheless, in a profound manner, at pivotal points, and throughout Deleuze's work. Deleuze also read and wrote on the same illustrious group of philosophers as Whitehead – Hume, Kant, Spinoza, and Leibniz – and intensively worked out his thought through others like Plato, while (for similar reasons as Whitehead) shunning some like Hegel. However, whereas Whitehead was more influenced by pragmatist philosophers like James, Dewey, and Santayana in simultaneously developing his pluralistic understanding of the world while criticising their potential 'anti-intellectualism' (including Nietzsche), Deleuze based his understanding of multiplicity, becoming, and the event on Nietzsche and, like Whitehead, Bergson.

Unlike many other philosophers related to poststructuralism, Deleuze was, with Whitehead, stubbornly interested in a new form of metaphysics that was not generated from generalizations of rationalist abstractions but as an instrument for limiting generalizations in light of the universal singularity of the event. Whitehead's 'fallacy of misplaced concreteness' appears throughout Deleuze's opus, reversing classical metaphysical formulations on how universals might construct the real world; namely, in no way. If it is impossible to reconstruct the becoming of events through abstract universals (in attaching eternity to them and even divinising them), we must instead ask: where is universalisation coming from and why do we find abstractions accompanying the occurrence of singular events?

Deleuze confesses that he always thought of himself as a pluralist and empiricist in the sense of Whitehead, one who does not reconstruct the world of becoming from abstractions (being), but seeks the multiplicities underlying and hidden in false unifications, simplifications, and rationalisations that exclude the multiplicities from whence they are constructed. Hence, Deleuze revered Whitehead's *Process and Reality* as one of the greatest books in philosophy because of how his empiric-ideal concepts express multiplicity; Whitehead's concept of the event appears in the midst of *The Fold*, instead of Leibniz's, as the expression of a divergent world of differences unable to be united; and in *What is Philosophy?* Deleuze links his concepts of event and (plane of) immanence directly to Whitehead's analysis of infinite becoming.

Deleuze models his transcendental empiricism by naming the condition of a world not under the paradigm of eternity but on the radical novelty expressed in Whitehead's divergent series of incompossible events, of which Deleuze understands even Whitehead's God to be an expression rather than a distraction. Moreover, with the concept of the chaosmos, Deleuze cumulatively labels Whitehead's strategies to establish the paradigm of novelty: the notion of creativity, the multiplicity of events of becoming, the immanence of all processes (that are not preformed by any law), the infiniteness of becoming, and the restatement of 'world' as a multiplicity of intensities. In fact, Whitehead's 'entirely living nexus' is a direct precursor of Deleuze's Body without Organs, and Deleuze considers their common deconstruction of organic orders into pure (orgiastic) life to be the aim of philosophy.

Whitehead and Deleuze remain intimately related both by their refutation of idealism and materialism, and by refusing to divide philosophical categories into reality (actual) and abstraction (ideal). Instead, their logic of multiplicity always intertwines event-multiplicity as actual and virtual (ideal). Deleuze considered Whitehead's eternal objects to be pure virtualities instead of potentials-to-be-actualised from a pre-give law. Moreover, in their late writings both Whitehead and Deleuze addressed the question of abstraction with virtuals and values, respectively, such that the mutual immanence and determination of actualities and virtualities/values becomes the condition for a world of multiplicity, novelty, immanence, and becoming; in other words, their treatment of abstraction becomes the condition for avoiding dualistic warfare.

Connectives

Becoming
Bergson
Event
Multiplicity

WHOLE

Jonattan Roffe

As early as his first book, *Empiricism and Subjectivity*, Deleuze rejects the idea of total unities, and works to analyse how things which are practically speaking unified – like human beings, societies and ideas of God and the world – come to be so.

Deleuze's procedure for coming to grips with the thought of unity throughout his philosophy is threefold. First of all, he maintains that there are no pre-existent wholes. Not only does nature itself not make a whole, but things themselves exist only one by one. They do not fit into an overarching structure and cannot be 'added up' to make a total picture of existence because everything is unique.We simply do not have any grounds for taking the unique things which make up existence as members of a species which could ground a unifying perspective. This point is closely connected to Deleuze's concept of 'multiplicity' that describes unique things in terms of their own complex constitutive relations. The most substantial treatment of the concept of the 'whole' in this sense is given in the discussion of Stoic philosophy in *The Logic of Sense*.

Second, it is important to note we seem, in fact, to be surrounded by unities of many kinds: human subjectivity, a unified and coherent basis for thinking, the unity of natural languages, and so on. For Deleuze, these kinds of transcendent totalities are fundamentally illusory. They are the product of certain habitual ways of thinking common to western culture and the metaphysical tradition Deleuze calls 'dogmatic image of thought'. The most significant discussion of the illusory nature of such totalities is undertaken in *Difference and Repetition*.

Finally, Deleuze goes on to argue that there are, in fact, unities but that these are produced by and in very particular social contexts. The unity of human experience, for example, or the idea of the world as a whole, is the very real and concrete result of the kinds of social experience that we have. As such, produced wholes are subject to the variations in the social context that is theirs. Their wholeness cannot be guaranteed, since it has no transcendental principle of unity but only the support of the social forces of its genesis and the maintenance of its consistency. Taken together, these three points describe the constructivist methodology of Deleuze concerning all unities. A totality is at once non-existent (in the transcendent, absolute sense), illusory (with regard to thinking), and concretely produced in a certain way by our social context.

At certain points, Deleuze himself seems to be advocating a kind of primary oneness to existence, particularly concerning his thesis of ontological univocity, or the univocity of being. In short, this is the position that claims all existing things are within a single world – everything that exists is 'said' in the same way ('uni-vocalised'). Univocity disqualifies in advance any thought of a transcendent ordering realm that is higher or more pure than the world of events. Ontological univocity is closely related to the thesis of monism that claims there is a single substance from which individual things are formed. Whilst this emphasis in Deleuze's work involves a certain thought of unity, we cannot consider him to be a 'holist' in any direct sense. Univocity must be understood rather as the emphasis on the common world of relations for everything that exists – a certain thought of general interconnectedness and proximity that would allow us to consider Deleuze's ontology as a kind of ecology of being. As he states in *Empiricism and Subjectivity*, nature is unique – but this does not mean that it is unified.

Connectives

Multiplicity
Singularity

WOMAN

Rosi Braidotti

Like all formations of identity in Deleuze's thought, 'woman' is a molar entity that pertains to and sustains the political economy of a majority. However, in a much broader phallogocentric historical system 'woman' is also positioned as 'other'. Deleuze shows great sensitivity in his treatment of 'woman' neither casting her as the mistress of alterity, nor fetishising her as the privileged object of masculine desire. Rather Deleuze avoids the tropes common to philosophical discourse on the feminine, choosing toremain polymorphous on the topic of sexuality, all the while performing a double displacement at the level of both Platonic theories of representation and psychoanalytic theories of desire.

Deleuze rejects the speculative self/other relationship of dialectics and argues instead that these terms are not linked by negation, but are two positively different systems each with its specific mode of activity. Thus 'woman' is not the sexualised 'second sex' of the phallic system, but a positive term: as the other, she is a matrix of becoming. Deleuze also rejects the psychoanalytic emphasis on negativity (lack) and the equation of bodily materiality with the originary site of the maternal. Instead of the régime of the phallus and of its specular other – woman – Deleuze prefers heterogeneous multiplicities and internal differentiation. In this sense he empowers 'woman' through positive figurations such as the non-Oedipal little girl of Alice in Wonderland, who has not yet been dispossessed of her body by the phallic law of the father; or in the equally empowered position of Ariadne, the philosopher's fiancée who expresses the feminine face of philosophy and is also the source of ethical transmutation, turning negative or reactive values into affirmative ones. Transcending the negative passions that the Oedipalising economy of the phallus induces is in effect a Deleuzian engine of the transformation, what Deleuze otherwise calls 'becoming'.

The role of 'woman' in Deleuze's theory of becoming is noteworthy. 'Becoming' is the actualisation of the immanent encounter between forces which are apt mutually to affect and exchange parts of each other in a creative and empathic manner. The notion of 'forces' accomplishes a double aim, which is central to Deleuze's emphasis on radical immanence: on the one hand it gives priority to affectivity in his theory of the subject; and on the other, it emphasises the embodied structure of the subject and the specific temporality of the embodied human. A force is a degree of affectivity or of intensity, in that it is open and receptive to encountering other affects. The transformation that occurs in the process of becoming asserts the affirmative, joyful affects over and above the negative ones.

Woman not only can enact processes of becoming-minoritarian but also, especially for Guattari, constitutes the main bloc of becoming for all processes of deterritorialisation. 'Becoming-woman' is both integral to the concept and process of becoming and also uncomfortably written into it as a constitutive paradox of Deleuze's nomadic subjectivity. The woman in question here is not an empirical referent, but rather a topological position, which marks degrees and levels of intensity and affective states. It expresses impersonal and ungendered forces; and, as is to be expected, this has generated a lively and often critical debate with feminist poststructuralist philosophers.

Moreover, 'becoming-woman' is a moment, a passage, a line of flight which bypasses empirical women per se. Processes of becoming are not predicated upon a stable, centralised 'self' who supervises their unfolding. Rather, they rest on a non-unitary, multilayered, dynamic subject. Becoming woman/animal/insect is an affect that flows; like writing it is a composition, or a location that needs to be constructed in the encounter with others. All becomings are minoritarian, that is to say they inevitably and necessarily move into the direction of the 'others' of classical dualism (such as sexualised, racialised and/or naturalised 'others'). Yet becomings do not stop there; they become displaced and are reterritorialised in the process. Thus, 'becoming-woman' marks the threshold of patterns of 'becoming-minoritarian' that cross through the animal and go into the 'becoming-imperceptible' and beyond. There are no systematic, linear or teleological stages of becoming; each plateau marks a framed and sustainable block or moment of transformation that is actualised immanently.

Alternatively, patterns of becoming can be visualised as an affirmative deconstruction of dominant subject-positions (masculine/white/heterosexual/ speaking a standard language/property-owning/urbanised and so on). Or else, becomings can be understood as stepping stones to a complex and open-ended process of depersonalisation of the subject. Internally self-contradictory, becoming can best be expressed by figurations: the wasp and the orchid; the woman and the turning of the waves; the sound and the fury, signifying nothing. In this way, the process of becoming is not about signification, but about actualising new modes of affective interaction: it asserts the potency of expression. Expression is the non-linguistically coded affirmation of an affectivity whose degree, speed, extension and intensity can only be measured materially and pragmatically, case by case. And it is therefore interesting to note that women are not *a priori* molecular; they too have to become woman.

Connectives

Becoming
Expression
Force
Lines of flight
Molar
Psychoanalysis

WOOLF, VIRGINIA (1882–1941)

Claire Colebrook

One of the challenges Deleuze presents to late twentieth-century philosophy and theory is his critique of linguisticism, or the idea that we can only think within a language and that language structures our perception. His idea that true thinking must plunge back into the life from which language emerges, rather than remain within a language, is profoundly modernist and continues an early twentieth-century concern with the genesis of systems of signs. Although Deleuze writes positively about a series of modernist writers and artists, including James Joyce, his and Guattari's celebration of Virginia Woolf in *A Thousand Plateaus* is significant for two reasons. First,Woolf 's own work is contemporaneous with Henri Bergson who was so important for Deleuze. It is possible that Woolf 's concern with pre-linguistic perception may well have emerged from the same intellectual milieu to which Deleuze appeals. Woolf 's Bloomsbury circle was concerned with the autonomy of the aesthetic and its difference from the fixed categories of logic. Bergson's appeal to the undivided flow of creative life from which fixed terms emerge was part of a broader modernist reaction against reification, intellectualism and technological rationalisation of which Woolf 's style is perhaps the greatest expression. Second, the most explicit appeal made by Deleuze and Guattari to Woolf is in the 'becoming-woman' section of *A Thousand Plateaus*.

If modernism in general shares the Bergsonian distaste for a world reduced to clock time, mathematical space and impoverished experience, Virginia Woolf 's response is uniquely positive and affirmative. Unlike other modernists who used techniques such as the fragmentation of language, quotation, allusion, punning and parataxis – linguistic techniques – to show signs operating as machines beyond human intent,Woolf used literature to think and express the extra-literary. This is perhaps why, when Deleuze and Guattari want to think about becoming, they turn to becoming-woman and Virginia Woolf.

Whereas 'man' is the presupposed universal subject of the system of speech and the being to whom all becoming is represented, woman is the key to all becomings. Woman is not the Other of man, not that which lies outside language as unrepresentable, negative and undifferentiated. If we want to think the life, becoming or perceptions from which the subject emerges then we need to move beyond 'man' as subject or ground to woman as becoming, expression and creation. Woolf is crucial here not because she is a woman writer, expressing women's experience in language (for she argues in *A Room of One's Own* (1929) that it is fatal, when writing, to think of one's sex). Rather, Woolf 's style is becoming-woman.

On the one hand, Woolf 's writing is about perception; her sentences in *The Waves* (1931) create characters who are their perceptions, and whose world is not a set of static objects so much as a perception of others' worlds. Characters receive impressions not as extended objects in time but as intensities or becoming, 'blocks of becoming'. On the other hand,Woolf's work is not just about perception and a world of impressions; she also enacts becoming and intensity at the level of style, with many of her sentences complicating and subverting the subject-predicate structure of standard speech and logic.

Connectives

Becoming
Bergson
Power
Woman
Writing

WRITING

Rosi Braidotti

Deleuze's philosophical monism makes no categorical difference between thinking and creating, painting and writing, concept and percept. These are all variations of experimentation, more specifically, an experimentation with intensities that foster patterns of becoming. Experimentation expresses different topological modes; they enact a creative process that is not configured by unfolding a fixed essence or *telos*. Creativity is understood as a multiple and complex process of transformation, otherwise the flux of becoming. Put simply, creativity affirms the positive structure of difference.

Writing then, is not the self-assertion of a rationally ordained imaginative subject, rather its eviction. It has to do with emptying out the self, opening it up to possible encounters with a number of affective outsides. The writer's eye captures the outside world by becoming receptive to minute and seemingly irrelevant perceptions. During such moments of floating awareness, when rational control releases its hold, 'reality' vigorously rushes through the sensorial/perceptive apparatus. This onslaught of data, information and affectivity simultaneously propels the self out of the black hole of its atomised isolation, dispersing it into a myriad of dataimprints. Ambushed, the self not only receives affects, it concomitantly recomposes itself around them. A rhizomic bond is thus established that, through the singular geometry of the affects involved and their specific plane of composition, confirms the singularity of the subject produced on a particular plane of immanence.

One needs to be able to sustain the impact of affectivity: to 'hold' it. But holding or capturing affectivity does not happen dialectically within a dominant mode of consciousness. Instead, it takes the form of an affective, depersonalised, highly receptive subject which quite simply is not unified. The singularity of this rhizomic subjectivity rests on the spatio-temporal coordinates that make it coincide with nothing more than the degrees, levels, expansions and extensions of the 'outside' as it rushes head-on, moving inwards and outwards. What are mobilised are one's capacities to feel, sense, process and sustain the impact in conjunction with the complex materiality of the outside; a sort of fluid but self-sustaining sensibility, or stream-of-consciousness that is porous to the outside. Our culture has tended to code this as 'feminine'. Pure creativity is an aesthetic mode of absolute immersion along with the unfolding and enfolding of one's sensibility in the field of forces one inhabits – music, colour, light, speed, temperature and intensity.

Because of the historical bond that ties writing to régimes of power, the activity of writing plays a special pragmatic role; it is a tool that can be used to decode the despotic power of the linguistic signifier. In this way, the intensive writing style particular to Deleuze spells the end of the linguistic turn, as he releases the subject from the cage of representational thinking. Writing is therefore, not explained with reference to psychoanalytic theories of symbolic 'lack', or reduced to an economy of guilt, nor is it the linguistic power of the master signifier. Writing is an intensive approach that stresses the productive, more than the regressive. Put differently, Deleuze insists writing is the structure of affectivity that animates the subject. At the heart of Deleuze's rhizomatics is a positive reading of the human as affirmative, a pleasure-prone machine capable of all kinds of empowering forces. It is just a question of establishing the most positive or even joyful connections and resonances.

For Deleuze what is at stake in writing is not the manipulation of a set of linguistic or narrative conventions; nor is it the cognitive penetration of an object; nor even the appropriation of a theme. Writing is an orientation; it is the skill that consists in developing a compass of the cognitive, affective and ethical kind. It is quite simply an apprenticeship in the art of conceptual and perceptual colouring.

A new image, or philosophical concept, is an affect that breaks through established frames and representations. It illuminates a territory through the orientation of its coordinates; it makes visible/thinkable/sayable/hearable forces, passions and affects that were previously unperceived. Thus, the question of creation is ultimately technological: it is one of 'how?'. It is also geological: it is about 'where?' and 'in which territory?'. Ultimately, it is ethical: it is concerned with where limits can be set and how to sustain altered states or processes of change.

Connectives

Black hole
Creative transformation
Difference
Immanence
Power
Representation

Bibliography

DELEUZE

D 1956 Deleuze, Gilles (1956), 'La conception de la différence chez Bergson', *Les Études Bergsoniennes*, vol. 4, Paris: Presses Universitaires de France, pp. 77–113.

D 1965 Deleuze, Gilles (1965), *Nietzsche*, Paris: Presses Universitaires de France.

D 1971 Deleuze, Gilles (1971), *Masochism: An Interpretation of Coldness and Cruelty*, trans. Jean McNeil, New York: G. Braziller.

D 1977 Deleuze, Gilles (1977), 'Nomad Thought', in David B. Allison (ed.), *The New Nietzsche: Contemporary Styles of Interpretation*, New York: Delta Books, pp. 142–9.

D 1983 Deleuze, Gilles (1983), *Nietzsche and Philosophy*, trans. Hugh Tomlinson, London: Athlone Press.

D 1984 Deleuze, Gilles (1984), *Kant's Critical Philosophy*, trans. Hugh Tomlinson and Barbara Habberjam, London: Athlone Press.

D 1986 Deleuze, Gilles (1986), *Cinema 1: The movement-image*, trans. Hugh Tomlinson and Barbara Habberjam, Minneapolis: University of Minnesota Press.

D 1987 Deleuze, Gilles (1987), *Dialogues with Clare Parnet*, trans. Hugh Tomlinson and Barbara Habberjam, London: Athlone Press.

D 1988a Deleuze, Gilles (1988), *Bergsonism*, trans. Hugh Tomlinson and Barbara Habberjam, New York: Zone Books.

D 1988b Deleuze, Gilles (1988), *Foucault*, trans. Sean Hand, Minneapolis: University of Minnesota Press.

D 1988c Deleuze, Gilles (1988), *Spinoza: Practical Philosophy*, trans. Robert Hurley, San Francisco: City Light Books.

D 1989 Deleuze, Gilles (1989), *Cinema 2: The time-image*, trans. Hugh Tomlinson and Robert Galeta, Minneapolis: University of Minnesota Press.

D 1990 Deleuze, Gilles (1990), *The Logic of Sense*, trans. Mark Lester with Charles Stivale, ed. Constantin V. Boundas, New York: Columbia University Press.

D 1991 Deleuze, Gilles (1991), *Empiricism and Subjectivity: An Essay on Hume's Theory of Human Nature*, trans. Constantin V. Boundas, New York: Columbia University Press.

D 1992 Deleuze, Gilles (1992), *Expressionism in Philosophy: Spinoza*, trans. Martin Joughin, New York: Zone Books.

D 1993a Deleuze, Gilles (1993), *The Fold: Leibniz and the Baroque*, trans. Tom Conley, Minneapolis: University of Minnesota Press.

D 1993b Constantin V. Boundas (ed.), *The Deleuze Reader*, New York: Columbia University Press.

D 1994 Deleuze, Gilles (1994), *Difference and Repetition*, trans. Paul Patton, London: Athlone Press; and New York: Columbia University Press.

D 1995 Deleuze, Gilles (1995), *Negotiations*, trans. Martin Joughin, New York: Columbia University Press.

D 1997a 'Desire and Pleasure', trans. Daniel W. Smith, in A. I. Davidson (ed.), *Foucault and his Interlocutors*, Chicago: University of Chicago Press, pp. 183–95.

D 1997b Deleuze, Gilles (1997), *Essays Critical and Clinical*, trans. Daniel W. Smith and Michael A. Greco, Minneapolis: University of Minnesota Press.

D 1997c Deleuze, Gilles 'Immanence: A Life . . .', trans. N. Millet, *Theory, Culture, and Society* 14: 2, pp. 3–9.

D 2000 Deleuze, Gilles (2000), *Proust and Signs: The Complete Text,* trans. R. Howard, *Theory out of Bounds*, vol. 17, Minneapolis: University of Minnesota Press.

D 2003 Deleuze, Gilles (2003), *Francis Bacon: The Logic of Sensation*, trans. Daniel W. Smith, Minneapolis: University of Minnesota Press.

D 2006 Deleuze, Gilles (2006), *Two Regimes of Madness: Texts and Interviews 1975-1995*, ed. David Lapoujade, trans. Ames Hodges and Mike Taormina, New York: Semiotext(e).

DELEUZE AND GUATTARI

D&G 1983 Deleuze, Gilles and Félix Guattari (1983), *Anti-Oedipus: Capitalism and Schizophrenia*, vol. 1, trans. Robert Hurley,

Mark Seem and Helen R. Lane, Minneapolis: University of Minnesota Press.

D&G 1986 Deleuze, Gilles and Félix Guattari (1986), *Kafka: Toward a Minor Literature*, trans. Dana Polan, Minneapolis: University of Minnesota Press.

D&G 1987 Deleuze, Gilles and Félix Guattari (1987), *A Thousand Plateaus: Capitalism and Schizophrenia*, trans. Brian Massumi, Minneapolis: University of Minnesota Press.

D&G 1994 Deleuze, Gilles and Félix Guattari (1994), *What is Philosophy?*, trans. Hugh Tomlinson and Graham Burchell, New York: Columbia University Press.

DELEUZE AND FOUCAULT

D & F 1977 Deleuze, Gilles and Michel Foucault (1977), 'Intellectuals and Power' in Michel Foucault, Language, Counter-Memory, Practice, trans. Donald F. Bouchard, Ithaca: Cornell University Press.

OTHER TEXTS CITED

B 1974 Barthes, Roland (1974), *S/Z*, trans. Richard Miller, New York: Hill and Wang.

B 1911 Bergson, Henri (1907), *Creative Evolution*, trans. Arthur Mitchell, New York: Henry Holt and Co.

B 1994 Bergson, Henri (1994), *Matter and Memory*, trans. N. M. Paul and W. S. Palmer, New York: Zone Books.

C 1986 Le Corbusier (1986), *Towards a New Architecture*, translated by Frederick Etchells, New York: Dover Publications.

C 1995 Cache, Bernard (1995), *Earth Moves: The Furnishing of Territories*, trans. Anne Boyman, Cambridge, MA: MIT Press.

E 2008 Eisenman, Peter (2008) *Ten Canonical Buildings: 1950-2000*, New York: Rizzoli International Publications.

JD 1973 Derrida, Jacques (1973), *Writing and Difference*, trans. Alan Bass, London: Routledge and Kegan Paul.

F 1956 Fitzgerald, Scott (1956), *The Crack Up*, ed. Edmund Wilson, New York: New Directions Publishing Corporation.

G 1972 Guattari, Félix (1972), *Psychanalyse et transversalité*, Paris: Maspero.

G 1979 Guattari, Félix (1979), *L'inconscient machinique*, Fontenaysous-Bois: Recherches.

G 1986, Guattari, Félix (1986), *Les Années d'Hiver 1980-1985*, Paris: Barrault.

G 1995 Guattari, Félix (1995), *Chaosmosis: An Ethico-Aesthetic Paradigm*, trans. P. Bains and J. Pefanis, Bloomington and Indianapolis: Indiana University Press.

H 1999 Holland, Eugene (1999), *Deleuze and Guattari's* Anti-Oedipus: *Introduction to Schizoanalysis*, London: Routledge.

HR 2000, Hardt, Michael and Antonio Negri (2000), *Empire*, Cambridge, MA: Harvard University Press.

K 1992 Kant, Immanuel (1992), *Critique of Judgement*, trans. J. C. Meredith, Oxford: Oxford University Press.

K 1993 Kant, Immanuel (1993), *Critique of Practical Reason*, trans. Lewis White Beck, 3rd edn, New York: Macmillan.

K 1996 Kant, Immanuel (1996), *Critique of Pure Reason*, trans. Werner S. Pluhar, Indianapolis: Hackett.

K 1998 Kant, Immanuel (1998), *Critique of Pure Reason*, trans. Paul Guyer and Allen W. Wood, Cambridge: Cambridge University Press.

L 1977 Lacan, Jacques (1977), *Écrits*, trans. A. Sheridan, New York and London: W. W. Norton and Co.

L 1982 Lacan, Jacques (1982), *Feminine Sexuality: Jacques Lacan and the École Freudienne*, trans. J. Rose, ed. J. Rose and J. Mitchell, London: Macmillan Press.

L 1993 Lynn, Greg (1993), 'Architectural Curvilinearity: The Folded, the Pliant and the Supple', *Architectural Design* 3–4.

M 1992 Massumi, Brian (1992), *A User's Guide to Capitalism and Schizophrenia: Deviations from Deleuze and Guattari*, Cambridge, MA: MIT Press.

M 2002 Massumi, Brian (2002), *Parable for the Virtual: Movement, Affect, Sensation*. Durham: Duke University Press.

M 1998, Margulis, Lynn (1998), *Symbiotic Planet: A New Look at Evolution*. New York: Basic Books.

O 2000, Oyama, Susan (2000), *The Ontogeny of Information: Developmental Systems and Evolution*. Durham: Duke University Press.

R 1984 Rossi, Aldo (1984), *The Architecture of the City*, translated by Diane Ghirardo and John Ockman, Cambridge, MA: MIT Press.

RU 2006 Reiser + Umemoto (2006), *Atlas of Novel Tectonics*, New York: Princeton Architectural Press.
S 1974 Smithson, Alison (1974), 'How to recognize and read mat-building', *Architectural Design* 9: 573-90.
S 1989 Somol, R.E. (1989), 'Between the Sphere and the Labyrinth', *Architectural Design* 11-12.
W 1994 Willemen, Paul (1994), 'Through the Glass Darkly: Cinephilia Reconsidered', in *Looks and Frictions: Essays in Cultural Studies and Film Theory*, London: British Film Institute, pp. 223–57.
W 2007 Weizman, Eyal (2007), *Hollow Land: Israel's Architecture of Occupation*, London: Verso.
WE 2003, West-Eberhard, Mary Jane (2003), *Developmental Plasticity and Evolution*. New York: Oxford University Press.

USING DELEUZE (AND GUATTARI)

Ansell Pearson, Keith (ed.) (1997), *The Deleuze and Philosophy: The Difference Engineer*, London: Routledge.
Ansell Pearson, Keith (1999), *Germinal Life: The Difference and Repetition of Deleuze*, London: Routledge.
Badiou, Alain (2000), *Deleuze: The Clamour of Being*, trans. Louise
Burchill, Minneapolis: University of Minnesota Press.
Bell, Jeffrey A. (2006), *Philosophy at the Edge of Chaos: Gilles Deleuze and the Philosophy of Difference*, Toronto: University of Toronto Press.
Bell, Jeffrey A. (2009), *Deleuze's Hume: Philosophy, Culture and the Scottish Enlightenment*, Edinburgh: Edinburgh University Press.
Bogue, Ronald (1989), *Deleuze and Guattari*, London: Routlege.
Bogue, Ronald (2003), *Deleuze on Music, Painting and the Arts*, London: Routledge.
Bogue, Ronald (2003), *Deleuze and Cinema*, London: Routledge.
Bogue, Ronald (2004), *Deleuze's Wake: Tributes and Tributaries*, Albany: State University of New York Press.
Boundas, Constantin V. and Dorothea Olkowski (eds) (1994), *Gilles Deleuze and the Theater of Philosophy*, New York: Routledge.
Braidotti, Rosi (1994), *Nomadic Subjects: Embodiment and Sexual Difference in Contemporary Feminist Theory*, New York: Columbia University Press.
Braidotti, Rosi (2002), *Metamorphoses: Towards a Materialist Theory of Becoming*, Cambridge: Polity.

Braidotti, Rosi (2006). *Transpositions: On Nomadic Ethics*, Cambridge: Polity.

Buchanan, Ian (ed.) (1997), *A Deleuzian Century?*, special issue of *The South Atlantic Quarterly* 96: 3 (Summer).

Buchanan, Ian (2000), *Deleuzism: A Metacommentary*, Edinburgh: Edinburgh University Press.

Buchanan, Ian (2008), *Deleuze and Guattari's* Anti-Oedipus: *A Reader's Guide*, London: Continuum.

Buchanan, Ian and Claire Colebrook (eds) (2000), *Deleuze and Feminist Theory*, Edinburgh: Edinburgh University Press.

Buchanan, Ian and John Marks (eds) (2001), *Deleuze and Literature*, Edinburgh: Edinburgh University Press.

Buchanan, Ian and Adrian Parr (eds) (2006), *Deleuze and the Contemporary World*, Edinburgh: Edinburgh University Press.

Buchanan, Ian and Marcel Swiboda (eds) (2004), *Deleuze and Music*, Edinburgh: Edinburgh University Press.

Clet-Martin, Jean (1993), *Variations: La philosophie de Gilles Deleuze*, Paris: Payot et Rivages.

Colebrook, Claire (2002), *Gilles Deleuze*, London: Routlege.

Colebrook, Claire (2006), *Deleuze: A Guide for the Perplexed*, London: Continuum.

Colebrook, Claire (2006), *Philosophy and Post-Structuralist Theory: From Kant to Deleuze*, Edinburgh: Edinburgh University Press.

Colebrook, Claire (2010), *Deleuze and the Meaning of Life*, London: Continuum.

Colebrook, Claire, Jeffrey Bell, and James Williams (2009), *Deleuze and History*, Edinburgh: Edinburgh University Press.

Critical Horizons: Journal of Social and Critical Theory, (2002) 4: 2.

De Certeau, Michel (1984), *The Practice of Everyday Life*, trans. Steven Rendall, Berkeley: University of California Press.

Delanda, Manuel (1997), *A Thousand Years of Non-Linear History*, New York: Zone Books.

Delanda, Manuel (2002), *Intensive Science and Virtual Philosophy*, London: Continuum.

Delanda, Manuel (2006), *A New Philosophy of Society: Assemblage Theory and Social Complexity*, London: Continuum.

Goodchild, Philip (1996a), *Deleuze and Guattari: An Introduction to the Politics of Desire*, London: Sage.

Goodchild, Philip (1996b), *Gilles Deleuze and the Question of Philosophy*, London: Associated University Press.

Grosz, Elizabeth (ed.) (1999), *Becomings: Explorations in Time, Memory, and Futures*, Ithaca: Cornell University Press.

Grosz, Elizabeth (2001), *Architecture from the Outside*, Cambridge, MA: MIT Press.

Grosz, Elizaveth (2005), *The Nick of Time: Politics, Evolution and the Untimely*, Durham: Duke University Press.

Grosz, Elizabeth (2008), *Chaos, Territory, Art: Deleuze and the Framing of the Earth*, New York: Columbia University Press.

Guattari, Félix (1977), *La révolution moléculaire*, Fontenay-sous-Bois: Recherches.

Guattari, Félix (1980), *La révolution moléculaire*, Paris: Union générale d'éditions.

Guattari, Félix (1989), *Cartographies schizoanalytiques*, Paris: Galilée.

Guattari, Félix (1992), *Chaosmose*, Paris: Galilée.

Guillaume, Laura and Hughes, Joe (eds) (2010) *Deleuze and the Body*, Edinburgh: Edinburgh University Press.

Hallward, Peter (2006), *Out of this World: Deleuze and the Philosophy of Creation*, London: Verso.

Hansen, Mark (2000), 'Becoming as Creative Involution?: Contextualizing Deleuze and Guattari's Biophilosophy', *Postmodern Culture* 11.1 http://muse.jhu.edu/journals/postmodern_culture

Hardt, Michael (1993a), *Gilles Deleuze: An Apprenticeship in Philosophy*, Minneapolis: University of Minnesota Press.

Hardt, Michael (1993b), *Gilles Deleuze*, London: UCL Press.

Hardt, Michael and Antonio Negri (2000), *Empire*, Cambridge, MA: Harvard University Press.

Holland, Eugene, Daniel W. Smith, Charles Stivale (2009), *Gilles Deleuze: Image and Text*, London: Continuum.

Kaufman, Eleanor and Kevin Jon Heller (eds) (1998), *Deleuze and Guattari: New Mappings in Politics, Philosophy, and Culture*, Minneapolis: University of Minnesota Press.

Lorraine, Tamsin (1999), *Irigaray and Deleuze: Experiments in Visceral Philosophy*, Ithaca: Cornell University Press.

Massumi, Brian (1992), *A User's Guide to Capitalism and Schizophrenia: Deviations from Deleuze and Guattari*, Cambridge, MA: MIT Press.

Massumi, Brian (2002), *A Shock to Thought: Expressions After Deleuze and Guattari*, London: Routledge.

Olkowski, Dorothea (1999), *Gilles Deleuze and the Ruin of Representation*, Berkeley: University of California Press.

O'Sullivan, Simon (2008), *Art Encounters Deleuze and Guattari: Thought Beyond Representation*, London: Palgrave Macmillan.

Parr, Adrian (2003), *Exploring the Work of Leonardo da Vinci in the Context of Contemporary Philosophy and Art*, New York: Edwin Mellen Press.

Parr, Adrian (2008), *Deleuze and Memorial Culture*, Edinburgh: Edinburgh University Press.
Patton, Paul (ed.) (1996), *Deleuze: A Critical Reader*, London: Blackwell.
Patton, Paul (2000), *Deleuze and the Political*, London: Routledge.
Patton, Paul and John Protevi (eds) (2003), *Between Deleuze and Derrida*, London: Continuum.
Pisters, Patricia (ed.) (2001), *Micropolitics of Media Culture: Reading the Rhizomes of Deleuze and Guattari*, Amsterdam: Amsterdam University Press.
Protevi, John (2001), *Political Physics: Deleuze, Derrida and the Body Politic*, London: Athlone.
Protevi, John (2009), *Political Affect: Connecting the Social and the Somatic*, Minneapolis: University of Minnesota Press.
Rajchman, John (1998), *Constructions*, Cambridge, MA: MIT Press.
Rodowick, D. N. (1997), *Gilles Deleuze's Time Machine*, Durham: Duke University Press.
Semetsky, Inna (2003), *Nomadic Education*, Rotterdam: Sense Publishers.
Semetsky, Inna (2006), *Deleuze, Education, and Becoming*, Rotterdam: Sense Publishers.
Shaviro, Steven (2009), *Without Criteria: Kant, Whitehead, Deleuze, and Aesthetics*, Cambridge, MA: MIT Press.
Stivate, Charles J. (1998), *The Two-Fold Thought of Deleuze and Guattari: Intersections and Animations*, New York: Guilford Press.
Thoburn, Nicholas (2003), *Deleuze, Marx and Politics*, London: Routledge.
Thoburn, Nick and Ian Buchanan (2008), *Deleuze and Politics*, Edinburgh: Edinburgh University Press.

OTHER REFERENCES IN ENGLISH

Foucault, Michel (1966), *The Order of Things*, London: Routledge.
Foucault, Michel (1977), *Language, Counter-Memory, Practice*, Oxford: Blackwell.
Foucault, Michel (1979), *The History of Sexuality: Volume 1: The Will, the Knowledge*, London: Allen Lane.
Foucault, Michel (1980), *Power/Knowledge*, Brighton: Harvester.
Foucault, Michel (1986), *The History of Sexuality: Volume II: The Use of Pleasure*, London: Penguin.
Foucault, Michel (1988), *The History of Sexuality: Volume III: The Care of the Self*, London: Penguin.

Freud, Sigmund (1939), *Moses and Monotheism*, trans.K. Jones, New York: Vintage Books.
Freud, Sigmumd (1950), *Totem and Taboo*, London: Routledge.
Genosko, Gary (ed.) (1996), *The Guattari Reader*, Oxford: Blackwell.
Genosko, Gary (2002), *Félix Guattari: An Aberrant Introduction*, London: Continuum.
Guattari, Félix (1984), *Molecular Revolution*, trans. Rosemary Sheed, London: Penguin.
Guattari, Félix (1995), *Chaosmosis: An Ethico-Aesthetic Paradigm*, trans. Paul Bains and Julian Befanis, Sydney: Power Publications.
Guattari, Félix and Antonio Negri (1990), *Communists Like Us*, trans. Michael Ryan, New York: Semiotext(e).
Harraway, Donna (1991), *Simians, Cyborgs and Women: The Reinvention of Nature*, London: Routledge.
Hume, David (1985), *A Treatise of Human Nature*, Harmondsworth: Penguin.
Hume, David (1993), *An Enquiry Concerning Human Understanding*, Indianapolis: Hackett.
Johnson, Linton Kwesi (2002), *Mi Revalueshanary Fren: Selected Poems*, New York and London: Penguin.
Kafka, Franz (1954), *Dearest Father*, trans. Eranst Kaiser and Ethne Wilkins, New York: Schocken Books.
Leibniz, Gottfried (1973), *Philosophical Writings*, ed. G. Parkinson, London: Dent.
Leibniz, Gottfried (1988), *G. W. Leibniz: Philosophical Texts*, trans. R. S. Woolhouse and Richard Franks, Oxford: Oxford University Press.
Nietzfche, Friedrich (1969), *Thus Spake Zarathustra*, trans. R. S. Hollingdate, Harmondsworth: Penguin.
Reich, Wilhelm (1961), *Selected Writings*, New York: Farrar, Straus and Cudahy.
Reich, Wilhelm (1969), *The Sexual Revolution*, London: Vision.
Solanas, Fernando and Octavio Getino (1983), 'Towards a Third Cinema: Notes and Experiences for the Development of a Cinema of Liberation in the Third World', in Michael Chanan (ed.), *Twenty-Five Years of the New Latin American Cinema*, London: British Film Institute, pp. 17–27.
Spinoza, Baruch (1989), *Ethics*, ed., with rev. trans. G. H. R. Parkinson, London: Dent.
Uexküll, Jakob von (1957), 'A Stroll through the Worlds of Animals and Men', in Claire H. Schiller (ed.), *Instinctive Behavior*, New York: International Universities.

Weismann, August (1893), *The Theory of Heredity*, trans. W. Newton Parker and H. Ronnfeldt, London: Walter Scott.

Willemen, Paul (1994), 'The Third Cinema Question', in Paul Willemen, *Looks and Frictions: Essays in Cultural Studies and Film Theory*, London: British Film Institute, pp. 175–205.

Notes on Contributors

Bruce Baugh is Professor of Philosophy at Thompson Rivers University. He is the author of *French Hegel: From Surrealism to Postmodernism* (2003), as well as several articles on Deleuze.

Ronald Bogue is Distinguished Research Professor of Comparative Literature at the University of Georgia. He is the author of *Deleuze and Guattari* (1989), *Deleuze and the Arts* (2003), *Deleuze's Wake* (2004), *Deleuze's Way* (2007) and *Deleuzian Fabulation and the Scars of History* (forthcoming).

Jeffrey Bell is Professor of Philosophy at Southeastern Louisiana University. His publications on Deleuze include *The Problem of Difference: Phenomenology and Poststructuralism* (1998), *Philosophy at the Edge of Chaos: Gilles Deleuze and the Philosophy of Difference* (2006) and *Deleuze's Hume: Philosophy, Culture, and the Scottish Enlightenment* (2009). He is currently at work on a book on political theory and aesthetics.

Constantin V. Boundas is Professor Emeritus in the Department of Philosophy, the Center for Theory, Culture and Politics, and Adjunct Professor at the Cultural Studies Programme of Trent University. His most recent publications include the editing of *Deleuze and Philosophy* (2006), *The Edinburgh/Columbia Companion to the 20th Century Philosophies* (2007) and *Gilles Deleuze: The Intensive Reduction* (2009).

Rosi Braidotti is currently a Distinguished Professor in the Humanities at Utrecht University, founding director of the Centre for Humanities and Honorary Visiting Professor in the Law School at Birkbeck College, London University. She has published extensively in feminist philosophy, epistemology, poststructuralism and psychoanalysis. Her books include *Patterns of Dissonance* (1991), *Nomadic Subjects: Embodiment and Sexual Difference in Contemporary Feminist Theory* (1994) and *Metamorphoses: Towards a Materialist Theory of Becoming* (2002). Her latest book is *Transpositions. On Nomadic Ethics* (2006).

Adam Bryx is an Associate Instructor and doctoral student at the University of California, Irvine. He has co-authored with Bryan Reynolds *The Masochistic Quest of Jean-Jacques Rousseau: Deleuze and Guattari to Transversal Poetics with(out) Baudrillard* (2009), and with Gary Genosko *After Informatic Striation: The Resignification of Disc Numbers in Contemporary Inuit Popular Culture* (2005).

Claire Colebrook is Edwin Erle Sparks Professor of English at Penn State University. Her most recent book is *Deleuze and the Meaning of Life* (2009).

Felicity J Colman is Senior Lecturer in Film & Media Studies at Manchester Metropolitan University, UK. She is the editor of *Film, Theory & Philosophy* (2009) and her book *Deleuze and Cinema* is forthcoming in 2010.

Tom Conley, Lowell Professor of Romance Languages and Visual & Environmental Studies at Harvard University, is author most recently of *An Errant Eye: Poetry and Topography in Renaissance France* (2010). Other books include *Cartographic Cinema* (2006), *The Graphic Unconscious* (1992), *The Self-Made Map* (1997) and *Film Hieroglyphs* (1991). He has translated works by Marc Augé, Michel de Certeau, Gilles Deleuze and others.

Verena Andermatt Conley teaches in Comparative Literature and Romance Languages and Literatures. She has written on feminism, contemporary theory and the environment. She has recently completed a book on space in contemporary French thought.

Roland Faber is Inaugural Kilsby Family/John B. Cobb, Jr., Professor of Process Studies at the Claremont School; Professor of Religion and Philosophy at the Claremont Graduate University; Co-Director of the Center for Process Studies; and Executive Director of the Whitehead Research Project. He is the author of *God as Poet of the World: Exploring Process Theologies* (2008) and co-editor of *Contemporary Whitehead Studies* (Rodopi).

Gary Genosko is Canada Research Chair in Technoculture in the Department of Sociology at Lakehead University in Thunder Bay, Canada. His latest book is *Félix Guattari: A Critical Introduction* (2009).

Eugene W. Holland is the author of *Baudelaire and Schizoanalysis: The Socio-Poetics of Modernism* (1993) and *Deleuze and Guattari's*

Anti-Oedipus: *Introduction to Schizoanalysis* (1999) and has published widely on Deleuze and Guattari and French poststructuralism in anthologies and journals such as *Angelaki, South Atlantic Quarterly*, and *Substance*. His book of political theory on nomad citizenship is forthcoming from the University of Minnesota Press in 2010. Dr Holland is Professor and Chair of Comparative Studies at the Ohio State University.

Graham Livesey is an Associate Professor in the Architecture Program (Faculty of Environmental Design) at the University of Calgary where he has taught design, architectural history, and urban design since 1991. He has been the Associate Dean (Academic – Architecture), Director of the Architecture Program, and was a principal of Down + Livesey Architects. He is the author of *Passages: Explorations of the Contemporary City* (2004) and *Gordon Atkins: Architecture 1960-1995* (2005) and he serves on the editorial board of the *Journal of Architectural Education*.

Tamsin Lorraine is an Associate Professor at Swarthmore College. She has published various articles in the area of feminist theory and recent continental philosophy. She is the author of *Irigaray and Deleuze: Experiments in Visceral Philosophy* (1999) and has nearly finished her latest project, *Deleuze and Guattari's Immanent Ethics: Theory, Subjectivity and Duration*.

John Marks is Associate Professor in the Department of French and Francophone Studies at the University of Nottingham. He is the editor of a special issue of the journal *Paragraph* on Deleuze and Science (2006).

Kylie Message is Senior Lecturer in the Research School of Humanities at the Australian National University. She is author of *New Museums and the Making of Culture* (2006), co-editor of *Compelling Cultures: Representing Cultural Diversity and Cohesion in Multicultural Australia* (2009) and the author of numerous journal articles. She has recently been awarded an Australian Research Council grant to investigate the formation and contestation of citizenship at the National Museum of the American Indian.

Brett Nicholls is a senior lecturer in the Department of Media, Film, and Communication at the University of Otago in New Zealand. His current research spans the political economy of the media, critical theory, and games studies. He has published on the work Homi Bhabha and Gayatri Spivak, along with articles dealing with video games, television police drama, conspiracy films, and aboriginal art. The question of time and politics is the conceptual thread that binds this array of material.

Simon O'Sullivan is Senior Lecturer in Art History/Visual Cultures at Goldsmiths College, University of London. He is the author of *Art Encounters Deleuze and Guattari: Thought Beyond Representation* (2005) and *The Production of Subjectivity* (2012), as well as co-editor, with Stephen Zepke, of *Deleuze, Guattari and the Production of the New* (2008) and *Deleuze and Contemporary Art* (2011).

Adrian Parr is Associate Professor in the Department of Women's, Gender and Sexuality Studies and the School of Architecture and Interior Design at the University of Cincinnati. She is also a Distinguished Fellow of iCinema at the University of New South Wales. She is the author of *Hijacking Sustainability* (2009) and *Deleuze and Memorial Culture* (2008) and co-editor, with Michael Zaretsky, of *New Directions in Sustainable Design* (forthcoming).

Paul Patton is Professor of Philosophy at The University of New South Wales in Sydney, Australia. He is the author of *Deleuze and the Political* (2000) and *Deleuzian Concepts: Philosophy, Colonization, Politics* (2010). He has translated work by Deleuze, Foucault, Nancy, and Baudrillard and published widely on French poststructuralist philosophy and political philosophy.

John Protevi is Professor of French Studies at Louisiana State University in Baton Rouge, Louisiana. He is the author of *Time and Exteriority: Aristotle, Heidegger, Derrida* (1994) and *Political Physics: Deleuze, Derrida and the Body Politic* (2001) and co-author, with Mark Bonta, of *Deleuze and Geophilosophy: A Guide and Glossary* (2004). In addition, he is editor of the *Edinburgh Dictionary of Continental Philosophy* (2005). His latest book is *Political Affect: Connecting the Social and the Somatic* (2009).

Jon Roffe is a lecturer at the Melbourne School of Continental Philosophy and an editor of the open access journal Parrhesia (www.parrhesiajournal.org). The co-editor of *Understanding Derrida* (2004) and *Deleuze's Philosophical Lineage* (2009), he is currently completing a comparative study of Deleuze and Badiou.

Alison Ross is Senior Lecturer in Critical Theory at Monash University, Australia. She is the author of *The Aesthetic Paths of Philosophy: Presentation in Kant, Heidegger, Lacoue-Labarthe and Nancy* (2007) and the editor of *The Agamben Effect* (2008).

Inna Semetsky is a Research Academic, Faculty of Education and Arts, University of Newcastle, Australia. She is the author of *Deleuze, Education* *and Becoming* (2006) and *Nomadic Education: Variations on a Theme by Deleuze and Guattari* (2008). She is on the Editorial Boards of *Studies in Philosophy and Education* and *The European Legacy: Toward new paradigms.* She has published several articles on the work of Gilles Deleuze.

Lee Spinks is an Associate Professor in the English Department at Edinburgh University, He is the author of *Friedrich Nietzsche* (2003), *James Joyce: A Critical Guide* (2009), *Michael Ondaatje* (2009) and numerous books on modern and postmodern literature and theory.

Cliff Stagoll completed his Ph.D. as a Commonwealth Scholar at the University of Warwick, with a dissertation on Deleuze's theorisation of the human individual. He is currently researching American pragmatism on self-transformation in the Department of Philosophy at the University of Western Australia.

Kenneth Surin is based in the Literature Program, Duke University.

Marcel Swiboda received his Ph.D. from the University of Leeds in 2003 where he currently works as an associate lecturer in the School of Fine Art, History of Art and Cultural Studies. He is the co-editor, with Ian Buchanan, of *Deleuze and Music* (2004).

Alberto Toscano teaches sociology at Goldsmiths, University of London. He is the author of *Fanaticism: On the Uses of an Idea* (2010) and sits on the editorial board of the journal *Historical Materialism*.

Constantine Verevis is Head of Film and Television Studies in the School of English, Communications and Performance Studies at Monash University. He is the author of *Film Remakes* (2006) and co-editor of *Second Takes: Critical Approaches to the Film Sequel* (2010).

Janell Watson teaches French and critical theory at Virginia Tech University. She is the author of *Literature and Material Culture from Balzac to Proust* (1999) and *Guattari's Diagrammatic Thought* (2009). She is the incoming editor of *The Minnesota Review*.

James Williams is Professor of European Philosophy at the University of Dundee. He has published widely on contemporary French philosophy, including books on Deleuze, Lyotard and poststructuralism. His latest book is *Gilles Deleuze's Logic of Sense: A Critical Introduction and Guide* (2008). He is currently working on Deleuze's philosophy of time.